HARRY REASONER

FOCUS ON AMERICAN HISTORY SERIES

Center for American History
University of Texas at Austin

Edited by DON CARLETON

HARRY
REASONER

A Life in the News

Douglass K. Daniel

UNIVERSITY OF TEXAS PRESS, AUSTIN

Page iii: News writer Harry Reasoner at WCCO in Minneapolis, circa 1950.

Unless otherwise noted, all photos in this book
are used courtesy of the Harry Reasoner estate.

Copyright © 2007 by the University of Texas Press
All rights reserved
Printed in the United States of America
First edition, 2007

Requests for permission to reproduce material from this work should be sent to:
PERMISSIONS
University of Texas Press
P.O. Box 7819
Austin, TX 78713-7819
www.utexas.edu/utpress/about/bpermission.html

⊗ The paper used in this book meets the minimum requirements
of ANSI/NISO z39.48-1992 (R1997) (Permanence of Paper).

Library of Congress Cataloging-in-Publication Data
Daniel, Douglass K.
    Harry Reasoner : a life in the news / Douglass K. Daniel. — 1st ed.
        p.   cm. — (Focus on American history series)
    Includes bibliographical references and index.
    ISBN-13: 978-0-292-71477-9 (cloth : alk. paper)
    ISBN-10: 0-292-71477-7 (alk. paper)
    1. Reasoner, Harry, 1923–1991.   2. Journalists—United States—Biography.   I. Title.
    PN4874.R34D36   2007
    070.92—dc22
    [B]
                                                                    2006028619

To my mother, Dorothy

CONTENTS

ACKNOWLEDGMENTS

Harry Reasoner had many friends and a large, loving family. They shared their memories to allow me to depict Harry as the many-sided human being they treasured. As an independent biographer, I alone decided how to tell the story of his life and career.

Members of the Reasoner family were most generous. The Reasoner children with whom I spoke provided memories of their father and their mother, Kay, including personal reflections. They believed their father would be understood best in the light of accuracy, and I thank them for trusting me to present him in that light. Ellen Reasoner was particularly helpful in providing family letters and photographs that contributed so much to my understanding of her father. Elizabeth Reasoner provided academic records, took time to discuss family history, and assured me that her father could withstand any scrutiny—to my mind an altogether accurate prediction.

Special thanks also go to Peg Reasoner Hansen, an affable correspondent long after answering my questions about her cousin, and I have enjoyed her friendship.

Quoting from Harry's writing was critical to presenting a portrait of him. I thank those who granted permission to quote from correspondence and other writings by Harry and those close to him: Stuart A. McKeever, executor of the estate of Harry Reasoner, and Dennis Newby, the son of Harry's sister, Esther, and brother-in-law Chester Newby. My gratitude goes as well to Kevin Tedesco of CBS News for assisting me in gaining permission to quote at length from network scripts and broadcasts.

I interviewed more than 120 people for this biography. Most of their names lie within the text and the bibliography. I am grateful to all for taking time to speak with me. Three of Harry's colleagues at CBS News—Andy Rooney, Mike Wallace, and Don Hewitt—were the first to open their doors, making it much easier for me to ask others to follow their example.

I am indebted to those who helped me to gather documents and other archived material. Without question the major resource has been the Harry Reasoner Papers at the Center for American History, located at the University of Texas in Austin. Center Director Don Carleton opened the papers to me before they had been catalogued, and his staff made the weeks I spent sifting through them an enjoyable experience.

Many others assisted me: Marie C. Anderson, a genealogist of the Reasoner clan; Elinore Barber, historian and archivist for Hastings College in Nebraska; Ruth Bartels, archivist with the State Historical Society of Iowa;

Mary Jo Bruett, referral specialist with the Iowa Department of Education; Monroe Dodd of the *Kansas City Star;* Vivian Hansen, librarian with the Humboldt Public Library in Iowa; JoEllen Haugo, special collections librarian with the Minneapolis Public Library; Robert H. Jansen of the *Minneapolis Star Tribune;* and Hazel A. Schelper, registrar for Buena Vista University in Storm Lake, Iowa. In addition, I thank Reasoner family friend Jane Purcell and CBS News alumni Ed Bliss and Merv Block for sharing material.

Research institutions that provided assistance include the presidential libraries of Dwight D. Eisenhower in Abilene, Kansas; Lyndon B. Johnson in Austin, Texas; Gerald R. Ford in Ann Arbor, Michigan; and Jimmy Carter in Atlanta, Georgia. My thanks also go to the Central Plains regional office, in Kansas City, of the National Archives; the Minnesota Historical Society in St. Paul; the Museum of Television and Radio, in New York and Los Angeles; and the National Military Personnel Records Center and the Civilian Personnel Records Center, in St. Louis.

Four organizations provided grants to assist with expenses. The most generous came from the Freedom Forum Journalism Professors Publishing Program. I also enjoyed the financial support of Kansas State University's College of Arts and Sciences, Ohio University's College of Communication, and a fund of the Text and Academic Authors.

Several university colleagues and friends helped me to assess the information I gathered: Bonnie Bressers, Ron and Betty Johnson, Carol Oukrop, Charles Pearce, and Todd Simon at Kansas State University; Marilyn Greenwald, Joe and Phyllis Bernt, Tom Hodson, and Pat Washburn at Ohio University; Janice Hume at the University of Georgia; and Paul Parsons at Elon University. Special thanks go to the University of North Carolina's Larry Lamb; I am certain his insight found its way into these pages.

I benefited from the encouragement of many friends: Russell Fortmeyer, Kelly Furnas, Brandi Hertig, Linda Hickok and Cort Anderson, Miranda Kennedy and Zach Baze, Mark Lemke, Claudette Riley, and Jason Schaff. Special thanks go to Alan Wild, who applied his expertise as an editor to the manuscript.

Finally, I owe a debt to my family. My sister, Holly, and my brother, Phillip, were steadfast as always. In researching Harry's life I often thought of my mother, Dorothy, several years younger than Harry but also growing up in the Midwest during difficult times. She helped me to understand what it meant to be a child of the Depression, a young adult during and after the war, and a person trying to find the right path in life. Like Harry, my mother benefited from the influence of an educated father, a strong-willed mother, and an older sister on whom she could always depend. I dedicate this book to her with gratitude and love.

HARRY REASONER

In the days when Americans relied on just three television networks for news and information, the world must have seemed to many a simpler place. It was not, of course, but there likely was a reassuring feeling to know that, whatever was going on, CBS and NBC and ABC would explain events each weeknight. Three out of four people watching television in the early evening were tuned in to the networks' news broadcasts in the 1960s and 1970s. Back then, before twenty-four-hour news channels, only a handful of anchormen enlightened a national audience. They helped shape what tens of millions of people thought was important and how they thought about it.

One was Harry Reasoner. For much of the 1960s, he was the regular substitute for CBS evening news anchor Walter Cronkite, who became known as the most trusted man in America. "Harry reflected in his personal work that almost mystical quality it seems to take for good television reporting, exuding this atmosphere of truth and believability," Cronkite recalled. "He looked like a rather handsome but regular fellow. He looked like a man who came from Middle America. He didn't have any special air of region or accent. He was immediately acceptable as being imminently believable."[1] Surveys near the end of the decade showed Harry Reasoner to be second only to Cronkite among viewers' favorite newsmen.

ABC took notice of Harry's popularity—and his desire to anchor his own newscast. Hired in late 1970, he was ABC's leading broadcast journalist for nearly eight years. Unlike Cronkite, he also delivered commentaries on Vietnam, Watergate, and other current events. Even with the smallest audience among the network newscasts, Harry and coanchor Howard K. Smith often reached from twelve million to fourteen million viewers each night. With their newscast, ABC began its long and eventually successful climb from last to first among the evening news programs.

Cronkite retired from the evening news in 1981, prompting *TV Guide* to ask its readers who on television they now trusted most. More chose Harry than anyone else.[2] By then he had left ABC and was a correspondent on the CBS news magazine *60 Minutes*, one of the most-watched television series on the air. For most of the decade, and for the rest of his life, Harry could be found on Sunday night reporting on an offbeat topic as more than twenty million people tuned in.

Harry's features—the hint of a smile, a knowing look in his eyes when he was being ironic or downright humorous—had been televised nationally since he had joined CBS News in 1956. Those who worked with him considered him one of the great writers of television news, facile with language yet insightful. "It was the grace of his language," longtime evening news anchor Dan Rather remembered, "whether it was something he had written out or was speaking ad-lib."[3] Even more than his writing, his ability to read a script with authority but a conversational tone—honed through a variety of news and feature assignments—put Harry in the first rank of broadcast journalism.

Yet there was much more to Harry. After he died in 1991 at age sixty-eight, his frequent collaborator and close friend Andy Rooney observed: "If you have a clear impression of what Harry Reasoner was like from having seen him on television, I can promise you, you are wrong. Whatever you think he was like, he was not like that. I could not possibly explain to you what Harry really was like, even if I was sure I knew myself."[4]

Those words presented a challenge to me as a biographer. In these pages I explore Harry Reasoner's life in the news—and his life beyond the newsroom. It began in rural Iowa in the 1920s and encompassed the Depression, a world war, and the beginning of the medium that would bring him national acclaim. Harry met the great men and women of his day and traveled around the world, but he kept many of the best qualities of small-town America.

As Rooney suggested, Harry's life contained surprising contradictions. He built a career on reporting but revealed little about himself, even to those close to him. He rose to the top of a highly competitive field but could appear lackadaisical. He sought the spotlight and public attention but was shy and quiet. He was a writer who did not enjoy writing. He was intelligent and well-read yet allowed indulgences to damage his work and his health. He was a man of morals who likely felt guilty for not living up to his own ideals. *60 Minutes* producer Don Hewitt put it this way: "Harry Reasoner had only one enemy . . . Harry Reasoner."[5]

He was an uncommon observer of life who carried with him some of life's common flaws—and, from the standpoint of journalism, a thoughtful man in a profession that has never had too many thoughtful men. How that came about is one story Harry never told.

The Most Wonderful Place in the World

Whenever anyone asks me where I'm from I always tell them Iowa. I don't know why. I haven't lived there for years. Perhaps Iowa and the Midwest are reality to me. **H. R.**

No one chooses the place of his birth or the circumstances surrounding it, only how he wishes to remember such things. In a 1981 memoir Harry Reasoner chose to reveal few memories of a childhood spent in five different communities in two Midwestern states. When interviewers asked, he usually called Humboldt, Iowa, his hometown. He was not born in Humboldt, did not attend its schools, and spent less time with its people than with those in any other place he lived as a boy. Yet he remembered most fondly this small town in north-central Iowa, a place of summer adventures, Christmas holidays, and family roots.

The Reasoner family history handed down over the years is a mixture of fact and folklore featuring a black-sheep forebear. Harry's great-grandfather, Samuel Reasoner, probably was born in Ohio around 1836. He and his wife, Sarah Jane Fleming of Illinois, were raising a six-month-old son, and farming near New Boston, Illinois, when he enlisted in the 27th Illinois Volunteer Infantry in August 1861. His exploits during the Civil War, including a battle at Mission Ridge, Tennessee, that left him with a limp, likely would have been a favorite family tale had Samuel returned to his wife and child. Instead, family lore contended, Samuel was mustered out of the Union Army in 1864 and appeared only briefly in New Boston to tell his wife he had fallen in love with a Southern belle and was moving to the South.

Frederick William Reasoner grew up without his father. In his middle years he rejected opportunities for contact with Samuel, who married a second and then a third time before dying in Florida in 1919. As a young man Fred Reasoner moved to Humboldt when, in 1880, his mother married an Iowa native, William Medler, who lived in the little town along the Des Moines River. Unlike his father, Fred took to farm life. In 1882 he married Carrie Zentz, the daughter of Wisconsin hotel keepers. On their Pine Lawn farm northeast of Humboldt, they raised four sons and two daughters. Two other children died before reaching adulthood, evidence of the fragility of life in the nineteenth century.[1]

Of the Reasoner boys who worked on the Pine Lawn farm, Harry Ray Reasoner, born in 1890, took after his grandfather in his lack of interest in agriculture. At seventeen Ray attended Humboldt College, a private institution that specialized in training teachers, but he ended his studies in 1911 without a degree.[2] That year he married Eunice Grace Nicholl, born in Canada in 1887 to parents from Ireland.[3] Eunice was a 1904 graduate of Bellevue College in Hastings, Nebraska. She taught at Humboldt College—she probably met Ray there—and later at public schools in Humboldt and Dakota City, the county seat and a rival to the town from which it was separated by railroad tracks.[4]

One family story contended Eunice planned to marry one of the Reasoner brothers, and it did not matter to her which one she landed. Another story was that Eunice nearly married Frank Gotch, a world-renowned wrestler who was Humboldt County's most prominent native until the airwaves carried Harry Reasoner's face around the country. Harry later told an ABC News colleague, "It could have been 'Harry Gotch and the News.'"[5]

The year Ray Reasoner began his career in education is difficult to pinpoint. The 1920 Census listed his occupation as farmer and noted that his wife, by then a naturalized citizen, had no job, at least not as defined by the conventions of the day. In fact, she was a homemaker, caring for a husband and a daughter, Esther, born in 1913, and about to begin another pregnancy.[6] Other records indicate Ray soon was working in the Dakota City school system, perhaps as principal or superintendent, and Eunice was a teacher, which would explain why the three were living in town and not on the Reasoner farm when their son was born on October 17, 1920.[7] They named the child after Ray's father, but William Frederick Reasoner lived for only four hours.[8]

Three years later Eunice was pregnant again, giving birth on April 17, 1923, in a modest frame house on First Street North in Dakota City. An issue of the *Humboldt Republican* noted, "Harry Truman Reasoner arrived last week to gladden the home of Mr. and Mrs. Ray Reasoner."[9] The origin of Harry's middle name did not survive in family records or lore. (At the time of the birth, the Harry S Truman who would become president was a county administrator in Missouri.) Throughout his life, Dakota City represented little more than an official place of birth for Harry. The Reasoner ties, in every meaningful way, were to Humboldt.

Even those meaningful ties did not keep Ray from leaving the area for a better prospect. Opportunity, at least the promise of it, guided him throughout his life. "Uncle Ray was a great one for adventure. There was always a rainbow over the next hill," Peg Reasoner Hansen recalled of her uncle. "He was changing jobs so often. My dad would say, 'Oh, he's got another wild hair.' I think my grandmother prayed for him a lot. It was a family joke. What would he be doing next?"[10]

Within months of Harry's arrival the family of four left Dakota City for Varina, a Pocahontas County community thirty-five miles west of Humboldt. Ray began work as superintendent of a consolidated school at an annual salary of $2,000. He taught physics, geometry, and algebra while serving as chief administrator for a school that averaged fifteen students a year. His six-person faculty included Eunice, herself earning $1,000 a year as assistant principal and teacher of English and history. His contract also called for a modern house for his family, which meant a dwelling that did not require them to carry water indoors or to use a privy.[11] The school board arranged for an old school house to be fitted with electricity and plumbing in time for their arrival that summer. Living with the Reasoners was a nurse for Harry.[12]

As a community, Varina was a step down from Humboldt and Dakota City. Its population was around three hundred, and it was beginning the slow death common to many small Iowa towns in the 1920s. A few vacant buildings already marked the two blocks of unpaved Main Street, but the town still supported several businesses as well as a restaurant, drug store, soda fountain, movie house, and pool hall. The telephone office shared a building with the light plant, which shut down service to businesses and the doctor's office by ten o'clock each night. A livery stable, blacksmith shop, pig yard, and two grain elevators near the train depot marked Varina as a farm town. The tracks of the Milwaukee Railroad separated the Catholic school and church on the northeast side of town from the Protestant churches and the public school on the northwest side. Irish Catholics tended the farms to the east and north, German Methodists the land to the west. Ray, not known as a churchgoer, had been raised in the Methodist Church in Humboldt. Eunice was a follower of Christian Science.[13]

Ray came to Varina full of ideas and initiative, and with a touch of bravado. His enthusiasm won over the community. He began a Boy Scout troop, encouraged playground sports at the school, and one afternoon marched all of the students to the movie house for a special afternoon showing. He organized school trips to the town of Fort Dodge, picnics, treasure hunts, and visits by entertainers and lecturers as part of a Lyceum program. To raise money for his Scout troop, Ray produced a traveling play to be put on by a cast of eight boys. Its debut in Spencer, Iowa, sold just twenty tickets for two performances, ending his dream of crisscrossing the state. Another idea called for the Scouts to build a houseboat on Clear Lake north of Varina. The realities of purchasing lumber and other materials turned the project into a log cabin on a farm outside of town.[14]

As he tried to broaden the horizons of the children in his charge, Ray sought ways to improve his own. He worked in the summers for a Chautauqua circuit, cultural tent shows that traveled from town to town featuring lectures, music, and other performances designed to educate and entertain small communities. In the summer of 1926 Redpath Chautauquas of Cedar Rapids hired Ray as circuit manager. Behind the wheel of a new Model T Ford, he drove thousands of miles through the upper Midwest while supervising a series of five tent shows.[15] Eunice, Esther, and three-year-old Harry spent that summer, as they did many others, with Ray's family in Humboldt. During extended visits they rented an apartment or stayed with Ray's parents, Fred and Carrie Reasoner, in the house they had built in town after retiring from the farm.[16]

Harry's earliest memories of Humboldt were linked to these visits to his grandparents' house at 206 Third Street North, the center of family activities until their deaths in 1933. The Reasoner clan celebrated Christmas there as lavishly as the times allowed, with plenty of roast turkey, dressing, vegetables, and four kinds of pie. Children put up stockings on Christmas Eve while adults ate oyster stew. Santa's gifts were not wrapped and were available to the children when they awoke on Christmas morning. Wrapped gifts from family were not opened until after breakfast. Harry cherished these childhood traditions and brought them to his home as a parent.[17] (A stickler for custom, he once told CBS News viewers that President Lyndon Johnson's family, spending the holiday at their Texas ranch, had actually opened their gifts the night before Christmas. "All I can say," Harry reported, "is it's a good thing the news didn't get out before the election.")[18]

In the summer, Humboldt was an open playground for Harry and other children. "Because it was small, everyone knew and cared about everyone else," recalled one of his cousins, Donna O'Hare Hopkins. "You could walk anywhere, not only because it was not big but because it was so safe. All we had was a sheriff and a night watchman."[19] Children rode their bicycles along Humboldt's unusually wide streets and played endless rounds of "chalk the corner" and other games. The Des Moines River provided a swimming spot, and Indian trails ran through the hills near its banks. The county fair and Fourth of July parade were traditions Harry enjoyed as a summertime visitor.

The Redpath Chautauquas fulfilled Ray's creative drive, and the entertainment aspects of the work encouraged his own interests in public performance. More important to his career as a school superintendent and educator, Ray took classes through Buena Vista College in Storm Lake, Iowa. He was a nontraditional student, performing extension studies instead of traveling regularly to the Storm Lake campus. Eunice, already a college graduate with a classical education as a teacher, took one Buena Vista course when they arrived in Varina. But Ray had set a path to completing a baccalaureate degree.[20] Graduation in fall 1926 coincided with another move for the family. Ray and Eunice had made a lasting impression on many of their students in Varina. Forty years later, after he had become a regular presence on television, Harry received letters from Varina school alumni who warmly remembered his parents.[21]

Napier, Iowa, could hardly be called a town when Ray became the superintendent of its consolidated school in 1926. Its location, just six miles west of Ames and the Iowa State College campus, made it seem less isolated than Varina. To be within the city limits of Des Moines required a trolley ride of just forty-five minutes. Yet Napier itself supported only a few dozen residents, a grocery and hardware store, a single grain elevator, and a machine shop. Students from farms in the district arrived by horse-drawn buses. Its teachers remained under strict rules set by many Iowa communities concerned about the habits of those who taught their children. They were forbidden to smoke in public and were required to attend a local church.

For the Reasoners, the move made good economic sense. With the job came a $200-a-year raise for Ray and another residence. Eunice continued to teach, now for an additional $150 a year. The family lived in a frame house behind the three-floor brick school building.[22] Harry's playground was the vast school yard, his neighborhood the handful of houses along the dirt streets of Napier, all surrounded by planted fields of corn.

With teachers as parents, Harry learned to read long before entering school as a student. He watched other children come and go each day, returning to their houses on the farms nearby. At first he wished he, too, lived on a farm. But after a year in Napier he came to think of the house, the school, and the yard as the home he wanted. He still enjoyed overnight trips to the homes of school friends, helping to milk cows, and other farm chores. When he began to attend classes himself, he considered himself nice and well-liked by other children, and thought of school as a pleasant place.[23]

Writing a short story when he was not yet thirty years old, Harry remembered this time with pride rather than whimsy, but with a touch of longing: "He tried in later years to tell people, people in the city, how he felt about those years . . . but never succeeded very well. He did not feel at all patronizing toward the small boy he had been, and the rustic pleasures and associates, and the little games, and the thinking that a tiny town in Iowa was the most wonderful place in the world."[24]

Ray and Eunice organized their lives much as they had in Varina. They hired a woman to care for Harry while they were in class and during their trips to the theater in Des Moines, a regular weekend outing. The school was open to students at all hours, and the Reasoners' home was a gathering spot for young people.[25] Esther, a teenager when she arrived, would graduate with the Napier Class of 1930.

At the end of the first school year, Ray skipped the Chautauqua circuit and organized a trek of his own, a ten-week family trip to visit Eunice's brother, Will Nicholl, in Claremont, California. With Ray at the wheel of an Essex, the Reasoners, Harry's nurse, and the family sheepdog traveled to Colorado's Pikes Peak, across New Mexico's pueblo country, and along Arizona's Grand Canyon on their way to the Pacific. "He must have had amazing confidence," Harry recalled. "The family collie rode on the fenders and hopped off to chase prairie dogs when we drove through the desert. There were no paved superhighways or motels. We stopped to cook our meals on the side of the road, and we beat the heat by swimming in municipal pools."[26]

During the typical academic year at Napier, Ray busied himself with school-related projects, such as establishing a school band, landscaping the schoolyard, and buying the school's first microscope.[27] He also sought venues for lectures and addresses. His interest in public speaking would grow over the next few years to the point that he printed a four-page brochure promoting himself as a man who "has made the problems of young people his hobby." Included were a dozen testimonials from letters and newspaper stories praising his speaking ability. A typical lecture, "Know Thyself," urged students to consider their relationships to their communities, their parents, each other, and God. The *Cedar Rapids Gazette and Republican* reported after a presentation by Ray, "Packing words of wisdom between humor and human interest, the speaker entertained and educated his audience for an hour."[28] A similar style would mark Harry's commentaries for CBS and ABC, although he would reach more people in one broadcast than his father reached in a lifetime.

Speaking engagements in small towns, Ray's favorite venues, were not money-making ventures even if they fed his ego. He kept a watchful eye for other ways to earn extra money for the family. Few of them succeeded as he had hoped. One expensive scheme began with an advertisement in a pulp magazine for a food steamer, a two-foot array of stainless-steel trays that cooked an entire meal over a single stove burner. Ray paid ninety-nine cents apiece for 144 cookers and planned to sell them for three times as much using a network of saleswomen he would recruit. He and his partners sold not one cooker, and some of the contraptions ended up as flower pots.[29]

Ray returned to the summer Chautauqua circuit, this time hoping to be a featured lecturer. Joined by a few older Napier students, he organized a variety show with music and a presentation. Their pitch failed to win over a Des Moines man beginning his own circuit, but he hired Ray as a superintendent for the new company, United Chautauquas, for the summers of 1928 and 1929. Ray eventually contributed lectures of his own in 1929 before laryngitis cut short his efforts.[30] To make up for the spoiled plan, he took the family on an eastward trip that brought them to Tarrytown, New York, where Ray studied for a Boy Scout training course, and then to Washington, D.C., before they returned to Napier in August. He had decided, for the moment, to become a professional Scout. To make an impression with the organization, he established a Sea Scout post, unusual for landlocked Iowa. In spite of the lack of a ship, much less a sea, Ray signed up twenty boys from Napier. In the summer of 1930 they put on variety shows across Iowa to raise money for local Scout troops.[31]

Perhaps it was a drive to do something different somewhere else as well as an opportunity to earn more money that led Ray to abandon the security of his superintendent's job in spite of the deepening economic depression that beset the nation. Before the beginning of the 1931 school year, and with two years left on his contract, he resigned as superintendent in Napier to work for a business college in Minneapolis. It is doubtful he intended to remain in that position for very long. Yet to leave Napier meant to be apart from his wife and son. Esther already had left the household, marrying one of her Napier teachers, James Baird, and moving with him to Illinois. Eunice and eight-year-old Harry remained in Napier for the 1931–1932 school term; records indicate they lived apart from Ray for another two years.[32] Considering Ray's Chautauqua summers and his speaking engagements, periods of separation from his family were common. The reaction of Eunice to her husband's plan can only be guessed. With millions of Americans out of work and facing life homeless and without food, leaving a good salary and a house was risky at best.

Minneapolis must have appeared attractive to a man just over forty and still looking for a business he could operate on his own terms. At first, Ray managed the Educational Counselors Association of Minnesota. Little came of it, and by the next year he was teaching at the Minneapolis Business College.[33] About the same time, Ray and a few partners from earlier endeavors used their Chautauqua experience and his background in education to create a new business, Northwest Assemblies, Incorporated. Ray would work part-time for the business college and spend the rest of his time on the road, selling and supervising assembly programs and recruiting students for the business college. Northwest Assemblies began with a desk and typewriter in the college's offices in the Physicians and Surgeons Building at Ninth Street and Nicollet Avenue in downtown Minneapolis.[34]

In those days schools, large and small, sought special programs to supplement their curricula and to enhance the cultural backgrounds of their students. Often, the programs offered unusual entertainment, motivational speakers, and music. In an era before television, such live programs showed students the variety of life that lay beyond their hometowns.

For its first year Northwest Assemblies organized an eight-act tour, contracting with schools for one act each month. The acts would travel from school to school, performing as many as four times a day if short distances separated schools. They included a singer accompanied by handheld organ chimes, a quartet of Southern blacks who sang spirituals, a violinist, a whistler who performed birdcalls and popular tunes, and a woman from the Middle East who lectured about the mysteries of harem life. Ray booked himself and a pianist as an act, together offering a program of classical music and inspirational lectures with such titles as "The ABC's of Life," "Our Greatest Asset," and "The Crime of Being Ordinary."[35]

If Ray worried he might be ordinary, the children in the Reasoner family did not. They saw a man who was big in every way, from his six-foot, heavyset frame to his sense of fun. "There wasn't a shy one in the family," Paul Reasoner said of his father, Harold, and the other Reasoner brothers. "Harry's dad was the character of the family. He was the most lovable of all of them. He was just full of the dickens all of the time. Not boisterous but a good-feeler, ho-hum and jolly, typical outgoing individual, very outgoing. Everybody loved Ray. He was just a big, lovable guy."[36]

On the road so much of the time, Ray would appear unannounced in Humboldt and stay overnight with his parents or a brother. "I loved to see him come," Peg Reasoner Hansen said. "He could charm a person, and had a very glib way of expressing himself. He had the same kind of humor Harry would show. I would call it dry wit, a very subtle humor."[37] Ray enjoyed the huge meals that were a Reasoner family staple. "After dinner Uncle Ray would stretch out on the couch in the living room," another Reasoner cousin, Donna O'Hare Hopkins, recalled. "He had an ashtray shaped like a tire with glass where the hub would be, and he would put this on his ample stomach and smoke a cigar."[38]

Eunice was different in both pursuit and personality. She was a studious woman of quiet strength but as respected and as loved by the Reasoners as her husband. "She was not at all like Ray. She had the English humor," Peg Reasoner Hansen said. "Harry got his tremendous vocabulary from his mother. She had a tremendous vocabulary and was a very, very intelligent woman. She was much more quiet and more subdued. She was definitely English. She loved to read."[39] Straitlaced as she might be, Eunice was not beyond the Reasoner brothers' sense of humor. One day when she had a toothache, the brothers persuaded her to sip a little liquor and hold the alcohol against the tooth. "Then she'd swallow it, and so they'd get another little sip for her," Paul Reasoner remembered. "Soon she didn't have any pain at all, and they had a marvelous afternoon."[40]

In the beginning, Northwest Assemblies showed promise to be the business Ray hoped would pay off handsomely. Nearly 260 schools signed up for the series during its initial year. Yet Ray soon risked losing his share of the business by selling portions of it to other investors for quick cash. Looking back over the sixteen years they worked together on the Chautauqua circuit and then in the assemblies business, Chester Newby offered this assessment of Ray's strengths and weaknesses: "Reasoner was a good salesman, a good lecturer along 'inspirational lines,' he was a great organizer, he could inspire people to become 'pioneers' in his schemes and gain their cooperation and assistance. As a practical businessman he couldn't add two and two together and get four and was absolutely stupid as to the consequences of his decisions involving money and property." To Chet, Ray was hopelessly small town. "He was uncomfortable and shy in front of 'important people.' He liked to work in small town schools but the city systems scared him and he avoided them."[41]

By 1935 the future of Northwest Assemblies seemed bright enough for Ray to bring Eunice and Harry to Minneapolis, where they rented an apartment. Leaving the classroom for good, Eunice became office manager for the business. Then Ray persuaded his son-in-law, James Baird, to join them as a booker, reuniting Esther with her parents and young brother.[42] Harry, though, hated to leave the rural life of Napier and the only home he had known. Living in an apartment district in the city, he attended Emerson public school and then Jefferson for ninth grade. He found the adjustment difficult and had trouble making friends.[43]

Ray continued his life on the road, traveling across the upper United States while delivering motivational lectures throughout the school year. The business prospered, although Ray was earning just $1,500, well below his superintendent's pay in Napier. Yet he was in his element, driving through small-town America, holding an audience rapt with his words before speeding off to another engagement. He frequently planned side trips with family, friends, and those in the assemblies programs to enjoy fishing and camping, opportunities for him to practice his skills as an outdoor cook and to loaf. He gave his dishes silly names, such as "Dirty Sandwich," a concoction of hamburger, sausage, and homemade sauce. In his own way, Ray refused to acknowledge the country was in the doldrums. Chet Newby later called Northwest Assemblies "kind of a party on the road, a holiday escape from the Depression, by the talent, the bookers, and the management. Do not discount it. Everyone had a great time."[44]

For young Harry, accustomed to Napier and the slow, quiet life of an Iowa hamlet populated by children from farm families, his father must have seemed as unique as some of the assembly performers he sent on the road. Ray was a mimic of sorts, enjoyed singing, and thought nothing of embarrassing his son by breaking into song and dance on a crowded Minneapolis sidewalk. Reflecting on the Northwest Assemblies crew, Harry described his father as "the merriest of them all: indefatigable promoter, organizer, practical joker."[45] The years were passing by, and Ray had yet to settle down in one place and establish the kind of stable home in which he had been raised in Humboldt. That probably was never his intention. "He was not what I would call tremendously dependable and a big money-maker," Peg Reasoner Hansen said of her uncle. "He just had itchy feet. He just had to be on the go."[46]

During the school year, Ray had appeared in Napier and later in Minneap-olis as his schedule and his mood allowed. In the summer, there was less dis-tance between father and son. For two consecutive summers, Ray packed the Reasoners and the Bairds, plus two pet bulldogs, into a car for a long vacation at a lodge near Swan Lake, Montana. At night, after everyone had turned in, Ray would sing Negro spirituals. "The halls of the building would resound as we variously joined in," Harry recalled. "Mr. Covington, the lodge-keeper, said that that was why the fish didn't bite well that summer: twenty resound-ing choruses of 'Seek and You Shall Find,' at two o'clock in the morning, be-ing too much even for trout."[47]

The summer of 1935 was the last Harry would enjoy with his parents and sister. Pain from a hip injury Eunice had suffered while hiking in Montana would not leave her. In Minneapolis, she dismissed Ray's pleas that she see a doctor, keeping faith in her Christian Science beliefs. She finally agreed to an examination by an osteopath, but even the diagnosis of cancer did not change her outlook. Eunice visited a Christian Science practitioner, and together they studied church literature.[48]

Harry's only words in print about his mother's illness may have come in a novel he completed a decade later. The protagonist reflects at one point about his mother: "I remembered my mother, the first and only woman I ever slept with in an innocent love and trust, and how she died, wanting to die, wanting to get the hell out of the world, sorry only because I was young and afraid and vulnerable."[49]

Eunice died in January 1936 in their Minneapolis apartment. Ray chose to place her body near his family's graves in Union Cemetery in Humboldt. The town's worst blizzard on record nearly postponed the services but did not prevent Ray from leaving town for the diversion and comfort of work. His grieving son stayed behind for a few more days with an aunt and uncle.[50] Upset as he was, his cousin Peg Reasoner Hansen recalled, Harry was not one to cry.[51] "I'm sure it was harder on him than I, for one, realized," said another cousin, Paul Reasoner. "This was part of life, and we accepted it that way. I don't think I had the sympathy that I've had in later years or the un-derstanding. Just didn't understand."[52]

For a while the Reasoners in Minneapolis continued much as they had be-fore Eunice's death. Esther took care of her younger brother while her father and husband traveled the country, both returning to their shared apartment when their work allowed. Their household soon fell apart. By the end of the year, Jim Baird had left the road for the classroom. Then Esther and Jim separated, the first step toward ending their marriage. In the same period, Ray decided to spend several months with a friend roaming the West Coast in a travel trailer, not returning to the city until the following spring. Esther moved to St. Paul, perhaps as part of divorce proceedings. In his sophomore year in high school, Harry took his bulldogs to live in an attic apartment with Chester Newby.[53]

Chester had been a regular presence in Harry's life almost from the beginning. He had been a student in Varina when the Reasoners arrived in 1923. He had accompanied the family to Napier to work as the school janitor, had worked summers with Ray on the Chautauqua circuit, and had joined them on family vacations. As a partner in Northwest Assemblies, Chet spent thousands of miles on the road selling the program to schools. He approached life with the calm analysis of a scientist—he had studied geology at the University of Iowa. Now just twenty-six, Chet was practically a son to Ray, even if they fought at times over the business, and was like an older brother to Harry.

In the spring of 1937, Chet would have a more formal relationship with the Reasoner family. He married Esther and brought her to the tiny apartment he shared with Harry and the bulldogs. Chet considered himself too much of a rational thinker to join St. Marks, the Episcopal church that Esther had chosen for herself and Harry, but he usually attended services with them.[54] Much as Eunice had, Chet brought to Harry's home life the security and common sense needed to balance the whimsical ways of his father.

Harry's first two years in Minneapolis public schools were unremarkable. His marks that second year dipped from three B's and one C in the first term to a pair of B's, a C, and a D in the second (his math scores fell from above average to below average while his English scores remained at a B). Teachers noted that he was interested in college and a career in journalism or printing. They thought him to have special abilities or interests in public speaking, and they described him as well mannered and friendly. He needed help with attendance, however, and was cited for being tardy too often.[55] Given that he had spent the fall watching his mother die of cancer, Harry had managed to cope with school rather well.

West High School would be a greater test of Harry's abilities. With more than 2,400 students, West High would be a social challenge as well. His studies would lay the foundation for any bid for college and career, yet he would undertake them while living with Ray during his junior and senior years. He probably was highly independent for a teenager, even if he lacked the maturity to handle such freedom. He was not one to get into serious trouble, but he needed direction and discipline. A high school transcript labeled Harry "optimistic, friendly and easy-going" during his first year at West High, an evaluation that would be repeated each year. A less positive label—"lazy"—appeared more than once, and he was criticized for lacking ambition. Such behavior, according to the teacher who made those judgments, could be modified by "firmness."[56]

Viewed as amiable if unmotivated, Harry at least gained credit for a consistent interest in writing. One outlet was the four-page *West High Times*, an award-winning school paper that published every other week. Harry wrote at least three short pieces for the *Times*, including a fictional sketch titled "Migration" that described a couple and their child as they drove west to an uncertain future.[57] The others were brief essays, each only 250 to 300 words in length, one on the value of essays and the other about the positive nature of uncertainty.[58] Harry's name never appeared on the paper's masthead, suggesting that he might have decided his talents were better used elsewhere or that he did not wish to make the commitment required of a staff member.

If Harry thought of himself as a writer, not just a reporter, he would have been more attracted to the Script Club than the *Times*. "Do you like to write poetry? Do you write short stories?" went a pitch for the club. "Has anything of yours appeared in the *Times*? Have you a desire to study radio writing? Have you written a one-act play? Would you like to compete in creative writing contests?"[59] The group's adviser was West High's creative writing teacher, Wanda Orton, a mentor for the school's writers with her love of literature and belief that writing was a worthwhile activity for anyone regardless of talent. "She was wonderful. I've never seen anything like her," one student, Betty Alexander James, recalled. "We were all just transfixed when she was speaking. She was amazing." Orton pushed her creative writing students to try any kind of writing. Out of class, they read John Steinbeck and other writers of the day, sharing their ideas with each other.[60]

With straight black hair, stocky build, and a serious manner, Harry seemed more mature than the typical boy of fifteen or sixteen. When he spoke, a voice of warm bass with much inflection added a few more years to his appearance. He was not athletic—his classmates remembered him as chunky if not fat—and he did not participate in school sports. "He didn't give the impression of moving fast or being energetic," James said. "He was a kind of couch philosopher."[61]

Whether Harry was popular or not did not matter to him or to the other high school intellectuals with whom he spent much of his time. "We were a little cell of left-wing radicals and literati. We wrote poetry, we were all left-wingers, we were intellectual chums," James Cooke Brown, a West High friend of Harry's, remembered. "I think we all believed the policies of the president and the New Deal were in the right direction but that they hadn't gone far enough and we hoped they would go farther. It's the sort of position that today would be called social democracy or democratic socialism."[62] Harry gained a reputation among his friends for a dry sense of humor, a sharp wit, and a quick mind.

When spending the summer with relatives in Humboldt, Harry may have dropped the leftist ideas from his conversation but not the wisecracks. Unlike many of his summer friends, Harry did not play baseball or other sports. As a visitor he did not have a coveted summer job, but he probably did not want one, either. Little was asked of Harry when he stayed with his Reasoner relatives. He enjoyed reading and seeing movies at the Humota Theater with the other kids and going to the coffee shop next door for chocolate Cokes and sandwiches. "He would say things that would just stop the group, something that he had been thinking about," cousin Paul Reasoner said. "He was a wit, and a lovable wit, not something that was derogatory or outrageous at all, but something that would fit in the situation. He would come up with something clever to say."[63]

Harry enjoyed a reputation as a kid from a big city but usually was careful not to make himself an outsider in Humboldt. He was different, though, reading a book in his cousin Paul's recreation room while the other boys shot pool. "We all felt that he thought he was a little bit sharper and a little bit more urbane than the rest of us country boys," a Humboldt friend, Alden Chamberlin, recalled. "But he was all right. Lots of times he had his nose in a book, reading. I can't ever remember him really coming down there playing pool with us very much, but he'd come down there in the rec room and maybe sit around there and read, with his nose in a book."[64] They accepted that side of Harry. "As far as being with us was concerned, he was just one of the guys. Everybody felt comfortable with him," another Humboldt friend, Jerry Rapp, remembered. "I think we just were glad to have somebody from some other culture, if you will, to come down and tell us all about the things that went on in the big city that we didn't know anything about."[65]

One teenage pastime was smoking. "You got into high school and, boy, you weren't one of the crowd unless you smoked a cigarette," Chamberlin said.[66] By age fifteen Harry was carrying a cigarette case, stocked with English Ovals when he could get them. "There weren't all of my friends that smoked, but some of them did," Rapp said. "When Harry came to town I had to find out whether he smoked or not. And sure enough he did. So that was when he and I would sneak off." The pair would light up in a garage or any other place out of sight of adults. They smoked tobacco when they could buy it or have someone else buy it for them. If not that, then they made cigarettes from cornhusks, grapevine, string, or Indian tobacco, a local weed that turned brown. "We saw it in the movies," Rapp said. "All the movie actors smoked. They'd go to some place, they'd all have to get out a pack of cigarettes, they'd all have to light up and have a cigarette. It was just one thing that we wanted to do because we thought we were all grown up. Now, fifty, sixty years later, I wish we hadn't."[67]

In Humboldt Harry had to hide the smoking from his aunt and uncle, who expected him for meals and in the house at a reasonable hour most nights. During the school year in Minneapolis, Harry could make his own schedule much of the time. His father was on the road, and his pregnant sister was preparing to raise a child of her own. He smoked cigarettes, as many of his friends did, and—when he could pass as old enough—he drank beer at bars in suburbs like Spring Park and Vine Hill. Out late one evening after drinking, Harry and West High friend Paul Norby had to run to catch the last streetcar home. In the darkness Norby slammed into a telephone pole and broke his front teeth. Harry commemorated the incident in Norby's yearbook with the inscription, "For teeth."[68]

He was no troublemaker or truant, but Harry enjoyed breaking a few rules. "He had some really go-gettin' friends," Paul Reasoner said in recalling a visit with his cousin. "One night we went down the trolley tracks in Minneapolis, lowered the air pressure on the car so that the tires would just fit on the trolley tracks, and we could ride right down the trolley tracks without steering the car at all."[69]

Harry dated girls in Minneapolis and Humboldt when he could, which friends remembered as not often. "He was very romantic about women. He was quite romantic, putting them on a pedestal," West High classmate Bill Landis said. Harry spent most of his time reading and writing, talking with classmates, and listening to them. "He was a pretty witty guy," Landis said. "He had a sparkling wit and a satirical bent, certainly far above anybody else around there. So he must have done a lot of reading to get that kind of slant on life. He was quite smart, but I don't think he ever studied at all."[70]

Harry's grades during his three years at West High were erratic. He would earn an A in English one term and a C in the same subject the next. As a junior he earned three A's and one C during both terms. But in his senior year he earned just one A amid a collection of C's. No doubt he was capable of high marks. His transcript noted his IQ as 129, placing him in the 96th percentile of the school's IQ scores. Although he was considered lazy by the school's administrators in his senior year, they did note near the end of his school career that Harry planned to attend Stanford University or the University of Minnesota and study international law or foreign diplomacy.[71]

As Harry struggled with adolescence, Ray was having troubles of his own. Even with Northwest Assemblies providing thousands of shows across the country and his frequent speaking engagements, Ray continued to try other enterprises that he thought were ripe for yielding profit. One year he bought a small carnival, providing a manager and a large truck to transport the acts and their gear across Minnesota. A summer of working small towns earned no money for Ray and his partners, and they disbanded the company and sold the truck. Another time, Ray met a man who sold motion picture entertainment to schools. The idea of providing a series of films instead of unpredictable human talent impressed Ray enough that he drove to Hollywood. He eventually contracted with Bell and Howell to buy a few projectors and then leased some old movies.[72] It was a modest success but only an addition to the assemblies business rather than a replacement for it.

In spite of its heavy bookings and its prominence as the leader in the field, Northwest Assemblies had been in trouble in the middle of 1937. A row with the other partners over money threatened the jobs of both Ray and Chet. More ominous was the lack of working capital and the need for a $5,000 loan to work through the summer. A loan secured, Ray and Chet closed their offices, moving operations to Ray's apartment, and spent the summer planning the 1937–1938 schedules. Chet understood, however, that the business could not continue under such management. The business had great potential, so much so that a Des Moines entrepreneur agreed to buy out all the other partners and create a new company, the National Program Service, with Ray and Chet each having a twenty-five-percent stake. Its offices remained at Ray's apartment, which he now shared with Harry.[73] Chet and Esther were expecting their first child. Dennis Newby joined the family on December 18, 1937.

Chet's days on the road were ending, but not because of the baby. In January 1938 Ray petitioned the district court to order the National Program Service into receivership. He may have hoped for ready cash or merely wanted out of one deal in order to begin another. The company, by Chet's reckoning, had 25,000 shows booked into 4,000 towns and was on track for an annual gross of $350,000. The court ordered the business to continue to meet its contracts through the spring of 1939.[74] Ray began full-time work at the Minneapolis Business College, although he likely still traveled a great deal. Chet, for his part, was relieved when the court mandated a $2,500 annual salary for his role in the liquidation. Hoping one day to earn a master's degree in geology, he did not mind. The end of the partnership also put Ray and his son-in-law on more friendly terms.[75]

Three events marked Harry's final year at West High. In addition to creative writing, Harry gave acting a try that year. His motivation may have been to put himself closer to Maura Anderson, a cast member and the object of a terrible crush by more than one West High boy. For its class play the graduating seniors of June 1939 presented *The Music Master* by Charles Klein. The contemporary story, set in New York, featured Harry in the lead role of Herr von Barwig, a middle-aged foreign musician who plays piano in a dime museum and falls in love with a young woman taking lessons from him.[76] His stocky build and mature voice conferred an appropriate illusion of greater age on the sixteen-year-old actor. "Harry did a fine job, a bang-up job," remembered Landis, himself an actor in later years. "He probably could have been an actor if he had chosen that profession. He had a good voice, a wonderful voice, even in those days."[77] Good as Harry was in the play, there would be no dates with Maura Anderson, at least not that year.

His senior year brought him his first taste of fame as a writer. In the spring Harry won the *Atlantic Monthly* national contest for high school writers for a short story titled "Milestone in Alkali," submitted by Wanda Orton. For

the Depression-era story, Harry created a voice distinct from his educated
upbringing. He described, in first person, the view of an Oklahoma teen-
ager traveling the upper Midwest in a Model T Ford with his father, mother,
older brother, and baby brother. Harry likely drew from his travels with Ray
and Eunice as he added fine details to the family's stop at a Dakota oil station
to fix a tire. The story begins:

> It's so hot all the time! The dust in the middle of the street rises in little
> whirls, and then settles down. These Dakota towns! I wouldn't live in
> one for love nor money. There ain't a soul stirring except the oil-station
> man and us. The oil-station man ain't shaved for maybe two-three days,
> and the sweat makes dirty little bubbles over his beard. He dunks our
> tire tube in the water and the steam shoots up. Those tires sure get hot
> on the gravel roads. I holler back to the car and ask Mom if she wants a
> drink. She's sittin' in the front seat with the baby and hardly turns her
> head. "Alkali, ain't it?" she says. I tell her yes and she says never mind.
> The baby is wet all over, partly from sweat, partly because he ain't been
> moved since morning. The calico dress Mom wears is wet underneath
> the baby, and clings to her skin. Mom don't move much any more. She's
> a big woman and she says it's too hot to move. She just sits and stares at
> the windshield all day. I say "at" 'cause she don't seem to see through it.
> She just looks at it. She don't even yell back when my old man yells at
> her any more.

The young narrator, doubtful of his father's efforts to find work, begs a dime
from a passerby, angering the proud father. He responds to his father's demand for the money with a curse, and he and his brother buy two Cokes at
a hotel soda fountain, forgetting their thirsty parents in the hot car. In an
economy of words, Harry had sketched the moment a family begins to break
apart under the pressures of bad times.[78] The maturity of the theme as well
as its execution must have impressed the judges. The *Atlantic Monthly* award,
which came with $25 in prize money, likely encouraged Harry to continue
putting his thoughts into prose.

That final year of high school also brought Harry notoriety of a different kind. Harry and classmate Jim Brown had decided the *West High Times*
was not publishing the real story of life at the school and, worse, was boring.
They began planning their own paper with the help of a few others. "We
were anti-establishment at that time," classmate Paul Norby said. "It was
nothing exactly extreme or anything like that."[79] Other classmates remembered the paper as a scandal sheet of sorts. One story reported the rumor that
the school principal, Noble B. Schoonover, was obtaining supplies from the
school board to build a house. There were gossipy items on who was dating

whom. Another story profiled a new female student under the headline "The Wench of the Week." Typed and mimeographed, perhaps at Ray's office, the maverick newspaper sold for five cents. "I was selling the newspaper out of my notebook in between hours," Norby said. "It was going like hotcakes."[80]

Which story angered Schoonover the most can only be guessed, but the notoriously humorless and strict administrator cited the "Wench of the Week" profile as the prime offender. "I'm not sure whether it was Harry or I who came up with this alliteration," Brown said. "But this stupid, damned principal decided that the word 'wench' meant prostitute. Well, we were taken up to his office and, on hardly any other grounds than that, threatened with immediate, total, and permanent expulsion and God knows what." Brown was expelled, in fact, although he had enough work completed to enroll in college the following year. Harry was expelled, too, but allowed back into school following a plea from Chet Newby.[81] "As we were being expelled we were told by this confused, irate, and illiterate principal that we had the two highest IQs in the school," Brown remembered with a chuckle. "It was a hilarious episode in my life, one I was very pleased about. You can't lay any shame on me, and I'm sure dear old Harry would remember it with glee as well."[82]

Harry did not escape penalty. The West High Class of June 1939 graduated without him. Not until January 1940 did Harry officially graduate, although by then he was studying at Stanford University.[83] West High classmates joked years later that the now-famous broadcaster who attended their reunions did not really graduate with them.[84]

Not that it mattered for his future. Harry had long been interested in joining the foreign service. Stories, novels, and movies had romanticized life overseas, and Harry shared his father's interest in traveling. Barely into his teens, Harry had spent one summer in Humboldt reading about foreign countries. "I was amazed a boy at that age would do that," his cousin Paul Reasoner recalled. "He brought this whole box of books. He said, 'I'm going to be a foreign diplomat and I'm going to study all summer.' He was not a real athletic-type individual but a real brain."[85] Stanford University offered a program that would complement his ambitions.

Going west became a family matter. Both Harry and Chet, with Esther and little Dennis in tow, would move to California to attend Stanford in the fall, Harry as a freshman and Chet as a graduate student in geology. Ray would join them later.[86]

The family planned one last vacation in the Midwest. In early August, Chet, Esther, and Dennis vacationed along Lake Superior. They invited Ray and Harry to come up the weekend of August 12 for a few days at the Naniboujou Lodge near Grand Marais, a favorite of Chet and Esther's for its fine food.

After breakfast on Monday morning, they viewed the lake from an overlook atop a rocky, twenty-five-foot cliff in front of the lodge. Ray and Chet, holding Dennis, leaned against a pine-log rail fence while chatting as Esther sat on a bench nearby. When Ray shifted his weight, the railing broke. Chet jumped forward, but Ray lost his balance. His body pitched backward over the cliff.

Chet handed Dennis to a bystander and rushed down a gully. He found Ray trying to lift his damaged body from the rocks along the shoreline. "I clasped him in my arms and said, 'Just rest a bit.' He struggled only a few seconds, then relaxed," Chet recalled. "In a couple of minutes his features turned bluish-gray in color and there was no evidence of breathing. I said to the others, 'I am afraid he is dead.'"[87]

Neither Chet's account, written nearly fifty years later, nor a story in the *Humboldt Republican* the week after the accident placed Harry at the scene.[88] He told an interviewer in 1972 that he had watched his father fall.[89] If Harry were not a witness to his father's death, his imagination made the horrible moment vivid. In an autobiographical novel published in 1946, he wrote these words for his protagonist, Joe:

> I remembered my father, the big dark man with the laughing eyes and
> lines under them, the tireless energy, the lust for life. I remembered the
> breathless bright morning on a northern lake when the support gave
> way and he fell, down to the rocks, with me running and people scream-
> ing. He was calm as he fell. I saw his eyes and they were just disgusted.
> "Oh, *damn!*" he said. There was a good deal of the whole ironical answer
> there: the silly rules and the reasonless frustrations, the grandiose plans
> and the meaningless, taunting accidents.[90]

Those likely were the only thoughts about his father's death Harry put onto paper, a sign of how much they hurt and how private or pointless he considered the act of expressing them. He seldom spoke of the accident to family or to close friends later in life. To his close friend Andy Rooney, Harry mentioned the accident just once in all the years they spent together.[91] Most people in his circle never knew from Harry that his mother had died when he was just twelve and his father when he was sixteen, let alone the circumstances. What family and friends would remember, however, was the uneasy feeling that overcame Harry whenever he or his children were near high places.[92]

In less than five years forces beyond Harry's control had changed his world. He had been taken from the comfort of rural Iowa and dropped into the big city, had watched his mother waste away from illness, and had lost his father in a freak accident. He had become, of all things, an orphan with little but the family name left to him. The impact of those years was not lost on Harry a quarter-century later. "A basic philosophy of life came out of that period," he told a reporter. "I felt like an outsider. There's a tendency among such people to join up with other outsiders. The basic decision I made was not to seek that kind of comfort. Not to indulge the emotions that bugged me. Not to be a rebel out of personal pique."[93] Learning not to indulge emotions was understandable, but denying them and avoiding dealing with them and their causes could be damaging.

In interviews about his background Harry usually referred to his parents as Iowa teachers. They were much more, of course. The core of Harry's personality drew from those of both Eunice and Ray. His mother had been a steady, quiet force in his earliest years. She nurtured his lifelong interest in reading and writing while providing a stoic model for dealing with the unexpected turns life could present. Like his father, Harry enjoyed other people and was naturally social while still retaining a degree of shyness. He learned from his father that he could excel at the things that interested him and even fail at those that did not while still enjoying the friendship of others. After observing the colorful life Ray had led, Harry may have thought drifting along in life was not necessarily a detriment.

There were other influences. Chet and Esther had provided a stable household. Wanda Orton had led him to the joys of writing. His West High classmates had exercised his mind and wit. Friends and relatives in Humboldt had given him a place to belong. For its part, fate had taught Harry he could survive the unthinkable tragedy of losing both his mother and his father.

His parents had done well in the few years they had with their son. They had raised a young man with good manners, an appreciation of culture, and a sense of kindness and charity. With Ray laid to rest beside Eunice in Union Cemetery, Harry now faced life on his own.

CHAPTER TWO

A Comfortable Life Upended

The thought of my youth and creative years slipping away
in absolute uselessness begins to bother me.   **H. R.**

A stunned silence fell over the Reasoner-Newby family on the long drive from Grand Marais to Humboldt. They had been prepared for Eunice's death three years earlier, but the unexpected loss of Ray had shocked his children and son-in-law. The tragedy shook their confidence in themselves and in their future, bringing into question their plan to move to California and creating an unexpected set of problems.

In the days that followed, Chet Newby, now the leader of the family, decided that the reasons to matriculate at Stanford University had not changed for him or for Harry even if the mood of the family had turned somber. In fact, Ray was to have had little to do with the initial move out west and with the educations both young men hoped to attain there. Before they could leave Minnesota, they needed to conclude the details of Ray's life.[1]

First, Chet agreed to take over a small school assemblies circuit Ray had booked for the fall in nearly one hundred towns in the Dakotas and Montana, meeting a final business obligation for his longtime partner and earning a few thousand dollars for the family. It was no surprise that Ray, seemingly indestructible to all, had died without a will. His estate was $1,000 in cash, a $2,000 life insurance policy that doubled because of the accident, an automobile, and little other personal property. To settle a legal claim threatened by the Reasoner family, the North Shore Hotel, already near bankruptcy, agreed to pay $50 each month until the estate had received $1,000. By court order Chet became Harry's guardian and oversaw a $4,000 trust fund for the sixteen-year-old orphan.

This sad business concluded, Chet joined his wife, brother-in-law, and toddling son for a farewell visit to Humboldt before setting out by car in late August 1939 for Palo Alto, California.[2] By the time school started the following month, the family had rented a three-bedroom home in the Menlo Park area for $50 a month. Harry's tuition was $100 per quarter, his college expenses financed by the trust fund. Chet had been designated a scholar-in-residence at Stanford but discovered upon their arrival that the professor with whom he had hoped to work had died and the geology department had fallen into what he considered a state of mediocrity. Not that it mattered at the moment. Chet had a hundred school programs to deal with by Christmas and returned to life on the road.

Harry attended classes and joined Esther for services at the Episcopal church, even becoming an acolyte. Their new home soon was alive with visitors from campus, the church, and the Midwest. They made the most of their first year in California, visiting the old World's Fair site in San Francisco and attending a city premier of *Gone With the Wind*. But Chet grew disenchanted with Stanford's geology program—he took no classes in either the fall or spring—and realized that the West Coast was a poor base from which to operate school programs or any other education business aimed at the Midwest territory he had come to know so well.[3]

Harry, too, had an unenthusiastic response to their new home and to his classes at Stanford. Chet would later contend that Harry found college to be too much a continuation of high school.[4] His grades reflected that notion in their uneven nature. Harry earned one B, two C's, and a D and withdrew from a fifth class during the first quarter. An average classroom performance, this time three C's and a B, continued in the winter term, but his grades rose to two A's—in history and philosophy—and two B's in the spring.[5] Why, then, would he leave Stanford so readily after a reasonably respectable year that ended on a positive note? "I ran out of money," Harry would tell inquiring reporters in later years.[6]

Money was more of a problem for his brother-in-law. With Chet wanting to return to Minneapolis to ensure the family's monetary stability, perhaps Harry decided his own money would be better spent at the less-expensive University of Minnesota. There probably was little thought that Harry would remain at Stanford on his own. He was too close to Esther and young Dennis and relied too much on Chet to go it alone. Chet would say later that Harry lost interest in the foreign service program that had brought Stanford to his attention.[7] Brushing over the fact that he attended classes there for just three quarters, Harry always cited Stanford as part of his college education. And why not? For a shy Midwestern teenager of modest means during the Depression, to have attended Stanford at all was an accomplishment not to be forgotten.

After another leisurely trek by auto, Harry and the Newbys arrived in Minneapolis in the summer of 1940. California had not turned out to be the answer to anyone's dreams. At least it had offered a respite from the calamity and sadness brought on by the loss of Ray. "We returned to Minneapolis fully confident in the future," Chet recalled.[8] He turned from pursuing higher education to the more familiar path of selling school programs, giving lectures on geology, and crafting and selling rock charts and other geology supplies for educational purposes. Chet moved his family into an apartment on Franklin Avenue and Harry into his own apartment across the street; some fifteen months later, the Newbys rented a basement apartment at 1927 Hennepin Avenue, where they would live, at times with Harry, for nine years.[9]

Harry sought his future at the University of Minnesota, enrolling in the fall of 1940. He still thought of himself as a writer, and the university was earning high regard for its writing programs. In addition to journalism studies, the university offered a fine campus newspaper, the *Minnesota Daily*, and a humor magazine called *Ski-U-Mah*. The university had nurtured the next generation of writers, among them humorist Max Schulman, novelist and playwright Tom Heggen, and broadcaster Eric Sevareid.[10]

Harry entered the social whirl of the university by joining a fraternity, Theta Chi. "He was a fun guy to be with," fraternity brother George Gates remembered. "We enjoyed ourselves. He had a good time on a low budget. He and I and a couple of others did a fair amount of socializing, doing college-boy stuff. We laughed a lot and drank a little beer, checked out the girls, that sort of thing."[11] In terms of grades, however, Harry's sophomore year was a replay of his freshman season at Stanford. Worse, he was not earning enough credit to advance to junior standing. He completed just six of eighteen hours attempted in the fall, dropping the other twelve during the term. He completed no classes that winter quarter and added only six more hours in the spring session. (He failed a geography class.) His cumulative grade-point average of 1.76 at the end of the 1940–1941 academic year brought Chet to campus for a talk with administrators about his brother-in-law.[12] Harry was allowed to enroll for fall classes, still a sophomore.

Considering the changes that followed, Chet may have demanded that Harry practice more self-discipline. The teen-ager started his first job, working as an attendant at the university garage from September to December.[13] He also moved into the Theta Chi house, which Chet thought might help Harry concentrate on his studies.[14] Focusing on school work must have been a challenge for any young man who wondered what future there was in college when the United States seemed poised to join the war in Europe. Before the winter term began, students were leaving campuses across the nation to avenge the attack on Pearl Harbor and to fight alongside their allies around the world. Those who did not join the armed forces waited for word from their draft boards.

The most important change for Harry in his second year at Minnesota came when he took his first college news-writing class, the first step in what would become a career. The move toward journalism brought Professor Mitchell Charnley into his life in a role similar to that of West High School English teacher Wanda Orton. "He was a Mr. Chips kind of guy, well-liked by students and respected, a good teacher," Gates said. "He insisted that we observe some good principles of writing and investigation."[15] Charnley and another professor, Sig Mickelson, encouraged Harry as a reporter and writer and became valuable references for his work and character.

Now part of the journalism program, Harry began landing writing assignments from the *Minnesota Daily* editors. "We considered it a serious daily newspaper with pretty high professional standards," remembered Victor Cohn, a *Minnesota Daily* editor. "Some college newspapers were always putting out joke editions and juvenile stuff, and we were way above that. We may have been sophomoric in our own way, but it was a pretty professional operation."[16]

The *Minnesota Daily* assignments for Harry were mostly theater reviews. Several appeared under his byline during the first few months of 1942. As a critic he tended to praise rather than punish. A negative comment—"There are a few defects in the play, mostly in the writing," he wrote of the thriller *Ladies in Retirement*[17]—was rare. Most often, Harry urged readers to attend University Theatre productions and explained why he had enjoyed himself. His later reviews took on the breezy tone of a seasoned theater-watcher on personal terms with his readers. "I went over to the Music building the other night and took a look to see how the *Faculty Follies of 1942* was shaping up," he wrote in March. "I came away with the conclusion that if you can still get tickets you shouldn't miss it. Take the word of your own Uncle Harry."[18] After reviewing two plays presented in their languages of origin, he wrote: "Last week I was a rude, unlettered journalist, and now I know three French words and two in Swedish, which makes me cultured as all get-out."[19]

When Harry substituted for a *Minnesota Daily* columnist he wrote "Some Notes on Formal Dress," a humorous view of his social manners and those of his classmates.

> The problem of borrowing clothes to go to any formal has always bothered me, inasmuch as I am only haltingly equipped in a sartorial way for the most informal of living, let alone the precise and expensive clothes needed for the more elegant affairs. I have a friend by the name of George Gates who is in much the same condition, and the fact that George and I have managed to go formal as often as we have is a tribute to the patience, love, and linear variety of our fraternity brothers, and the cheerful credit sometimes extended by certain campus cleaners.[20]

Students edited *Ski-U-Mah* in Murphy Hall, the journalism building, and the magazine presented another opportunity for Harry to share his writing and understated wit. Harry's *Ski-U-Mah* essay "Homecoming" poked fun at the organization of the annual campus event. "The secret of Homecoming is a thing called a committee. A committee, briefly, is a homogeneous group of men and women charged with the responsibility of mimeographing releases for *The Daily*. A committee functions through a chairman, called 'Chairman,' and various subcommittees, called 'the subcommittees,' with subchairmen, or 'algae.'"[21]

Favoring the personal essay over other forms, Harry's writing for *Ski-U-Mah* and the *Daily* showed a tendency for light but thoughtful musings about everyday things rather than weighty matters. His work found a receptive audience among other students, both editors and readers, and suggested a practical career path for a writer. "We thought it was terribly hot stuff, in terms of journalism and literature, and I suppose that it was," Harry would say of his and his peers' college writing. "In effect, I saw journalism as a way of making a living writing—as opposed to creative writing."[22] Journalism also helped Harry begin to overcome the shyness and feelings of inferiority he had felt in school.[23] Finding a career and becoming more at ease with himself would be the most tangible benefits of his college years.

Overshadowing these successes were the usual problems in the classroom. Harry failed American History that fall, recorded a B in basic news reporting, and earned no other credit, having dropped two additional courses. He failed history again in the winter term, dropping two classes during the session, but passed newspaper reporting with a C and American Government with a B.

After Harry had dropped all three classes he had attempted in the spring quarter, including another reporting course, the university decided to drop Harry. He left campus with a D-plus average, hardly befitting his talents.[24] "He was skipping classes," according to Chet. "He had a good deal of writing ability and could write effective news stories, but he wouldn't meet the class requirements."[25] Harry enjoyed himself but was no scholar. Of the qualities required of a college graduate, drive and desire rather than intellect and ability had eluded him. As many postwar journalists would discover, skill and professional experience still carried more weight than formal education.

Harry moved into the Hennepin Avenue apartment. But there was friction at the Newby home concerning Harry. Chet, in his memoir, recalled that Harry had gotten himself into some difficulties around this time. Harry himself later acknowledged the "rows and jams" and his own "bastardly" behavior that marred the good times he usually enjoyed with Esther and her husband. There were recriminations about laziness and ingratitude.[26]

One jam that put him at odds with Chet may have taken place after he had left the university. In an undated letter, Harry confessed that he had forged checks written to his brother-in-law to obtain a quick $125 in cash. A girl, he claimed, had become pregnant, and he needed the money for an operation. Harry denied he was the father or even had enjoyed relations with the girl, but he contended she had him "over a barrel." He asked Chet to forgive him and to reimburse his accounts from the trust fund, nearly depleted by three years of college expenses. His letter of confession and regret was almost whimsical, concluding that "I never had the damn girl. Now I wish I had."[27] A few years later, he placed the protagonist of his first novel in a similar bind.[28] The episode was another sign that Harry, still a teen-ager, could be irresponsible and even reckless.

Chet and Esther insisted Harry find a job. For two months he worked as a standards checker at the Swift and Company meat plant in South St. Paul.[29] Then he became a copy boy for the *Minneapolis Times*. In September the *Times* promoted Harry to reporter, the newsroom depleted by the draft. At nineteen he was a $90-a-month reporter for the city's afternoon daily, not at all the equal of the morning *Tribune* and morning *Star*.[30] But the *Times* had character. Old equipment filled the musty newsroom. A pneumatic tube carried copy to the composing room. The clacking of thirty-year-old typewriters had become much quieter since the staff had been reduced by wartime needs and budget cuts. Harry thought the reporters and editors were good, just too few in number and supported by too few dollars from its owners, the Cowles family, which put their resources into the morning *Tribune*.[31]

Still, Harry was earning a living as a writer, even though he mostly rewrote stories from the *Tribune* and made phone calls for additional facts. Few *Times* articles carried bylines, and Harry and others worked in relative anonymity. Columnists, however, lived by their name recognition. On the back page, below Walter Winchell's "New York News Scene" column and beside "Blondie" and other comic strips, the *Times* ran a local column, "Under Your Hat," with various bylines. Much like the Winchell piece, it offered a half-dozen or so brief items, often funny, gossipy, irreverent reports on people and places in wartime Minneapolis.

The first of twelve "Under Your Hat" columns written by Harry appeared on November 30, 1942. He relied on family, friends, and his own observations to come up with material. Chet obviously was a source for one item: "A Minneapolis geologist who just returned from a field trip through Utah, Montana and the Dakotas reports that in Utah especially the manpower situation is really acute. He says that in nearly every town he was stopped by men on the street and offered employment."[32] He began his next column by reporting that four-year-old Dennis Newby had received a War Savings stamp book, the kind that when filled with twenty-five-cent war stamps could be traded for a $25 war bond. "Dennis pasted in his first two stamps, then got a sheet of one cent postage stamps his father had, filled up the book, wanted his bond...."[33]

Harry filled his columns with observations about his hometown. He even served as a source for pithy comments in the "Under Your Hat" columns written by others. "The Sage of Humboldt," wrote Jack Weinberg, "says he's

willing to have Uncle Sam feed the entire world, but what he's afraid of is
we may have to do the dishes, too."[34] Harry enjoyed playing with words and
phrases and the many facts he had stored up after years of reading and con-
templation. With "Under Your Hat," he was further developing a style of
storytelling that relied on observation and wit, colored at times by a sense of
irony.

> *December 17, 1942*: Whatever happened to the yo-yo? Looking for one
> the other day (never mind why) couldn't find any in the first five stores.
> Can't it be that they contain critical materials?...Hitler has barred the
> play "William Tell" from the German stage on the grounds it is pro-
> Swiss. Everything would have been all right, probably, if Willie had
> missed the apple and hit the son...There ought to be some sort of a gag
> on those New Guinea town names. How about: "The Japs have Buna
> and now they're Gona?"[35]
>
> *January 11, 1943*: Private Bob Young reports from Fort Snelling on
> a group of three newly inducted men who were dreading the occasion
> for the first salute. It came as the three men were walking down a nar-
> row walk between two three-foot piles of snow, and a major approached.
> Nervously, they saluted all right, but forgot to concede the right-of-way.
> Tolerantly, and undoubtedly with a wide experience with rookies, the
> major stepped off into the snow, polished boots and all.[36]
>
> *January 19, 1943*: If you cherish a soft-lead pencil for any particu-
> lar reason, take care of it. A long-threatened shortage has materialized.
> Reason is graphite that makes 'em soft is going to war. Maybe comman-
> dos rub it on their faces. Some scribblers, incidentally, may be figuring
> on getting the lead out of Hitler's pants....Minneapolis man who used
> to work for power company reading meters on hot water heaters is now
> in malaria-infested south Pacific district. In other words, and it sounds
> good if you say it out loud, he's a heater meter reader in a malaria area.[37]
>
> *March 1, 1943*: Hazel Crawford reports that a friend of hers went to
> Washington last week and got a hotel room immediately. A congressio-
> nal investigation starts tomorrow....Did you hear about the Nazi scien-
> tist who created an ersatz sausage, but was shot because he couldn't make
> both ends meat?[38]

Harry enjoyed his first real taste of adulthood. He earned some money for
a change and probably found more satisfaction writing for the *Times* than he
did struggling with onerous classes at the university. He also realized a high
school dream by dating Maura Anderson, his costar in the school play and
the most popular girl at West High. She made an appearance in "Under Your
Hat" on December 30: "Maura Anderson waited for traffic light to change to
green at Seventh and Nicollet other noon, changed her mind and just stood

there. Complained the traffic cop: 'What's the matter, lady? Ain't we got no colors to suit you?'"[39]

More than four years had passed since Harry and Maura had been classmates, enjoying sodas with their friends at the Hasty Tasty. To her, Harry had seemed older than the other boys even then. They saw little of each other while both attended the university. Sometime in the fall of 1942 they began going out. Harry became a confidant for Maura, listening to her describe the crush her psychology professor, B. F. Skinner, had on her.

Harry took the relationship more seriously than Maura. "Harry had this kind of fantasy about me off and on all his life," she recalled nearly sixty years later. "That's a straight little fact. I'm not bragging."[40] Indeed, Maura Anderson would influence two of Harry's triumphs, the novel that appeared immediately following the war and a memorable segment of *60 Minutes* some forty years later. The latter had its roots in the date to see the movie *Casablanca* that Harry and Maura enjoyed early in 1943. It would be easy to think of Harry, ever the romantic, imagining himself as the world-weary Rick faced with danger, intrigue, and a lost love. Maura Anderson remembered, "He used to say to me, 'Here's looking at you, kid.'"[41] Harry eventually gave her a ring.[42]

The job at the *Times*, the public audience for his writing, and the romance with Maura, even if unrequited, ended for Harry when he received his orders to appear in March 1943 for induction into the United States Army. His last "Under Your Hat" column noted his imminent departure, and he filled the space with the viewpoint of an unusually thoughtful and mature young man being shipped off to war. There was no bravado brought on by Hollywood images of glory or youthful naiveté. Instead, his words revealed the sentiment for home and the uncertainty about the future that other inductees likely felt but could not or would not express. He wrote, in part:

Yes, the hot breath of selective service has fallen on the necks of this year's crop of 19-year-olds. Nicollet Av. looks dearer in the thin winter sunlight, and nostalgic harbingers of spring touch a deeper chord. We won't be here, most of us, to see the last defiant trickle of snow in the gutters as the lawns turn green and the papers carry the first stories on the Millers' pennant chances. The Aquatennial will be just a rumor to us. Your civic pride will have to carry on alone.

But just remember—it's an expanded civic pride that makes us fight. We'll be thinking of you, and we'd like to believe you'll be thinking of us. These are the things we'll remember—the things we're fighting for:

How on the first warm days of spring the streetcar motormen drop the windows down and you can hear the water running in the gutters as you sit pensive and unfettered in the first real shirt-sleeve weather.... How glad the people are on the first days on the beaches, and how friendly. This is a friendly city. We'll remember that, when we meet our first real unfriendliness....

There are all sorts of things we ought to say before we go, to our folks, to our girls, to our friends. But we probably won't get time to say most of them, and maybe it isn't important anyhow. One thing to the girls: This is an unfortunate but necessary interim in our lives. Don't make it more than that in yours.[43]

Harry dutifully reported to the reception center at Fort Snelling in Minneapolis on March 13, 1943.[44] He received a week's furlough before being ordered to return for assignment. Harry was a reluctant soldier. For all the maturity in his writing, he had enjoyed a sheltered life. Except for the year at the Theta Chi house, he had never lived away from a home maintained by a close relative. Little had been demanded of him. He had worked but three jobs, the *Times* position lasting the longest at seven months. His taste for adventure and travel had developed from books read on a couch and the cross-country trips he had enjoyed with family. Now, he was undertaking the greatest adventure a young man could experience in 1943.

Understandably, the uncertainty of its outcome weighed heavily on Harry. In an uncompleted novel begun after the war, he wrote of a young man's feelings as he prepared for basic training:

> Just before I had left town in the army I had come home from the induction center very unhappy: I had been in the army about a week and it seemed I could not do it. I have never felt quite so trapped before or since, nothing in my life had prepared me for being a soldier. I lay down and cried and my sister came in and comforted me, and I cried and talked for an hour and cried because the folks had died so long ago and because of all the things that seemed wrong.[45]

When he left Esther, Chet, and young Dennis at the Minneapolis rail station on March 23, he needed all of his strength to keep from sobbing. That night, on a troop train bound for California's Camp Roberts, Harry lay in an upper berth of a Pullman car and wrote to Esther that he already was thinking of ways to get out of the army, even if it proved him to be cowardly. "If the goddamn war ever ends all I want to do is to come back to the *Times*, see you and Chet for dinner, etc., and bully Maura into marrying me," he wrote. "This could go on forever. Don't pass around what a sissy I am. Even Chet probably wouldn't understand and I'll probably regret it some day. It's a cinch I can't go on feeling like this."[46]

From that night on, for the next three years, Harry wrote to Esther once or twice a week if not more often. His letters contained whines and complaints, demands for everything from soap to cigarettes, and reports of excitement over new experiences and depression over drudgery, all brought on by a life completely foreign to what he had known. Yet the letters also showed the steady maturation of an American boy preparing to face death on the battlefield. There was little talk of duty, honor, and country. Harry had no ambivalence about the task before him. He did not want to be there. He hated the army and the way the war had upended his comfortable life in Minneapolis just as he had begun to find his place. He was convinced at times that he would never again see his family or home. At weak moments he schemed, at least in his own mind, for ways to get out of it. But, as did millions of others, Harry went along with the army at every turn and probably never truly believed he would fail to do his duty when called upon to face the enemy. When that call would come was the maddening question for all.

Private Harry Reasoner arrived at Camp Roberts, his home for the next thirteen weeks, on March 28, 1943. He was assigned to Company D, Third Platoon, 80th Training Brigade, 17th Infantry Training.[47] So recently the raconteur of the pages of the *Minneapolis Times*, he now was just one of 50,000 men on fifty-four square miles of hilly land north of Paso Robles.

After an opening ceremony and a propaganda movie, Harry underwent his first two-mile march.[48] The rumor mill that operated in overdrive among enlisted men had Harry's ear by the end of the day: One in three Camp Roberts graduates was sent directly overseas, probably to the Pacific theater, that summer. He could not help but pass along every bit of news and every thought, good or bad, to Esther. "In case anything does happen to me before I see you—accidents in training, etc.—remember that I loved you and tried to be a good boy. I tell myself that lots of fellows will come through alive and that the war will be over some day. There is nothing else on my mind at any time." In the meantime, though, he asked for socks, slippers, a washcloth, a belt, a hat, and a toothbrush.[49]

The routine of basic training swept over Harry. He was up at five-thirty in the morning for nearly twelve hours of supervised activities. He marched so much that his feet ached and soon began to swell. He hoped the doctors at the infirmary would transfer him out of the infantry; instead, they gave him arch supports and sent him back on the field. When his feet were too swollen for marching, he found himself on kitchen duty. By day he drilled with a rifle, learned military courtesy, crawled atop the dirt of the Salinas River valley during mock combat, ate from a mess kit, learned to head for cover during an air raid, and tried not to become one of the recruits who passed out during hikes or calisthenics. Lights were out at nine-thirty most nights.

There were movies some evenings—the first was titled *Happy Go Lucky*. He saw it twice in ten days, a break from the strain he was feeling. "This (the infantry) is a tough, hard branch and we know what we have to do," he wrote

Esther. "We don't have the frills and glamour of the air force or motor out-
fits, but we've got the rifles and the guts and the stamina. You should see me
hit the sand with a 30 lb. pack and assorted equipment. I suppose it's good
for me." [50] He was less impressed with many of his fellow recruits. "The kids
in this outfit are pretty good kids on the whole, you know—but unbelievably
filthy-minded, uneducated, stupid. The two or three college men or at least
men from better-class homes who happened to be assigned here feel it pretty
badly. Me too. There's a difference between the vulgarity of newspaper-
men, smooth and with some knowledge and fact behind it, and the sewer-
conversation we live in. You can't imagine." [51]

Even as Harry grew in strength and confidence, he connived ways to leave
the infantry and the army. When one recruit earned a discharge because of a
weak heart, he told Esther, "Wish I could fake something like that." [52] In several early letters he begged her to feign illness herself so he could be granted
emergency leave for a visit home. "It's done all the time," he assured her.
"You are smart enough to work it and I'm pleading with you to do it now." [53]
After he reported qualifying for a sharpshooter's medal with a range score
of 170 out of 210, he admitted he enjoyed firing a Browning automatic and
learning to handle a new antitank weapon called a bazooka. There were two
or three trips off base, including a bus ride to Los Angeles to visit Eunice's
brother, William Nicholl. By mid-May he had become resigned to remaining at the camp. [54]

Esther's cheery letters with news from home and her reassurances soothed
Harry. The rugged discipline he was being forced to undergo helped him appreciate what he had left behind. "Except in my more depressed moments, I
am determined to come out of this army an un-ruined man, and go on stronger than before," he told Esther. "I think I can write—as a matter of fact, I
think I'm a pretty damn good writer. With your continuing help, the years
of war will pass, and I can go on to make you proud of me—as proud as I am
of you, all of you." [55]

With basic training nearing an end, Harry waited for his next assignment.
To pass whatever free time he had, he began working on a novel. "We'll see
if Professor Charnley and the rest of the people who have believed in my
prose and insight were right," he wrote Esther. [56] Harry also applied for the
Army Specialized Training Program, which selected men from the ranks of
the military and placed them in college programs to study medicine, engineering, and other professions deemed vital. He told his sister he hoped to
be chosen for language school to study French, which might put him in occupied areas away from combat. "I like to think of a job like Claude Rains had
in *Casablanca*—you know—selling visas to beautiful women, etc." [57]

Being accepted into the ASTP became Harry's new obsession. While he
waited he worked for the Camp Roberts public relations office, writing news
for the base paper and for hometown publications. [58] A spotty college tran-

script proved to be no hindrance, and being classified for limited duty because of trouble with his feet may have helped. In early July he received his
orders to report to Stanford University for ASTP testing and processing to
determine a university and course of study.[59]

The workings of fate were not lost on him. "Stanford is much the same,
only with a lot of uniforms," he wrote Esther. "It's kind of weird being here
in uniform and marching to chow across the quad. I can't help but feel if I
go up to the post office and wait long enough Chet will pick me up in the
green Chevy."[60] Yet Harry faced a dilemma. He did not want to be a part of
the regular army. But to be accepted in the ASTP program, he had to study
engineering, which meant math, physics, and chemistry, the sorts of courses
that gave him the most trouble in high school and in college. At the end of
each term his progress would be reviewed in order to determine whether he
should continue in the ASTP. Failure meant either being sent to troop duty
or trying to enter Officer Candidate School.

There really was no choice, in his eyes. He accepted the challenge to spe-
cialize in electrical, chemical, or civil engineering. He boarded a train for
Los Angeles to begin studying engineering at City College. He had hoped to
go east to be closer to Minneapolis, but he admitted to Esther that he liked
the idea of living in Los Angeles.[61] After the demands of boot camp, an assignment to a campus near Hollywood would seem like a dream come true.
Over the next several months he sent Esther far fewer letters marked by complaint and regret. In their place was a constant request for money, if only a
few dollars here and there, and the typical gripes about the army. He did give
the service some credit: his weight had fallen from 215 pounds to 196.[62]

Harry joined other soldier-students in the dormitories at Chapman College, across the street from City College. He and three others shared a room
with twin bunk beds, a bookcase, a table with a typewriter, and a window
overlooking Madison Avenue.[63] Before long he even had a steady date, a divorced mother who had been a girlfriend of his cousin Bob Nicholl. (Maura
Anderson was out of his life; she would marry a Marine by the end of the
year.)[64] Two weeks later he was talking of marriage, which sparked a rare moment of introspection about his feelings for women. "What worries me is not
the factors of her age and the child or my position as much as the fact that I
apparently always think I'm in love only until or unless I elicit a response—
when I lose interest," he wrote. Infatuated with her "while she was unattain-
able," Harry admitted that "now that she isn't I begin to wonder, especially
in the morning. What can I do about this characteristic?" In two more weeks
he decided he wanted to stay single after all.[65]

Classes gave Harry little time to ponder the solution. Two weeks of rest
ended with a full schedule: six hours of math, seven hours of physics, three
hours each of English, chemistry, history, and geography, and five hours of
military training. For twenty-six hours each week they would undergo super-

vised study. There would be no time for novel writing.[66] Skipping classes or
dropping subjects was not an option.

Trigonometry defeated him after the first few weeks. "I'm too set in my
lazy, non-scientific habits of mind to start in on a technical course now—
while I'm here I'm merely living a lie. I'd rather go back to the infantry....
The whole idea of my going back to school as a freshman engineering student is ridiculous anyway."[67] His attitude had not changed a few weeks later:
"I hate to feel that I'm licked, but I just haven't got the intellectual drive to
learn a bunch of stuff that bores me to tears."[68] He did not quit, however,
and his midterm grades, above average in all but math, renewed his hope that
he could stay in the program and thus avoid the war a little longer.[69] Writing occasionally for the campus paper, the *Los Angeles Collegian*, boosted his
spirits.[70]

Allotted free time for the students in uniform granted them one hour at
night and then from lunch Saturday until study period at seven o'clock Sunday evening. Harry had friends among his classmates, of course, and Los Angeles was a playground for servicemen, even those like Harry who had just
$37 a month after deductions—and $8 of his pay went to cigarettes.

One night he saw bandleader Jimmy Dorsey play at the Palladium. When
the mother of one of his army buddies took them to dinner at a Sunset Boulevard restaurant, comedian Jimmy Durante took the table next to them. Actors Gene Kelly and Robert Cummings were seated nearby. After a crowd
gathered on the sidewalk to gawk at the comic through a window, Harry
turned to Durante and asked, "Are they looking at you or me?" Amused,
Durante invited Harry and his party to attend the *Command Performance*
show at the radio studio next door. Bob Hope was the emcee, the featured
singers were Betty Hutton and Judy Garland, and sweater girl Lana Turner
joined Durante for the fun. At the Finlandia Bathhouse with his army pals
Harry shared the steam with actors Franchot Tone and Burgess Meredith.
"Friendly guys, both of them," he wrote to Esther, "and for Chet's information, well-hung."[71]

An order that nightly free time be spent either in the library or in their
quarters—no more late runs for a beer as Harry had been doing—enraged
him. "I'll get the goddamn degree and give my diploma to whatever officer
is nearest and tell him what he can do with it," he wrote to Esther. "Sorry
to subject you to all this, but no civilian can possibly understand the terrible
hopeless futile rage that any intelligent man gets into in the army. When I
finish exposing the goddamn organization after the war they'll have to abol-
ish it. Jesus."[72] But watching a few of his classmates flunk the program and
ship out to other assignments, likely in harm's way, spurred Harry to renew
his focus on his own studies.[73]

He admitted later to Esther that the discipline had helped him learn to use
his time, although he predicted he would slip back into his lazy ways when

the war ended.[74] By the end of the year he was even more philosophical about the effect the army had had on him, including getting him in good physical condition. "I've learned to deal with all sorts of people and to accept discipline and to take orders from people whom I know absolutely to be vastly inferior to me in every way. I've become absolutely realistic about the way the world is set up, and learned some attitudes, not especially pretty, that I think will be useful to me if I am ever a civilian again."[75]

The first month of the new year brought Harry an eight-day leave and what he had longed for since Camp Roberts—a visit to Minneapolis. When he returned to the ASTP he was transferred to the campus of the University of California at Los Angeles to pursue a new field: premedicial training. He had been one of eight young men from his City College unit to be selected from the applicants for the program. He thought medicine made more sense for him than engineering, but within weeks he decided the program was a waste. By then he had been reclassified as fit for combat duty.[76] When he turned twenty-one on April 23, his dorm friends paddled him and carried him up and down the hallway. With little spare time and less spare change, it was the only celebration he could afford.

The never-ending quest for money led Harry to his first national broadcast. The Young Republicans had offered a war bond or an expense-paid trip to the national political convention in Chicago in the summer of 1944 for the best essay extolling GOP virtues. Harry was a Roosevelt man, but $100 was $100. Besides, persuading voters of any stripe to change administrations in the middle of a war would be a challenge for a writer.

He submitted an essay titled "A First Voter Looks at the Republican Party." It read, in part:

> The vote this year is a tremendously significant thing. I firmly believe that in this election the choice is between two fundamentally different ways of life.
>
> Nobody imagines that we can elect a Republican candidate and "go back." No American can close his eyes to the hard facts of a changing world. But an increasing number of Americans, I think I can say an increasing majority of Americans, recognize the choice of two ways to go forward, and that majority is determined that the nation shall proceed forward under the leadership of the Republican party.
>
> Nobody is more anxious than a service man that in winning the war we do not lose our national soul. We want something more than a directive and a pension to come home to. Many of us believe that a continuance of an old, tired, cynical and fumbling Democratic Administration may do irreparable damage to the country we are serving.
>
> The Republicans will offer this nation a new birth of freedom and a forward-looking policy of production and employment after the war,

with American initiative once again free to move toward better and happier ways of living in a free world.[77]

A telegram informed Harry he had won. He was pleased, if a little sheepish
when he thought of his Iowa relatives reading about him promoting a Republican.[78] Insincerity aside, Harry decided to take the trip to Chicago. The
possibility of a side trip to Minneapolis may have helped persuade him to
forgo the war bond.

More than one thousand delegates gathered at Chicago Stadium on
June 27, 1944, for the opening day of the GOP convention. Among the first
speakers, Chairman Harrison Spangler announced, was a young private in
the United States Army. The chief of the Young Republicans, Mrs. Clyde
Corbin, introduced Harry to the convention and to the nation via radio.
An NBC radio announcer described him as "a tall, black-haired, broad-
shouldered lad." To an ovation befitting a man in uniform, Harry went before the microphone. It was the first time a national audience would hear the
voice that would become so familiar.

> I don't believe that any young man has ever stood before an assemblage
> like this and felt as deep a humility as I feel right now. This convention
> is a big thing, and I am fully sensible of the honor I am receiving this
> morning. To me there is only one thing that makes it understandable:
> the fact that all of us, old Republicans, young Republicans alike, are
> here with one mind, all believing in the same principles and gathered
> to do something constructive about them. Thank you.[79]

His remarks lasted just thirty-five seconds, but Harry had sounded like a seasoned professional, smooth and sharp without a single misstep. If only he had
believed what he was saying.

After his return from Chicago, the days of going to class and the nights of
hobnobbing with the stars of Hollywood ended quickly for Harry. The term
at UCLA was over by midsummer, and Harry professed to be glad to be rid
of it. Whether he dropped out or flunked out is not clear from his letters to
Esther. Like the Republican essay, he knew that spending time studying to
be a doctor was a sham. Besides, a longer hitch in the army to compensate
for the free education might be a possibility, and Harry would have none of
that. Still, planned or not, the year he had spent in college in uniform had
kept him out of some of the bloodiest fighting of the war.

The army reassigned Harry in August 1944 to an ordnance evacuation
company at Camp Chaffee, about ten miles southeast of Fort Smith, Arkansas. "Don't worry," he wrote to Esther before leaving Los Angeles. "I'm sure
that I will be a good deal happier mentally if not physically once I stop this
masquerade. And I have no intentions of getting killed. I shall try to get back

into army journalism of one kind or another....It's all going to be over in a year or so anyway, I think."[80]

The 3613th Ordnance Evacuation Company was a newly activated unit. Harry learned upon his arrival that an overseas assignment would follow eight weeks of basic training and ten weeks of special technical training. Joining him for the duration of their service was another ASTP alumnus, Walt Kingsley, who had been a premed major himself at a different college. "Our company was trained to evacuate tanks that were either knocked out of battle, or somehow or other became disengaged in battle, and to bring them back to ordnance to be repaired. We evacuated all kinds of ordnance but mainly tanks and treads," Kingsley remembered. "All we did was pull tanks out of the Arkansas River."[81]

With his typing and writing experience, Harry soon was named the company clerk. That meant handling the morning report and the other paperwork of the company. He even learned to drive the jeep afforded the first sergeant and the clerk. "He worked in the office, so he didn't have to do anything other than go in there and bang a typewriter," Kingsley said. "He had it made in the shade, as they say. It was good duty to draw, and he had the skills to do it."[82] His letters to Esther now lacked the angst of his earliest correspondence, reflecting a greater ease with his circumstances. In October he was promoted to corporal.

Life at Camp Chaffee was relatively easy. "We were serving our time," Kingsley said, "and after a while it got pretty pedestrian."[83] Hanging over them was the possibility of orders to head to Europe or, worse, to the Pacific. A few times they were told to prepare to move out, only to stay put at the last moment. With each week it seemed less and less likely the company would go overseas.

Fort Smith was no Los Angeles, but it was a friendly town open to soldiers. Walt Kingsley brought Harry to his girlfriend's home for meals. They attended movies and occasionally took a trip out of town, hitchhiking once to Fayetteville to try to meet some college girls. "There we were in our army uniforms," Kingsley said, "and we went to some sorority. And we knocked on the door and said, look, we're fraternity men....We didn't get anywhere."[84] Harry had dated other girls since his close call with marriage and now began seeing a cadet nurse he had met in Fort Smith. "About once a year I fall madly for some sharp girl," he wrote to Esther, "but one of us always gets over it."[85] In January 1945 the company moved to Camp Gruber near Muskogee, Oklahoma. "What a hole," Harry told Esther.[86] With plenty of time on his hands, Harry had returned to work on his novel. He completed it in February and waited to hear from the New York agent showing it to publishers.

There was another move up for Harry, a promotion to sergeant in June, and a series of moves for the company: to Camp Bowie near Brownwood, Texas ("a complete flop" as a town, Harry determined, but he allowed that the camp itself was beautiful), to Camp Hood in Texas, and finally to Camp Breckenridge in Kentucky, near Evansville, Indiana.[87] Harry and Walt Kingsley, who had married a Fort Smith girl, were appointed to the information and education department to work on a camp newspaper. "We had a separate little barrack where we worked while the rest of the troop was out in the field doing their maneuvers," Kingsley recalled. "We had a nice time up there in that little shack. It was sort of isolated from the rest of the troops. I thought it was a privilege, in a way, for us to be up there."[88] By then Harry was spending most of his time shooting pool and going to the movies, waiting for his discharge to come through.

That day arrived in January 1946. Harry and Kingsley, joined by Walt's wife and another GI, took a car to Camp Atterbury in Indiana to be separated from the army. The moment Harry had prayed for was at hand and he was still in one piece—better off physically, in fact, than when he had been drafted. On the drive their Pontiac crested a hill on an icy road and smashed into the back of a disabled truck. Betty Kingsley was cut and bruised worse than the men; all had to be pried out of the wreckage and treated for injuries.[89] The accident accounted for Harry's only wounds suffered in uniform.

Harry concluded his active duty as a staff sergeant on January 26, 1946, just shy of a three-year hitch.[90] The scores of letters he wrote to Esther, revealing his most personal thoughts, showed little appreciation for the good fortune he had enjoyed. Hundreds of thousands of Americans had been killed or maimed or scarred in ways he could never fully understand. He was not the only soldier to hope he would be denied a trip to the front lines; he always went where the army told him to go. However, what Harry had missed by remaining stateside was the awesome experience that marked his generation, and it separated him from many of the newsmen with whom he would later work. His brilliant mind would never have the opportunity to try to make sense of war and all of its qualities. So much from his own experience would shape his writing in the years to come, but Harry had passed by the greatest experience of all.

CHAPTER THREE

Secure at Home, Adrift at Work

Every time I go through my resume I can't decide whether I was
becoming well-rounded or merely drifting.　　**H. R.**

S ervice in the military has a way of changing a man. It takes him from
his home, sends him to unfamiliar places, forces him to live and work
with all kinds of people, and often provides the spark for a different
life out of uniform. In these ways, World War II changed untold numbers of
lives. For other servicemen, their ambitions remained unchanged by the new
world they had encountered. They sought only to return to the lives they had
left. Within a month of his discharge, Harry had moved back in with Esther,
Chet, and Dennis at the Hennepin Avenue apartment. To help servicemen as
required by law, the *Minneapolis Times* offered Harry a job on the news staff
he had left three years earlier. He had considered an advertising job in Chicago but decided he would rather be a news writer.

Not much had changed at the *Times*, still the poor stepchild of Twin Cities
journalism. "It was just playing out its string," Harry commented later. "It
had no chance to be a real, successful newspaper."[1] Not that the *Times* was
without character. "This was such a strange, laid-back kind of newspaper,"
recalled Barbara Flanagan, who had been hired at the *Times* in 1945. "There
didn't seem to be any great pressure except once in a while when there was a
big event. It was a different kind of place."[2] The *Times* had a small but loyal
readership even if the Cowles family did not invest more money and other
resources in the faltering afternoon daily.

When Harry returned from the army, slim and handsome, he soon became a staff favorite. Harry and his friend Al Woodruff would play gags and
cut up to their colleagues' delight. "They were two of the funniest people I'd
ever met," Flanagan recalled. "One of them would do a perfect imitation of
the city editor. They did different members of the staff. They had a whole
coterie of people that they imitated. They'd yell 'Stop the presses!' and all of
this kind of foolishness."[3] Harry's humor could go too far. Once, he wrote an
all-too-accurate parody of *Times* columnist Brenda Ueland's personal musings. It hurt Ueland, an established staff writer, and she wrote Harry a long
memo that elicited an apology.[4]

Harry probably covered the police beat or city hall for the *Times*. Bylines
were rare, making it impossible to know exactly what he may have written

during a routine day. He reflected on the job of a police reporter in a manuscript a few years later:

> It is one of the pleasantest jobs in the world. I have noticed that most
> people in the news seem to have been police reporters at one time or an-
> other, and they all liked it. It is one of the easiest ways to spend time that
> I know of. There is the danger that it is a backwater, that the years can
> slip by in the city hall filled with the small and sordid parade of police
> news and that before you are aware of it you have become a courthouse
> fixture, an old man. I became conscious of this danger after I had been a
> police reporter for about a year, but it didn't seem to matter. There was
> always something of interest happening, the days went fast. There was
> always plenty of free liquor, plenty of passes to shows, plenty of night-
> club people willing to pick up the check as a hedge against future public
> relations problems. Nobody respects a police reporter much, but nearly
> everyone is nice to him. Sometimes I wish those days had never ended.[5]

In his forties, Harry was nostalgic but realistic about his work at the *Times*,
once telling listeners to his radio commentary at CBS that the first six months
of a young reporter's career are the happiest. "You have not yet found out
that the glamour of the newspaper business is largely an illusion, that your
importance is highly qualified, that the free passes to the burlesque shows
are in lieu of salary," he said. "You are meeting the old hands, the good men
who have stuck it out, and gradually being accepted as an equal, and there is
a sense of excitement that a lot of men never get anytime in their lives. You
cherish little stories, cynical or sentimental or illustrative, and you never forget them."[6]

Sentiment aside, the seamier side of the profession as practiced in the
1940s came through in a story Harry shared from his days as a reporter.
At the time, newspapers published the names of people arrested for driving
drunk. An old hand at a newspaper explained to a new reporter that anyone
who came to the press room in city hall should be told that their paper published names because the competing paper published names, too. If the competing paper did not publish a particular name—and its reporter was known
to accept a $20 bribe to keep a name out—then their paper would not be ex-
pected to publish it. Meanwhile, the other reporter for the other newspaper
would tell the same story to anyone who came to him. At the end of the day
the reporters for both papers would split the money they had collected, usually $200 a week. In recalling this bit of chicanery, Harry never said whether
he participated in such a practice at the *Times*.[7]

Just two months after he had returned to the *Times*, Harry celebrated a
milestone for any writer, particularly one just twenty-three: the publication

of his novel. The genesis of the book reached back to his army days when he had access to a typewriter and the time to write whatever he wished. He had finished the untitled manuscript during his stint with the 3613th Ordnance Unit, even managing to land a New York literary agent, Eleanor King, to send the novel to publishers in the fall of 1945. Rejections from Little, Brown and Company and other publishers had followed, including one from a Houghton Mifflin editor who found it well written but, at times, imitative and forced, even exceedingly melodramatic.[8]

Better news came from Bernard Ackerman, Incorporated. It agreed to publish the novel in exchange for ten-percent royalties and a promise of better terms for his next book. By November, when no title had yet been determined, King told Harry someone had suggested *Tell Me About Women*.[9] The title came from a request posed by the protagonist, Joe Wilson, to a friend in the opening of the story and then repeated near its end.

The Book-of-the-Month Club recommended the novel to its members, publishing a photo of Harry in uniform and a favorable review in the club newsletter. "The writing has been compared to James Cain's, and it does have that author's direct attack," the review contended. "Yet Mr. Reasoner has something definitely his own. It is, I think, an underlying compassion which lets him speak with such uncanny clarity for other idealists of his generation. One fact is sure. Only a young man of today could have written this particular story."[10] With a first printing of 3,500 copies and a cover price of $2.50, *Tell Me About Women* arrived in hardcover from Ackerman's Beechhurst Press on April 12, 1946.[11]

Spread over just 189 pages, the plot of *Tell Me About Women* is easy to encapsulate: Young reporter Joe Wilson marries the girl of his dreams, Maris, after she returns from an affair with her college professor. When only a month later Joe discovers Maris is pregnant, he leaves her briefly but reconciles with her before he is inducted into the army. She asks for a divorce during his first furlough, then reconsiders when she realizes she loves him after all. Joe walks out of her life as she sleeps, deciding his love cannot overcome a lack of trust. Plot likely did not drive Harry as he typed the manuscript on his army-issue typewriter. He appears to have sought to present a coming-of-age story as seen through the eyes of a young idealist more interested in commenting on the world than changing it.

Critics tended to be kind and complimentary. The *Chicago Sun* reported that the book "tells a great deal more of the confusion which befogged his generation—the children of the Lost Generation, the kids who couldn't get lost because they were never found in the first place. Its importance, aside from the very fine writing, lies in the fact that it might be any young man's story—any very young man."[12] The *New York Herald-Tribune* called it "a young man's book…it has power, and if it oscillates between immaturity and

maturity it still stands as a first effort of unusual pith and brilliance." It disputed the jacket's claim that the author was cynical in the Cain style. "Reasoner seems not cynical at all, but sensitive and perceptive, and often saying
things, in a few words, that strike you as true and keenly observed."[13] A *New
York Post* columnist called it "the best novel about the war generation that I
have yet read. Watch Mr. Reasoner!"[14]

Harry had drawn so much from his own life that readers who knew him
could be excused for questioning how much of *Tell Me About Women* was actually fictional. His protagonist, Joe, lived in a Minnesota town during the
war, worked for the afternoon newspaper, had written for the college paper
and magazine, and had lost his mother at an early age and then his father to
a fall from a cliff. Joe drank a good deal, had paid for an abortion, and loved
a high-school classmate with blond hair and a slightly chipped front tooth.
The physical description of Maris was so close to that of Maura Anderson,
she was irritated when the book came out. "I think it was a fantasy that was
like therapy for him," Anderson said years later. "He married me and things
worked out and he left me. I think that was very satisfying."[15] Being linked to
a character who slept with a classmate as a sophomore, became pregnant by
a college professor, and generally treated her loving husband in a cold, confused manner was nothing to boast about.

Examining the novel in light of Harry's life, what may be most interesting in *Tell Me About Women* is what it revealed about the way he saw himself
at age twenty-three. After looking back on his parents' deaths and his own
struggles, Joe discloses the personal philosophy he had developed:

> So, after I went to work on the *News*, I formulated the whole thing into
> a precocious design for living. Friends are faithless, I said; friends sicken
> and die; friendship is the excess of companionship. Watch how you give
> yourself in friendship, therefore. Love is an illusion; confine your activi-
> ties to sex and secure a recommended contraceptive. Understanding is
> a myth; do your job and figure things out for yourself. Avoid the ex-
> cess, every time. Avoid the soul-stirring part; avoid the part that fills the
> throat; avoid the part that energizes you and makes you plan. You can
> do it, Joe; you can construct a tradition of mediocrity, you can pass on a
> stronghold of reserve to whoever comes after. In time, you might even
> be able to write a little bit about it.[16]

With the exception of the novel's final scene, in which Joe writes a good-
bye note to Maris and leaves her asleep in their apartment to return to the
army, Joe reacts to events with an almost lackadaisical attitude. He avoids
confrontations with his wife although their marriage is at stake. Throughout
the novel Joe analyzes the world but does not seek to shape it by exerting his

will upon it or even rebelling against it. In later years Harry would ask himself whether he was drifting through his own life. As a writer he would not employ such cynicism again until his political commentaries for ABC News. As a man he seemed to carry some of Joe's attitude over the many years ahead, nearly always remaining reserved in his emotional ties.

Harry had little time to savor the personal victory the book represented. His agent and publisher pushed him for a second book well before *Tell Me About Women* had reached bookstores.[17] Harry dutifully complied, working on a second book as his enlistment wound down and continuing with it upon his return to Minneapolis. By April, just a month before the second novel had to be completed in order to appear in the Ackerman catalog for the fall, Harry was having trouble. He needed more time—and perhaps less pressure.[18] In July, King asked again about his progress, reporting the good news that his book had entered its third printing. She later returned a short story, *The Tough Guy*, with news that *Esquire* and six other magazines had rejected it.[19]

Harry did write another novel, shorter than *Tell Me About Women* but revisiting the kinds of sexual tensions and ruminations that had marked his previous work. Its main character, Paul Hansen, was a veteran whose left arm had been impaired by a freak accident during the war. Reporting from Los Angeles for a Minneapolis newspaper as the war winds down, Paul seeks the normal life he had once enjoyed. Then he meets a boyhood friend, Buddy Todd, also inexperienced with women. The story shifts to Buddy's hopes that his new girl may be the one with whom he could spend his life. The pitfalls and entanglements he faces raise the question of whether a man can honestly commit to one woman without compromising his free will.

Whether too short in length or too shallow in its objectives, the untitled manuscript failed to find a publisher.[20] *Tell Me About Women* remained Harry's only published novel.

In his postwar personal life Harry was having far more success. He had met a University of Minnesota law student, Kay Carroll, the eldest of three daughters of a Minneapolis attorney, Lynn B. Carroll, and his wife, Evelyn Bremmen. Kay had graduated from West High School in 1942 but, three years younger than Harry, did not know him. Family memories place their first encounter at a café, the Bridge, among mutual friends from the university, not long after *Tell Me About Women* was published. Being a published novelist impressed Kay, and Harry later said she had reminded him of Ingrid Bergman, the actress in *Casablanca*. Kay was pretty, with black hair and an attractive build developed by years of swimming. She was a reader, too, and an optimistic person who was ready to try new things.

Months later her youngest sister, Lynn, could not believe Kay and Harry were to be married. "He was stocky and our family was tall and thin," Lynn recounted. "With all the grace of an eleven-year-old I said, 'But he's fat!' She was furious. 'He is not fat!' She was plainly very much in love." [21] Kay's intellect, her quiet way, and a wry sense of humor likely attracted Harry.

One possible impediment was her strong Catholic faith. While Harry may not have given it much thought, his sister, Esther, was plainly upset. "She was still firm in the belief that Catholics should marry Catholics and Protestants marry Protestants," Chet Newby recalled later. "Besides she felt Catholics had rather more children than they could cope with." [22] Dennis Newby remembered his mother's unhappiness over the idea Harry would marry a Catholic. "I don't think anybody had anything but affection for Kay because there was nothing not to like," he said. "But I think there was a lot of problem over that religion thing." [23]

Nevertheless, Harry and Kay married on September 7, 1946, at the Minneapolis Court House, a justice of the peace presiding and the Newbys and the Carrolls attending. They drove Chet's Pontiac to Lake Superior for a honeymoon. One of the other guests where they stayed was the mayor of Minneapolis, Hubert Humphrey, who later became a friend of Harry's. [24] At one point the newlyweds walked along the lake. The sky had turned gray, and waves crashed along the shoreline.

"Oh, isn't this eerie?" Kay exclaimed.

"No," Harry replied, "it's Superior." [25]

Housing in the city was tight after the war. At first the couple rented rooms in private homes, then stayed for a time with the Newbys, and eventually shared part of a Quonset hut in south Minneapolis. They had moved to a small house on 50th Street when the first of their seven children, Stuart, was born in June 1947. Kay had continued to study law, even as raising a child and caring for a husband slowed her progress. Her sister Lynn once visited overnight and saw the next morning how Kay managed. "She was sitting with the baby hooked in her arm with the bottle and the law book open on the kitchen table," Lynn recalled. "That's how she got through law school." [26] Harry, meanwhile, wrote news and movie reviews for the *Times*, although it must have seemed like a dead-end job given the general dearth of enthusiasm on the part of readers, advertisers, and owners.

Harry probably enjoyed the languid pace of the *Times* newsroom and the fact that as movie critic he had one of the few regular bylines in the paper. "You worked as a regular reporter in the morning and were allowed to see movies, free, in the movie screening rooms in the afternoon," he remembered years later, "and then for the Friday paper you wrote reviews of the movies, with the implied restriction that the reviews had to be favorable." [27]

Such recollections of his stint at the critic's desk were more whimsical than accurate. From the time Harry began reviewing movies in July 1946 with *Smoky*, an undistinguished Western starring Fred MacMurray, the contents of his notices ranged from high praise to outright rejection. [28] He usually found a middle ground, commending some aspect of a production and criticizing another. The reviews carried a neighborly tone, as though Harry were telling a friend whether the new Humphrey Bogart movie was worth seeing. (Usually it was, he determined.) He understood how different genres appealed to different audiences and seemed to judge most films by their own ambitions.

He punctuated the rote form of the reviews (few were more than 100 words and many just two or three paragraphs) with humorous, telling, or sarcastic observations:

Make Mine Music: It's got an awful lot of things in it, a few of which are very good, some of which are mediocre, and some of which are terrible. It's an uneven sort of hodgepodge.[29]

Diary of a Chambermaid: Paulette Goddard is the improbable and uninteresting heroine. Burgess Meredith, Hurd Hatfield and Francis Lederer all leer at her from time to time.[30]

The Searching Wind: Off hand it sounds like a pretty dull idea, and that's the way it turns out.[31]

Anna and the King of Siam: Linda Darnell plays Linda Darnell, distinguished as a harem girl.[32]

Till the End of Time: Obviously intended as a searching poignant inquiry into the readjustment problems of returning service men, certainly a fertile field, but it gets bogged down in a swamp of poor dialog, puerile conceptions and almost unbelievably poor acting.[33]

Angel on My Shoulder: Paul Muni, who has more white in his eyes than the Redcoats at Bunker Hill, returns to the screen of the State this week in an ambitious fantasy.[34]

My Darling Clementine: Victor Mature, cast as a tubercular and alcoholic surgeon turned gambler, is so much less bad than he usually is that he looks extremely good by comparison.[35]

Two Smart People: Lucille Ball and John Hodiak play a pair of gay, romantic swindlers....As always happens to Hollywood swindlers, they are at last trapped by dull, unromantic policemen.[36]

His tastes varied, but he could spot a classic, from *The Big Sleep* and *It's a Wonderful Life* to *Miracle on 34th Street*.[37] The dark of the theater would have been a welcome break from the *Times* newsroom for Harry, and Kay could accompany him on the cheapest of dates for a couple getting started in life.

Harry may not have remained content writing news in the morning and reviewing movies in the afternoon, but other forces spurred a change of employment. The *Times* announced its merger with the *Star* and *Tribune* on May 17, 1948, contending that rising costs in terms of wages and newsprint, along with other expenses, had prompted the paper to close when it could not find a buyer.[38] The *Star* and the *Tribune* absorbed most of the 230 employees, but Harry was not among them.

Why he was passed over is unclear because of conflicting stories. In later years Harry told interviewers that he had lost his position as drama critic for writing an unfavorable review of a traveling theater production. Indeed, his last movie review appeared in September 1947, seven months before the newspaper folded. In an employment application he completed in 1951, he cited the merger of the *Times* with the *Star* and *Tribune* as the reason he left.[39] In a radio essay he delivered on CBS in 1967, Harry noted that he was not offered a job on the surviving newspapers as most of the staff had been, leading him to feel as though he had been fired.[40] Whatever the case, for the first time as a husband and father, he was out of work. Within weeks of the merger his second child, Ann, was born.

The offer of a job with a Chicago newspaper tempted him, but Harry decided to remain in Minneapolis.[41] He tried selling microscopes for Chet Newby, driving a Durant sedan across Minnesota to pitch the instruments to schools. He was no salesman—rejection cut too deeply.[42]

Later in June he was back to writing, although for corporate communications rather than the press. Northwest Airlines had hired Harry to supervise publicity and public relations projects. As assistant director of publicity he earned $6,000 a year, a $1,200 boost from what he had been earning at the *Times*.[43] Unlike the faltering newspaper, Northwest promised vitality and adventure as it pursued postwar expansion that included routes to Tokyo, Seoul, China, and Manila. In December the airline added Honolulu to its Pacific routes.[44] Harry and Kay flew to the Hawaiian Islands as part of his job, a greater perk than going to an afternoon movie without needing a ticket. A year after Harry joined the company, Northwest added Boeing 377 Stratocruisers to its fleet.[45] Working from corporate headquarters on University Avenue in St. Paul, he could see a future with the company.

Publicity and promotions meant travel, another new wrinkle for Harry. The public relations staff, made up of four or five writers and two secretaries supervised by Joe Ferris, a former newsman himself, wrote press releases, articles, and items for radio and television for the entire Northwest route. They also wrote for the company newspaper. Harry flew to Milwaukee, Portland, Chicago, and any other city served by Northwest in order to produce copy that might be used in the news media. Publicity writers would meet with business editors to publicize the airline, linking its services to the needs of the business community.

When celebrities such as comedian Bob Hope or baseball's Babe Ruth or statesman John Foster Dulles traveled on Northwest, Harry or other members of the department noted their arrival in town, often with a quick interview and photograph developed in an airport darkroom to be provided to the media.[46] "He was an excellent writer," recalled Harold Peyer, who joined the department as a writer the same month Harry was hired. "He had a command of the English language that was fabulous. He was a good editor too. He was a very precise man."[47]

Harry and Harold Peyer worked together for nearly eighteen months, and the young family men became friends. They shared simple dinners at their homes, spaghetti and a few beers. "It was that kind of a time when everybody was trying to get their feet on the ground and watching a career of one sort or another," Peyer remembered.[48] His wife, Eileen, recalled a visit that found Harry watching the children while Kay was occupied. "Harry met us at the door with diaper pins in his mouth and one kid under his arm. I said, 'Whoa! What happened?' And he said, 'Kay is studying, and this is my job.' He was changing one kid and watching the spaghetti boil. He was pretty versatile."[49] Money remained tight, especially for a single-income household with two children.

At Northwest Airlines the Reasoner sense of humor had toned down from the newsroom days. He remained easygoing. "As a matter of fact he was almost unflappable. There wasn't anything that really got his goat or upset him. He sort of took life the way it came," Harold Peyer said. "He could also be so deadly serious, in the sense that he wanted everything perfect. He wanted the job done right."[50] Harry assigned stories, critiqued them, and turned them back to the writers if they needed revision. He was cool under pressure, confident, and not at all lazy. Even as he wrote publicity for the airline, Harry retained his newsman's senses of observation and reflection, if just in conversation with his friends. "Harry was kind of a philosopher in some ways," according to Peyer. "He could be talking on a serious subject but do it in a very lighthearted way. He was very observant of the human race and some of its foibles."[51]

Harry remained restless and uncertain of the career he desired. In casting about for an answer, he turned for a moment to politics. He ran for alderman from Minneapolis's 13th ward in the May 1949 primary elections. He was one of eight candidates seeking a four-year term on the twenty-six-member council and, by virtue of the alphabet, the last listed for the ward. The top two primary candidates would vie for the position in the regular election. Harry ran as a Republican and, at twenty-six, was the youngest in the field.

In answer to questions put to each candidate by the *Minneapolis Tribune*, he contended that he favored changing the form of the city government but offered no specifics. He called for a reappraisal of where the city obtained its revenues, with considerable relief for taxpayers as a goal. He criticized the city system of putting each alderman in charge of liquor licensing and control in his ward as "ridiculous—a real encouragement to venal and irre-

sponsible men" but had no specific alternative other than a system he called
aboveboard, responsible, and simple. When asked his qualifications, he cited
his experience as a college student, army veteran, and newspaper reporter. "I
have had many opportunities to observe city government at first hand and I
believe I have both of the primary qualifications of a responsible public ser-
vant," he added. "Liberal but realistic and flexible principles, and the political
ability to make my principles count in every-day government. Most 'practical politicians' lack the first quality; most liberals lack the second." [52]

Voters were not swayed by Harry's responses or the campaign fliers he
distributed while canvassing neighborhoods. With 381 votes, or four percent
of the 8,626 votes cast, he came in seventh. [53] Politics would not be the answer
to Harry's question of where he belonged.

Not long before Christmas in 1949 Harry surprised Harold Peyer by telling him good-bye. He had quit the publicity department. Peyer never knew
exactly why, although he suspected it involved a conflict with the publicity
department director, Joe Ferris, whom Peyer considered fairly easygoing as
a boss. "I don't know if anybody in the office knew what caused Harry to
leave," he said. "Harry never talked about it, and neither did Ferris. I sensed
that, while there was some animosity involved, it was one where they had
agreed to disagree." [54] On an application form a few years later Harry contended he left the airline because of a "personal disagreement" with his supervisor. [55] The Peyers never talked to Harry again, seeing him only when he
turned up on television.

For Harry the Northwest stint had become just another job in the search
for a career that could bring him satisfaction as well as money. He spent the
first six months of the new year and new decade as a freelance writer, handling public relations accounts and other writing assignments. He also returned to college, earning three B's and an A in four journalism classes in
the winter term at the University of Minnesota. His spring term report was
as good—two B's and an A—but included incompletes in two courses. [56]
Whether he ran out of money or just lost interest in completing a degree,
Harry never returned to the classroom.

Journalism still presented the easier path for making a living as a word-
smith. In the summer of 1950 Harry began writing for WCCO, the radio
station owned and operated by CBS that ruled the Minnesota airwaves and a
large part of the upper Midwest by means of a 50,000-watt transmitter. The
station had been founded in 1925 and purchased in full by CBS in 1932. Sig
Mickelson, one of Harry's former college professors, had created its radio
news bureau in 1942. [57]

The star attraction at WCCO was Cedric Adams, the best-known and
best-loved writer and broadcaster in the region. He had been a gag writer for
a cartoon magazine and had been writing a column for the *Minneapolis Star*

by the time he began broadcasting at WCCO in 1931.[58] When Harry joined the station Adams was writing a daily column for the *Star* and *Tribune*, serving as emcee at all sorts of public functions, and firmly established as a regional celebrity. A weekly program on the CBS national network spread his fame even farther. A description of Adams written for the 40th anniversary of WCCO could be applied to Harry as a national audience would come to know him: "He was not a comedian—yet, he could be uproariously funny at times. He was not a master of ceremonies, but he could be entertaining. He was not a public speaker, though he did appear before countless audiences in the Northwest. He was simply 'Cedric.' His hallmark was an eye for detail, the trivia of life that comes from living in a small town."[59]

Adams was distinctive whether on radio, in print, or in person. "He had a deep, mellow voice and robust laugh," a WCCO colleague, Allen Gray, remembered. "He was the kind of person you gravitated toward. He could write a column double-parked while he waited for his wife to finish shopping. He'd have a little portable typewriter with him."[60] Sig Mickelson recalled that Adams had no training as a broadcaster or news writer but brought a human quality to the job. He was personable and likable, keys to his enormous appeal and popularity with listeners.[61] Harry, asked to reminisce about Adams for a biography of the broadcaster, said: "I suppose nobody ever really did figure out why he was as great as he was…I suppose it was believability that came across, not only in his column, but over the air. He was always completely at home with the people he was talking to. And I suppose that's what made him a success."[62]

Not surprisingly, Cedric Adams once had spoken to West High School students while Harry attended classes.[63] How much influence he may have had on Harry at any time of his life can only be guessed. By the time WCCO had hired Harry to write the news for Adams he was twenty-seven and already shared many of Adams's qualities as a writer and as a person. Perhaps Harry saw in Adams the success that was possible by writing for broadcast, by focusing on the news instead of fiction, and by becoming a public personality. "It is amazing," Bob Hope observed, "that one man can wield the power that Cedric holds on the Twin Cities and suburbia."[64] But Adams had a formidable trait that Harry seemed to lack: drive. By his own reckoning Adams produced twenty-three broadcasts a week, fifty road shows a year, and a daily newspaper column. He answered 2,500 fan letters each week.[65]

Yet, Harry and others remarked later, Adams was easy to work for. Writing for him, though, paid poorly. Harry earned just $3,000 a year, $1,800 less than he made at the *Times* and less than half of the $6,250 he was earning when he left Northwest Airlines. He supplemented the WCCO salary with a half-time job directing public relations for the 18,000-member Minnesota Education Association in St. Paul, earning another $1,800 annually.[66] Harry may have recognized that writing for Adams could lead to a career in broadcasting. "This was a tremendous job for a kid twenty-six, twenty-seven years old," Gray said. "It wouldn't have paid a lot of money, but the credits you could take anywhere."[67]

Harry was one of six people working on WCCO news broadcasts. Five teletypes brought news to the station, and Harry and others rewrote the information for the 12:30 p.m. and 10 p.m. newscasts handled by Adams, who was too busy to write news himself.[68] "He insisted, because he was such a fine writer, that he have a good writer for the news," Joyce Lamont, another WCCO broadcaster, remembered. "It's very possible Cedric influenced Harry. He was very fond of him. It was mutual. They admired each other."[69] Adams's style—a fast delivery, with each word pronounced clearly but with an informal tone—included an occasional ad-lib. He demanded a story that could end the broadcast on a humorous note. "People would wait for that delightful little remark, a double entendre, and they loved it," Lamont said. "Everybody else was reading copy and you could tell they were reading copy. But that Cedric. He had that informality."[70] Broadcasting folklore in the Twin Cities has it that Adams drew so many listeners at 10 p.m. that airline pilots watched the lights across the prairie go out at 10:15 when he finished his broadcast.[71]

The Adams style would have fit Harry's own writing preferences. He, too, enjoyed spicing up a routine report with a turn of phrase or a play on words. It was hard work, of course, and Lamont remembered Harry taking the job seriously while remaining friendly with his colleagues.[72]

His reputation as a writer, whether he knew it or not, was moving beyond Minneapolis. Mickelson, who in 1949 had left WCCO for CBS News in New York, remembered the name of his former college student when the station's general manager boasted about him. "I began to hear stories about the fact that CCO had one of the greatest news writers in the business," Mickelson said. "He would frequently tell me what a find they had in Harry Reasoner."[73] However, Harry did not remain at the station long enough to build on his reputation. When he announced after little more than a year at WCCO that he was leaving, the staff was surprised to learn where he was headed: the Philippines.

As far back as high school Harry had dreamed of working in the foreign service.[74] What motivated him to seek such a position with three children— daughter Elizabeth had been born in January 1951—may have been an unsatisfied wanderlust. Or perhaps he simply was tired of working two jobs in the only town he had known as an adult. In February he completed an application for employment with the government of the United States. He cited a "long ambition for foreign service" as his reason for wanting to leave WCCO. He also asked for a base salary of no less than $6,000 as a press officer, public affairs officer, or radio officer.[75] The Minneapolis recruiting team that interviewed Harry later that month admitted he was impressive. "Anyone should be interested in this young chap. He is absolutely tops," an interviewer wrote in a memo. "He has poise, charm, a wonderful mind and fine personality traits....Let's be sure to hire this one."[76] The government deemed Harry acceptable in June but waited until August to assign him to the State Department's United States Information Agency operation in Manila.[77]

In September Harry traveled alone to Washington, D.C., for training. Following a three-week passage to the Philippines, he arrived in Manila on November 11, 1951, and moved into the Manila Hotel and later to the Bayview Hotel. "It must have been quite a sumptuous town before 1941," he wrote to Esther. "Now the big palms along Dewey boulevard are gone—cut down by the Japanese to make the street a landing strip. I haven't seen the downtown areas, but even along the boulevard there are still skeleton buildings, ruined by artillery fire. And there's a general air of economic decay. And millions and millions of people. So far I've seen a few lizards, including one which lives in my hotel room. We don't bother each other."[78]

Harry worked at the Regional Production Center (RPC) of the USIA, located in an American Embassy compound in a suburb called Pasay City. The editorial offices had been a club for enlisted Navy men. Harry's desk sat on a balcony that ran around the top of the building, with one entire side simply screen. "The rain on the tin roof is quite loud," he wrote Esther, "and the breeze is picking up a little. It's kind of pleasant in a way but not too conducive to much work."[79] Cockroaches, large and sturdy with wings enabling them to fly, were a Manila mainstay. Harry found that bug spray was ineffective, and he had been advised that a Philippine kitten would kill the bugs when they came out at night. "Kittens are cheaper than DDT," he later observed, "and more fun."[80]

Almost immediately Harry became consumed by his duties. The American staff, aided by Filipinos in the printing plant, produced publications aimed at spreading the U.S. point of view throughout the Far East. "Production, of course, was magazines and propaganda," recalled Ken Landgren, the plant manager at the time Harry arrived. "We did the printing right there. We had a big plant, lots of natives running a lot of equipment. We turned out a lot of stuff."[81] Harry and two or three others wrote articles for the monthly *Free World Magazine*, the RPC's major publication, as well as various printed material. "*Free World* was the big thing," according to Bob Thompson, who supervised printing at the RPC. "It was telling the truth about America throughout the whole Far East. You could call it propaganda, but that didn't seem to be nice words. We printed the truth."[82]

Taking a human-interest approach and featuring lots of photographs in more than forty pages, the magazine promoted life in the United States and other democracies in dozens of languages and dialects. "He was writing good things," Landgren said of Harry's work. "Of course, much propaganda is saying how great the world is if you behave yourself, this sort of thing, and bringing the American picture to the Far East." Harry saw the work as worthwhile and the writing as a way to extend his professional skills while enjoying a new adventure.[83]

The newness soon wore off. Loneliness and boredom, both linked to the absence of the family, marked Harry's first months in Manila. So did a brief return to the freedom of single life. There were evenings with Ken Landgren and his wife, Lynn, and the friends he quickly made among the other Americans. "They used to kid him all the time, calling him Shufflefoot," Ken Landgren remembered. "His feet were not pigeon-toed but the opposite. He walked like that, like a little duck. But what a neat guy."[84] He visited a rice plantation, dined in his dinner jacket at the Seafront Club, and visited the Riviera nightclub and casino.[85] While the Landgrens and other friends played bridge, Harry lounged in a corner reading a book. There were food and drinks at the Port Officers' Club, the Here's How bar with its renowned singer Ricky, the Marco's nightclub, and other places around the city.[86]

In Minneapolis, Kay completed her law studies—she graduated magna cum laude—and spent two or three months preparing for the voyage to Manila. She was excited about the adventure that lay before all of them.[87] She did have one request: She asked that the children be baptized in the Roman Catholic Church before they had their tonsils removed prior to undertaking the journey across the Pacific.[88] To his sister, Harry expressed misgivings. "I have said to anyone concerned many times, and say again, in writing, that I will use all of my influence to prevent my children being raised as Roman Catholics," Harry told Esther in a letter. He had no objection to the baptism, however, because of a "clear understanding that it means no strings, implied or otherwise."[89] Perhaps Harry was posturing for Esther—she had thought going to Manila was a silly idea to start with—or at a later time he relented; all of the children were raised as Catholics and Harry eventually became, according to a priest who was a close friend, the most Catholic non-Catholic he had known.[90] At the time, though, the issue was fractious.

The Minnesota family, reunited in March 1952, began to adjust to the tropical climate. Harry had rented a newly built house with six rooms in a Manila suburb called Paranaque. The house had concrete pillars instead of columns, white woodwork, and a large patio in the same red tile found throughout the first floor.[91] Like most of the American families, the Reasoners employed Filipino servants to cook, clean, and wash clothes. Kay, optimistic and not prone to Harry's sort of complaining, told Esther in letters shortly after her arrival that the house had become her immediate project. "We are very anxious to make the house comfortable, get the babies used to a strange land," she said, "and then I think we can have a lot of fun."[92] Adjusting to the lizards that joined them was an effort for Kay but not for Stuart and Ann, who hoped to make one a pet.[93]

One of their diversions was the community theater. In May, Harry and Kay took parts in a fifteen-minute scene from the play *Medea*—he as Creon and she as one of the women. That summer Kay won the lead in a presentation of *The Moon Is Blue*. In December, Harry found himself in rehearsals for *The Philadelphia Story*, presented by the Manila Theater Guild. The *Manila Bulletin* noted that Harry would be making his stage debut in the lead role of C. K. Dexter Haven. (Cary Grant had played the part in the 1940 film.) In a review, critic Vicente Rivera Jr. called Harry "properly suave, personable, and after a momentary woodenness of expression gets rolling smoothly. He has the kind of voice audiences pray for in a play. As the bantering, knowing Dexter, perhaps Mr. Reasoner should unbend a little more. Just that much little more."[94]

The pressures at the RPC were minimal—"Nobody was busting their pick on deadline," Ken Landgren recalled. "It was an easy life." Yet, the restlessness and uncertainty that seemed to guide Harry's outlook had not abated. In his letters to Esther, he was skeptical of the long-term appeal of the life he had found in Manila. "The attractions of the service—servants, cheap liquor and cigarettes, travel—hold no permanent appeal for me," he told her.[95] Travel that fall took him to Bangkok, Rangoon, and Hong Kong, the very activity he had yearned for as a teen-ager. In Phnom Penh, Harry joined a Cambodian businessman and his wife for dinner. Unable to use chopsticks, and having no fork available, Harry stared at his food. The Cambodian woman fed him, bite by bite through course after course, for the evening. (He later observed, "I suppose that's why I'll always like Chinese food.")[96] In spite of the travel, he soon complained of the work itself, producing the magazine, a weekly photo review sheet, and various books and pamphlets.[97]

Harry began pondering a return to the United States as soon as his two-year tour ended, if not earlier, and possibly even rejoining the staff at WCCO. The plotting and scheming that marked his letters from the army began to appear in his missives from Manila. Plans to ship goods from the States to the islands to resell, rejoining WCCO in its television department, persuading Senator Hubert Humphrey to help him obtain a transfer to Washington, where he could quietly resign from the USIA—it all may have been mental diversions, daydreams to pass the time, or the thoughts of a dissatisfied if not unhappy man.[98]

For the three years Harry worked at the RPC he earned good to excellent evaluations even though he questioned the efficiency of the department and felt underused.[99] "Harry could do the work of four men, he did his stuff so fast. He could put stories together," Bob Thompson observed. "He was disgruntled at times and he just felt that he could do so much more for the operation and he wasn't given enough work to do." [100] One supervisor suggested he was lazy and indifferent, a charge both Harry and another supervisor disputed. [101]

Harry turned back to fiction for a creative pastime. He began at least one novel and completed several short stories during his stay in Manila, placing his characters in settings familiar to him. One story featured a new arrival to Manila watching the lizards crawl on the ceiling of his hotel room. Another story told about a police reporter hired by an airline public relations firm; disillusioned by executive politics and an incompetent boss, he returns to the courthouse beat. Later, Harry wrote about a man who works for a propaganda center in the Orient. Notes for an unfinished novel tell of a young army man enrolled in college courses and then sent to Arkansas to work for an ordnance company. [102] Years later Harry dismissed these efforts as third-rate Irwin Shaw. [103] No magazines bought the stories he wrote, which would have provided him a sense of validation as well as an extra paycheck.

Money remained a concern. Harry had earned raises in grade and pay, but it did not seem enough to him. By November 1952 the family had left the suburban house for a prefabricated home within the American government's Military Plaza, partly to save $50 a month but also to enjoy the added security and the presence of other American children. [104] "Now if we could just solve the family income problem, gross, net or otherwise, everything would be fine," Kay wrote to Esther. "Only the threat of impending bankruptcy keeps this from being a most enjoyable trip." [105] The move placed Harry a short walk from the RPC offices. By the following June they had sold their car for $2,250 and planned to make do with cabs. The family would move again, into a four-bedroom home, that summer. They would use the fourth bedroom as a study, at least for a while. Kay was pregnant again, and in October 1953 she gave birth to Jane, their fourth child. [106]

Returning to the United States remained Harry's immediate goal. He told Esther he had a firm offer of a job with the television department of WCCO, although the money was less than what he had been earning at Northwest Airlines. He believed it was the opportunity that mattered, and he wanted the change. [107]

Esther worried about Harry. She had been against the move to the Philippines, and now her fears of trouble for the growing family seemed to be realized. She chose an unusual way of checking on them. Reading that Adlai Stevenson, former Illinois governor and Democratic nominee for president the previous year, planned to visit Manila in March 1953, Esther wrote him a letter asking him to look in on her brother. [108]

Harry thought nothing would come from Esther's letter—until a Stevenson aide informed the American embassy that Stevenson wanted to see

Harry in his suite at the ambassador's residence. Harry spent the day worrying about the meeting. When Harry walked into the suite, Stevenson was busy changing clothes for a dinner that evening. Standing before Harry without his trousers, Stevenson looked him over.

"Ah, you are the young man whose sister is concerned about his health," he said. "Tell me, how are you?"

Harry assured him he was well.

"Good," Stevenson replied. "Thanks for coming up and giving me that authoritative firsthand report. You look to be in good health." [109]

After barely a minute of pleasantries, their meeting ended. Esther later received a letter from Stevenson assuring her that her brother was healthy and well. A few years later Harry recalled the episode after the Democratic Party had once more nominated Stevenson for president: "I don't suppose that again in my lifetime would I have a chance to say that I have talked to a President of the United States, or even a candidate, with his pants off." [110]

Little else out of the ordinary took place during the Reasoners' remaining months in the Philippines. In spite of their money problems and Harry's ongoing soul-searching regarding his career, the family enjoyed their island lifestyle. "We were out at this club one day and the girls were sitting there in their swimsuits and we're sitting there and the kids are in the pool," Bob Thompson recalled with a chuckle. "And Harry just looked at me and looked at the girls and kind of shook his head and had that little smile. 'You know, Bob, we got a couple of lovely broads.'" Throughout their friendship, well beyond Manila, they enjoyed recalling that moment of bliss. [111]

Another theater role came up that fall, the lead in a production of *The Seven-Year Itch*. Focused on the possibility of a television news job, perhaps Harry was trying to acclimate himself to performing before an audience. Kay spent her days caring for baby Jane and the other children. By the spring of 1954 the Reasoners had planned their home leave for May. What it held for their future was uncertain. Harry wanted to visit Minneapolis, St. Louis, New York, and Washington in the search for a stateside job. He even began considering another hitch with the foreign service, perhaps in Europe, but seemed adamant that he would not return to the Philippines. [112] In trying to balance his economic needs—the foreign service probably would pay a bit better than the WCCO job or another news position—with what might be his best chance to see Europe, he struggled to decide the best course.

When Harry arrived in New York he called on Sig Mickelson, now the head of CBS News. "He said he wanted to get into television," Mickelson recalled, but Harry admitted he knew nothing about the medium. "So I said, 'Why don't you go out and find yourself a job for a year at a television station somewhere and come back at the end of the year,' not knowing exactly what was going to happen." [113] Harry's timing, for once, was fortuitous. A new television station preparing to go on the air in Minneapolis needed a news director. With his experience as a writer and his knowledge of the Twin Cities, Harry was a strong candidate. On August 31, 1954, he resigned from the USIA, citing an offer by KEYD-TV and "the economic future of myself and my family."[114] He may not have known it, but the USIA was considering him for another assignment, possibly to Greece or to Cambodia.[115] By the time the USIA officials in those nations had inquired about his availability, Harry had returned home.

KEYD, Channel 9, was the fourth television station and the first independent to go on the air in the Twin Cities. Its owner, Baker Properties, began laying the groundwork for its first broadcast six months before its scheduled debut in January 1955. It hired staff, obtained programming, and built a studio in the twenty-eight-story Foshay Tower in downtown Minneapolis, topped by the station's antennas. The associate general manager, Bob Fransen, was a *Minnesota Daily* and *Ski-U-Mah* alumnus from his days at the University of Minnesota, and he had been hired for his first job in radio by Sig Mickelson.

Those connections, as well as having known Fransen from his Minneapolis days, would have helped Harry be considered for the position of KEYD news director. "We thought he was a pretty good candidate," Fransen recalled. "We also knew that we weren't going to be able to get, because of budget and things, Walter Cronkite or somebody huge. Even among the local news anchors none of them would have been interested in going from a well-established newscast at a network affiliate to taking a chance with a brand-new independent station." Harry looked good on the air, and he understood news and the market. Yet there was concern over his lack of television experience.[116]

When Channel 9 began broadcasting on January 9, 1955, Harry was the news department, writing and producing newscasts at 6 p.m. and 10 p.m., the late-night program later moving to 10:30. Lacking network film because of its independent status, KEYD used still photos, slides, and other graphics to supplement its news, weather, and sports. Each night he sat behind a desk on the set, a nameplate in front of him, a globe to the right, and a map of the world as a backdrop.

Even with his skills and talents Harry was not a natural, and he was learning with every broadcast. "At first he looked like a hayseed, when he first got on the air," KEYD's chief announcer, Stuart Armstrong, recalled. "He just gave that impression of just coming off the farm. He was very green and rough when he started out. This was something very, very new to him."[117] Glenn Smith, the station's operating engineer, also remembered the difficult adjustments Harry went through. "He always did have a little trouble speaking on air," Smith said. "When he first started he mumbled a lot. He did stumble quite a bit."[118] There were plenty of goofs in the KEYD studio, of course, as there would be for any new station that broadcast live in the early years of television. Videotape did not exist, and each newscast had the feel of a stage production.[119]

One night in the early weeks of his KEYD broadcasts Harry simply froze on camera. He could not speak or read a word of the script, and the camera went to a black screen or to other programming. The next night, just minutes before going on the air, he realized he could not speak. Someone had to take his place.[120] Such stage fright was not uncommon in broadcasting. "You can sit there and look at that dumb camera twenty-four hours a day, but when those two little red lights go on it is a horrifying thing," Armstrong said. "Here I am, in front of God and everybody, what do I say and how am I going to say it?"[121] Harry regained his voice and called Kay, who reminded him in no uncertain terms that the family needed the money and told him not to do it again.

Harry was back on the air the next day and never had the problem again. "I sometimes think that if she had felt sorry for me," he said later, "I never would have gone back."[122] Indeed, broadcasting had frightened him in the beginning. He later told friends that Kay had suggested that, if need be, he drink some whiskey before sitting in front of the camera.[123]

The unique quality of his scripts and his straightforward demeanor distinguished Harry if his delivery did not. "Harry was not a real colorful person," said Jack Horner, the sports anchor for KEYD. "He was kind of dull on the air. Actually, people did not take to him right away. Harry did not appeal to the run-of-the-mill news fellow. Harry appealed to the more erudite class of people. He just wanted to give them straight news, very authentic, and once in a while he would throw a very funny quip in there."[124] He began to draw an audience as well as attention from his peers. "He had an honesty about his approach and a sincerity that just seemed to click pretty well with the viewers," Fransen said.[125] Horner attributed Harry's growing popularity to his tone as "a real down-to-earth newsman. People really, truly appreciated the sincerity and the quality of his news."[126] Armstrong believed Harry's years as a news writer gave his reports a different quality than most television news writers. "Most of us, as we were coming up in the news business, we were not trained news people. Harry was," Armstrong said. "I would go in and I'd rip off some news and read it and that was it. But Harry would rewrite it in his style. It was a lot different and, in my opinion, much more listenable."[127]

While working at KEYD, Harry began writing what he came to call "end pieces," newscast wrap-ups that allowed him to comment on a news item while reporting its salient facts. They tended toward the humorous observation or subtly sarcastic response. His end pieces sealed a relationship with viewers that was unique in the market. One end piece followed reports about the romantic life of Princess Margaret:

> You may remember that last week on our inside story of the Margaret-Townsend romance we predicted there would be no marriage. We are now able to tell you exclusively why, from the same drunken sailor who gave us the other inside story.
>
> It's because of Elsa Maxwell. Margaret, considering the thing from all angles, has made a fairly deep study of the married life of her Uncle Edward, who gave up the throne for a woman named Wallis.
>
> Margaret could probably foresee herself and Capt. Townsend in a few years, when the glamour of a daring marriage had worn off, when her face had begun to sag like Wallis's, and when Capt. Townsend, his waistline gone, had let his membership expire in the Gentlemen Jockeys Club. She could probably foresee those gay parties at which she and an aging Uncle Edward might stare at each other with the same inexpressible boredom you can see in his eyes now in news pictures.
>
> Better spinsterhood and a box of souvenirs tied up in a lavender ribbon, Margaret decided, than marriage and a string of parties with Elsa Maxwell and her lavender friends.[128]

In a column for the *Minneapolis Tribune*, television writer Will Jones called Harry's newscast the most quotable in the area. "The sad truth, I'm afraid, is that most of the other newscasters don't come up with quotable material when they're on the air," he told readers. "That KEYD-TV allows him to present his news with this extra penetration and spark is a big factor in his favor."[129]

To attract viewers KEYD tried to do as much live coverage as possible, including local sports and news.[130] "It was so clumsy to get all that heavy equipment in one place and get it all working and everything and get a good signal through," remembered Tom Carlyon, the station's technician and cameraman. One of the memorable stories Harry covered live for the station was the first-degree murder trial of dentist A. Arnold Axilrod, accused of strangling a twenty-three-year-old patient he had been accused of impregnating. Harry and KEYD's managing director, Robert Purcell, tried but failed to persuade the judge in the case to allow the station to broadcast the trial. Still, the station aired live reports outside the courtroom.[131]

Outside of the regular newscasts, Harry learned the basics of writing and producing other news programs. He served as host of a half-hour news documentary show, *Twin City Heartbeat*, at 8 p.m. Wednesdays. Each week he took viewers behind the scenes of a community-service organization with both live and filmed segments.[132] In the summer of 1956 he produced an unusually frank program about racial prejudice in Minneapolis and St. Paul. "The Invisible Fence" featured interviews with middle-class black residents of the Twin Cities and examined their lives, focusing on what they endured in a supposedly tolerant Northern city. Presenting incidents of inequality and injustice, the program closed with a plea for tolerance. *Variety* praised the program and Harry, and it won an honorable mention in the Robert E. Sherwood Freedom and Justice TV Awards.[133]

KEYD-TV won other honors for its news programs. The University of Minnesota Journalism School presented its news and community service award to Harry and KEYD-TV in 1955.[134] It won the top television news award in February 1956 from the Northwest Radio-TV News Association, which cited the station's "depth of coverage and individualist treatment" of the news.[135] What it could not win was a larger audience. The station remained in fourth place in a four-station market. "We were a little station competing against three giants," Tom Carlyon said. "They had a lot of money and our station didn't."[136] In later years Harry told people KEYD earned high ratings only twice—when it carried the state high school basketball championships, and when it showed a film on water safety instead of a speech by Adlai Stevenson that the other stations aired at the same time.[137]

The uphill battle to gain viewers at KEYD as well as the low pay may have led Harry to a pessimistic view of his future at the station—and in television news in general. Or he may have tired once more of Minneapolis and the routine he had reestablished there. "I think he was kind of casting about, to try to find out what he was going to do with his life," said his sister-in-law, Lynn Carroll. "Whether he was unsure about what he wanted to do, I don't know. I think that he waffled."[138] Some sense of dissatisfaction spurred him to apply for reinstatement with the USIA. Whatever pitch Harry made to rejoin the agency did not impress its personnel department, which still had the resignation letter citing the Reasoner family's monetary considerations. "This case fits [department] policy of not rehiring a man who resigns for personal gain like a glove fits a hand," stated a note dated March 15, 1956.[139] That door closed firmly in Harry's face, another bridge burned.

Still, Harry had one more avenue left to explore. Close to a year and a half had passed since Sig Mickelson had suggested Harry learn about television news. "He was back in the office," Mickelson remembered, "and said, 'I've had my year.'"[140] Harry had impressed Mickelson as a superb writer and editor, and the news executive had hoped the time would come when CBS News would have a place for him. Mickelson did not hire people for the news, public affairs, or sports departments at CBS News. He sent Harry to John Day, the director of news for the network. Day's offer gave Harry more than a moment's pause: He could join the television news department as a temporary member of the writing staff. He would be paid just under $158 a week for a guarantee of no more than eight or nine weeks. "He took a real gamble coming in on a temporary job at a very small salary," Mickelson said.[141]

Harry was unsure he should take the risk. His fifth child, Mary Ray, had been born in May. How could his family live on half of what he had been making—and in New York? They had settled into a good life in Minneapolis and enjoyed their friends. There were Dixieland concerts with Bob and Jane Purcell, bridge games with Jack Horner and his wife, and shows to see at the Radisson Hotel's Torch Room. Harry had slipped into a routine at the station.[142] On the other hand, KEYD had changed hands in May and the new owners decided eliminating the news department was a good way to save money. Harry, they reasoned, could work in the announcer's booth or handle public relations. He tried to find a job with the other stations in town.[143] Even with the changes at KEYD, the CBS News offer, with its great potential but great drawbacks, weighed upon him.[144]

Finally, Kay spoke up. "You'd better go," she told her husband. "I don't want you spending your forties blaming me and the children for keeping you from your chance in the big time."[145] Harry accepted the offer the next day and was asked to report to New York by the end of July.[146]

The CBS News job would be his sixth position since he had left the army ten years earlier. Was Harry drifting through life, displaying the kind of "itchy feet" that had taken his father from one job to another? Oddly, though, the experiences he had collected in the decade before he joined CBS News would benefit him as a journalist and as a writer who observed life and commented on it. By the time he packed for New York he was a thirty-three-year-old husband and father who had seen a good deal of the United States and a part of the world few had known. The work itself—as reporter, public relations man, political candidate, freelancer, radio writer, government propagandist, news writer, and broadcaster—had kept him writing. More important, perhaps, it had kept him thinking—about the world, about people, about himself.

Writing and thinking would be at the core of the skills Harry brought to New York. Both would become critical to the success he hoped to achieve.

CHAPTER FOUR

Taking a Chance at CBS News

I'm really grateful to journalism. I don't know how I would
have earned a living without it.　**H. R.**

T he risk Harry took in leaving Minneapolis for New York in July
1956 was not small, professionally or personally. The pay was poor,
and there was no guarantee of a full-time, permanent position. The
sole breadwinner for a family of seven, he would earn just $157.50 a week for
four months as a summer replacement on the CBS News assignment desk. If
he were to succeed, however, he would be part of a growing organization that
offered many opportunities to a well-spoken, good-looking young man who
could write and broadcast the news.

The early months were rough going. Harry stayed for a while with his
Army pal Walt Kingsley in Stamford, Connecticut. Then he moved into a
room at a YMCA in the city, paying fifteen dollars a week in rent and riding
the subway to work. As a new hire, he found himself in the office from four
in the afternoon until midnight. But he did have confidence in himself. "It
seems like kind of a limited job, after a small station where I did everything,"
he wrote to Esther, "but this end of it—the acquisition of film news, and occasional appearances on the film—would probably be the best place to lead
from into correspondent status."[1] If it were possible to become a CBS News
correspondent with only one year of broadcast experience, then the place to
begin was the assignment desk, the hub of activity for the young television
news operation.

CBS News, much like Harry, was still learning the craft of television
news in 1956, even though the medium had existed for a quarter of a century. CBS was not the first network to televise images, but it was the first to
televise news on a regular basis. In 1930, using an antenna atop the Empire
State Building, RCA broadcast a toy model of Felix the Cat during NBC's
first experimental telecast.[2] A year later CBS went on the air with its experimental station, broadcasting a variety program featuring composer George
Gershwin and singer Kate Smith. The same year, CBS aired the first regularly
scheduled news program, *Bill Schudt's Going to Press*, an interview program
with reporters as guests.[3] A decade of experimental broadcasts followed. Not
until July 1941 did CBS and NBC begin regular television service, providing
fifteen hours a week of commercial programming that included two fifteen-

minute newscasts each weekday on CBS.[4] Its antenna rose from the roof of the Chrysler Building. The news staff for WCBW in New York totaled two people, one writer and one announcer, and broadcast from a studio in the Grand Central Terminal Building. A graphic artist provided visuals—mere symbols that accompanied the announcer's words.[5]

The Japanese attack on American forces at Pearl Harbor was a milestone for television news in two ways. First, it provided the medium its first major news event. For its part, WCBW stayed on the air for ten hours that Sunday with reports from radio correspondents in the studio and panel discussions featuring a variety of analysts. When President Franklin D. Roosevelt asked Congress to declare war on Japan, WCBW carried the audio from the Capitol but had no video line. Instead of images from the speech, the station transmitted an American flag as Roosevelt spoke—the ripples in the flag provided by an off-camera electric fan.[6]

More important to the future of television news, America's entry into the war brought a freeze in the development of television as all efforts turned toward the war. Ten commercial television stations were on the air in early 1942; only six aired programming during the war. Both CBS and NBC curtailed all general programming and discontinued regular news in favor of news specials. The station operated by the upstart engineer-inventor Allen B. DuMont, WABD, remained on the air with a regular schedule throughout the war.[7] Not that it mattered; there were only a few thousand television receivers in New York and not many more elsewhere in the United States.

In 1946, with the world at peace, the networks resumed their development of television in full force, stopping only when the federal government in 1948 ordered a freeze on building new stations as it worked out regulations for the medium. More than 100 commercial stations were on the air when the freeze ended in 1952. In the next three years the number of stations grew to more than 400; nearly 90 percent were part of networks linked coast to coast. By then two out of every three American homes had television sets.[8]

With the growth of television came the television networks (ABC joined the fray in 1948) with their entertainment shows and news programs. In 1946 both NBC and CBS had begun airing regular evening news programs. The weekly news program on CBS gave way in 1948 to a nightly news roundup each weekday by relative newcomer Douglas Edwards. No one of greater prestige wanted to be involved with or, in the eyes of network executives, had the special on-camera appeal the new medium demanded.[9] Not even coverage of the 1948 conventions and election persuaded the radio correspondents that television was worth their talents. At that time it was not.

The fifteen-minute Edwards broadcast at first reached only viewers in New York, Washington, Boston, and Philadelphia. Soon, however, other stations began to carry the program. By fall 1951 *Douglas Edwards With the News* went coast to coast, thanks to coaxial cable. Yet the content of the program remained tied to wire service reports and whatever filmed reports CBS News bought from a newsreel service, Telenews. The Edwards program provided pictures with stories well after the events had occurred. "We had no bureaus, we had no correspondents, no reporters, no nothing," recalled Philip Scheffler, who joined CBS News in 1951. "I don't think any of us were prepared for the kind of explosion that happened in broadcast journalism." [10]

When Scheffler left the network in 1953 for two years in the Army, CBS News had sixteen or so people on its staff. He returned in 1955 to a network news operation with nearly 300 people across the nation and even overseas. Two men had provided much of the spark at CBS News. One was Sig Mickelson, Harry Reasoner's former college professor, and the other Don Hewitt, just twenty-five when he left the newspaper business in 1948 to try something new.

Mickelson realized that television, as a visual medium, relied on its pictures but had no system for obtaining film that matched its specific needs. In order to cover stories that were visual and to do so according to the editorial goals of the network, he began in 1953 to set up a CBS News film service. He realized that reporter and cameraman had to work together to create in the field the report that would air from the studio. Thus, CBS News set about looking for reporters and cameramen who could be a unit. However, building film crews was just part of the effort to create the television news division at CBS over the next five years.

As Mickelson designed the framework, Hewitt became the primary force for building it. He began directing the Edwards evening news soon after it started in 1948. His background as a photo editor gave him a visual sense lacking in many with a broadcasting background. More important, Hewitt understood the unique demands of television news as well as the equal importance of what was aired, in terms of words and images, and how it was aired, in terms of the technical side of television broadcasting. Combining ceaseless energy with a rapidly flowing stream of ideas and a willingness to try anything, Hewitt directed major CBS News broadcasts well into the mid-1960s.

The equipment for gathering news in the field was evolving too. "Nobody had anticipated television, and there wasn't a camera for shooting film for television," recalled Wendell Hoffman, a stringer cameraman in Nebraska and Kansas who later joined the CBS News staff. The 35 mm cameras used by the newsreels weighed a few hundred pounds and required a tripod. Hoffman used a ten-pound Auricon camera, which shot 16 mm film and could be held in one hand. When its 100-foot film magazine proved too small, Hoffman cut open the camera with a saw and added a 400-foot film magazine from a Bell and Howell camera, which gave him twelve minutes of film.

In the early 1950s, event coverage was still seen as the work of Pathe News, Fox Movietone, and other newsreel crews, especially outside major cities. When Hoffman attended an event in Nebraska with his little camera, he drew more than stares from the other cameramen. "I was the only man on God's earth representing a network," Hoffman said. "I was the laughingstock of all the newsreels." Often, in the early days, Hoffman worked as a one-man unit across the Midwest for both CBS and NBC. "They had not worked out the hierarchy of how you covered a story. They just said, 'Wendell, go out and cover the story.'" When sent to Texas to cover a blizzard that had killed tens of thousands of livestock, Hoffman provided images and words by filming the damage, writing a script, and then reading it in front of the camera he had balanced on a fence post.[11]

In spite of these efforts to lift the medium to the status of radio and print, television still had to win over journalists who, believing the news hierarchy began with newspapers, only grudgingly accepted radio. Many broadcasters had contempt for television in the mid-1950s. "In radio if you were an editor or a manager of one kind or another and your wife didn't want you to work nights or if you were totally incompetent or you had personality problems or something, they would ship you up to television where nobody gave a damn," said Bill Crawford, a CBS News alumnus from 1954. "Radio was the dog that wagged the television tail."[12]

The stodgy attitude of the radio generation had its benefits. Young, unproven reporters new to CBS had opportunities they would not have had in radio. They were willing to participate in the evolving system Mickelson, Hewitt, and others crafted in order to build a television news program that could earn the respect newspapers and radio enjoyed. "There was no precedent for this kind of operation," remembered Ralph Paskman. When CBS News decided to stop buying film from Telenet in favor of gathering its own film, Paskman left his job as a radio news writer around 1954 to become the assignment editor for television news. "We had to sort of devise systems and procedures on our own based on our own particular needs."[13]

In the CBS News system, the assignment desk was the firehouse that dispatched people to respond to newsworthy events. With no bureaus outside of New York or Washington, CBS News relied on the assignment desk to determine what needed coverage. The men at the desk watched the news wires and decided what needed coverage by CBS News correspondents or its affiliates, how to get film from events, and whether people on the desk should go into the field with camera crews to provide on-site reports.

The desk mainly served the Douglas Edwards broadcast but also provided reports for the national morning news and local reports for the New York station, WCBS. Its staffers, called reporter-assignment editors or reporter-contacts, were required to use news judgment and exercise their news-gathering abilities, including the skills needed to write in the field and to report on camera. "All of our people had to be able to write their own material," Paskman said. "We didn't send writers out. We had a couple of correspondents who needed that kind of hand-holding. The reporter or correspondent had to write their own pieces. If they couldn't do that they wouldn't be working for us." [14]

The assignment desk became a proving ground for anyone hoping to become a CBS News correspondent. "In those days you had to be an absolutely self-confident person," said Phil Scheffler. "You were making decisions, particularly at night and on the overnight when there wasn't any management there. You were making decisions about coverage all the time. At a very young age we were responsible for a lot of effort on the part of CBS News." [15] Working under the command of Paskman brought out a staffer's ability to succeed or fail under pressure. "Paskman was the boss," said David Buksbaum, who worked on the assignment desk. "He was a very stern taskmaster and a wonderful man. Everybody that worked for him hated him and loved him at the same time." [16] Competing with NBC News and ABC News drove Paskman to push the members of his staff to their limits. "If you don't demand, you don't get," he said. "A lot of them just dropped by the wayside. The ones who stuck with it were the ones who eventually became staff correspondents. We considered being named a correspondent was like graduating from school." [17] It was far more common to quit the assignment desk than to be promoted from it.

Into this pressure-filled world came Harry Reasoner. Considering his laid-back personality and lack of aggression, it would seem likely that Harry would be one of those who would drop by the wayside. But he had ambitions, and he had talents. Sig Mickelson told Walter Cronkite as Harry began working, "Here is a fellow who can really write." [18] Harry also faced an uncertain future if he were to lose his job.

That did not happen, of course. Harry did well enough on the assignment desk that summer for Kay and the children to join him, and the family settled into a small, split-level house on Guyer Road in Westport, Connecticut. When he was on the day shift, Kay drove him to the train station in time to catch the 6:59 to the city. He usually was back home shortly after five in the afternoon. [19] "Money was very tight," recalled his daughter Elizabeth. [20] There were days when Harry had trouble finding a clean shirt to wear. Kay was learning to feed the family on half the salary Harry had been earning in Minneapolis. "My mother got very good at stretching things," Ann Reasoner remembered. [21]

Soon, the temporary job melded into a permanent one, but that did not mean a promotion to correspondent was imminent. The competition inside CBS News would be keen. Others on the assignment desk were eager to prove themselves, too, including a twenty-three-year-old North Carolinian named Charles Kuralt, who came to the network within a year of Harry.

Kuralt saw the assignment desk as a chance to move from writing for the evening news to reporting for it. Harry and Charlie became friends, sharing as they did a fondness for writing, for people, and for a drink after work. Most of all, they loved covering the news.

Harry's work during his stint on the assignment desk left a favorable impression on his superiors. He performed well in the field in the few opportunities he had to leave New York. He joined Douglas Edwards in Louisiana to cover a hurricane that struck Lake Charles. When the network needed extra staff in Galveston, Texas, to report on a Teamsters' Union convention, it sent Harry. When the desegregation of schools in Little Rock, Arkansas, became a running story in the fall of 1957, Harry filled in at the scene for a day. "What first attracted CBS to him was his writing ability," Cronkite remembered. "They only discovered, I think, after getting him in the shop that he had this appeal to the general public. He had a neighborly quality, sort of a Midwestern neighborly quality that I think was very appealing to people. He wasn't obviously smooth. He didn't seem to be a performer. He seemed to be somebody who dropped in to tell you a story." [22]

In just eighteen months Harry established himself as one of the leaders of the next generation of CBS News reporters. Actually, his was a new generation, one that came directly out of television rather than the network's radio tradition. Harry and those who followed were not burnished in broadcasting for the ear alone; from the beginning they were learning the craft of writing words to accompany images transmitted to televisions around the nation. On December 1, 1957, CBS News made it official: Harry was a CBS News correspondent, the same position held by Edward R. Murrow, Eric Sevareid, Howard K. Smith, and others who were part of the finest broadcast news corps yet assembled. [23] To Harry, it was the greatest day of his professional life. [24]

Working as a field correspondent meant greater visibility for Harry, both at CBS News and with viewers. Yet it was not the most lucrative move, at least at first. Leaving the assignment desk and its pay system based on overtime actually cost Harry. Now a salaried employee, he earned less money at the beginning. The benefit, in terms of money, came in joining those who were paid talent fees. The complicated system boiled down to this: Harry and others earned extra money each time they appeared, either in image or in audio, on radio or television. The amount depended, in essence, on the esteem of the broadcast program or its regular host. For Harry and similar correspondents, there was no higher talent fee than the one paid for appearing on the evening news. Simply put, getting on the air meant more money. Who wrote what the correspondents read was inconsequential when payday came. As good a writer as Harry was, it was airtime that brought in the largest paychecks. This fact could not have been lost on him as his career developed.

Any boost in Harry's earnings was a blessing to the growing Reasoner family. A fifth daughter, Ellen, arrived in 1959. By then the family had moved from Westport to a house in Weston, known affectionately as "the Barn." It had been just that before being converted into a house. Harry and Kay may not have enjoyed the more rustic qualities of the Barn—a metal ring remained in one of its beams, and the large unfinished summer living room was another reminder of its earlier use—but their children loved the Barn. Living amid acres of woods with footpaths and just across the road from a creek and a pond, the siblings never ran out of games and adventures. At night they often gathered in Stuart's room to hear Harry read to them of the exploits of Peter Pan, Huckleberry Finn, and other favorite characters.[25]

The years 1958 and 1959 brought Harry the variety of assignments that seasons a correspondent and builds his credibility with the network and with viewers. For the science series *Conquest*, Harry helped report on open-heart surgery at the University of Minnesota, the first coverage of this kind of procedure for television.[26] By the spring of 1958 he was host of a weekly news program, *Harry Reasoner With the News*, at 10:55 Sunday mornings. He became an honorary member of the Royal Order of Swinging Tailhooks by taking off and landing on the *USS Leyte* the day before Christmas 1958.[27] He was among the reporters who appeared on the year-in-review program *The Big News of '58*, joining Robert Trout, Howard K. Smith, David Schoenbrun, Winston Burdett, and other senior correspondents.

Harry was becoming a television personality himself, earning quizzical stares on the sidewalks of New York. "They really appear annoyed because they recognize me, but can't place me," he told newspaper columnist Earl Wilson. "If I was a TV comedian, or even an actor, it would be easier for them. But a newscaster, they can't remember."[28] Best of all, from the standpoint of a family man, his salary was growing. On his 1958 tax form he listed his gross earnings at just under $25,000.[29]

Decades later Harry's colleagues from those early years remembered his ability to tell the story for television as well as a sharp sense of how to write it. "The best broadcasters, in my view, are the same on the air as they are across a lunch table or a dinner table at home," Bill Crawford said. "There's something about the camera that smells out phoniness. If you are genuine on the air, it shows. Harry had that quality."[30] The son of schoolteachers in the Midwest, his plain manner appealed to viewers. It was neither forced nor faked. "He was a believable person," Phil Scheffler said. "He had a way of speaking to the camera as if he was speaking to one person, which made him a person that was believable. I think when you saw Harry on camera you identified with him, you believed him, really just like the guy down the block."[31]

Complementing that quality was his skill in writing for television. Longtime producer and executive Robert Wussler, a young CBS News staff member in those days, described the requirements of good television writing: "Being able to convey messages in as few words as possible but with an adverb or adjective punctuated here or there, sentence structure, paragraph structure, and then being able to deliver that line in a very believable way, and being able to write to the visuals."[32] Harry did it better than almost anyone. "He wrote very well, and writing was much prized in those days," correspondent and producer Ernest Leiser recalled. "It was extremely simple and direct. It was a very classy style."[33] Another veteran of those years, Sanford Socolow, remembered Harry and Charles Kuralt as the standout writers of the period. "There wasn't much room for expression," Socolow said. "The pieces ran a minute, a minute and a half. Two minutes was a major take-out. If you could be succinct and stylish both at the same time you really stood out. Harry and Charlie were about the only ones that pulled it off."[34]

One story in particular marked Harry's first five years as a CBS News correspondent: the ongoing drama in Little Rock as the city struggled with school desegregation. Harry was the principal reporter for coverage beginning in the fall of 1958, the second year of unrest. More than most stories, Little Rock coverage demanded detachment and fairness, no matter what the reporter thought of the merits of anyone's position on the question of school desegregation. Everyone would be watching for any signs of bias.

The story in Little Rock had more than just two sides. First, there were the segregationists who wanted to continue to keep black children from white schools. There were the black parents who wanted the same rights and privileges for their children as their white neighbors. Then there were the school administrators, the federal troops, the public officials, the business community, and citizens with various opinions. Good reporting called on a journalist, print or broadcast, to develop trust, on all sides, that he would present their points of view accurately and fairly. It was a difficult task.

At first Harry merely followed the lead of *New York Times* reporter Claude Sitton, a veteran observer of Little Rock tensions by that time. In a few days Harry began developing his own sources and his own instincts for where the story lay.[35] The school year had begun with a vote by the school board to close the public high schools rather than allow blacks to attend them. The school board resigned and a board of moderate businessmen coupled with segregationists took their place. The story became one of economics rather than race when more and more business interests declined to locate in Little Rock because of the controversy. When the segregationists took over the board and fired dozens of teachers—a purge aimed at hobbling schools to prevent desegregation—public opinion turned. By the next year the high schools were opened with a small number of black children in class.

In later years, Harry believed television reporting influenced the outcome by bringing the story to living rooms around the country. But viewers had to believe they were seeing all sides. As a CBS News correspondent, Harry worked to provide balance. "That was the primary principle of news coverage back in that day—trying your best to be objective," recalled Sitton. "Reasoner was right down the line. His questions were good. His discussion with me and other reporters was level-headed and to the point."[36] True to character, Harry went about his work quietly. "He did it in a very sensitive and sensible way without any flamboyance or without any hyperbole," Phil Scheffler remembered. "He also had great sources in Little Rock on both sides, in all camps."[37] Awards and accolades came later in Harry's career, but he believed covering Little Rock that year was the best work he ever did as a correspondent.[38]

There were other stories, too. Harry was in the corps of correspondents that covered the September 1959 American tour of Soviet premier Nikita Khrushchev. The entourage visited Des Moines and the farm of Roswell Garst near Coon Rapids, Iowa. Part of Harry's job was reporting the reaction of his fellow Iowans to the friendly invasion by the man many saw as their enemy. The natural rapport Harry enjoyed with people, not to mention the fact that he was one of them by birth, made it easy for him. "People were a little afraid of television," said Robert Wussler, "and Harry was great at putting them at ease. I think it was just his manner. It was the way he treated people always, not just when the camera was rolling."[39] There also were trips to Cuba as Fidel Castro's revolution took over the island nation, and he traveled to Rome with President Dwight D. Eisenhower in December 1959 and was with him again in June 1960 when he visited the Far East.

The presidential campaign dominated the news that year and served, as campaigns usually did, as the bellwether of a network news operation. Harry had been assigned to cover his old friend Hubert Humphrey while the senator from Minnesota campaigned for the Democratic nomination for president. It also led to his biggest embarrassment as a correspondent.

West Virginia had become a pivotal state in the contest between Humphrey and Senator John F. Kennedy to collect enough votes for the Democratic nomination for president. On the night of the West Virginia primary, it became clear that Humphrey would lose. The senator confirmed to Harry that he would concede the state to Kennedy later that night. Harry dutifully reported the news for CBS radio and then went to bed, not bothering to cover the actual announcement. Why wait up for a brief statement, he reasoned, when he needed sleep?

The next morning Harry found a cool New York supervisor on the other end of the phone when he checked in with the news department. Humphrey, it turned out, not only conceded West Virginia to Kennedy, he had dropped out of the race for the nomination. The CBS News correspondent covering the Kennedy campaign had provided the coverage while Harry slept. It was an error serious enough to warrant dismissal. Not only did CBS News keep Harry, he went on to cover the 1960 political conventions. But Harry felt humiliated, especially when his supervisor suggested he had been enjoying the company of a woman that night instead of doing his job. Whether or not that was the case—and Harry insisted it was not[40]—he was tagged as being lazy.

Harry's high-school report card had used that word nearly twenty-five years earlier: "He's lazy." Exactly when the word began being applied to him at CBS News is difficult to pinpoint. More important, colleagues disagreed, at least in hindsight, on whether it was a fair description of Harry during his first decade as a correspondent for the network. On one side were those who believed he simply did not work any harder than required, allowing his talents as a writer and broadcaster to provide an above-average performance when more time and effort would have produced excellence. "I think Harry was a little lazy," cameraman Wendell Hoffman said. "I don't think he was as well-prepared on the story as some of the other guys. I wouldn't say that in the time I knew him Reasoner was a star reporter. He didn't dig into the story. I can remember being kind of panicky that we didn't know what we were doing."[41] Ralph Paskman, the assignment editor, thought Harry was lazy: "If I had a story that really called for a lot of get up and go and competition and tough going, I would pick a man like Dan Rather, not Harry Reasoner."[42]

On the other side were people who believed Harry, a quiet man without histrionics, did not show the intensity that went into his work. "Lazy is too simplistic and I don't think gets at the heart of it," Sanford Socolow observed, contending that people misread Harry. "You can't be a major anchor as he was unless you've got drive and ambition and the skin of a rhinoceros and an ego that goes beyond anything I understand. Harry had that. It was just better hidden than it was in people like Cronkite."[43] Dan Rather, who began working with Harry in the early 1960s, took offense at applying the word to Harry, comparing him to the star outfielder who almost effortlessly catches a fly ball no matter how difficult the play. "Harry's style was frequently every feather in place, above water," Rather said, "but underneath paddling like hell."[44]

Did the perception, at least in some circles, that he was lazy hinder Harry's rise at CBS News? Even if the cause was unclear, at the end of 1960 he felt a career slowdown, marked in his mind by the fact that Charles Kuralt beat him into prime time with his own news program, *Eyewitness to History*. Kuralt had been named a correspondent just six weeks after Harry, an even greater accomplishment given the fact that Kuralt was twelve years younger. Harry was downcast that his chief rival and friend had a plum assignment while he could no longer get even substitute jobs on the local news on WCBS. The program director had determined that Harry had no presence on camera as an anchor, and Harry admitted years later that he had been stiff and somber in his few opportunities to substitute for a regular anchor. Nor was he getting many stories outside of New York to cover for the national evening news.

Another sign that he might become a journeyman rather than a star at the network was his new regular assignment: writing radio news. By then Harry had the view of radio that the writers and broadcasters in that medium had once had for television. The money was good—as much as $1,000 a week added to his pay—but he knew the real action lay in television. He did as he was asked and started writing and reading reports for CBS radio, ten minutes each and twice a day.

Until then Harry had been part of a team, whether with a cameraman or as one of the correspondents in a broadcast. Now he was unto himself. "On radio it's harder to do the right kind of job because you must do it all," he observed. "If you're writing for a newspaper and you haven't made yourself clear, somebody else can read it and do something about it before it appears in print. On television you have the help of films. On radio, if it's bad, it really shows."[45] To avoid bad writing, Harry began to have fun with the task of covering the world's news in these reports, drawn primarily from wire stories. Mainly he wanted to keep listeners from being bored. As likely, he wanted to avoid boring himself. He provided some welcome, if unexpected, humor to the news or presented it from a different angle if such approaches would not compromise the story.

When the hijacking of a Portuguese ocean liner turned into a ten-day event, Harry began to write the updates as if they were for a soap opera. After Ernest Hemingway died, he wrote an obituary in the Hemingway style. When the secretary of a newly appointed Washington official praised her boss for making ninety-five trips across the Atlantic, Harry noted on the air that he must still be in Europe.[46]

Millions listened, but one listener mattered more than others, at least to Harry's career. He was Jack Gould, the television critic of the *New York Times*. No one writing about television had the cachet of Gould, and industry executives took note of what he wrote about Harry for the March 12, 1961, issue of the *Times*. Complimenting Harry for providing a lively news summary with an attention-getting turn of phrase and dry humor, Gould praised him for taking "the curse off the lifeless wire service prose of hourly newscasts." Gould went on: "If the individuality of Mr. Reasoner's broadcasts reflects a broader CBS policy to encourage members of its news staff to be themselves and not echo a corporate pear-shaped tone, the network could discover that its news problems were not as formidable as it may have thought."[47]

Suddenly, Harry was in demand again. In a matter of weeks WCBS invited him to become the anchor for its regular evening television news programs, with stints on weeknights before he settled into a Saturday night schedule beginning in June 1961 that lasted for nearly two years.

At seven o'clock on Saturday nights Harry delivered a five-minute news report, followed by sports and weather. Then at eleven Harry had ten minutes of news for late-night viewers. The stint on radio had seasoned him for writing news and reading it from a studio, albeit one without a camera. Viewers discovered what radio listeners had been enjoying, a different take on the events of the day. Weekends were notoriously slow news days. Harry and his producer, Irv Drasnin, decided the broadcast did not have to be dull even if the news was. For example, one night Harry promised viewers an interview with the winner of that day's big sports event. Most probably expected the victor of the prize fight or the horse race that had been highly anticipated. Instead, Harry interviewed the winner of the annual Charlotte–to–New York homing-pigeon race.

Trying to be different also made up for a small budget. There was no money for remotes and feeds that would have brought strong film and on-site reports to the broadcast. To make the point of how little they had to work with, Harry and Drasnin decided to play up this weakness one night. All they had was a story on the new mail pouches that postal workers carried, a feature on ice sculptures, and other inconsequential reports one could hardly call news. Harry wrote a throwaway introduction for all of them. "He stuck it to CBS management and he put it on the air," Drasnin recalled. "It was terrific." The general manager called after the broadcast to say he got the message.[48]

Had there been complaints, Harry was ready to argue that providing viewers with a sense of wit, insight, or comment was no sin.[49] That attitude led Harry to return to what had been a signature for his news broadcasts at KEYD. Each night he would write an end piece, a story a minute or so long, sometimes much shorter, that would close the broadcast. It might be slyly funny or whimsical or even poignant. But it was different from what almost anyone else was doing for television news. "There were damn few who could do what he was able to do with language and with words," Drasnin said. "It's not just the turn of phrase, it's not just the glibness. It's language. It's what you have to say and being able to do it in that format...to do it without being obvious, without cliches, to be able to get at the heart of something in a straightforward, conversational way."[50]

When the studio received the news that the popular comic actor and television star Ernie Kovacs had died in Los Angeles in a car accident, Harry went into his office and wrote that night's end piece:[51]

Ernie Kovacs died in a car accident in Hollywood this morning, and the guess has to be it was the most widely discussed news event of the day—one man's death in a world where everybody dies. This always happens when a man who belongs to the public, a man whom everyone knows, comes to a sudden end. The sense of loss and tragedy is heavy and immediate.

An event like this hits us wherever we are on a Saturday morning— in a supermarket, on a skating rink, self-satisfied in a late bed—with the old promissory note of our own mortality in a way that generalized warnings from the National Safety Council never could.

All prayer books ask for protection from sudden death. It is nice to think we will have a warning, time to think things out and go in bed, in honor and in love. Somebody dies in an unprepared hurry and you are touched with a dozen quick and recent memories: the sweetness of last evening, the uselessness of a mean word or an undone promise. It could be you, with all those untidy memories of recent days never to be straightened out.

There's a shiver in the sunlight, touching the warmth of life that you've been reminded you hold only for a moment.[52]

"Very few people can do that in that kind of time constraint and that kind of pressure," Drasnin said, "and he did."[53] People close to Harry would recall the Kovacs obituary as one of his finest moments as a writer for television.

Harry's talents on Saturday night enjoyed the fortuitous support of the CBS entertainment schedule. The late news followed the Western series *Gunsmoke*, at that time television's most popular series. Following the news was a popular late-night movie series. Broadcast in America's largest television market, with a solid lead-in and a solid program following it, the eleven o'clock news with Harry Reasoner would become, by October 1961, the most-watched news program in the nation.[54]

Up to that time he had been writing and broadcasting elsewhere for CBS News, from television specials for the national network to other WCBS news programs, the sort of full slate befitting a correspondent. What Harry needed to reach the top level of CBS News—anchor of a regular news program broadcast to the nation—was an opportunity for a stronger venue than the weekend news for New York. Such an assignment would bring Harry regular talent fees, meaning more money. It also would allow him to bring his style and persona to a national audience, perhaps developing a following—that would mean even more money when it came time to negotiate a new contract. The opportunity came on October 2, 1961, at ten o'clock that Monday morning, with the debut of *Calendar*.

For years CBS programming had languished in the morning show race against NBC's *Today* show. Network executives decided to try something different in order to bolster its audience throughout the morning. Timing and the television landscape favored a more creative approach. The networks, still smarting over the quiz-show scandals of the 1950s and the description of television as a "vast wasteland," were putting more money into public-affairs programming. "We were given free creative reign," recalled John Kiermaier, the vice president of the public affairs department at CBS News. "We took chances and we did things that nobody else had done."[55] Developing a morning show that was not merely a version of *Today* but a valuable program for people at home became a goal.

Who was at home at ten o'clock in the morning? Mostly women, some of them single and not working outside of the household and others who were married or single and caring for children. Their choices on television were limited to children's programs, soap operas, or game shows. This reality was not lost on Madeline Amgott, a reporter and writer who had joined CBS in 1956 and had become a writer and researcher for a morning show, eventually serving as an associate producer for the 1960 presidential campaign coverage before turning to writing and producing for radio. "I knew there was an audience of intelligent women who might want to see something on in daytime other than soap operas," Amgott said. "They were very much interested in what was happening in the world and how it related to them. And there was no program for them."

Amgott took her idea for a weekday program tilted toward women's interests to Kiermaier, expecting that even if such a program were undertaken she would not be the main producer for it. "Women didn't get jobs as producers in those days," she said. "Every time I went to a meeting at CBS, I was the only woman there who wasn't a secretary for many years." Amgott had decided to continue writing and producing for radio until Kiermaier insisted she become assistant to Tom Wolf, the executive producer of the new program.[56] The idea of a half-hour live program, broadcast in the morning five days a week, and produced by the news department rather than the entertainment division of CBS, surprised Kiermaier. "We were just trying to see if you could do intellectually a show that had some content," he said, "and which also would reach people perhaps at a different level than other programs at that time period, ten o'clock." While enthusiastic, he thought it was a long shot.[57]

With his reputation as a newsman and his light touch, Harry was Kiermaier's choice to be the host. "Harry's test was just so obviously head and shoulders above all the rest. I was convinced, and certainly the people at CBS News I reported to were convinced, that Harry was the right host for this."[58] Amgott thought Harry would be a good choice, too, at first. "I felt that if he was able to have a wife who was a lawyer, he would be more readily aware of what women's intellectual needs were than most men," she said. "It wasn't true, though. I think that Harry was not at all impressed with feminine intellect." That said, she liked the news judgment and engaging personality he brought to the broadcast.[59]

Others at the network wanted someone identified with entertainment rather than news. Singer Mel Tormé was considered, for example.[60] James Aubrey, the president of CBS Television, preferred Alan Ludden, later the host of the game show *Password*. Aubrey was less against Harry than he was against having a newsman as host, but Kiermaier insisted that Harry be given the position. Aubrey warned him: "You can have Reasoner, but if he doesn't work out, you know where the Hudson River is."[61]

Harry's cohost, a woman, would provide the balance on *Calendar* between news and entertainment, between male and female perspectives. She could also do commercials, which Harry, as a CBS News correspondent, was not allowed to do. The producers tried to interest a well-known woman, such as former Miss America Bess Myerson or author Betty Friedan. They approached actress Bette Davis, who was not interested even though her film career was in the doldrums.[62] Then they auditioned another actress, Mary Fickett, who was in her late twenties. Fickett had no news background, although both of her parents had worked for newspapers. She had acted in a few films but was better known on Broadway, having appeared in *Tea and Sympathy* and then as Eleanor Roosevelt in the drama *Sunrise At Campobello*.

When she tested for *Calendar*, she just chatted with Harry, answering questions he posed to her. "I got into this silly, silly thing about what my mother said happened to me when I chewed gum," Fickett remembered. "She said, 'I don't know what happens to you, but you lose all sense of being a lady. You start chewing gum like you were a whore.' For some reason I was glibly repeating this story to Harry, who was falling all over his chair at this point."[63] Not only had she amused and charmed Harry and the other people on the set, Fickett had shown in her audition that she could listen and ask questions. She was naturally curious and likable, and she and Harry made an attractive television couple viewers would like to see each day.

Fickett understood her role on *Calendar* from the beginning. "It was going to be a news and public affairs show. We were going to be interviewing people. I was not supposed to do any hard news. Harry was to do the hard news but there were a lot of aspects of news that were not considered hard news by the network—writers and performers, you know," she said. "I got into it before I knew what I was getting into. I didn't have time to get scared."[64]

The staff of *Calendar* was coming together. In addition to hosts and producers, the show would need a news writer to handle the two- to three-minute news segment that closed each broadcast (it was shifted later to the opening), as well as writers to handle the introductions for each program and the introductions for specific segments. A live show, *Calendar* was heavily scripted but used a conversational style that did not make it seem written.

Before he joined the broadcast Harry had been working a stint as the host of another public-affairs program for WCBS, *Eye on New York*, the television version of a popular radio program. He had enjoyed working with its writer, John Mosedale, and talked to him about the new opportunity *Calendar* presented. "They're bringing in a really good writer," Harry remarked. "You ever hear of a guy named Andy Rooney?"[65]

Andrew A. Rooney had been writing for CBS radio and television since 1949. Four years older than Harry, Rooney was the more accomplished reporter and writer of the two. He had worked for the campus newspaper at Colgate before serving in the Army. Writing for the service newspaper *Stars and Stripes* during World War II, he had flown on bombing missions over Europe and had covered the invasion of France and the subsequent battle across the continent. Rooney had written four books about the war when CBS hired him to write for the radio and television shows of entertainer Arthur Godfrey. He had written for Garry Moore and other CBS personalities and had completed a fifth book by the time he joined the staff of *Calendar*.[66]

It may be the effect of hindsight—their association lasted well beyond *Calendar*—but many of their colleagues came to think of Harry and Andy as sharing a similar view of the world and style in which they wrote about it. "Harry drew his images from home and hearth. Andy Rooney was home and hearth," said John Sack, a writer for *Calendar* who called Harry's style "very intelligent cracker barrel."[67] Some believed Andy was the more sardonic of the two men. To Mosedale, Harry and Andy had a similar tone in their writing. "It was witty and understated and unpretentious," Mosedale said. "But there was a difference in the way they arrived at that sense that I can't lay my hand on."[68]

As *Calendar* developed, the producers and writers stayed away from what they considered "ladies features," such as cooking and sewing. "We decided this was not going to be a how-to from that point of view," one of the show's producers, Mel Ferber, recalled. "We were interested in more important issues, even if the issues were light. They were not how-to. Women were interested in more than cooking."[69] A program might cover a single topic or it might cover several. "It could be anything from one day to the next," said Irv Drasnin, Harry's writer and producer from WCBS and later a writer and producer for *Calendar*.[70] Topics were avoided if Harry was not interested in them or if, as in the case of fine art, he had little background in them. With Harry's wide interests and curiosity, few subjects presented a problem. To the delight of the writers and producers, he also had few subjects he wanted to push.[71]

When *Calendar* first aired the focus was decidedly on the gender more likely to tune in at ten o'clock. The program featured CBS News commentator Eric Sevareid, on hand to discuss with Harry the rise of feminism in Great Britain; the president of the National Council on Child Care, who discussed problems facing working mothers with Harry and Mary; and a segment featuring the young man who caught the record-setting sixty-first home run of Yankees player Roger Maris. Harry's champion at the *New York Times*, Jack Gould, applauded the effort in his review the next day. "They are herewith nominated for the head of the class in daytime television," Gould wrote. "Their half-hour promises to be a delightful oasis of fun and intelligence."[72]

For the staff, *Calendar* was a playground filled with hard work by creative, intelligent people given the freedom to follow their interests. "The idea was if we enjoyed it, the audience would enjoy it," writer Ron Bonn said. "That's the core of knowing what to do for an audience."[73] For example, one segment about the equinox featured a poetic dialogue between Harry as winter, reading the poetry of Robert Frost in front of a snow-covered New England fence, and Mary as spring, reading selections of A. E. Housman before cherry blossoms. When astronaut John Glenn orbited the earth, the show put into context this important early step in the space program. Harry sat in the middle of the studio with a globe and Mary's morning grapefruit, showing that Glenn's orbit was but a tenth of an inch above the globe. Then he walked twenty or more feet across the studio to represent the distance to the moon. Observed Bonn, "You have better ideas in television if you don't have any money."[74]

On a typical weekday, Harry would meet with the producers and writers early in the morning to learn what was on the program for the day. He would review the introduction written for the broadcast as well as other parts of the script, including questions he might pose to guests. He preferred not to meet the guests before they appeared live on the program, believing that the interview would be more spontaneous and fresh, and his responses, including laughter, more genuine.

After the program he might perform other tasks for CBS News, such as broadcasting news for radio or for television or working on a television special. But *Calendar* was his key assignment for the next two years. Behind the camera, *Calendar* was a writers' show, and Andy Rooney was the chief writer. Rooney wanted scripts to sound the way people spoke and not carry a literary quality. When John Mosedale joined the staff, his first assignment was to write an introduction Mary Fickett would read for the Texas Boys Choir. "This is good writing," Rooney told Mosedale. "Take it back and dumb it down."[75] Drasnin believed the tone of the *Calendar* scripts reflected the staff's strong points. "Rooney and Mosedale were very gifted at that kind of conversational writing. And Reasoner was very gifted at just taking it or the idea of it and just going off on his own," he said. "Mary, coming out of theater, probably felt much more tied to the script than Harry did. Harry adored her and, on air and off, was very supportive and would do nothing to embarrass her."[76]

Harry wrote little himself, perhaps only the end piece that might close a program. "He was one of the best writers I've known," Amgott said, recalling an essay Harry wrote when phone numbers grew to eleven digits with the advent of area codes. "There were a lot of other things he did like that. He was incredibly perceptive."[77] Most of the time, Harry was content to have Rooney, Mosedale, and others provide the scripts. His job was to read them, and he had confidence in the writers with whom he worked. "If something were clumsy or awkward he would tell you," Mosedale said. "You could tell immediately he was not just another throat, as they say."[78] Harry did have a few pet peeves. One was a preference for the words "in spite of" rather than "despite." Another was a refusal to use the word "pontiff" in place of "pope."[79] The point was that he knew good writing. "That's why Harry was so easy to write for. He was an excellent writer himself," Rooney said. "He could have done it all without anybody, but he didn't want to take the time."[80]

When Harry did take the time to write for *Calendar* he offered his observations about the American scene and American life. Speaking just two to three minutes on the air, Harry offered these sorts of observations to *Calendar* viewers:

> *The occasion of Lincoln's birthday*: I'm surprised every four years at how badly several people in this country want to be president. The fact that a man wants to be president enough to run for it as hard as you have to to get it is almost reason enough for me to vote against him. You can't do that, of course, because the only people running are the people who want to be president.[81]
>
> *First lady Jacqueline Kennedy*: No matter what else you think about what he's done, President John Kennedy has done an unkind thing to us. He has brought a first lady to the White House who is younger than most of our wives. This makes us feel bad and our wives even worse. The first thing you know there will be a president younger than we are. Presidents and doctors should be older than anyone.[82]
>
> *Daylight-saving time*: It may be part of the great American tradition of fooling itself to pieces. It (time) might be compared to the water coming from a faucet. The water that hits your hand is the first of more to come and the tail end of that disappearing down the drain. That's the way it is with time. This instant is the last we'll see of what's disappearing behind us into history and simultaneously our first look into the future.[83]
>
> *Turning forty*: So, now the forties, after finding out the thirties weren't so bad, just short. It seems to me the forties ought to be fine. A man in

his forties ought to have more time for pleasant little things, like going to football games or sitting on the gravel of his driveway in the spring and feeling stones that are warmer than air. The forties ought to be the time a man gets some respect. This is the time of the fullness of years, and even in the parliament of your own home you ought to be able to feel like a statesman. But most of all, the forties ought to be a time for the gaining of knowledge and conclusions that you'll need so from then on....It seems to me the forties ought to be the time a man learns to live with the memory of his youth and the anticipation of his age. I'll let you know, ten years from now, how it works out.[84]

End pieces aside, Harry's major contribution to *Calendar* came in front of the camera. His ability to read a script and then deliver his lines flaw-lessly, developed over the years as a broadcast newsman, was a valuable skill for his first daily studio work. Interviewing was another skill he brought to the program. Although Rooney prepared questions for the guest segments, Harry understood that the best interviews flow according to the answers and not the questions.[85] He often obtained a revealing interview because he lis-tened to what a person had to say. "Reasoner was very good at connecting with people because he would look at them and listen to them," Drasnin said. "That's true of any good interviewer."[86] Ron Bonn recalled an interview by Harry with a Swiss engineer as builders completed the Verrazano-Narrows Bridge as one of many warm exchanges on *Calendar*. "Harry liked people, and people liked Harry," Bonn said. "He was good-looking, he had a good voice and a quick wit, and you really wanted to talk with him. You wanted to spend time with Harry."[87]

Mary Fickett had her own style. Unlike Harry, she enjoyed meeting guests before the broadcast. She felt more comfortable during an interview if she held a card with questions. "I didn't use it all the time," she said. "I wanted to do it one way and he felt more comfortable the other way. He would wing it."[88] Their differences—he was the newsman from Iowa, she the Broadway actress from the East Coast—probably contributed to their appeal as co-hosts. It was obvious, too, that they liked each other. "She greatly admired Harry professionally," Andy Rooney said. "You wouldn't think that comes through on the air, but it does."[89]

Mary's laughter in response to Harry's dry humor sounded genuine on the air, such as the time they began to banter about a report on the launch of a satellite.

"I don't understand what happens when the satellite gets around on the other side of the world," Mary said.

"Well," Harry replied in a serious tone, "you're working, of course, on the assumption that the world is round."[90]

Everyone involved in *Calendar* had only luck to thank for the success of the pairing and the positive chemistry it produced. Yet *Calendar* was Harry's program in many ways. It catered to his interests and showcased his talents as an interviewer and as a broadcast personality. "Harry loved *Calendar*," said Bonn. "*Calendar* was his show, in a sense that he never had one again where it was his show. Harry was young and eager and had a good imagination and just loved what he was doing." [91] Mary Fickett had no qualms about her place. "I didn't feel slighted because I was a woman. I was not competitive in that field the way, say, Barbara Walters is," she said. "I was in awe of the guys. I had nothing to do but to learn from them. Harry, being the kind of person he was, was very solicitous of me, very loving, very caring, very helpful. It was a very productive period for me." [92]

To her dismay, Madeline Amgott watched as her idea for a program for women was taken over by men and featured a woman in a decidedly second-ary role. "For her sake, in terms of the show, she always let Harry take the lead," Amgott remembered. "She didn't in any way try to compete with him, which made it good for him and good for Andy and bad for me. I would get very angry sometimes." More and more *Calendar* turned toward subjects of interest to men, the outcome of having men in charge. "Nobody thought of it as my idea," Amgott said. "I certainly didn't go around broadcasting that because that was not what you could do to get along or get anywhere." She left *Calendar* after a year or so, disappointed she was not given a producer's position when there was an opening. [93]

Guests on *Calendar* ranged from government officials and political fig-ures—Attorney General Robert Kennedy, Supreme Court Justice Wil-liam O. Douglas, socialist Norman Thomas, and India's Indira Gandhi ap-peared—to film and theater performers such as Olivia de Havilland, Peter O'Toole, George C. Scott, and Robert Preston. (When actress Lillian Gish realized *Calendar* was a television show and not a radio program, she refused to allow the camera to show her face. Only after a producer's cajoling did she agree to appear.) [94] Music was represented by Japanese violinists, mem-bers of the New York City Opera, Boston Pops conductor Arthur Fiedler, folk artists, and a tribute to George Gershwin. Painter Salvador Dali visited, as did novelists James Jones and Joseph Heller. Topics discussed by experts included marriage counseling, presidential press conferences, sterilization, drug addiction, deafness, and the use of tranquilizers and other drugs. [95]

The program had a playful side. Comedians Bob and Ray explained taxes. On a segment on abstract art, an art critic appeared with Harry to explain a bizarre painting, but it turned out it had been upside down all the time—an April Fool's prank played on Harry. [96]

Although a live half-hour, *Calendar* was not bound to the studio. It trav-eled to London for a week of shows, including one about American soldiers who married British women and stayed in the British Isles. ("Everything is just as reported, only better," Harry wrote to his sister, Esther, about Great Britain. "Unbelievable politeness, friendliness, efficiency. Perhaps 1776 was a mistake.")[97] *Calendar* broadcast from the Mall in Washington during Martin Luther King's march. The program visited John Glenn's hometown of New Concord, Ohio, with Mary interviewing Annie Glenn as Harry reported on the spaceflight.

A visit to the World's Fair in Seattle provided an amusing behind-the-scenes drama for the men on the *Calendar* staff. According to Ron Bonn, the budget allowed Harry and Mary to take the train to Seattle, but much of the staff remained in New York. Ever the romantic, Harry already had a crush on Mary, and his male colleagues urged him to use the trip to his advantage. They even worked out a signal Harry was to give on the air if his love were no longer unrequited: He would take his left finger and casually pull it across his left eyebrow. Only the boys in the studio would know.

That Monday the staff in New York gathered around a television screen. "Every segment we're watching Harry," Bonn recalled, "and there's no movement. Nothing." No signal appeared Tuesday or Wednesday. They began to despair, the tension grew, and by Friday they watched intently the last broadcast from Seattle. "The camera is full on Mary," Bonn said. "Mary turns to the camera and slowly tracks her little finger....Harry, with his total inability to keep his mouth shut, well, they were about an hour out of New York when he blurted out the whole thing to Mary. That is so *Calendar*, so Harry and Mary."[98]

Romantic feelings toward beautiful women were not the only indulgences Harry enjoyed. He treated himself to a drink before each broadcast, an act that had become almost a ritual for him. As early as eight or eight-thirty in the morning he would seek a drinking companion. "I don't know the extent to which this was a confidence builder, whether this was a reflection of his insecurities, which we all had," Irv Drasnin said. "He was so good at it and he made it seem so effortless that you wouldn't have thought. But I'm sure beneath the surface...that's a lot of pressure."[99] After the program Harry would visit a bar before returning to the CBS News offices. He told John Mosedale, "There's nothing less moral about having a drink at eleven o'clock in the morning than there is at eleven o'clock at night."[100] The alcohol seemed to have no effect on his ability to do the work, and drinking was looked on as just part of the business at that time. But Harry had not always been careful about his before-broadcast drink. One Saturday night at WCBS he had read the late news with a discernible slur.[101]

The heavy smoking did not abate, even though Andy Rooney was nearly violent in his opposition to it. For Ron Bonn, tobacco rather than alcohol was the more evident danger facing Harry. "The thing I would chide him about was the smoking, much more so than anything to do with drinking," Bonn said. "He made Murrow look like a teetotaler on smoke." [102]

Over the two years it aired, *Calendar* developed into one of those programs described as having a small but loyal following. That meant it had weak ratings but critical acclaim and the aura of high-quality television. But ratings mattered, even for a public-affairs program. The number of CBS affiliates carrying the show dwindled during its run, and CBS decided to end the program in August 1963. In its place was a more traditional news program featuring broadcast journalist Mike Wallace.

"*Calendar* got no ratings," Bonn said, "and yet every time I would mention the name somebody would not only say, 'I love that show,' but would then begin recounting their favorite segment on that show. That never happened with anything else I did at CBS. That was the essence of *Calendar*. It was on a very personal and direct level, and the people who watched it, watched it." [103] For years afterward people would stop Harry and tell him how much they had enjoyed *Calendar*, always asking about Mary Fickett. She returned to acting and later starred for twenty-five years on the daytime drama *All My Children*, winning the first Daytime Emmy Award for best actress. Most of the staff went on to other CBS assignments, many of them working again with Harry.

Calendar had been a pivotal step in Harry's CBS News career, crowning a phenomenal seven-year rise from summer hire to top correspondent and broadcaster. The daily grind of reading a script, conducting interviews, and looking poised and polished on air had provided the seasoning and experience a routine news assignment could not. A strong performance on the air, supported by favorable reviews in the *New York Times* and other newspapers, gave him greater cachet as a broadcaster. The program advanced his reputation as a writer, even though he had done relatively little of the writing himself beyond the end pieces.

Significantly, *Calendar* had joined Harry and Andy Rooney. Not only would they remain lifelong friends, they would become a successful team on several public-affairs and news programs in the future, furthering both of their careers. These early years at CBS News also established what would become a commonly held view of Harry as a person: an intelligent, witty companion and a loyal friend, but also a private man who held back his emotions and could appear cold to those he did not know or trust.

Life at home had taken root for the Reasoners. The family had moved from the Barn to a house on Buttonball Lane in Weston around 1961. A second son, Jonathan, was born the following year, the last of Harry and Kay's seven children. Maintaining the home continued to be Kay's responsibility. Attending Mass each Sunday was a family tradition, but Harry usually drove Kay and the children and skipped the service. As respectful as he was of the church, he was not ready to convert to Catholicism. "The only thing that he ever said to us, which I think was a snow job, really, was that with all the babies and stuff that someone had to stay home and take care of the children on Sunday," his daughter Jane said. "My father said he was sort of Catholic by association."

The children were becoming more aware of their father's fame. Harry's name began to appear in the *TV Guide* crossword puzzle. "That was the big time to me," Jane remembered. "He had to be somebody famous to be in *TV Guide*."[104]

Harry had come to enjoy the trappings of being the star. As one of many field correspondents covering breaking news, he had had to develop sources, interview them, and deliver reports on air wherever the event occurred. It could be a grueling task. But with a studio assignment, writers provided scripts and producers arranged for guests and handled all the details. Harry arrived at the office in the morning and returned home by the evening. He could write as much or as little as he wished. The money was better—he reported earnings of $81,444 on his 1961 tax return[105]—and he was not required to curtail his vices. *Calendar* showed Harry that having his own program provided too many benefits to justify remaining content with being a television reporter.

CHAPTER FIVE

On the Air and Everywhere

I am aware that I have a reputation for getting along with people, for being calm and not being temperamental. That's the exterior. It's always been the exterior, and it works well, it becomes part of the personality. But, despite my placid exterior I am ambitious. I am competitive, but I am also determined not to look bad.   **H. R.**

F or all the protestations about its cancellation and the fact that he would miss the good company of its staff, Harry Reasoner was not unhappy to see *Calendar* leave the air. He had too many opportunities to explore to remain with a low-rated program beyond its usefulness to him. As early as January 1963 he had lobbied CBS News executives for its demise that fall, contending the show should be allowed to die gracefully after two years. He opposed a plan to replace it with a half-hour news program, contending that the network would not provide the resources required to produce a strong broadcast. He also believed a straight news program would attract only about one-third of the already small *Calendar* audience.

More to the point, Harry did not want to be the host of whatever CBS decided to air. He questioned whether such an assignment would prevent him from working on *CBS Reports*, the network's showcase news and documentary program.[1] Besides, he probably realized that being host of a morning program would put him too far from the evening news and prime time.

The CBS News president at this time, Richard Salant, was well aware of Harry's popularity with viewers.[2] Harry probably did not need to remind Salant that his contract with CBS News was nearing its end, and Harry insisted that he assumed he would remain at the network even though he was unsure of what the network executives had in mind for him.[3] Indeed, Salant planned a major role at CBS News for Harry. He would continue working on *CBS Reports* but would also serve as a roving correspondent on major stories for both the morning and evening news programs.[4] Harry would perform other duties as well, some of them having begun before *Calendar* left the air.

In this way, a series of assignments marked Harry's career in the 1960s. Some were daily, such as the essay he broadcast for the CBS radio network, and others weekly. Many involved special programs, and they could be scattered over the course of a year. All would make for stepping-stones to the anchor chair of the evening news, and he began taking those steps well before *Calendar* ended. Significantly, his work on television in the 1960s relied mostly on his skills as a broadcaster, reading the words of Andy Rooney and others, and not on his own writing.

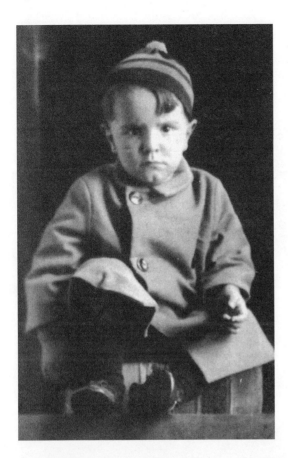

Harry Truman Reasoner,
circa 1924.

Harry on a camping trip
with his parents, Eunice
and Harry Ray Reasoner,
circa 1930.

Harry, circa 1932.

Army private Harry
Reasoner at Camp
Roberts in California,
1943. (Minneapolis Public
Library, Minneapolis
Collection.)

Harry and Kay Reasoner on their wedding day, September 7, 1946.

Comedian Bob Hope aboard a Northwest Airlines flight, with airline publicist Harry Reasoner in background, circa 1949.

Reporter and news anchor Harry Reasoner prepares to broadcast live with KEYD-TV cameraman Tom Carlyon in Minneapolis, 1955. (Minnesota Historical Society.)

CBS News Correspondent Harry Reasoner at a news event, circa 1962.

CBS News White House Correspondent Harry Reasoner (third from left) with President Lyndon B. Johnson (far right), circa 1965.

Former President Dwight D. Eisenhower (center) reminisces at his childhood home in Abilene, Kansas, with brother Milton (left) for a CBS News special with Harry, 1966.

CBS News Election Night 1966 newsroom with correspondent Roger Mudd, director Vern Diamond, and Harry Reasoner.

ABC evening news coanchors Howard K. Smith and Harry Reasoner, circa 1972.

Harry broadcasts from the Great Wall of China during President Richard M. Nixon's 1972 visit to Beijing.

President Gerald R. Ford and Harry take a walk at the presidential retreat at Camp David, 1974.

ABC News coanchor Barbara Walters makes a point to Harry, circa 1977.

Away from the television camera, Harry relaxes.

With *Calendar* on a slow march toward cancellation, Harry would need another regular broadcast to remain in the public eye and in the exclusive club of correspondents with their own programs. Early in the year an opportunity opened because, oddly enough, veteran CBS News correspondent Eric Sevareid suffered from camera fright.

Among the legendary "Murrow boys" who covered World War II for CBS radio, Sevareid had never been comfortable before a microphone.[5] Adding a television camera only made his jitters worse. He anchored the fifteen-minute national news at eleven o'clock on Sunday nights, a high-profile assignment a generation before twenty-four-hour news became the norm. "It was a little-known fact around CBS News that Sevareid was so camera-shy that we used to videotape his program at ten o'clock and then stick around and be ready to update it if that ever became necessary," recalled Bob Siller, a news writer for the broadcast.

One night in early 1963 when a civil rights story required a last-minute revision, Sevareid reluctantly returned to the set in order to report the news live. At the end of the broadcast, he was so shaken that two people had to help him out of the anchor's chair. Sevareid, who had recently turned fifty-one, told Siller, "This is a job for a younger man."[6]

Harry, just two months shy of his fortieth birthday, began anchoring the Sunday night news in February 1963. Unlike the brooding Sevareid, Harry was approachable and friendly in the studio. Their writing styles reflected their personalities. Sevareid tended to conclude his broadcasts with a weighty piece while Harry favored lighter subject matter most of the time. "I think it was simply a personality thing," Siller said. "I think Harry was sort of a light-hearted fellow and Eric was a pontificator in a lot of ways. There was room for all kinds of variety in the stable of anchors and correspondents."[7] Harry had conquered his own camera-fright long ago and was unflappable under the pressure of a breaking news story. "He made it all seem so natural," said Hal Haley, the producer of the Sunday night broadcast. "He simply had a wonderful delivery. He was just at home in front of the mike and in front of the camera."[8]

Although the Sunday night news came to be thought of as Harry's show, others actually shaped the weekly broadcast. Haley, the producer, would come to work around ten o'clock in the morning. Others on the small staff would arrive in the early afternoon. Harry could appear as late as six or seven in the evening, well past the time he could have a meaningful impact on the program. He would read the news copy, edit it, and deliver it on the air without complaint. "Harry was really a God's gift to the producer," Haley said. "He came in, participated in planning the broadcast. He didn't write it, but he certainly made sure the copy was his style and acceptable to him. He was very cooperative, really a nice guy to work with."[9] Harry's main contribution was the end piece, which he wrote himself.[10]

With the broadcast lasting just fifteen minutes, the closing piece had to be short, usually less than a minute and often just thirty seconds or so. That was enough time for Harry to make an impression with the audience or, in the long term, to maintain the impression of a likable, respected newsman who brought a wisp of a smile and an ironic or humorous touch to a newscast.

Harry enjoyed understated irony. On the day Elizabeth Taylor and Richard Burton married following a torrid affair that had made headlines around the world, Harry told his audience: "Elizabeth Taylor, the American actress, and Richard Burton, the Welsh actor, were married today in Montreal. They met two years ago while working on the movie *Cleopatra* in Rome and have been good friends ever since."[11] Promoting *The National Citizenship Test,* a quiz-oriented news program to air in prime time the following week, Harry told viewers: "Incidentally, there have been some feelers extended by people who know I've been involved and who would like the answers so they can dominate the audience in their particular living room. In general, I'd like to say the offers have been insulting to a man of principle. And inadequate to a man of avarice."[12]

As he had with the Saturday news and with *Calendar,* Harry at times would close the broadcast with a more serious observation. When investigators of an Eastern Airlines plane crash determined that its pilot had died while helping passengers escape the burning wreckage, Harry commented: "The pride in a man like this radiates out in lessening circles of intimacy—from his family, to his fellow employees at Eastern, to all pilots, to all his countrymen, and finally the pride you have in just being a member of the same species."[13] The defining events of the decade—civil rights marches, Vietnam protests, the growing drug culture, and assassinations—also turned Harry away from fun and frivolity.

Another example of Harry in a contemplative mood was a piece he delivered on a Sunday night in 1965 after a weekend of war protests at campuses.

> First of all, it would be a good thing if the interest in this dangerous and important war leads both demonstrators and observers to a study of it. Many reporters who have been to Vietnam, even those who disagree strongly with U.S. involvement, believe many of the marchers are naïve, a few of them knowingly specious, but most of them merely uninformed. James Reston of the *New York Times* notes that they seem to be carrying last year's banners. At the same time, defenders of U.S. policy are not always as well informed as they might be: this is not a war of bellicosity or jingoism, and these emotions do our cause no service.
>
> Secondly, there would be wide agreement that the demonstrations, and the reactions to them assiduously gathered among servicemen in Vietnam, would be a good thing if they pointed up unfairness in the

contributions to this war, unfairness in our whole system of apportioning the burden of military service. General Hershey, the Selective Service director, for instance, would be glad if a new consciousness of inequities prodded Congress into basic reforms.

And third, many people hope that the exhilaration of the demonstrations moves demonstrators to an awareness of their responsibilities. Citizenship in a democracy is a loaded gun and used in uninformed or frivolous ways it is dangerous. George Washington, who had some worries about the nation that he fathered, once said that if you are going to have a democracy you must provide for the enlightenment of its citizens or it simply will not work, and that was never clearer than this weekend.

Most college students, of course, were not demonstrating this weekend. At Purdue, for instance, they held a highly successful dance in which the couples were paired off by computers, and that may represent a more dangerous trend than marches of protest. But one student wrote home from a college in Pennsylvania: "I have two alternatives this weekend, to fast for thirty hours in front of the Vertol helicopter plant or to go to a fraternity beer party. It's a hard choice."

It's even harder than that.[14]

In mid-August 1965 when race riots plagued Los Angeles, Harry told his Sunday night viewers:

What the great mass of Negro citizens are feeling is, ironically, what great masses of white citizens have felt in the past ten years when small groups of white hoodlums brought disgrace to whole communities. And in judging what is happening, the uninvolved citizen needs to remember the same kind of arithmetic—when there were a thousand jeering cretins out in front of Central High School in Little Rock, there were a hundred thousand residents at home, sick at heart and ashamed of the people who were speaking for them....The country owes it to Negro Americans to give the same credibility to the citizenship of the majority as it does to White Americans at times when it has been a few men of that color bringing shame and disgrace to all.[15]

A quiet man who avoided conflict and confrontation in his own life, Harry often urged conciliation and understanding in human nature. (He deplored racial and religious prejudice and had little time for those who practiced either.) CBS News policy supported commentary rather than outright editorials favoring a particular side on a specific matter, yet Harry himself probably preferred to offer ideas for his audience to ponder rather than a course of action for them to take.

In the studio, Harry gave the Sunday night operation a lighthearted camaraderie rare at the news division, perhaps raising a few eyebrows over the notion that they might be having too good a time. After each broadcast, he led the staff from the Grand Central Terminal studio to a saloon, the Pentagon, for a drink. A round of drinks, always bought by Harry, lined the bar upon their arrival. When the Sunday night news moved to a studio at West 57th Street, Harry took the after-broadcast meeting to another bar, P. J. Moriarty's, which agreed to stay open just for them. Associate producer Norman Gorin remembered, "It was like a little party every Sunday night, and it went on for years."[16] With a drink in his hand and friends at his side, Harry enjoyed talking about anything and everything.

At such times Harry would engage in the kinds of word games that delighted his companions. A favorite for years was an all-star football team composed of clichés and other overused phrases from the wire services. There would be Mounting Tension, a Sherpa tribesman at fullback; Bodes Ill, the Scandinavian tackle; Grinding Poverty, the Eurasian split end; and Fragile Peace, the lovely cheerleader. He encouraged attacks on double redundancies, citing from Houston a "rich Texas oilman" and from Dublin a "crowded Catholic pub." Faint praise amused Harry in such descriptions as "Singapore, the cleanest city in Asia" and "Ecuador's finest playwright." He liked to point out that the Dire Straits kept moving, appearing in Vietnam one day and the Middle East the next, and he asked if any photographs were available of the giant pall over Rome.[17]

Harry held the Sunday night anchor position throughout the 1960s, even when his regular assignment took him to Washington. It was one slice of airtime that was his alone. Some things were worth sharing, the evening news anchor desk among them. In the middle of his *Calendar* assignment Harry found himself one of the beneficiaries of an upheaval at the evening news.

Douglas Edwards, who had been the only CBS evening news anchor in its fourteen-year history, was pulled off the broadcast in April 1962. Edwards had had his detractors for years, those who criticized his delivery as bland and faulted him for not being more active in production. The beginning of the end came when the NBC team of Chet Huntley and David Brinkley scored well with critics and viewers with its political convention coverage in 1960. As a result the nightly *Huntley-Brinkley Report* gained viewers and pulled far ahead of CBS in terms of its share of the evening-news audience. CBS executives replaced Edwards with someone they believed would be his opposite, bringing a strong hand to the program and providing a voice brimming with authority.[18] He was Walter Cronkite, a broadcast journalist with deep roots in print.

Cronkite had declined an opportunity to join CBS News during World War II, remaining with United Press in London even after Edward R. Murrow tried to recruit him. He had been with UP since 1937 and enjoyed the wire service, with its focus on hard news and straightforward reporting. After serving as UP correspondent in postwar Moscow, Cronkite decided to return to the United States in 1948 to look for opportunities in news that offered a better financial future than journeyman reporter for the wires. He had worked for two years as the Washington correspondent for radio stations in his native Midwest when, in 1950, Murrow offered him another job with the network.

Cronkite became a CBS News stalwart, the network's choice to anchor its 1952 convention coverage (a great success for him and for CBS) and the host of such popular historical series as *You Are There* and *The Twentieth Century* in addition to a full roster of regular news assignments.[19] When Murrow left the network in 1961, Cronkite became its top correspondent. He then replaced Edwards, his junior by just one year, determined to make the evening news competitive with NBC. But he could not work every day of every week of every year. CBS began using Harry and correspondent Charles Collingwood as substitutes when Cronkite was needed elsewhere or went on vacation. For Harry it was more national exposure and extra dollars in talent fees.

The changes in the evening news did not stop with its anchor. In the summer of 1963 CBS News began designing a thirty-minute evening newscast. For several weeks Harry took over the fifteen-minute program while Cronkite and a team of producers and writers worked on test versions of the expanded program, ending each test with a critique. Its executive producer, Don Hewitt, conceived a new set, one that was an actual working newsroom with desks for writers and wire-service machines close at hand. The theatrical setting of a desk with maps, a throwback to the earliest days of television news, gave way to reality and practicality. Cronkite would work at a U-shaped table not unlike that used by the managing editor at a newspaper. He would read the news from the same spot.

The first half-hour evening news program on any network aired on CBS on September 2, 1963. (NBC broadcast its first half-hour program the following week. ABC did not go to thirty minutes for another four years.)[20] Cronkite and company scored a coup for the first broadcast by persuading President Kennedy to grant an informal interview at his home in Hyannis Port, Massachusetts, that morning. His comments on the *CBS Evening News With Walter Cronkite* made front-page news, especially when he said that he was dissatisfied with the policies of the Diem regime in Vietnam and that the war was "their war." Kennedy added, "They have to win it, the people of Vietnam."[21]

Ten weeks later Kennedy was the focal point of the event that brought television news into maturity. Ed Bliss, the news editor for the Cronkite newscast, remembered walking past the wire machines as they churned out

the bulletin from Dallas that shots had been fired at the president's motorcade. Cronkite was eating lunch at his desk but could not go on the air immediately: It took several minutes for a television camera in the studio to
become "hot," and no one had conceived of a reason to keep a camera on at
that time of day. From then on the studio always maintained a hot camera.[22]

For fifteen minutes or so, Cronkite delivered the news by audio to CBS
viewers, who saw only a placard announcing a news bulletin. When he came
on the screen he was in shirtsleeves, having forgotten to slip on his jacket
amid the uproar to cover the biggest story in the brief history of national
television news. As such, any CBS News staff member who heard about the
shooting immediately came to the office. "It was a mighty hard line of work,"
writer and producer Bill Crawford recalled. "We were all half in tears part of
the time."[23]

Cronkite remained at the anchor desk for the rest of the day, but the evening coverage was turned over to Harry. By his own custom, Harry had been
enjoying lunch at a New York restaurant that Friday.[24] Had Cronkite dined
out that day and had Harry been in the studio, it likely would be Harry's
face forever associated with the news that Kennedy had been assassinated.
Charles Collingwood also sat in when Cronkite was off the air, but Harry
was the principal fill-in for Cronkite. With all of the talent available at CBS
News, it was a sign of the regard in which Harry was held.

Little could be prepared in terms of a script because no one knew where
the story was going. A suspect, Lee Harvey Oswald, had been captured by
Dallas police. What would happen next? Through it all Harry worked with
as much script as the writers could produce, but often he ad-libbed—and in
a masterful way. "That was his greatest job that I ever saw," a producer of
the evening news, Les Midgley, said. "It was a terrific three days. And he did
a great job."[25] The news dominated television all day on Saturday as police
questioned Oswald, reaction came in from around the world, and the nation
prepared for the funeral of the first president to die in office since Franklin
Roosevelt in 1945.

Harry offered a unique observation in a prime-time commentary, focusing as he often did on the way in which an event fit into a broader context:

> At the end of this second day of concentrated national grief and atten-
> tion to one event, it may be time to stop for a moment and think about
> our own attitude. Introspection is proper in sorrow as it is at any time,
> because mourning—if it becomes a fixed and purposeless moan at the
> cruelty of fate—can be habit-forming.
>
> In Norwalk, Ohio, today a fire burned up a home for the elderly, and
> about sixty-three old men and women died.
>
> There is a way of thinking about our knowledge of God which might
> make you say that in His sight that event was sixty-three times as im-

portant as the death in Dallas. In the national attention those sixty-three have scarcely had a place. They get six inches of type in the Sunday edition of the *New York Daily News*, for instance, just above a little item about a man who stole some money from a department store. You might think that we are out of proportion, that the national dirge that fills these days is inappropriate. Either we should do more, mourn all the time for everybody, or maybe do less.

There were, for instance, some calls last night to CBS in New York from citizens complaining about missing their normal Friday night programs. Our operators, I understand, were polite.

We are not out of proportion. We are not dishonoring the sixty-three old folks or the thousands of others who died yesterday and today and will die tonight and tomorrow. We are not God. We are a nation of men who tempt with honor and reward all kinds of men to serve us. When one is especially worthy, especially important to us, and becomes a sacrifice as well as a leader, it is entirely appropriate that we do him great honor. We are all dying and what we feel about John Kennedy is not so much sadness that he met his appointment a little sooner, but a gratitude and love for a man who would make that appointment for us.

There is only one reservation: It must not be a habit. When President Kennedy announced the quarantine of Cuba, one reporter suggested that what he wanted from his countrymen was intelligent support, not intoxicated belligerence. It seems likely that what this man would want from his martyrdom would be a considered dedication, not a pointless self-pity.[26]

Among his other contributions was the narration of a portrait of the dead president, also put together under intense pressure.[27]

Officials scheduled a memorial service in Washington on Sunday and a funeral procession to Arlington National Cemetery on Monday. Harry would anchor the live memorial coverage Sunday morning and offer another essay to accompany the images from the service. At the same time, it turned out, Dallas police planned to move Oswald from the city jail to the county jail.

Covering the transfer from the basement of the city jail about ten o'clock that morning, CBS correspondent Dan Rather implored New York to break from the memorial service in Washington when Oswald appeared. Looking back years later, Rather believed the decision to go from the church to the Reasoner essay before showing the accused assassin was a matter of taste as well as a technical decision. All the while, however, he and correspondent Nelson Benton were urging that New York switch to them in Dallas. "You've got to come to us, you've got to!" Rather yelled into his phone line as Oswald made his way to the basement for the transfer. The CBS broadcast remained on the memorial service in Washington as a gunman, Jack Ruby, burst from the crowd of onlookers in the city-jail basement to kill Oswald on live television—live, at least, on NBC. "In this moment we lost a step because they didn't come to Dallas," Rather remembered. "It was the first time of the weekend that we hadn't led our competition."[28] CBS had taped the shooting, but it was second-best compared to NBC's live report.

The four days of coverage that began with the assassination in Dallas and ended with the burial in Arlington tested the resources and resolve of television news. At one point a report came in that a black man may have been the killer. "Let's hold that until we get further confirmation," Harry told producer Robert Wussler. Confirmation never came, and the network was spared an embarrassment.[29] Producer Don Hewitt would say later that Americans needed a place to turn in their grief, and many turned to Cronkite to tell them everything would be all right. "He was the glue that held America together," Hewitt said.[30] Harry's performance solidified his stature at CBS as the Number 2 man for the evening news anchor desk. As the years went by, CBS News staff assumed that Harry was the heir apparent, even though there was no reason to believe Cronkite was going anywhere anytime soon.

Cronkite and Harry shared the basic qualities required of an anchorman. Both knew the news business, having worked in it most of their lives, and both had the look of someone viewers could take seriously as they explained the day's events. "They were more alike than they were different," news editor Ed Bliss contended. "They both spoke as though they knew what they were talking about, which is basic, it seems to me. They were credible. They both had warm voices. Their manner was a little different. I think Cronkite punched more than Harry in speaking. Harry was a little more conversational in reading the news. Murrow and Cronkite both delivered the news more."[31] There was a feeling, though, that Cronkite was more serious. "Walter was basically kind of a hard-news, wire service kind of guy, no nonsense, straightforward, no-bullshit reporter of the facts," said Sanford Socolow, an evening news producer. "Harry was a guy who delivered the facts in a not-so-straightforward way but in a very pleasant and effective way which was very appealing. It was so different from any other newscaster."[32]

Cronkite was more involved in the broadcast than Harry, which is understandable for a program called the *CBS Evening News With Walter Cronkite*. He arrived at the studio about ten o'clock in the morning. Around four o'clock, the staff would meet in an editorial conference to determine the lineup of stories. The producers supervised the stories appearing with film while the staff writers would handle the stories without film, the "tell" stories that Cronkite would read. He decided the order in which the typical twenty to twenty-two stories would be reported. Cronkite read the news stories, asked for revisions when needed, and timed the delivery of each in order to fit the lineup into the time slot. "A wonderful editor, Cronkite," Bliss remembered. "He wasn't the writer Sevareid and Reasoner were, but he wrote well and competently. He was a terrific editor. He could spot a hole in a story." [33] In late 1963 Eric Sevareid joined the evening news as its commentator, usually taping his segments a few hours before airtime.

The routine did not change when Harry substituted for Cronkite. Harry seldom turned back copy, although he might make small changes. "I think maybe he didn't want to hurt anybody's feelings," said John Mosedale, a *Calendar* alumnus who wrote for the evening news. "He should have. You can't worry about hurting anyone's feelings on a news broadcast." [34] Not only did Harry trust the writers, considering them the best in the business, he knew he was a substitute. "Harry acted as if he were a guest," Socolow said. "Although he was invited to participate in every way, he mostly acted as if he felt it was Cronkite's show and Cronkite's staff and he would do just whatever he was told to do. I think he felt he didn't want to rock the boat, and this wasn't his boat." [35] When Cronkite went on vacation and Harry filled in, the mood in the newsroom lightened. "We felt on holiday when he came on the show, we liked him so," Bliss said. "He wasn't as demanding as Cronkite. We could relax a little bit." [36]

Another upheaval at CBS News had a direct effect on Harry. In March 1964, with NBC ahead of CBS in the evening news competition, CBS Chairman William S. Paley and President Frank Stanton had agreed (Stanton somewhat reluctantly) to move Richard Salant to a corporate position and give Fred Friendly the reins of the news division. [37] Friendly had been Murrow's producer in the 1950s, and together they had made *See It Now*, the pioneering documentary series for television. Friendly refined the concept with *CBS Reports*, which he produced from 1959 to 1963. Paley hoped Friendly would inspire and motivate the news staff with the kind of enthusiasm, passion, and energy that had made him highly effective as a producer, if difficult to deal with at times.

Harry had admired Salant and waited, as did everyone at CBS News, to see what Friendly would do. When Friendly called him shortly after it was announced that he was taking over, Harry said, "You know, Fred, you are an executive in the sense that Willie Sutton is a banker." [38] The kidding aside, Friendly did not think Harry was being used to the network's best advantage and decided to involve him in a correspondent triple play: Alexander Kendrick would leave London for New York, Dan Rather would leave the White House for London, and Harry would become the new White House correspondent. Rather could use the experience in a foreign posting, in Friendly's view, and Harry would gain a daily assignment with the high exposure he deserved as a network star. [39]

Harry was not sure it was the best move for his career—he did not like the insularity of Washington and questioned whether he would be good at the job—but he tried to be optimistic.[40] "Well," he told friends, "at least it will be experience." Andy Rooney replied, "You're too old to be getting experience."[41] Harry dutifully went to Washington, and Kay and the children moved into a house on Cardiff Road in Chevy Chase, Maryland, after the school year had ended.

Politics was not particularly interesting to Harry. Having been a reporter he knew it was wise to be discreet about one's own political views, even at home. Once, in 1956, he had told one of the children he had voted for Adlai Stevenson, then regretted violating what he considered the sanctity of the voting booth. (Kay had voted for Eisenhower.)[42] At times Harry expressed privately his disdain for certain politicians, Joe McCarthy and Richard Nixon chief among them. "You have to have some standards," he told his daughter Elizabeth.[43] Most of the time, Harry avoided discussing specifics. "He made it very clear that it was sort of his job not to be political," his daughter Jane said. "I think that he would have felt that was unprofessional of him."[44]

When Harry joined the White House press corps in February 1965, he had not been a beat reporter since his days at the *Minneapolis Times* nearly twenty years earlier. He had enjoyed the general assignments he received at CBS News, where he might be interviewing an author one day and a farmer the next. He had also become accustomed to the studio work that required him to read a script rather than write one. Now he was returning to field reporting, a step backward had it not been for the fact that he would report regularly for the morning and evening news. "You tend to use your White House reporter more than anybody else in your stable of correspondents," producer Robert Wussler said. "So it's a great promotional vehicle."[45] Still, Harry thought of the White House as the most important police beat in the world. At the time the top cop, as it were, was Lyndon B. Johnson.

If Johnson believed the reporters covering him were damaging his administration, he could make their lives miserable. Worse yet for CBS News correspondents, Johnson owned CBS radio and television affiliates in Austin and would complain to network president Frank Stanton about coverage or, in the case of correspondent Robert Pierpoint, attempt to have people fired.[46] When veteran correspondent George Herman missed a news conference held by Johnson when he was majority leader of the Senate, Johnson called Stanton. (Stanton did not tell Herman the source of the complaint and accepted his explanation for his absence.)[47] Another time, Johnson, now president, announced an unexpected news conference one morning. Herman was live on CBS, desperately filling time while waiting and waiting for Johnson to appear. Meanwhile, the president watched the correspondents on his television set, enjoying their predicament. "It was nothing. No emergency was going on," Herman recalled. "He was just showing us who was boss."[48] More to the point was the phone call Johnson placed to Dan Rather after the evening news carried a report the president perceived as unfavorable. "Rather," the president asked, "are you trying to fuck me?"[49]

For a White House correspondent, Harry enjoyed an unusually pleasant relationship with Johnson. He reported the news with detachment, whether it was favorable or unfavorable to the administration. Yet he was sympathetic to the demands placed on the president, particularly those posed by the Vietnam War. The daily radio commentaries Harry wrote while in Washington often suggested that listeners empathize, as he did, with the chief executive.

Within weeks of his posting to the White House he commented on the conflicts that arose at times between the press and the president. "The competition between reporters to build stories, and the need for a large journalistic enterprise to have interesting stories to fill its pages and its broadcasts, is a basic part of our lives and, most people think, a basic guarantee of our freedoms," Harry wrote. "But this very competition and power imposes a special responsibility not only to dig out the news no matter who is hurt, but sometimes just to recognize that there isn't any news there." After questioning the aggressive tactics of the press and offering a view from the president's position, he concluded: "In complaining about the infrequency of full-dress news conferences, the press forgets that there is not a great deal of precedent for them and that every president has to operate in his own style. But Mr. Johnson doesn't forget that and maybe reporters should remember that there are some real reasons for the suspicion public officials have of the press."[50]

In another radio commentary, Harry noted that the mother of a soldier had asked Johnson why it was necessary for her son to have died in the war, and he provided Johnson's response that America's freedom was in danger and Vietnam was the best place to defend it. "The questions of mothers of soldiers must always be a substantial part of the burden a president must bear in making decisions that mean inevitably that soldiers are going to be killed," Harry wrote, "and there are no easy answers."[51] Later that year, after war demonstrators attacked Johnson's Vietnam policies, he wrote in support of the administration and deemed successful the president's efforts to prevent the collapse of South Vietnam and the enlargement of the war.[52]

Harry respected Johnson and was impressed by him, the only president Harry ever knew with any degree of intimacy.[53] "When you first go to the White House, I don't care who you are, it's an experience that is like no other," said Pierpoint, who began covering the White House in 1957. "I think Harry never quite got to the point where he could look on Lyndon Johnson as just another pol who had risen to the top."[54] Johnson was well-known for attempting to seduce as well as intimidate reporters in order to get what he wanted.

Harry had his own story about how the power-wielding president tried to impress him. Johnson had remarked that Harry ought to have his own program on CBS. Harry explained that he did, the Sunday night news, but it was not carried by CBS affiliate WTOP in Washington. The president made a phone call, the story went, and WTOP began carrying the broadcast.[55] "It's the kind of thing Johnson would do hoping to curry favor with a White House correspondent," said Pierpoint. "He would make sure Harry knew it, too."[56] On another occasion, Johnson made a show of asking Harry, in front of Lady Bird Johnson and a few others visiting his Texas ranch, what he would do about Vietnam if he were president. (Harry said he would be suspicious of the military and what its leaders told him.)[57]

Harry and his White House colleagues worked in offices in the CBS News bureau on M Street NW. Harry reported for the evening news, and Pierpoint provided reports for the morning news and for radio. At the White House, reporters tended to congregate in the lobby because the main press room was too small for the twenty or so members of the press corps. Restricted in their movements, reporters had to be aggressive to develop stories that went beyond press releases and other announcements.

At times Harry appeared indifferent toward covering the White House. Having waited with other reporters for updates about Johnson's gallbladder surgery at Bethesda Naval Hospital on October 11, 1965—a necessary if dull event to monitor—he told the audience for his radio commentary that many reporters played cards or worked crossword puzzles while waiting for news from the press office. "In the very nature of things," he said, "the complete and continuing coverage of the president of the United States by American journalism...involves a tremendous waste of a lot of people's time."[58] Barely a week had passed when Harry commented again on the Washington press corps, saying on the radio that he found the city to be a rather provincial place, not unlike New York. "Reporters here do get so overwhelmed with the minutiae of their daily contacts with the great and the fascination of the diplomatic and parliamentary games that are played there that they lose perspective, and insofar as they lose perspective they lose their usefulness," he said. "The trouble is that the city is so fascinating, so fascinating that you forget what a large percentage of the activity is intramural and irrelevant."[59] That was unusual, a White House correspondent giving the impression that he did not think much of the job.

It would be easy to envision Harry bored at the White House. "Most Washington correspondents are entranced by the politics of the city—national politics, not the infighting," said Bill Small, who managed the Washington bureau of CBS News. "Just the whole idea that the nation's movers and shakers are all in your city. Harry, I think, was less interested in that. He was not obsessed with Washington." Small respected Harry as a writer and reporter. "He was never lazy when I worked with him," Small said, "and I think that reputation was based on the fact that someone else might take an hour, hour and a half to write, and Harry could knock it out in thirty minutes." [60] Harry never complained to Small about the hours or the travel.

During the eighteen months Harry reported from the White House, he returned to New York for a few days each week to work on other programs and to anchor the Sunday night news. He probably never saw the White House assignment as anything more than a way station. By the time he moved back to New York, in mid-1966, he left behind colleagues who had enjoyed him as a person. Harry had also not challenged his White House colleagues on their own turf. Dan Rather, by comparison, had been highly aggressive both within the White House press corps and with Pierpoint. "Dan was competitive with everybody," Pierpoint recalled. "He was not easy to work with. On the contrary, Harry was very pleasant and very easy to work with. We got along a lot better than Rather and I did." [61] One reason may have been the fact that Pierpoint was the expert and Harry did not want to be seen as an interloper on Pierpoint's beat. But it also may have been that Harry just did not care much for the task at hand and felt he had nothing to prove.

Fred Friendly's decision to send Harry to the White House proved to be a mistake, especially for Harry. Whatever the reason, a lack of aggressive reporting blemished his reputation within CBS News. "I'm not sure he had a lot of heavyweight sources inside the White House and that sort of thing," said Bill Crawford, who worked for CBS News in Washington at the time. "That's not the way he operated. I don't think he was after scandal and inside dope and that sort of thing." [62] George Herman added: "He was extraordinarily lazy. Harry was one of the best news readers in the business and, I thought, an excellent writer. But he didn't have the nose for news and the drive and the inquisitiveness and whatever else it takes to be a good reporter, I didn't think." [63]

More people were taking note of his drinking, too. "He loved his martinis," said Kim Gregory, a CBS announcer in Washington. "He had a cot in his office, one of these metal cots. After lunch sometimes he'd come up and close the door and open up the cot and snooze for an hour or two." [64] Bill Small recalled Harry drinking a shot of whiskey before going on camera. "I never saw him drink too much," Small said, "but it was something that was a habit of his." [65]

In the eyes of CBS News management, Harry had established more firmly a reputation for being laid-back at best and lazy at worst. His good relationship with Johnson was among the evidence they cited. "Johnson loved him because he was easy on him. He didn't ask any tough questions," said Gordon Manning, who was in charge of hard news for CBS. "Harry is not a vindictive kind of guy. He has his standards. He just kind of treaded water. He didn't get beat on every story or anything like that, but he was not known for his energy or his pursuit of investigative efforts. You can break stories and you can be vigilant and curious, and Harry just rested on the oars and let the current take him." [66] Bill Moyers, Johnson's press secretary, remembered Harry as an amiable person. "He was very much a gentleman, not adversarial and not—on the surface—all that entrepreneurial as a reporter," Moyers said. "But he had a gift for absorbing what he saw, for listening to the swirl around him, for thinking his way through an idea, and then coming up with a report that got to the nub of the matter. His writing was unique, and he was among the best when it came to analyzing the situation or the story." [67]

In later years Harry acknowledged that he had not been a good beat reporter at the White House. In his memoir he pointed out that he disagreed with those who believed he got along well with the president because he was not tough on him, but he offered no explanation for the perception. "I think I did a good job in a principal requirement," Harry wrote, "which was understanding and reporting Lyndon Johnson." [68]

Harry left Washington for New York amid circumstances similar to those that had brought him to the District of Columbia. Fred Friendly had resigned from CBS News in March 1966 in a public dispute with corporate interests. The Senate Foreign Relations Committee, chaired by Senator J. William Fulbright, had begun a hearing in January that had turned into an examination of the Vietnam War. Friendly wanted to carry the hearings live, which meant canceling commercial programming. CBS did so for two days of hearings, but the president of the CBS Broadcast Group, Jack Schneider, refused a third day of live coverage even though NBC would carry them. Friendly complained bitterly and, when Schneider's order stood, left the network. [69]

Brought back as president of CBS News was Richard Salant, who told Harry that Friendly had erred in sending him to Washington. By August, Harry had been ordered back to New York and Dan Rather back to the White House. The Reasoner family left Chevy Chase and, with the Barn available for rent, moved back to Weston. "I am vaguely neutral," Harry wrote to an acquaintance, Naomi Burton of the publishing house Doubleday and Company, about the move, "but we have enjoyed the year in Washington except that we really weren't unpacked yet." [70]

Doubleday had been working with Harry on a collection of his end pieces, his first book since *Tell Me About Women* in 1946. As a renowned newsman rather than a first-time author fresh from the Army, he had enjoyed seeing his novel reprinted in 1964 by A. S. Barnes & Company. "I think, as a young man's book, it holds up pretty well," he wrote in an author's note to the new edition, "but perhaps the best reason for agreeing to its reissue is that the last time I looked at it I suddenly realized that it is now a period piece...an exercise in nostalgia for my generation." [71] In its first year the reissue sold about 700 copies, gaining Harry just $228.42 in royalties. [72]

Since then, Harry had been too busy or not sufficiently motivated to write another novel to capitalize further on his celebrity. Instead, he gathered his favorite end pieces from *Calendar*, the Sunday night news, and the daily radio broadcast, *Dimensions*, into a book titled *The Reasoner Report*. Doubleday released the collection, priced at $3.95, in September 1966. It was a modest book, just 168 pages, and Doubleday had provided an advance of $750. (Within five months the book sold more than 7,000 copies. A standard agreement of ten-percent royalty would have earned Harry less than $3,000.)[73]

A look at his 1965 tax return showed why writing books was not the best way for Harry to earn money. He reported to the Internal Revenue Service income of $130,746.02, more than $25,000 of it coming from lecture fees (at $1,500 each) and nearly the same amount from substituting for Cronkite on the evening news. He had been paid just under $12,000 for his work on *Dimensions*, the daily CBS Radio broadcast that featured an essay read by Harry but, unknown to listeners, not necessarily written by him.[74]

Dimensions on the CBS Radio Network and the Sunday night news on television were the regular recipients of most of what Harry wrote for CBS News during the second half of the 1960s. Of the two venues, *Dimensions* featured the longer pieces, generally three pages of script. Other correspondents had daily radio features and they, like Harry, could not write all of them if they also were expected to report the news, narrate documentaries, and appear on other programs. Harry usually wrote two radio scripts each week while other writers provided the additional scripts for him to read on the air. If he were on assignment and unavailable to tape the broadcast, then another correspondent, such as George Herman, Marvin Kalb, or Roger Mudd, would substitute for him.[75]

News items usually inspired Harry when he searched for topics, but he continued to look for an unexpected angle or an insight to which most of his listeners could relate. When two of Eleanor Roosevelt's children sold at auction many of her belongings after her death, Harry wrote: "It's always a little sad to see a person's worldly possessions spread out before everyone...price-tagged...handled...bought and carried off by strangers. Yet if scattering her possessions can help in some small way to remind people of Mrs. Eleanor Roosevelt, maybe the buying and the selling will have been well worthwhile."[76] The death of former president Herbert Hoover, turned out of office in 1932 but honored for his diplomacy and humanitarian work later in life, led Harry to remark: "Hoover was in many respects a victim of history, and it's good that history—and his countrymen—later vindicated him. It may be that in the national respect and grief right now is not only corrected judgment, but something of a guilty conscience."[77]

CBS News did not seek the kind of strident opinion found in some syndicated newspaper columns, and Harry leaned toward the sort of observation and comment suitable for a self-described "man of mild opinions."[78] He reminisced on occasion, honoring favorite authors when they had died and drawing a point from his early career as a reporter. He commented in a wry tone on modern annoyances, from obnoxious drivers ("It is obviously not only illegal, and possibly immoral, but certainly impractical to shoot them all") to the tradition of closing bars on Election Day ("I suppose nine hours of abstinence every other year never hurt anyone").[79] When he wrote about his family life, he often disguised it by referring to "a man I know," thus avoiding sounding self-absorbed or too much the complainer.[80]

A contemplative writer since high school, Harry was most eloquent on *Dimensions*, as he was on other broadcasts, when he pondered the nature of life. Perhaps his experiences with death at a young age had made him more philosophical about it. His view extended to deaths of family and friends, not just public figures. "He was very matter-of-fact but was very comforting," his daughter Elizabeth said. "You expected the loss was part of the life. It was an important thing that you felt bad about it because that really was a tribute to the person and to the connection."[81] In the days former British prime minister Winston Churchill was near death Harry noted that the great statesman had preserved his image and standing by withdrawing from public life before old age had taken its toll. "If the great mind dimmed, the public was not affronted by it; if the body weakened, there was no spectacle. In this as other ways, he was an example to the young and a reassurance to the old."[82]

The assassination of Martin Luther King Jr. in April 1968 led Harry to explore why the loss of the civil rights leader should be felt by all Americans. He could comment on this only briefly in an end piece for a television broadcast: "Tonight a great many Negroes have been asked for their reaction, but sorrow is not segregated, and if I am permitted a personal statement, I will say that this one white man bows to no black in his sadness on the occasion of the violent death of Martin Luther King. But anger is a more comfortable emotion than sorrow, and violence mitigates sadness. Perhaps in some sense, it is the white man who will sorrow most tonight for it is he who has no one to turn against in anger but himself."[83]

For a *Dimensions* commentary Harry gave a stronger, fuller, and deeper voice to the frustration he felt as an American.

> On the day after Martin Luther King was martyred, it's hard to think of anything amusing that doesn't dry up like a raisin in the sun, when exposed to a minute's sober thought. This report has occasionally been advertised as wry commentary, but at a time like this, it's a temptation to let wryness ferment into downright cynicism. Rather than yield to the temptation, we propose to discuss our feelings about Martin Luther

King honestly, trusting that as we go on, we'll find a note of hope some-where, rather than utter despair. Some reflections, in a minute...

The obvious irony in Martin Luther King's death, of course, was its instant commemoration with a rash of sporadic window-breaking, looting, rock-throwing, and scuffling with police, in scattered north-eastern and southeastern cities. Non-violence was such a hallmark of Dr. King, and senseless street-fighting such a desecration of his spirit, that it's a temptation for us to forget that non-violence was only his strategy; his objective was always social justice—first, legal rights for his own, disenfranchised people—later, economic equality for the poor—all the poor, black and white. Although Dr. King probably wouldn't have seen it this way, perhaps urban violence was a symptom not of his failure but of his success, though a success too slow in coming to satisfy either Dr. King or his followers. Dr. King's greatest achievement may turn out to be his key role in making American Negroes realize that after centu-ries of abuse and degradation, it didn't have to remain that way; it was really possible for Negroes to be just like the rest of us. His accomplish-ment along these lines was so complete that it's absurd for an American Negro today to feel any other way, whereas only a decade and a half ago, it was equally absurd, perhaps, for a Negro to feel he could really make it to full equality, in his lifetime. Dr. King's accomplishment was also so complete that the expectations of most Negroes today are bounding far ahead of white society's ability to adjust to them; hence the frustration on both sides—frustration expressed in the apathy of many whites, including some former sympathizers—and frustration expressed in the flaming bottle or brick or other missiles thrown from black hands at anything white.

There was another irony about Martin Luther King. He was so com-pletely identified as the foremost exponent of Negro rights by both blacks and whites that we tend to forget that King was really a figure of moderation. He was the leader who stuck his neck out for Negroes anywhere, but wherever he happened to be he always remained in touch with the white community, ready to maintain a dialogue, to keep ra-cial tension from ripping the community apart. Dr. King was really in the mainstream of a dynamic society; the proof is that he was so equally hated by both extremes.

White racists habitually refer to King in terms unsuitable for air—and they probably still will; but as black racists now prepare to exploit King's memory, we hope they and others remember they once were wont to refer to King, mockingly, as "De Lawd."

A final thought, in a moment...

America has traditionally impressed the world as a society of con-
spicuous waste. Perhaps it's economically healthy for us to buy a new car
every couple of years—and litter the landscape with our rusty discards.
But have we such an abundant supply of another commodity—the men
who'll go down the line for justice—that we can gun them down as pro-
miscuously as this? If we keep killing off our Martin Luther Kings, there
might, just might, come a time when we can't replace them. And then,
we're in real trouble.[84]

As fast and as thoughtful a writer as he was, Harry still could not meet the
daily demands of *Dimensions*. The usually mild tone of the broadcasts made
it easier for others to write with his voice in mind; they understood Harry's
point of view and knew what CBS News expected. A *Calendar* colleague,
John Sack, was among those who wrote *Dimensions* scripts for Harry. He discussed topics with Harry only if he were not sure of Harry's opinion. "You
could always tell when Harry was reading something of mine because it was
fairly erudite," Sack recalled. He often turned to research for details to give
his pieces depth. "In Harry's writing there were more basic truths about love
and life. Harry drew his images from home and hearth. I drew my images
from the library and the ivory tower."[85]

In spite of the money and the opportunity to practice his craft, Harry
at times considered *Dimensions* a terrible chore.[86] It was, of course, just one
more thing to do. After George Herman substituted for Harry for a week,
Harry asked him to write regularly for the radio broadcast, as many as three
or four scripts a week. "I thought to myself, 'That's not right,'" Herman remembered. "If it's a Harry Reasoner report, you write it yourself."[87] CBS
News saw nothing wrong with trading on its correspondents' names on radio
as it did on television.

There was one difference: Radio did not carry writers' credits. The evening news, *CBS Reports*, and other television broadcasts listed the names of
the writers. Only unsophisticated television viewers believed that Walter
Cronkite or any other anchor or host wrote his own scripts when a staff of
writers was at hand. With radio, listeners might be excused the assumption
that Harry and others were reading their own words.

Andy Rooney provided the words and Harry the face and voice for several unconventional broadcasts in the 1960s. The reputations of both rose
at CBS and among television critics who were delighted with these literate
reflections, written and produced by Rooney. The first, *An Essay on Doors*,
aired March 8, 1964, as part of a series called *One of a Kind*. It was a simple
idea only a fine writer and an appealing broadcaster could pull off: a discourse
on doors. Harry spoke to the camera in a studio filled with different kinds of
doors, and the program used film of doors of all sorts, from an ancient city in

West Africa to the Baptistery of the Church of San Giovanni in Florence, Italy, even from scenes in movies illustrating dramatic entrances. Harry offered Rooney's observations throughout, including this final reflection: "The best and worst takes place behind closed doors. The closing of a door can bring blessed privacy and comfort. The opening—terror. Conversely, the closing of a door can be a sad and final bang—the opening a wonderfully joyous moment."[88]

More collaborations followed. In 1965 came *An Essay on Bridges* and *The Great Love Affair*, which celebrated the American attachment to automobiles. In 1966 they teamed again for *An Essay on Hotels* and *A Bird's-Eye View of Scotland*, touring the countryside in a helicopter. That year the administrators of the George Foster Peabody Award, television's most prestigious honor, bestowed a personal award for television news upon Harry. The citation called him "a skillful and responsible reporter" who had "demonstrated a unique capacity for pinpointing the not-so-obvious and for holding up to inspection some of the absurdities with which we live." Noting the essays with "producer Andy Rooney," the citation commended their journalistic skill, taste, and imagination.[89] Rooney, who had written the scripts, was not even invited to the awards luncheon, one of the few times he was sore with Harry.[90]

Three more of their broadcasts appeared in 1967: *An Essay on Chairs*, *The Strange Case of the English Language*, which looked at the abuse of words and expressions, and *An Essay on Women*. Many women may not have been amused by its chauvinistic tone and lighthearted look at the women's movement. When a CBS News press release referred to the "Reasoner-Rooney view" guiding the broadcast, their friend Charles Kuralt responded with a poem that ended:

> We used Sperry-Rand machines and followed Harvard-Yale athletics
> And kept ourselves smelling good with Chesebrough-Pond cosmetics.
> And voted for Johnson-Humphrey, and never quite got sated
> Of a world so di-vi-ded, so over-hyphenated.
> But bear in mind the fate of the Aero-Willys Motor Car
> Your present hyphenation really goes too far.
> Collaborate blithely on my friends, but let me tell you true—
> The world will never-never buy a Reasoner-Rooney view.[91]

Harry and Andy worked so well together and so often during the decade that some people came to believe that Harry's reputation as a writer rested on Rooney's skill. That view, likely colored in part by the belief that Harry avoided hard work, ignored his years as a field correspondent and as an essayist. However, he seldom wrote half-hour and hour-long programs himself. The acclaim that money brought, though, lay in airtime. "He could have done it without me," Rooney contended years later. "That's the thing—he was a very good writer and he just didn't bother to do much with it."[92] Busy with other assignments, Harry wrote so little that he was in danger of being seen as merely a reader of scripts, a performer rather than a capable journalist.

The broadcasts produced by Rooney were a contrast to the hard-news specials for which Harry reported and to most of his work for *CBS Reports*, the network's prestigious documentary series on public affairs. As CBS News president Richard Salant had promised, Harry was often part of *CBS Reports* during the decade. He did not write for the documentaries, but he interviewed policy-makers and others and provided narration. He appeared alone or with other correspondents on programs about Defense Secretary Robert McNamara and changes he had ordered in the Pentagon, black leaders and the civil rights movement in the Northern cities, the perils of presidential succession, federal aid to parochial schools, conflicts between the tobacco industry and the office of the surgeon general, an update on school integration, and conflicts between the press and the legal profession.[93] Instant news specials, such as reports and analyses on congressional testimony, used Harry as host in part because he was a quick study for a script and had no qualms about appearing on hastily produced programs.

Harry's aura of friendliness made him the interviewer of choice when a news program called for a light touch and an ability to put at ease the person before the camera. For *Young Mr. Eisenhower* in 1966, Harry accompanied Dwight Eisenhower on a nostalgic visit to his hometown of Abilene, Kansas, and to the military academy at West Point. Eisenhower, not known for being talkative with the press, responded to Harry with an openness and warmth that probably surprised many viewers.

At one point Eisenhower reminisced about his upbringing by a stern father, remarking, "When his temper came to the fore he could be very harsh."

Harry asked, "Is that where you get your temper, Mr. President, from your father?"

Eisenhower thought for a moment. "Well," he said, "I learned to control mine pretty well. I suppose it is. As a matter of fact, I learned to control it from my mother and a little talk she gave to me when I was, oh, I guess when I wasn't over ten. And I didn't appreciate it until I was thirty-five or forty."[94]

For another broadcast, Harry joined Rose Kennedy for a tour of the home in which she raised John F. Kennedy. He profiled California governor Ronald Reagan, a broadcast that won an Emmy award for his script, and for another program he interviewed both Eisenhower and Omar Bradley, then the only living five-star generals, about the Vietnam War.[95]

Next to civil rights, Vietnam was the major story of the era. Senior correspondents often visited Vietnam for a few weeks to gain a sense of the conflict and to enrich their reporting about it. Harry prepared to fly to Saigon in September 1967 to report on the South Vietnam elections and provide a few spot stories for the evening news. "I haven't been in Vietnam since 1953," he told his Sunday night news viewers, "so I'll have to study up on it. I understand the French have left." [96] Within minutes President Johnson called Harry and offered to brief him before his trip.

Johnson arranged for Harry to meet with Defense Secretary McNamara. "Nobody got a briefing by the president, at least nobody I knew of," recalled Ed Fouhy, the Saigon bureau chief for CBS News. "But we all thought whatever Johnson had told him was a bunch of bullshit." [97] Harry was no fool, of course, and knew he had been primed for a reaction favorable to the administration. Still, he was a novice when it came to war coverage.

That first night in Saigon amazed him. "Jesus, there must have been a hell of a fight last night," Harry told Fouhy the next morning. "There was just bombing and fighting and shellfire all night." Fouhy discovered that what had kept Harry up all night had been the usual harassment and interdiction fire and the flares dropped around the city by C-47s each night. Old hands had slept through what to them was routine. [98]

To some, Harry may have appeared to be one of those newsmen derisively called a "three-day wonder," reporters who visited briefly and then evaluated the war on the whole based on little experience. "To use the military term, they came over to get their ticket punched," said Barry Zorthian, the chief spokesman for the U.S. military and embassy, "to come and see the Vietnam War on the spot to get some better feel for a thing than you would get sitting in New York or Washington." But Zorthian had a high regard for Harry and believed he visited with the intention of making an independent judgment and to report accordingly. [99]

Fouhy had been warned to keep Harry safe. "He's a star," Gordon Manning told Fouhy. "Let him hear some gunfire, but don't put him in any harm." Harry insisted on seeing a real battle. [100] He and a camera crew flew by helicopter to the north and stumbled onto more action than they had planned at a place called Gio Linh, which had been giving trouble to the Marines in the area. The helicopter carrying the CBS News crew stirred up the Viet Cong, to the consternation of the camp commander. Harry spent several hours talking to soldiers at the base and occasionally diving into a trench when a mortar round fell from the sky. The unit suffered one casualty that day, but by that night Harry was back at his hotel enjoying dinner and a drink—and feeling guilty about it.

That one day under fire had both terrified him and absorbed him. He also came away with a sense of the problem for the American military in the Vietnam War: Gio Linh was of no practical value, the Marines could not get at the Viet Cong to drive them away, and the American troops suffered casualties with no end in sight.[101] The days he spent in Vietnam in 1967 likely were on his mind when he commented on the war in the years ahead. As befitted a top newsman of the era, Harry had gotten his ticket punched.

Report from the field, anchor a newscast, serve as host of a late-breaking special, interview anyone from a peddler to a president, give voice to a television essay, broadcast weekdays on radio, garner awards and acclaim—Harry did it all. Yet he ran afoul of CBS News management for not bringing more energy and more gusto to his assignments. He was a better writer than Dan Rather, many believed, but he was no match for Rather as an aggressive reporter. He was as versatile an anchor as Cronkite and a better writer, but he did not show the same concern with the details that went into preparing a broadcast. He could interview presidents and Army grunts with equal empathy but relied on producers to develop the programs.

In sum, Harry was damned for not using his enviable talents to their fullest extent. "Harry had a bad rap," Irv Drasnin contended. "There were people that I remembered questioning his work ethic, who thought he didn't work hard enough. And I don't think that's true. I think Harry had the wonderful trait of not taking himself seriously, at least not so you noticed it, while taking the work very seriously. He didn't make a big show of it." [102]

If Harry's critics were looking for tangible evidence of sloth, he gave it to them on election night in 1966. Television news organizations built their reputations on their coverage of elections, even the midterm elections that came halfway through a presidential administration. They determined the political powers that would work with the president for the rest of his term. The House would be elected that day, about a third of the Senate, and numerous governors across the country. CBS News had created a special unit led by Bill Leonard to prepare for the election.[103] On the air, Cronkite would coordinate coverage, Harry would cover major issues and House races, Roger Mudd the thirty-five Senate races, Mike Wallace the gubernatorial elections. Eric Sevareid would offer analysis.

The CBS News Election Unit provided Harry and his colleagues notebooks thick with information about the issues and elections from state to state. They were expected to study the data so that, come election night, they could speak with authority and ease, providing insight and anecdote in reporting the numbers from the polls. It was just the kind of tedious work that bored Harry, and he was all too open about his lack of interest in it. "Harry never felt it was worth his time to do all that," Rather said. "He just didn't have the stomach for it, which I can understand." [104]

On election night, Harry's lack of preparation showed on the air. He turned in, by most accounts, a second-rate performance. "He blew it, plain out and out," Bob Siller remembered. "He knew nothing like what he should have known. It got to the point they wouldn't even come to him for a report because they knew he was lacking." [105] Cronkite blamed what he thought was Harry's lackadaisical attitude. "He didn't seem to take it very seriously where all the rest of us were really uptight about getting it right and getting it done and beating the opposition," Cronkite recalled. "Harry kind of at times annoyed me because we were such different characters in this respect. I had a feeling that Harry was kind of standing back and laughing at the rest of us for working so hard. I thought there was a kind of mental sneer there, never appearing on his lips, but perhaps I had a feeling that he was thinking, 'What are these people doing knocking themselves out for this particular performance?'" [106]

Bill Leonard was furious. "The Harry of wit, the Harry of style, the Harry of shrewd observation were all eclipsed by the Harry of comparative ignorance," Leonard contended in his memoir. "He simply had not done his homework. And I told him so." [107] Worse, in Leonard's view, Harry did not claim to have had a bad night but just pointed out that doing homework was not his strong suit. "He got along with the gift of gab, and he's a very genial gent," news executive Gordon Manning recalled. "He didn't take his assignment seriously enough. He would never go the extra mile to read up or to prepare himself with small talk about his assignment. He went through the motions. He did it and got away with it because he was charming and good-looking and affable and witty. But it's no substitute for good, hard-news reporting." [108] CBS News executives were, at minimum, disappointed with Harry and what they perceived to be his weak work ethic. His assignments remained relatively unchanged. His poor showing was forgiven, perhaps, but hardly forgotten.

Two years later, the presidential election between Richard Nixon and Harry's friend Hubert Humphrey would be the climax of 1968, an incredible year of political and social chaos. Harry, to his surprise, discovered late that summer that he would be excluded from election night coverage by Leonard, with the support of Richard Salant and Gordon Manning. "He just couldn't be counted on," Manning said thirty years later. "The national election had a lot more riding on it. You couldn't count on Harry, whatever you gave him to do, biting into it and making a contribution." [109] Prevented from joining the top correspondents that night was a slap in the face. "Harry was distraught," Andy Rooney remembered. "He was really hurt on that." [110] What angered Harry most was that Leonard had not told him about his displeasure with his work.

As election night approached Harry spelled out his feelings in a bitter memo to Leonard that rejected an invitation to meet with the executive: "The situation is so insulting and embarrassing I cannot find in myself the disposition to come down and defend a career to men who have found it impossible to be candid with me." He recounted, with traces of sarcasm, many of his successes as a correspondent, including the Reagan documentary he had written. "I said insulting. The way a reporter prepares for a story is a matter of individual style and the test is the result, not the preliminary mannerisms. The implication is not tolerable to me that I wrote the Reagan show out of some precocious indifference or that I read Rooney's stuff out of a simian ability to mouth." [111] It was a rare show of anger from Harry, another sign of just how deep the criticism had cut.

The slight turned Harry heartsick. "There's no doubt in my mind that he felt bad, that he felt it was a punishment and undeserved punishment," Dan Rather said. "It was not only humiliation, but humbling. Harry was a very, very proud man." [112] What could he do? CBS News was the best in the business, he believed, and even Bill Leonard thought Harry was second only to Cronkite in a glittering stable of correspondents. Hardly anyone of his stature left one network for another. Besides, what awaited him at NBC, where Huntley and Brinkley ruled? He probably could not conceive of joining ABC News, considered a distant third in a three-way race. Yet, by his own account, it pained Harry to work where he was viewed by management as adequate for some assignments and inadequate for others. [113] "I think he was disappointed and hurt, but it was his own making," Manning contended. "It was his own bed and he was lying in it." [114] From that time on, Harry felt less appreciated at CBS News and held less love for the organization. [115]

Even if election coverage were not to be on his agenda, Harry remained busy as the fall of 1968 approached. He still anchored the Sunday night news and substituted for Cronkite. Another prime-time news series was in the works at CBS, but one Harry had his doubts about. Don Hewitt, feeling unappreciated himself, had approached Harry with an idea for a new kind of news program. Its stories would not be as long as a *CBS Reports* documentary but would have more depth than a piece for the evening news. If they had been working in print, Hewitt thought, what he was proposing would be less like a newspaper and more like a magazine. The title for the broadcast came from Hewitt's lament that CBS, with all of the hours of make-believe entertainment taken up in prime time, surely could find the space for a little reality, even if just sixty minutes. [116]

CHAPTER SIX

60 Minutes and a Bruised Ego

On *60 Minutes*: I didn't think it would fly. I've been wrong a lot,
but never so happily wrong.   **H. R.**

Memories differed on just which executive had the dubious honor of being the first to turn down the idea for *60 Minutes*. CBS News president Richard Salant recalled rejecting Don Hewitt's proposal for a magazine-style news program as early as 1963. He believed that the single-subject, hour-long documentary was ingrained in television and that viewers would not enjoy being jerked from one story to another. He also feared creating a new vein of competition and bad feelings between the hard news and public affairs/documentary units of the news division, which already questioned each other's respectability and seriousness.[1]

Hewitt and news executive Bill Leonard contended it was Fred Friendly who initially declared *60 Minutes* to be a lousy idea.[2] That would be no surprise. Friendly created and refined the very kind of documentary Hewitt had come to dislike, and he was not inclined to give up precious airtime to an untested hybrid—and one he may have seen as frivolous. Besides, Friendly doubted whether Hewitt had the talent or the intellect to guide such a program.[3]

Whether for the first or second time, Hewitt did propose *60 Minutes* to Salant soon after Salant had replaced Friendly as CBS News president in 1966. There is no argument, however, that Hewitt alone conceived and lobbied for what would become the most successful news program in television history—perhaps the most successful television series of any kind.

People at CBS News wondered whether good ratings would ever attend television broadcasts that were not comedies, dramas, or variety shows. Even Edward R. Murrow gave in to ratings, serving as host of the popular but fluffy interview series *Person to Person* in the 1950s while anchoring *See It Now*. The audience for the typical *CBS Reports* program in the 1960s was half that of the entertainment shows the other networks aired.[4] Documentaries were important and prestigious but, to many viewers, boring and not the escapist fare they sought in their homes on most evenings.

Hewitt acknowledged this reality even though he had been a newsman from his teens, had directed *See It Now*, and had helped develop the CBS evening news from its inception in 1948. He too had a short attention span, a low tolerance for the dull, and enjoyed being entertained. Hewitt had begun to fear that serious television journalism would disappear from prime time because it simply could not attract a sufficient audience—and enough advertising dollars—when competing against entertainment programming aimed at the masses. He thought a magazine-style format was the answer if it could provide both types of news—hard-edge issue journalism and lighter personality journalism, a mix of what people need to know and what they want to know. His model was *Life* magazine, which published provocative articles on social problems and human-interest pieces under the same cover. An hour of television could accommodate three stories of sixteen or so minutes, with commercials in between, allowing Hewitt to satisfy all tastes.[5]

CBS had turned over the hour from ten to eleven o'clock Tuesday nights to CBS News in 1965. Since then, *CBS Reports* and other news programs had competed with movies on NBC and, on ABC, the popular drama *The Fugitive* and, from 1967–1968, the variety show *Hollywood Palace*.[6] Beginning in fall 1968, *60 Minutes* would appear every other Tuesday in the CBS News hour. Although *60 Minutes* would air just twice a month, Salant worried that a magazine broadcast, even one produced by CBS News, would take away too much airtime from the hour-long documentaries that were important public-service broadcasts if not ratings winners. He also questioned whether Hewitt himself was serious enough about journalism to make the magazine program a journalistic enterprise and not merely an entertainment vehicle.[7]

Fortunately, Hewitt found an ally in Bill Leonard, the CBS News vice president. Once Friendly had left CBS, Leonard had become more interested in Hewitt's idea and how it could be translated to a regular series. Together they watched a Canadian series, *This Hour Has Seven Days*, and its mix of public-affairs reporting and personality profiles in a single broadcast impressed them.[8] Pressed by Hewitt and Leonard (and perhaps stung by the idea of agreeing with Friendly about anything), Salant approved a modest $25,000 budget for a test version of the program. In creating a new format for broadcast journalism, Hewitt faced many choices. Would *60 Minutes* mix live reports with filmed and taped reports, long pieces and short pieces on serious topics and light ones, commentary from correspondents and from guests? Working out the details was a perfect job for Hewitt, an energetic idea man and problem solver willing to try anything to see if it might work.

One choice Hewitt made from the very beginning: The correspondent for *60 Minutes* should be Harry Reasoner. Hewitt and Leonard recognized Harry was an audience favorite and had the personality and skill to handle any type of assignment. "The program obviously suited Harry, who never looks out of place regardless of the subject," Leonard wrote in his memoir. "Beyond this, if Harry was not the best writer in the whole News Division stable, he was damn close to it."[9] In spite of their praise of his abilities, Harry was a curious choice given that he had at times disappointed both Hewitt and Leonard. Only a few years earlier Hewitt had vowed never to work with Harry again.[10] Leonard had criticized Harry's work ethic more than once, even pulling him off the election night team in 1968.

However, *60 Minutes* was a different kind of broadcast. It would not cover breaking news, nor would it require the correspondent to research the stories. "All the heavy lifting was done by the producers," CBS News executive Gordon Manning pointed out. "Harry contributed his personality and his interviewing skills to the assignments, but he's not in overall charge of marshaling all the facts and putting together the tapestry of the story."[11] For *60 Minutes*, as for many other news programs, a producer would handle the reporting (conducting initial interviews and gathering facts) and then write the first draft of the script. The correspondent would be brought in to interview people on camera, review and revise the script, and then read it. Only with several producers handling the basic legwork could a correspondent appear in several segments.

When Hewitt told him about *60 Minutes*, Harry did not think much of the idea and doubted the program would ever air. He believed that CBS News management would resist building a series around a single correspondent and creating another "star" who, like Murrow, could become too popular and too powerful. But he felt he owed Hewitt a debt from the early days of his career.[12] At Hewitt's request, Harry spent an evening filming the test episode. Hewitt did not have enough money to create new stories. Instead, he took a few hour-long documentaries and cut them into fifteen-minute segments.

Salant, Leonard, and another CBS News vice president, Bob Chandler, liked the pilot program, but Chandler suggested that one correspondent was not enough. As a practical matter the program needed a second correspondent. Serving as the correspondent for three segments for each broadcast, even at the rate of every other week, was too much for one person. Harry also might not be as suitable for some segments, perhaps those that needed a sharp edge to the reporting and interviewing.[13] Besides, two correspondents with contrasting styles could provide an appealing chemistry. For Harry's opposite Chandler suggested Mike Wallace.[14]

Wallace had been a controversial figure when he arrived at CBS News in early 1963. Wallace, forty-five, was not an established journalist in either the print or broadcast tradition. He had begun as a news writer and broadcaster in Detroit in 1939, working later as an announcer for *The Lone Ranger* and other radio entertainment programs. (One of his colleagues in Detroit was Douglas Edwards, the first evening news anchor for CBS.) Returning from the Navy after World War II, Wallace worked as a radio reporter and moved into entertainment with a radio show pairing him with his wife, actress Buff Cobb. Together, they went to New York in 1951 to serve as hosts of a CBS television daytime show, *Mike and Buff*. It ended in 1955 when they divorced. He had tried dramatic acting and presiding over a game show before joining, in 1956, a New York television show called *Night Beat*, an interview program that established him as a relentless and often cutting interviewer. A similar program, *The Mike Wallace Interview*, aired nationally on ABC until 1958, when his ratings fell amid criticism that he was too sensationalistic.

For the next few years Wallace worked in television as a reporter, announcer, host, game-show guest, and commercial spokesman for Parliament cigarettes. Wallace abruptly changed the course of his career when the accidental death of his son Peter led him to re-evaluate his own life. Rejected for news positions with the three national networks, he had accepted an anchor position with a Los Angeles television station when CBS News president Richard Salant reconsidered and hired Wallace as a correspondent.[15] His first major assignment was the *CBS Morning News*, the successor to *Calendar*. He eased into other assignments, including politics, and was covering the Nixon campaign in 1968 when Hewitt told him about *60 Minutes*.

Although Hewitt and Leonard wanted Wallace, Salant was not convinced Wallace was a serious newsman. Leonard argued for Wallace in a memo, and Salant approved him for the program.[16] Wallace himself needed persuasion to join Harry as a correspondent for the program. Like Reasoner, Wallace respected Hewitt but did not think *60 Minutes* would be more than a diversion for him. While he liked the idea of his interviews driving the program's hard-news segments, he did not believe CBS News had enough faith in Hewitt to entrust him with the kind of undertaking *60 Minutes* would require to be successful.

On the whole, Wallace figured he had little to lose. If the new series did not work out as he predicted, he assumed he would be sent to the Washington bureau to cover the White House if Richard Nixon were elected. (Earlier that year, Wallace had turned down an offer to become press secretary for Nixon.) More to please Hewitt than to show his faith in the concept, Wallace joined Harry for the taping of another pilot.[17] They reworked the opening and the story introductions for the broadcast before Wallace returned to the campaign press corps and Harry went on with his other duties.

Harry and Mike Wallace had not always been friends. When Wallace became the host of *CBS Morning News* his credentials were suspect to many in the rank and file of the news division. Among those giving him a cold shoulder was Harry, who, as Wallace was fond of saying later, looked upon him "as if I were a hair in his soup."[18] Wallace believed that Harry had been a leader of the anti-Wallace faction after his morning news program replaced *Calendar*.[19] Harry may indeed have resented Wallace, as many did, because he had not risen from the news ranks. But Harry knew *Calendar* was leaving the air from early 1963 and had supported the decision to cancel it. Moreover,

Harry should have been happy that Wallace, not he, had drawn the morning-news assignment, which Harry did not desire.

Whatever the reason for his icy regard for Wallace, after nearly a year Harry approached Wallace and offered to bury the hatchet. "We were very good friends after that," Wallace recalled. "We just hit it off."[20] Although they competed for stories and prominence on *60 Minutes*, the program did not harm their friendship, probably because each was comfortable with his unique role.

Hewitt thought of the pair as good casting: Harry wore the white hat, Mike the black.[21] Another analogy would be good cop/bad cop: Harry the likable and easygoing investigator who put people at ease and coaxed them into confessing their sins, and Mike the aggressive bulldog who confronted his subjects like a prosecutor. "He was such a good guy, such a good spirit," Wallace said of Harry, "that he needed a nasty and abrasive contrast."[22] To the surprise of the two correspondents, CBS News executives approved *60 Minutes* for the 1968–1969 television season.

Beyond the obstacles Hewitt had to overcome, little was remarkable about *60 Minutes* when it first aired on September 24, 1968. Harry and Mike introduced the program that night, with Harry telling viewers: "This is *60 Minutes*. It's a kind of a magazine for television, which means it has the flexibility and diversity of a magazine adapted to broadcast journalism."[23] What followed was the eclectic mix Hewitt had envisioned. The broadcast featured exclusive footage of Hubert Humphrey and Richard Nixon, each having allowed CBS News cameras in his respective hotel suite as their parties nominated them for president the previous month. Newspaper columnist Art Buchwald provided a humorous commentary, and Wallace reported about the strained relationship between police and the citizens of big cities. An excerpt from a film called *Why Man Creates* ended the broadcast.[24] The entertainment trade newspaper *Variety* contended that the premiere "showed great promise" and added that the program "should easily capture the thinking man's home in the Nielsen sample—both of them."[25]

Two weeks later Wallace reported for the first of two segments on biological warfare. Profiles of Georgia governor Lester Maddox and auto racer Graham Hill preceded an interview with Richard Nixon. Harry interviewed Hubert Humphrey for the next program, which included an interview with third-party candidate George Wallace and a report on the marriage of Jacqueline Kennedy and Aristotle Onassis. By this time *60 Minutes* was in stride, moving from serious subjects to entertaining pieces about culture and personalities.

Other CBS News correspondents contributed segments, such as Charles Collingwood's report from Paris on diplomat Averell Harriman, Morley Safer's examination of racial discrimination in Great Britain, and Robert

Trout's interview with German military hero Otto Skorzeny. As for the two regulars, Wallace was handling more of the hard-news assignments while Harry often reported on the lighter topics for the program. He examined the topical comedy of the Smothers Brothers and the television series *Laugh-In* and presented a piece on shoplifting at Christmas.

For one segment, Harry went to dinner with the food critic of the *New York Times*, Craig Claiborne, to find out what diners should expect in a first-class restaurant. Their forty-dollar meal, which included pigeon, was considered moderate to expensive at the time. In between bites at the Laurent in New York, Harry asked Claiborne about etiquette, such as trading bites with one's dining companion (permissible) and requesting that the waiter carve the meat (of course). He sounded like the average man he was, an Iowan visiting the big city, wondering aloud who supplied pigeons to the restaurant.

"It never occurred to me that people eat them," Harry said.

"I love them," Claiborne replied. "You're thinking of the steps of the public library." [26]

Harry and Mike made their first international trip for *60 Minutes* when they visited the Middle East. Mike reported on the Israeli side of the conflict while Harry looked at the Arab position. They took a similar approach to reporting on the war between Biafra and Nigeria, with a flip of a coin sending Wallace to Lagos and Harry to Biafra. Who had the better assignment depends on whether Wallace thought contracting dysentery was preferable to coming under fire as Harry and his crew did. [27] Later that year Harry reported on the Catholic side and Mike the Protestant during a trip to Northern Ireland.

Closer to home and closer to his heart, Harry presented "Essay on Whiskey," written and produced by Andy Rooney. Wallace introduced the segment: "I don't believe that in all the years I've known Harry I have ever seen him devote himself to a story more completely and with more apparent pleasure." [28]

Perhaps Harry's most interesting personality piece that first season was a visit with the Duke and Duchess of Windsor at their French country home, which they were putting up for sale. The royal couple took Harry on a tour of the place as if he were a prospective buyer. (Their asking price was $1.2 million.) The Duke appeared amused by Harry's asides about the plumbing and the gardens and did not seem to mind the occasional question about his abdication as king of England thirty-two years earlier:

> "How old were you when you became king?" Harry asked.
> "Forty-two," the Duke replied.
> "And you were king for ...?"

"Ten months."

"Is that long enough to be a king?"

"No."

Later, Harry inquired:

"If you had not abdicated, how much would that have changed history, do you think?"

"As a constitutional monarch, I don't believe it would have changed it at all," the Duke replied. "I might have tried to exert some, say, advice or pressure, to try and avoid the Second World War, but it was very unlikely that I should have succeeded."

"So the changes in your life and the big decisions have been personal rather than historical?"

"Sure, yes. I would say entirely personal."[29]

Hewitt tinkered with some of the elements of 60 Minutes in its first year. An occasional segment highlighting letters from viewers, positive and negative, became a regular part of the broadcast. A regular segment called "Digressions," featuring silhouettes dubbed Ipso and Facto exchanging caustic or witty remarks prompted by a story just aired, eventually disappeared. Other correspondents continued to supplement the work of Harry and Mike Wallace, and at times people without a CBS News connection offered commentary. The program also used material aired elsewhere, such as a British television interview with Alice Roosevelt Longworth, President Teddy Roosevelt's outspoken daughter, and a conversation about generational differences that Harry and his eldest son, Stuart, had taped for a Philadelphia television station. They discussed war protests, drugs, and the counterculture, each sounding skeptical of the other's views.

Unlike the correspondents who reported for the evening news, the 60 Minutes reporters seemed to be more involved in the stories they presented. Indeed, Don Hewitt wanted a kind of personal journalism to permeate their stories, which he saw as focusing on people rather than issues. Harry and Wallace were not performers, even though they read from a script. But they were personalities who brought something of themselves to their reports. For a segment called "Playing the Money Game," they played a board game while economist and author Adam Smith explained the international monetary system. At the end of a segment in which Harry reported on panhandling in big cities, Wallace came up to Harry on the street and asked, "Pardon me, sir, I wonder if you could let me have a hundred dollars for lunch at 21?" Harry replied, "Why don't you get a decent job like me?"[30] By participating in their stories, they developed a rapport with their audience not un-like the stars of the entertainment shows elsewhere on television.

A major difference, of course, was that Harry Reasoner and Mike Wallace were dealing with real-world facts rather than fantasy and make-believe. To retain their credibility as newsmen, Harry and Wallace did not stray from the conventions of journalism—mainly accuracy, fairness, and independence—even if they were playing roles within the program itself.

The program *60 Minutes* was turning out to be the perfect vehicle for Harry and his talents and interests. He could interview personalities and pol-iticians for profiles, sympathize with people wronged by the system, provide an easygoing authority to an investigative report, and even team again with Andy Rooney for offbeat segments.

On occasion he could provide one of his own trademark essays. A week before Christmas of 1969 Harry offered his favorite Christmas piece, which he had written seven years earlier for *Calendar* but now reprised for a larger audience. Even more people heard it when he delivered the essay again on the ABC evening news two years later. Harry later said it brought him more mail than anything else he ever did.

One week from tomorrow is Christmas Eve.

There are three ways to take Christmas: Cynically—as a welcome boost for the economy. Graciously—the appropriate attitude for non-Christians wishing their Christian fellow-citizens all the joys to which their belief entitles them. Or reverently. If this is the anniversary of the appearance of the Lord of the Universe in the form of a helpless baby, it is a very important day.

I suspect that a good many Christians, the priests and ministers and the men who have to arrange extra seating, sometimes resent Christmas and the Christmas-and-Easter Christians they never see at any other time. In a lot of ways, for custodians and theologians, it would be more convenient if Christmas had never happened. But it did; this fantastic annual burst of buying and giving and near hysteria is based on a quiet event that Christians believe actually happened a long time ago.

It's a startling idea. My guess is that the whole story, that a Virgin was selected by God to bear His Son as a way of showing His love, it's my guess that in spite of the lip service they have given it, it is not an idea that has been popular with theologians. It is a somewhat illogical idea, and theologians love logic almost as much as they love God. It is so revolutionary a thought that it could come only from a God who is beyond logic and beyond theology. It has a magnificent appeal. Almost nobody has seen God and almost nobody has any real idea of what He is like, and the truth is that among men the idea of seeing God suddenly and standing in the very bright light is not necessarily a very comfortable idea.

But everybody has seen babies and most people like them. If God wanted to be loved as well as feared, He moved correctly here, for a baby growing up learns all about people. If God wanted to be intimately a part of man, He moved correctly here, for the experience of birth and familyhood is our most intimate and precious experience.

So for Christians it comes beyond logic. It is the story of the great innocence of God, God the baby, God at the mercy of man, and it is such a dramatic shot toward the heart that if it is not true, then for Christians nothing is true.

So all the bustle and the putting of extra seats in the churches is all right. For if a Christian is touched only once a year, the touching is still worth it. And maybe on some given Christmas, some final quiet morning, the touch will take. Because the one message of Christmas is the Christmas story. When Christians hear it again at this time of year in all its tender glory, they are suffused with pride and love and, in a stroke of faith as lovely and illogical in the midst of what they see about them as the story itself, suffused with hope.[31]

Anything was open to *60 Minutes*, and Harry was not held back by the constraints of a regular beat. To a journalist easily bored by routine, the news magazine format promised him variety and stimulation.

If there were a dark side to being a *60 Minutes* correspondent in those first few years, it was not at all unexpected: low ratings. From September 1968 through April 1969 the program earned a rating, a measure of the size of the audience, of just 13 and a share of just 25, meaning that 25 percent of televisions in use were tuned to the CBS broadcast. It finished eighty-third out of 103 programs. The second season was worse. The rating and the share were lower, 11.6 and 21, and the program finished ninety-second out of 103 programs.[32] That did not mean cancellation was imminent. The competition on ABC that second year was a new medical drama, *Marcus Welby, M.D.*, which finished the year eighth among all programs.[33]

Meanwhile, in January 1969 NBC had begun airing its own magazine program, the two-hour *First Tuesday*, which appeared just once a month in place of a movie. People not interested in news turned to *Marcus Welby, M.D.*, at least once a month, which gave the show more exposure and contributed to its growing popularity. Aside from the fact that ABC now ruled the time slot, the cost of filling an hour of time helped keep *60 Minutes* on the air. Compared to a typical comedy or drama, it was relatively cheap to produce an hour of news, another positive factor in the face of low ratings. Another reason to continue the low-rated broadcast was the acclaim it received from critics, the television industry, and the journalism profession.

For Harry, *60 Minutes* was just one part of his professional world. He still delivered a daily radio broadcast, anchored the news on Sunday nights, and sat in for Walter Cronkite on the evening news. He remained popular with its staff. "I was a pretty hard taskmaster when I was there and obviously I don't think he would have attempted to take that kind of role," Cronkite said. "Harry was an easygoing fellow. He enjoyed life immensely. Everybody loved him on staff, as far as I know. He spent a lot of time lunching and drinking and dining with people in the shop, which I didn't do. Our personalities in that regard are quite different. But I know he was highly thought of as a bon vivant companion."[34] To the amusement of friends, Harry at times parodied Cronkite's serious, wire-service delivery.

The joking belied a stylistic difference between the two newsmen—Harry preferred the feature story while Cronkite was a hard-news reporter. He enjoyed a turn of phrase for a routine story and the inclusion of an offbeat news item. "You could be more creative in writing for Harry than writing for Walter," said Gary Paul Gates, for a time a member of the evening news staff. "What Harry would encourage, wouldn't insist on, but encourage was a little more creativity, a little more grace to stories. He'd be much more appreciative of a catchy lead than Walter."[35]

With the end piece now a signature of a Reasoner broadcast, Harry would provide one for the evening news whenever he substituted for Cronkite. "Sitting at the anchor desk he would swing around to his typewriter and in four or five minutes he'd compose a wonderful little feature to read at the end of the show," Ed Bliss remembered from his days as the broadcast's news editor.[36] For instance, on the fifth anniversary of the thirty-minute evening newscast Harry observed how times had changed:

Both Kennedys were alive then. President John appeared in an interview on that first broadcast, saying that the war in South Vietnam was theirs to win or lose. Hubert Humphrey was Democratic whip in the Senate. Richard Nixon was in semi-political retirement. Eugene McCarthy's high point in national publicity had been the nominating speech for Adlai Stevenson in 1960.

The word "hippie" hadn't been invented, "pot" to most people was something you put a chicken in, and "fascist pig" was something Europeans used to call each other. But there was enough news to take the step to go to a half-hour every night. As a matter of fact we thought we had plenty of news.

It's a measure of how fast the world accelerates that after only five years the troubled autumn of 1963 now has a nostalgic, peaceful sound.[37]

On the last day of 1968 he commented that it had not been the favorite year of most people:

The end of a year, of course, is artificial, a synthetic convenience for marking a point in time so we can see where we stand. As such there is great psychological value to it. Looking back on horrors and failures we can already say, at one minute past midnight tonight, that was last year, this year can be different. It's a point of division, and even on a new year's eve when it's hard to be nostalgic about the year behind, we can still be hopeful about the year ahead. Since all years are precious just because they are, finally, all we have, it's all right to have a cup of kindness for this one.[38]

Irony attracted Harry and was prime material for end pieces. His twinkling eyes and wispy smile probably told people watching him on their television sets that he, too, thought something was ridiculous. Reporting that army lieutenant Arthur Ashe had defeated Tom Okker of the Netherlands in singles play at the U.S. Open at Forest Hills, Harry noted: "Okker is something called a 'registered player,' halfway between a pro and an amateur, a classification not accepted in other activities where the taking or not taking of money is a key distinction. Okker gets $14,000 prize money because Ashe is a complete amateur. Lieutenant Ashe gets the cup and fifteen dollars for his day's expenses."[39]

When a new contract for the plumber's union in Philadelphia guaranteed its members more than $19,000 a year by 1971 if they worked a forty-hour week, Harry noted: "A Philadelphia school teacher with a master's degree can make up to $11,400 a year. Plumbing is an honorable trade. So is teaching."[40] Entertainer Barbra Streisand appeared in Las Vegas for her first nightclub performance in six years, and Harry reported these additional facts: "The occasion was the opening of a $60 million hotel. Her salary for the week will be at least $100,000. Her first number was 'I Got Plenty of Nuthin.'"[41]

Harry could also be sarcastic or irreverent, qualities unimaginable in a Cronkite broadcast. After a film titled *Satyricon* had been seized by authorities in Rome, Harry said: "Today's confiscation was based on the argument that the movie is obscene, shows corruption of minors, and violates a law safeguarding people under sixteen while making a film. It sounds like it should make a lot of money and get good reviews in New York."[42] With Cronkite coming off coverage of the moon landing in July 1969, arguably the biggest story of the century, Harry anchored the evening news on July 25. He began to end the broadcast with the usual words: "That's the news. This is Harry Reasoner for Walter Cronkite, who will be back on Monday." Then he added, "Walter, of course, has been…"—with that, Harry looked over his shoulder at the newsroom staff—"…where *has* Walter been?"[43]

Graceful under pressure whether at the typewriter or in front of the camera, Harry made it look easy to be witty, urbane, and thoughtful. "I watched him do it and envied his ability to write something so good so quickly," Bliss said. "It was always good copy, but what bothered me was that if he had run it through the typewriter one more time it would have been better. But he always went with the first draft. So often he could have taken a good thing and made it a real gem. I never quite forgave him for that."[44] Many others who worked with him, almost all of them admirers, questioned what more he could have done had he only taken the time.

It was not the only rub on Harry around the shop. Gossip about his drinking now circulated freely at CBS, and the evidence could be found during lunch at the Biarritz, a French restaurant a few blocks from his office. With evening news writer Charlie West and another friend or two, Harry sat at table 24, beneath a painting of olive trees in a French countryside, often eating veal scallopine or striped bass between cigarettes and sips of a Beefeater's martini. "He sent us all the big people at CBS. He was very good to us," recalled Marie Louise Vaillant, who owned the restaurant with her husband, Ambroise.[45] From the time it opened in 1966 the Biarritz had been Harry's turf—too much so to those who thought he was spending a great deal of time there drinking and smoking.

Harry made small gestures toward discretion. Once, after Walter Cronkite took the table next to his at the Biarritz, Harry quietly asked Madame Vaillant to seat Cronkite a little farther away next time. "He liked his privacy for lunch," she said. "He enjoyed his conversation with Mr. West and his friends—and his martinis."[46] It would be difficult for Harry to talk shop—at times poking fun at the news division and even Cronkite himself—with Cronkite sitting nearby.

Harry was not malicious or petty in his humor but could be playfully sarcastic, even on the air. On one of the days Cronkite reported from Cape Canaveral, Harry was asked to appear at a sales meeting for Bulova, the watchmaker that advertised heavily on the evening news. In gratitude, the Bulova people gave Harry an Accutron wristwatch. "I kept taking it in afternoons to tell Walter what time it was," Harry explained later, "and he didn't think it was very funny. He thought he ought to have had the watch." Harry eventually nicknamed the timepiece the Walter Cronkite Memorial Accutron. Some time later, he was covering the wedding of Luci Johnson at the White House when fellow correspondent Roger Mudd noted on the air that it was then noon and time to reveal the inscription inside the wedding ring. Harry replied, "Well, I'm sorry, Roger, but according to the Walter Cronkite Memorial Accutron it's only four minutes of twelve." Pleased with the free advertising, Bulova sent Cronkite his own wristwatch, which became known as the Harry Reasoner Memorial Accutron. Harry later remarked, "We've been good friends ever since."[47]

Another time, while closing an evening news broadcast by noting that Charles Kuralt had won a Peabody Award for his "On the Road" segments, Harry told viewers, "In receiving a Peabody, of course, Charlie joins a select group at CBS News who have won in previous years." (Harry had been awarded a Peabody two years before his old rival.)[48] On the way to the Biarritz one day, Harry ran into Jack Lawrence, a CBS News correspondent who had just received permission from North Vietnam to visit its capital. Lawrence already had been criticized by some conservative viewers and policymakers for what they saw as negative reporting that hurt the American war effort. "Congratulations, Jack, for getting the visas to go to Hanoi," Harry told him. "I just want to remind you of something—CBS News has a long-standing policy against accepting awards from foreign governments for meritorious reporting."[49]

During one of his stints on the evening news, Harry passed around an eight-by-ten photograph of himself, a publicity shot that had been rejected because it showed him looking glum and forlorn. He promised to buy a drink for the person who submitted the best caption. News writer Merv Block collected the prize for writing, "Gee, I sure hope nothing happens to Walter."[50]

To Harry it was all part of enjoying the work and the people with whom he worked. "I don't think anyone else would have had fun with that photo the way Harry did because you just don't joke about Walter. He was the emperor," Block said. "But Harry was an irreverent guy."[51] Not taking the job or himself too seriously endeared Harry to many of his colleagues but disappointed others, particularly those in management. "They perceived him as goofing off too much," Andy Rooney recalled. "They had a very accurate impression of him as a brilliant guy who was, to some extent, wasting his talent."[52]

The perception likely was a factor when, in 1970, it came time for Harry and CBS to negotiate a new contract. What was important to Harry at this point in his career? "Money and assignment," recalled his agent, Ralph Mann. "They were very tough on money, as they were tough on anybody except a guy like Cronkite, even though Harry was one of their top guys."[53] Harry already earned a base salary of about $100,000 and wanted another $50,000, which would still put him well below the $250,000 Cronkite reportedly earned but well above other correspondents. Instead, CBS offered a modest raise and little else. Harry turned angry over a counter-proposal he considered beneath him.[54] Not only did CBS management consider Harry lazy at times, now it was unwilling to pay him the salary he believed befitted his status as the Number 2 correspondent in the news division.

Complaints that he did not work as hard as he should were not part of contract talks with CBS, according to his agent. "Harry's facility to write something one time and get out got him labeled as lazy. He wasn't," Mann contended. "I think they were semi-jealous of the fact that he could do it so easily and so well. Harry was very sure of himself. He wrote it, it was good, and he walked away from it."[55] Another threat to his earning power was Bill Leonard's irritation over his appearances on the lecture circuit, which at times made him unavailable for unexpected chores at CBS News.[56] Dropping the speaking engagements—Harry was earning up to $2,500 per appearance and had collected more than $23,000 in 1969[57]—would be a blow to his income.

For a man with seven children to raise and educate, money was more than a salve to the ego. For one thing, it helped make up for the time Harry spent away from home and from his younger children. "I don't think he was real pleased about that when he thought about it," his son Stuart recalled. "He said to me one time they had more money but less of a father."[58] The Reasoners had moved to a seven-bedroom home on Long Lots Road in Westport around 1969, the last house Harry would own. The property included a swimming pool and a tennis court, and across the street was a country club.

The big house was perfect for entertaining, and Kay arranged dinners and other functions. Their New Year's Eve parties at Long Lots, black-tie affairs with formal dinners for dozens of guests, became a social staple. (When composer Richard Rodgers sat down at the piano during one of their smaller parties, Harry remarked, "It's like Jesus saying the Mass.")[59] The house could be abuzz with the children's activities. One family rule concerned the *New York Times* crossword puzzle: No one was allowed to work the original puzzle lest everyone else lose the opportunity. Harry arranged for a copying machine to be installed in the house so that copies could be made for all.[60]

Money was important personally and professionally. More problematic than money for CBS—and more important to Harry—was assignment. He wanted to be the evening news anchor, the top position at CBS News. But Cronkite's broadcast had become the ratings leader among the three networks. At fifty-four, Cronkite was showing no signs of wanting to leave. Considering that CBS enforced a mandatory retirement age of sixty-five, Harry would have to content himself with remaining the heir apparent for eleven or twelve more years. Just seven years younger than Cronkite, he likely would be passed over for a younger man by then. At the least, Harry would be anchor for only a few years if he were to replace Cronkite upon his retirement.

It was an unappealing prospect to an ambitious man at the midpoint of his professional life: Spend the rest of your career as a stand-in news anchor and as a correspondent for a program few people watched. (The ratings for *60 Minutes* were not improving. Its competition, *Marcus Welby, M.D.*, was on track to be the top-rated program on television for 1970–1971.)[61] Worse, Harry felt he did not have the appreciation and respect he deserved. When Ralph Mann suggested what once had been the unthinkable—to approach ABC News about a job—Harry agreed it was time.

ABC had been a castoff, a second thought, in broadcasting from the beginning. When government regulators ordered NBC to sell one of its two radio networks, the Blue Network and the Red Network, Edward J. Noble used $8 million he had earned manufacturing Life Savers candy to buy the Blue Network in 1941 and rename it the American Broadcasting Company. Twelve years later Noble sold ABC to a theater chain owned by Leonard Goldenson when Noble could not invest enough money to expand as aggressively into television as CBS and NBC had been doing. Goldenson began with just five owned-and-operated television stations and nine affiliates. Prime-time programming brought in the revenue, and Goldenson turned his attention toward the money-making operations of ABC and ignored the news division, which only cost money.

ABC was an unlikely innovator in entertainment. Goldenson negotiated the first deals with Hollywood production companies to produce programs for the networks, which nearly all movie studios were loath to do. One result was a partnership with Walt Disney, who used his ABC series to finance and promote his new amusement park. The ABC prime-time schedule featured many firsts—the first western (*Cheyenne*), the first medical drama (*Ben Casey*), and the first soap opera (*Peyton Place*) as well as such influential shows as the private-eye series 77 *Sunset Strip* and the controversial crime drama *The Untouchables*. Its focus on shows aimed at young audiences helped ABC build an audience less interested in the CBS and NBC shows that appealed to older viewers.[62]

The evening news on ABC, anchored by newsman John Charles Daly for most of the 1950s, limped along with a meager budget. "It was a laughingstock as far as the news operation," recalled Bob Siller, who worked at ABC for nine years before joining CBS News in 1962. "When the *Andrea Doria* went down, we couldn't even get a plane to go out to film it. We didn't even have pictures. We just dribbled along on our own. It was very discouraging."[63] Not only did Daly anchor the broadcast, he was in charge of ABC News and, as a vice president for the network, oversaw its sports, special events, and religious programming. Television viewers developed a habit of turning to CBS and NBC for news. Another sign of the times and ABC's lack of interest in the news operation: More people saw Daly on CBS when he served as host of the game show *What's My Line?* than tuned in to his evening news work.

By federal mandate television stations had an obligation to broadcast in the public interest. ABC already was under fire from those who believed *The Untouchables,* with its violent stories of the Prohibition era, was exactly the wrong kind of program to bring into American homes. As congressional scrutiny of television broadcasting grew sharper, Goldenson in 1960 heeded the suggestion of U.S. senator John Pastore that he bolster the public-affairs efforts of ABC.[64] To give the news division new direction and credibility, Goldenson hired James Hagerty, the former press secretary to President Eisenhower. Hagerty had been a newspaper reporter and was well connected in Washington, but he knew little about broadcast journalism. He hired print reporters and hoped they could make the transition to the screen. Another move toward legitimizing ABC News came in 1962 when Hagerty hired Howard K. Smith, who had left CBS in a disagreement over whether he had editorialized in a civil-rights documentary, to produce a half-hour news and commentary program.[65]

Hagerty left in 1963 when Goldenson replaced him with Elmer Lower, an executive at NBC who had worked at CBS. Much as Sig Mickelson had done at CBS a decade earlier, Lower began building the infrastructure ABC News needed to compete with its rivals. Hobbling his early plans was a budget of just $5 million a year, about one-sixth of what NBC and CBS spent apiece. "The general feeling was that ABC was going to make it eventually," Lower remembered, "but they had to do better in prime-time programming to have enough money to go around."[66] Making the best of what he had, Lower hired more news crews and invested in equipment, opened news bureaus overseas, and hired promising young correspondents.

The lack of resources at ABC was evident every night. Most noticeable was the length of the evening news. CBS and NBC had expanded their broadcasts to thirty minutes in 1963, but ABC lagged at fifteen minutes for another four years. Cronkite and the team of Huntley and Brinkley were mainstays at their networks. At ABC the evening news featured a parade of anchors during the 1960s, including a twenty-six-year-old Canadian named Peter Jennings, who left the desk in 1967 after two years. Lower removed Jennings's replacement five months later and put in White House correspondent Frank Reynolds, joined in 1968 by Howard K. Smith as coanchor.

Gathering the news itself was a challenge with limited resources. When Dallas police announced the transfer of Kennedy assassination suspect Lee Harvey Oswald, the ABC producer supervising coverage decided to send his only news crew to the county jail to film Oswald's arrival. Assuming nothing would happen at police headquarters, the ABC crew missed the murder of Oswald by Jack Ruby. NBC had the shooting live, CBS had it on tape, but ABC did not have it at all.

"The ABC bench was woefully inadequate," an ABC producer, Robert Siegenthaler, recalled. "There's an apt analogy. We could field nine players as a baseball team, no problem, but we had no bullpen. If anyone got hurt, the substitutes were not up to it."[67] Reporter Sam Donaldson left WTOP in Washington for the network in 1967 and was appalled by its lack of personnel and equipment. "CBS would show up with three camera crews, and we'd barely be able to have one," Donaldson remembered.[68] Comparing ABC to NBC after having worked at both news divisions, as well as at CBS, news writer Merv Block said, "It's the difference between riding on a stolen bicycle and riding on a battleship."[69]

In trying out correspondent after correspondent at the anchor desk, Lower had hoped to find the right person for the job. "The way to attract audience, in my opinion," Lower said, "one, you've got to have a good news organization. But the anchorman is important, in my opinion. People seem to follow them. People don't say, 'Did you see ABC News last night?' They say, 'Did you see what Jennings said last night?' That goes back to Ed Murrow and Huntley and Brinkley."[70] ABC came close to signing Charles Collingwood, but the veteran CBS correspondent could not break his ties to the network with which he had worked since Murrow had hired him to cover World War II.[71]

When Ralph Mann told Lower that Harry was interested in talking to ABC, Mann did not know that ABC had surveyed the television audience to determine how people rated the anchors. Cronkite was the favorite by a wide margin. Runner-up was neither Huntley nor Brinkley. Nor was it Howard K. Smith or Frank Reynolds. Viewers had pointed to Harry Reasoner as their second favorite anchorman.[72] Understandably, Lower welcomed Harry's interest in ABC. Besides, raiding CBS and coming back with one of its stars would please the affiliates and generate publicity for the evening news. When negotiations began with Mann there was no discussion of the criticism that Harry had been lazy at CBS. "We didn't know that at the time," Lower said. "I knew Harry from CBS and I don't think he had the lazy tag on him at that time."[73]

If money and assignment mattered most to Harry, ABC News offered him both. He would earn double what he was paid at CBS, $200,000 a year for five years, a million-dollar contract. Most important, the assignment was what he had long sought: anchor of an evening news broadcast on a national network. There was one catch. He would be the coanchor, taking the place of Frank Reynolds in New York while Howard K. Smith remained in Washington. Harry respected Smith and, Ralph Mann recalled, did not want to offend Smith by demanding that he anchor the broadcast alone. Harry did receive top billing. He and Smith would alternate the nightly commentary that came near the end of the broadcast. In addition to the anchor job, Harry would serve as host of the first newsmagazine produced by ABC and would provide a daily radio commentary.

CBS could not hope to match the ABC offer. "They desperately wanted to have him stay," Mann said. "We were in the middle of a negotiation for him to continue at the CBS network. They could not give him what ABC was willing to give him. Not only was the money good, but the most important thing was the job. CBS could not give him the job he had at ABC."[74] Harry and ABC had managed to strike the kind of deal that would take him away from CBS News after fourteen years.

Only a few hours after ABC News had concluded its election coverage on November 3, 1970, the phone rang in Howard K. Smith's room at the Plaza Hotel. It was two or three o'clock in the morning, but Lower and news vice president Bill Sheehan wanted to meet with Smith about an urgent matter. When they came to Smith's room, they told him they planned to replace Reynolds with Harry and wanted to know if Smith would be willing to work with Harry. "For some reason they were disappointed in Reynolds," Smith recalled. "I told them quite frankly I thought that Reynolds had done a marvelous job on the elections just that previous evening and I was surprised. They said, 'Well, we'll do better with Reasoner.' I said, 'OK, I'll adjust.'"[75] For Reynolds, the news was a shock, coming as it did after what he and others thought had been strong election coverage. "Frank's perceived failing was that he didn't excite viewers," said Bob Siegenthaler, an ABC News producer at the time. "They went for another name. It's a standard broadcast thing—if something isn't working you change to something else and hope you catch lightning in a bottle."[76] When Sheehan went to see Reynolds, the anchorman thought he would be praised for the election broadcast. He was—and he was told he was being replaced.[77]

Harry's departure stunned CBS News. No one of his stature had ever left voluntarily from television's premier news operation. "It was a huge jolt, a huge damn thing," remembered Sanford Socolow, an evening news producer. "The executives started pointing fingers at each other on who had let him go. Salant was beside himself. It really sent shock waves through the organization."[78] That Harry would go to ABC was even more startling. "To join the enemy, even though ABC was a fairly toothless enemy, you just didn't do it," correspondent Roger Mudd said.[79] For the executives of the news division, the simple answer—and the only one that could absolve them of mishandling the situation—was that Harry had left for a job they could not provide. "To those of us who didn't regard Harry as all that indispensable because of his attitude, his laziness, we didn't think we'd go out of business because Harry was leaving," news executive Gordon Manning said.[80] After all, the ranks of CBS News correspondents were rich with talent.

Ego and ambition, represented by the belief that he belonged in the anchor chair, had helped push Harry to leave. However, the lack of respect Bill Leonard and others held for him cannot be overlooked as a factor in his departure. Harry had never held CBS in quite the same loving regard after he was excluded from the 1968 election coverage. Other slights had followed and, even if they had had a legitimate basis, had hurt Harry's pride. Compliments were few and could sound hollow. There was no question that ABC had made him feel wanted, the salary had made him feel valued, and the anchor job would make him one of the elite broadcasters in journalism—all made possible, in large part, by the CBS executives who had taken him for granted. "Harry brought a sense of credibility ABC lacked," recalled David Buksbaum, who had left CBS for ABC in 1969. "That somebody as big as Harry Reasoner was at the time would be willing to come over to ABC was a big deal."[81] At ABC he was a hero of sorts.

Bitterness colored the farewell comments of Frank Reynolds at ABC. While he welcomed Harry and said that his anchor time had been wonderful, at times, Reynolds also told viewers, "I'm not going to suggest that I'm completely happy about what has happened to me, for it is also the truth that I don't like it one bit and see no reason to pretend that I do."[82]

Harry had reason to be gracious when he left CBS, and he was sincere because he had enjoyed the years he worked at the network and the many friends he was leaving. Walter Cronkite set the tone when he bid farewell to Harry on the evening news on November 5, 1970: "My colleague Harry Reasoner is about to become my competitor. After a long and distinguished career here at CBS News, Harry is leaving to become coanchorman of the ABC evening news report. We regret to see him go and we wish him well—not too well, of course."[83] The words had touched Harry when he heard them, less so when he learned they had been written by his friend Charlie West rather than by Cronkite.[84] But then Harry must have known Cronkite would not have spoken them had he not respected Harry.

The next night, his last on the CBS evening news, Harry returned the gesture—with a sly nod toward his new job.

As Walter said last night, this will be the last time I substitute for him on this program.

By a rough calculation I have said "Harry Reasoner for Walter Cronkite" some 350 times or more. I think the highest tribute I can pay to Walter and the people who produce this broadcast is to say that in my craft it is a higher honor to substitute for Walter Cronkite than to stand alone most places.

I hope that this honest and sentimental statement won't interfere with your viewing habits in the months to come...

That's the news. This is Harry Reasoner for Walter Cronkite. Good night.[85]

Congratulations and good wishes flowed to Harry from within the news division and from outside of it. "CBS will be a lonelier place without you," wrote Lyndon Johnson, "but your friends and admirers will undoubtedly be paying more and more attention to ABC news now." The chief rivals for the presidency in 1968, Hubert Humphrey and Richard Nixon, both wished Harry well and complimented ABC for its coup.[86]

Meanwhile, CBS News scrambled to fill the void his departure had created. London correspondent Morley Safer joined Mike Wallace at *60 Minutes*, Dan Rather took over the Sunday night news, and Roger Mudd became Cronkite's regular substitute on the evening news. "If I were so lazy," Harry later remarked, "why did it take three people to replace me?"[87]

CHAPTER SEVEN

At ABC, New Duties and Old Habits

I wanted to be an anchorman before I got too old, and it looked like a good time. As you grow up in journalism you find you do some things better than others. I am at home in front of the camera reading news, and I like to write. And when you find that which you do best, you try for the pinnacle.   **H. R.**

B y nearly any measure Harry had reached the pinnacle of television journalism when he sat down at the New York anchor desk of the ABC evening news. His was not the highest-rated news program among the three networks—nor would it ever be in the seven and a half years he worked at ABC during the Age of Cronkite. Yet Harry was among that elite corps of just four men who told Americans watching television news what was taking place in the world and, in commentaries separate from the news, what they thought about it.

Time magazine considered ABC's coup an important step in the network's effort to be more than a distant third among the three television news operations. Noting that Frank Reynolds had been ABC's ninth anchor in eight years, the magazine observed, "Even a whimsical and gentle man like Harry Reasoner does not kid himself that his tenure at ABC depends on anything but his future ratings." The magazine also reported that hiring Harry "made excellent journalistic sense" if ABC wanted to improve its dismal audience, never more than twenty percent of those watching a national evening news program. "Judging from Reasoner's past form, he will be empathic, bemused and, in the nonpejorative sense of the term, Middle American," *Time* wrote.[1]

Harry set that familiar tone in his commentary on December 7, 1970, after he and Howard had made their first appearance as a team. He noted that who reads the news does not improve the news itself, and he praised both Reynolds and Smith.

"The men at these desks, I think, are like format and type style of a newspaper," he said. "All we can do is not interfere with your understanding of what we can find out. We'll try to find out as much as we can and tell you as much as we know." He closed by saying, "I'd like to take this opportunity to thank all my friends who pointed out that this is Pearl Harbor Day."[2]

An outsider might assume that Harry's career would undergo a radical change with his departure from CBS News and his ascension to the anchor desk at ABC. Actually, little was different for Harry professionally. At ABC

News he applied his skills as a broadcaster to the evening news, a weekly magazine program, a daily radio program, and other broadcasts as needed, just as he had at CBS. Harry and the network itself still relied on writers for the words to read and on producers for the organization required to bring off a broadcast. Just as he had been at CBS, Harry was spread thin at ABC and mainly applied his face and voice to the work of others. "When Reasoner joined ABC," recalled its president for news, Elmer Lower, "everybody wanted a piece of him."[3] Once again, writing took a secondary place, although he did more of it at ABC in the form of commentaries for the evening news and his own weekly news magazine.

From the beginning, however, Harry made a mistake that colored his entire tenure at ABC: He worked and lived as if he were still at CBS. Perhaps it was ego or just the belief that he had to pay his dues only once, but Harry failed to realize that he was in new territory and had to prove himself all over again to writers, producers, and executives unaccustomed to his ways. They knew the Harry Reasoner on television—professional, cool under pressure, and an easygoing presence with just the right thing to say. They quickly discovered less endearing qualities—detachment, indifference, and indolence. Those traits had been part of Harry at CBS, but in the fourteen years he worked there his colleagues learned to accept them as part of a grander package.

At ABC, Harry's flaws stood out to those who expected him to work as hard as anyone, if not harder, to make ABC News as good as its rivals. "Think, if you have an anchor like Harry, who is so laid-back, who isn't passionate, who doesn't give his all twenty-four hours a day, that's not going to be received well," observed Joan Richman, one of the CBS News veterans who worked with Harry at ABC.[4] Consequently, the flaws that became all too evident at ABC—particularly the drinking—were seen in more of a negative light than they had been at CBS. As much as they liked Harry, his coworkers at ABC were less forgiving.

Patrons of the Biarritz did not notice a change when Harry moved to ABC. He could still be found at his table enjoying lunch and martinis in the company of Charlie West and other CBS cronies. When producer Les Midgely walked past most of the CBS evening news staff at Harry's table one day, he waved his hand dismissively and said, "You can have all of them, Harry."[5] The remark turned out to be as much a prophecy as it was a witticism. In previous years ABC had brought in several CBS News veterans, such as David Buksbaum and Av Westin, to shore up its operation. In Harry's wake, more CBS News staff began testing the waters at ABC. People from Ernie Leiser to Andy Rooney followed Harry to join the ranks of their long-suffering competitor. Harry did make full use of one quality of his new ABC office. The network news shared a building with the Café des Artiste restaurant and bar. Soon, he became as much a fixture at the des Artiste as the murals that adorned its walls.

Those at ABC who thought Harry was a drag on the operation because he lacked a take-charge attitude and spent too much time at the bar made their own ill-considered judgment. What mattered more than anything, of course, was the public view of Harry as expressed in ratings. That did not change. In hiring him ABC News bought his high standing with viewers and with peers in addition to that familiar smile and voice—in short, ABC traded on Harry's credibility as a newsman. His credibility was real, too, forged in the newsrooms of the *Minneapolis Times* and KEYD-TV and perfected over years of reporting and broadcasting major and minor events for CBS. His intellect and curiosity fed his credibility, and his talents as a broadcaster made believers of viewers. "He brings a freshness, a new authority to television journalism," wrote a television critic in Atlanta after Harry's first year at ABC. "His voice, his personality, his wonderful sense of humor make him one of the most appealing of all TV newscasters."[6] Above all, Harry remained a journalist, even if he was no longer reporting and writing the news.

ABC executives, as their CBS counterparts had discovered years before, had only to determine the best ways to use Harry in order to realize the highest return on their investment. "It was hard not to get along with him," Ernie Leiser said. "He was an attractive, intelligent, bright, easygoing-in-manner guy, even though he was driven by ambition."[7] Why ambition failed to fuel a stronger work ethic in Harry was not the point. If he could bring the network viewers as well as prestige while sparking a turnaround in its fortunes, then Harry and his warts would be worth every cent and any imposition.

Part of Harry's job was to gain viewers for the ABC evening news, and he went to work building the audience by glad-handing the affiliates at their annual meeting, in Los Angeles in May 1971. It was a tough crowd: Of the nearly 200 stations affiliated with ABC, just 138 were carrying the broadcast when Harry joined the network. ABC News would never be competitive with CBS and NBC as long as nearly a third of its affiliates did not carry its evening news.

At the meeting Harry did not stop with smiles and good cheer. In a speech to the affiliates, he tried to shame them into carrying the broadcast. "We can go head-to-head with anyone and win, because we have the best evening newscast on television. To go with the best news, we need the best affiliates. Without you we are nothing," he said. "Any station having a network affiliation and not carrying that network's news is a disgrace."[8] Whether being chastised had an impact or not, station clearances for the evening news began to rise after Harry came on board. In fifteen months all 172 primary affiliates and 18 secondary affiliates were airing the evening news, its biggest lineup ever.[9]

The rest would soon follow. In May 1972 the broadcast earned its highest national share of the audience ever when it gained 23 percent of those watching any evening news program. For the first time, the ABC evening news was Number 2 in the ratings, ahead of NBC. Its Nielsen average was up five points from May 1971 and had attracted an additional 2 million viewers, a 40 percent increase.[10] "It's no coincidence that there has been a healthy increase in viewership over the same period," wrote Wade Mosby, a television critic for the *Milwaukee Journal*. "Reasoner exudes a sort of calm, dispassionate attitude that inspires confidence."[11] Harry turned out to be a bargain for ABC—it finally gained the foothold it needed. Losing him had been a blunder for CBS that would have ramifications for both CBS and NBC in the decades ahead.

A typical workday for Harry began with the drive from his home in Westport to the ABC offices in the city. An extra $5,000 had been added to his $200,000 salary to allow him to hire a driver. (In later years he commuted by train.) Not wanting a limousine driver—they talked too much, Harry told friends—he hired a young college dropout, Adam Schloss, who was a friend of the Rooneys. Each morning they would meet at a Howard Johnson's near the Connecticut Turnpike, Schloss leaving his car in the parking lot and taking the wheel of Harry's leather-upholstered Mercedes for the hour-long drive. Harry would read the *New York Times* or a paperback novel by John D. MacDonald or another favorite writer. At times they would talk about what was in the news or baseball and other sports. On the days he would be reading a commentary on the evening news, usually Tuesday and Thursday, Harry made notes as he rode into town.[12]

The executive producer and a handful of senior producers set the lineup of reports for that evening's broadcast, beginning with morning meetings. Harry usually did not participate in the first morning meeting that determined the program's content, spending much of his time in his office. "Their only job all day is to put on the best possible evening news," he told a visitor. "I don't think I should try to do their job unless I can come in at nine-thirty and do nothing else. I do a good many other things."[13] The evening news reflected its producers' ideas more than Harry's. He was not the kind of anchor to direct coverage.[14] Harry trusted the producers to make those decisions and seldom objected to them. Besides, all were part of the same generation of journalists, sharing the same concepts of news. Asked if ABC had policies or guidelines for the news, Harry responded: "Only to be as professional as possible. And don't lie, don't libel, and don't talk dirty."[15]

However, if Harry did not think a story should air, it would not. If he objected to something in the script, the script would be changed. "My rule always was, you never can ask an anchorman, or anchorwoman nowadays, to say something that they don't want to say," contended Av Westin, the executive producer of the evening news when Harry began his work at ABC.[16] He disliked bullfighting, for example, and refused to have anything on the air about it, even a report by correspondent Peter Jennings.[17] On the whole, he made few demands. "Harry's interest in this kind of thing wasn't all that deep, frankly, and ultimately he was pretty happy to anchor the broadcast," news vice president Bill Sheehan said. "He had a strong feeling about what was appropriate material, content for the news broadcast, and he would speak his mind on that."[18] Although Harry expected to have a say in the editorial process and to travel to cover important stories, he followed the lead of producers and other news executives.

Most of Harry's work behind the camera on the evening news, besides writing his commentaries and end pieces, came in reviewing scripts and revising what did not sound right to him. The writing staff learned what he found unacceptable and developed an ear for his style and cadence. In time fewer and fewer notations of "DTSTL"(Droppable To Say The Least) and "OMDB" (Over My Dead Body) would appear on scripts.[19] "I think it's silly to have a fetish about writing for your own program if you are the voice of a network broadcast which represents the daily work of several hundred people," Harry told an interviewer. "I think you ought to be able to write any part of it. I think, in other words, you ought to be an experienced journalist kind of writer, and I think I am."[20]

Harry was not one to demand changes just because he could. "I worked with a lot of these guys, and a lot of it's ego," producer Bernie Cohen said. "He was not like that, not at all. He did his thing, you did your thing, and once he trusted you, sometimes he never even read the stuff until rehearsal."[21] Others thought Harry was not nearly as involved in the broadcast as he should have been, among them his partner, Howard K. Smith. "He was a good writer but he didn't like to work at it. He was interviewed once in my presence by a reporter and he was asked how much of his stuff he wrote and he said, 'As little as possible,'" Smith said. "Harry is actually an illusion himself. He's marvelous on television, but he doesn't work."[22]

More than a trace of bitterness marked Smith's memories of his career in the 1960s and 1970s. His generation had established the reputation of CBS News. He was the last American correspondent to leave Berlin in 1941 and the first to return after the fall of the Third Reich. He covered postwar Europe for CBS News for more than a decade before returning to the United States. Another career highlight came in 1960 when he moderated the first Kennedy-Nixon debate. But Smith left CBS in 1962 after management contended he had editorialized in his reporting on civil rights.

Two months later ABC News hired Smith as a commentator, reporter, and documentary host. He began anchoring the evening news with Frank Reynolds in 1969.[23] He had resisted being a coanchor even with Reynolds, whom he thought to be the perfect anchorman. "Generally, two men are no better than one man. In fact, they're worse than one man. One man can concentrate and do something to make the show better. Two men, you scatter responsibility so that you don't have any real authority," Smith said. He believed the Huntley-Brinkley team that had been so successful for NBC was a case of unique chemistry, not a model to replicate.[24]

By most accounts, Harry and Howard Smith—in spite of occasional friction and a lack of friendship off the air—were an effective broadcasting team. For instance, in 1973, when the evening news learned that former President Lyndon Johnson had died unexpectedly at his ranch in Texas, producer Dick Richter decided to interrupt the lineup and return, after a commercial break, with the coanchors reminiscing about the late president. "Howard and Harry were just absolutely fantastic telling stories for the rest of the half-hour," Richter remembered.[25] These opposites were thought to be attractive to viewers. In contrast to Smith's serious and somber tone, Harry lightened the program with that sense of warmth so many viewers enjoyed. "He and Smith were a pretty good team there for a long time and we were making some progress," news president Elmer Lower recalled.[26] More stations were coming on board, and more people were watching.

Smith reported political stories and other news from Washington while Harry handled national and foreign news in New York. Joined electronically on the air but separated physically by nearly 250 miles, the partners were not close in any way. "We were coanchormen, but we were not intimates," Smith recalled nearly thirty years later. "Reasoner was really ideal for television. The lines on his face indicated wisdom and warmth. Actually, I don't think he was that wise and he wasn't warm at all when you came to know him. He was good on television, he wrote well for television, and he practiced well on television." They worked together for five years and ABC News improved its standing with viewers, yet Smith considered Harry to be a disappointment.[27]

Their colleagues noticed the lack of warmth between the coanchors. "Not that they didn't like each other, it's just that they were so different," producer Walter Pfister said. "Their personalities were at opposite ends of the pole. Harry was a hail-fellow-well-met and Howard was a studious or reserved person."[28] Smith may have had little respect for Harry, producer Walter Porgess believed, and what chemistry existed between the two tended to be slightly negative.[29] "Harry thought Howard was a little too cerebral or fussy or whatever, and I think he thought I was a little too Germanic," producer Bob Siegenthaler said. "I like to run it very tight, and Harry was more, 'Come on, we'll be able to do it, why do we have to rehearse again,' and stuff like that."[30] Ernie Leiser, who produced the evening news with both men, contended that Smith worked harder on the broadcast than Harry. "Neither loved the other, and it wasn't an altogether pleasant relationship," Leiser said. "On the occasions when one would be off and the other would be doing the show alone, life was a lot easier for the people putting the shows together than when they were working together. When each was doing a solo, it was clear that person was happier."[31]

Serving as correspondent for a documentary program gave Harry the opportunity to be on his own, at least for a while. His close friend at CBS, Andy Rooney, had joined ABC after a dispute at *60 Minutes* had led him to work elsewhere for a time. Together again, their collaborations brought back memories of the literate documentaries on which they had worked in the 1960s. Although he remained at ABC less than a year, Rooney wrote, produced, and directed three programs that aired in 1972, each with Harry designated in the script as "The Star." They toured California by helicopter for *A Bird's Eye View of California*,[32] which recalled their excursion over Scotland a few years earlier. The interest they shared in matters of faith led to *An Essay on Architecture*,[33] which explored the designs of places of worship and how they revealed the lives and beliefs of people of all religions.

Close to Harry's heart was *A Small Town in Iowa*,[34] Rooney's reflections on life in small-town America. Shot in Humboldt, the program was a homecoming for Harry even if he did not write the script. Rooney and the television crew shot film for ten days in Humboldt while Harry spent just two days doing his on-camera work. The setting was personal for Harry, but Rooney's script took an everyman approach to the subject. "A great many people who grew up in small towns live in cities now, telling everyone how good it was back home," Harry observed at the beginning of the program. "You wonder if maybe small towns are better to remember than they are to live in." Rooney's style so suited Harry that when he remarked on camera, "There is no anti-Semitism in Humboldt, but there are no Jews, either," the words sounded natural for the man who once played in the streets from which he now broadcast.

Documentaries may have separated Harry from Howard Smith, but special events drew them together. Their work on camera went well in part because both were professionals but also because their producers played to their individual strengths and interests. Smith covered politics and understood the background and context to a much deeper level than Harry. During political conventions in 1972 and 1976 and in election-night coverage the difference was noticeable even though both had access to the ample amount of material gathered by the research staff. "This is a boast, so it sounds like a boast," Smith said, "but I don't think he knew as much as I did because I don't think he worked as hard. But he knew enough and it worked very smoothly, I thought."[35] Harry did manage to annoy Smith by being less than tidy during conventions and elections, allowing paper to pile up until Smith told him to clean up the desk they shared.[36]

ABC eschewed the gavel-to-gavel convention coverage of its competitors and instead offered a ninety-minute wrap-up each evening of the Republican and Democratic conventions in 1972. Producers used Harry as a sort of color commentator rather than a political analyst, relying on him to ask the kinds of questions a typical viewer might ask. "In any situation like that Howard would seem as though he had read nothing else for the last six months," producer Walter Porgess recalled. "Harry gave the impression, rightly or wrongly, that he glanced at the research. That was OK, too, because he always knew what to ask, he always knew what the story was. It came easily to him and he was very good at it without any great obvious effort." [37] Although he may not have considered it as such, Harry had a type of sweet revenge on the CBS naysayers who had removed him from election coverage in 1968. He still prepared very little for the special broadcasts but now was the prime anchor for a competing network—and earning twice as much money. Better still, several critics liked the ABC coverage, especially Harry's droll observations.

Politics was Howard Smith's preferred beat, but the space program was one area he avoided. Harry worked from New York or traveled to Cape Canaveral to anchor launches and other events with correspondent Jules Bergman, the network's space expert. Harry did not know much about the space program and did not bother himself with learning about it. "Bergman did all the mechanics and Harry put it in perspective for the audience and did a pretty good job of it," producer Walter Pfister said. "Harry's ability was to make a comparison or an analogy to something in real life. He brought it home to people, the guy next door. That was a pretty good duo." [38]

Harry liked to ad-lib, finding it easier to comment without a script.[39] At times, though, producers wished that he had made a greater effort to prepare in the hope that the very good work they expected from him would reach a level of excellence. "As a producer you wanted to like Harry a lot," said Pfister, who oversaw special-events coverage. "But sometimes he frustrated the hell out of you because he didn't do his homework." [40] Other producers were more content with his contributions. "Harry did not believe in showing sweat, whether literally or figuratively," Bob Siegenthaler said. "He liked to maintain a façade of imperturbability. If he's inscrutable, you don't know whether he's done his homework or not. But I would not make any charge that any air program suffered for his lack of preparedness." [41]

With Harry the network news at ABC was making strides in the quality of its coverage and the size of its audience. Who was willing to complain to its major asset that he could be better? He was their star and, besides, he was not going to change—and, most important, the results were an improvement over the past.

In February 1972, Harry and an evening news team traveled to Beijing to cover President Nixon's historic trip to China, the first by an American president. Sparse crowds greeted Air Force One at the Beijing airport and relatively few people lined the motorcade route. "The absence of huge crowds can be overestimated," Harry told viewers. "In China there is no such thing as news or news events as we know them. News is simply an instrument of national policy." [42] It was the perfect event for Harry. There was no real news beyond the fact that Nixon would shake hands with Mao Tse-Tung and be treated to a state visit. The trip opened China to American television viewers, and Harry focused on describing the pomp and circumstance as well as the colorful cultural curiosities.

While admitting that China seemed better off than it had ever been before, Harry shared his skepticism of the communist way of life in his evening news commentaries from Beijing. "The people we see are well-dressed and busy and healthy, and the food is good and the attitude toward visitors mostly polite and helpful," he told viewers one night. "But there's such a stuffiness about everything, such a proletarian pomposity. Life here must be like an eternity of service club lunches, an unending cliché, combined sometimes with a deep hypocrisy." [43] Harry visited the Great Wall and reflected on its symbolism for the revolutionaries now ruling the former empire. "China's leaders still think of themselves as inside some sort of great wall. It's made of thought now and it's more than the thirty-five feet high that those emperors twenty-two centuries ago thought was safe. That's what makes it especially interesting and significant that Chairman Mao and Premier Chou, whose law is impenetrable, sort of let Richard Nixon in the back way." [44] Several critics praised the ABC coverage and preferred it to the competition.

The next White House charter plane in which Harry flew took off in June 1974 when Nixon, in spite of being awash in Watergate, visited Moscow. "I think the day-to-day grind of covering the White House is for younger and livelier men, but I am perfectly willing to join a ceremonial parade like this," Harry joked with viewers before leaving the United States. "Howard, if I find out any news, I'll call you." [45] When Soviet technicians blacked out six news reports from the American television networks, Harry personally escorted one can of film, a report with Soviet dissident Andrei Sakharov, to London so it could be part of an ABC evening news broadcast. [46]

Not only were these adventures for Harry, such visits were respites from the annoyances of the increasing celebrity that came with a high-profile job on television. No one had known him in Beijing. In Yalta, Harry and producer Dick Richter strolled the boardwalk along an ugly, dirty beach as 200-pound female bathers beckoned the strangers from America to join them. "Harry loved it," Richter said. [47]

On the streets of New York, passersby stopped Harry occasionally to shake the hand of the man they saw on the evening news. To his amusement, a few mistook him for Howard Smith. Harry was five years younger but as silver-haired as his partner. On one occasion, F.B.I. Director J. Edgar Hoover asked an assistant to locate a Reasoner commentary he had been told was critical of the Federal Bureau of Investigation—only to discover that the commentary was actually delivered by Smith.[48] When a friend told CBS evening news writer John Mosedale that he had trouble telling Harry and Howard apart, Mosedale responded: "That's easy. One of them's a hawk, and the other one says 'Warshington.'"[49]

Howard Smith was indeed a hawk on the subject of the war in Vietnam. Believing that a firm stand had to be taken against the communists in Southeast Asia, Smith thought the Gulf of Tonkin Resolution had been an act of "high wisdom," and he spoke against anti-Vietnam rioters and in favor of continued fighting.[50] On the other hand, Harry saw the war as rooted in honorable intentions but ultimately a sad waste of lives, money, and prestige for all involved. Vietnam was one of the issues that separated their evening news commentaries. The most obvious distinction between the coanchors may have been the overall tone with which they delivered their commentaries. Howard Smith was a serious man and his commentaries, often heavy and analytical, reflected his personality. Harry was more interested in what issues and events told him about human qualities, and he usually found a lighter way to make a point.

The pair alternated commentaries during the week, a move designed to broaden the appeal of the broadcast.[51] What influence either had on viewers cannot be measured, but with a national audience each night they were certainly prominent figures in the arena of public opinion. True, Harry spent more time reflecting on trends, lifestyles, baseball, holidays, and other less weighty topics. Yet he also commented, even sharply at times, on the two critical issues of the early 1970s, the Vietnam War and Watergate. He added his voice to those skeptical of government policies that prolonged the war and kept secrets from its citizens.

By the time Harry began delivering commentaries on the ABC evening news, the Vietnam question had turned from whether to how soon the United States would extricate itself from the battlefield. In a commentary delivered on his fourth day on the job at ABC, Harry contended that the most serious casualties of the war might have been the morale, efficiency, and sense of purpose and mission of the military services. "The world, we hope, may come to an era when armies are not needed," he concluded, "but in the meantime it is frightening to see the erosion of our army by a task it cannot master and the country cannot fully support."[52] He returned to that thought in April 1971 when he commended the testimony before Congress of a decorated Vietnam veteran, John Kerry, and agreed with the view that the nation should admit that getting into and staying in the war had been a mistake. Noting that Kerry retained his pride in serving his country, Harry observed that the worst casualty of Vietnam, perhaps, was the pride and integrity of the military.[53]

Harry avoided emotion in the delivery of commentaries, probably due in part to his personality and to decades of objectively reporting the news. The tragedy of the Vietnam War did move him, however, even though he chose to express his deeper feelings in private. "I was always struck by how he talked about it in his commentaries," his young driver, Adam Schloss, recalled. "He talked about it with passion to me. He could step back from his emotions about Vietnam and express his opposition in his commentaries and do it in a way that would not offend and not polarize."[54] Harry seemed to understand that anger and vitriol alienated viewers and clouded the message.

Skepticism and disappointment in the way the military and the Nixon administration conducted the war marked Harry's reflections on Vietnam. When officials in Washington contended that officers in the field—and the press quoting them—were in error in criticizing the war and had failed to see "the big picture," Harry told viewers, "It would be easier to believe things were going according to plan if the plans didn't change retroactively to fit the situation." He concluded: "Ever since our involvement in Vietnam began, the big picture has been hard to see. I suggest that one of the poorest views has been from Washington."[55] Harry criticized advisers to President Johnson who had not shared with him their doubts about war policy, and then asked in regard to Nixon: "Is the president, as he ought to be, the best-informed man in the world? Or is he, as I think Mr. Johnson was, the man whose best friends won't tell him—the husband who is the last to know."[56]

A patient man by nature, Harry began to show his impatience for the Nixon administration when, in a May 13, 1971, commentary, he called on the president to seek a speedy end to the war rather than the slow track the president was pursuing. "I am not in the group that believes our involvement in Vietnam started for wholly bad reasons, or that the aims and principles at stake were always hopeless. But they are now," he told viewers. Questioning the logic of a gradual withdrawal of troops, Harry contended that a weaker force in Vietnam would not help negotiations. "President Nixon could have ended the war on more favorable terms to our allies in January of 1969 than he could now, and the trend is downhill, at home and on the scene," Harry concluded. "Mr. Nixon likes the phrase 'to bite the bullet.' It is time to do that now and end this interminable nightmare."[57]

From that day Harry cast a critical eye on plans that delayed the end of the war. Noting that Nixon had reduced American forces while also reducing American aims in Vietnam, he described the president as "like the man who was too kind to cut off his dog's tail all at once; he chopped it off an inch a day."[58] When American forces began heavy bombing of North Vietnam in April 1972, Harry observed that differing groups were coming together in opposition to the bombing. "For once principle and tactics tell us the same thing," he said. "Stop the deep bombing. Keep lowering our posture, not raising it. Don't slow down the already slow pace of our disengagement."[59]

One other constant in the swirl of Vietnam brought forth Harry's mild-mannered ire: the government's criticism of people who differed with its policies and its efforts to keep those policies secret. In June 1971 the press began publishing the Pentagon Papers, a secret history of how the United States had conducted the war. That a democratically elected government would hide information from its people disturbed Harry, and he called the effort "at the very least a particularly intense hypocrisy." Agreeing with those who said the secret study had shown the executive branch's contempt for the legislature, Harry added: "That, and even more, a contempt for the people, and their ability to understand and reason and make intelligent decisions. The North Vietnamese and the Russians and the Chinese are presumably used to that contempt from their leaders. We are not."[60]

When Nixon aide H. R. Haldeman contended that those who criticized the president's peace proposals were aiding and abetting the enemy, Harry called it "a shocking statement" and claimed it showed a "kind of intellectual arrogance, an arrogance which says in effect, once we have made up our minds to do something good for you, please do not question either our manner or our method." Harry concluded: "It is characteristic of an attitude which seems to feel timidly that we are at a hopeless disadvantage in a hostile world if we are candid with ourselves and face our divisions. That is not so, and I hope Mr. Haldeman's boss doesn't think it's so."[61]

Reports of government misdeeds and hypocrisy rankled Harry as the Watergate drama played out. Unlike Vietnam, Watergate began and ended with Harry at the anchor desk. At least thirty of the commentaries he delivered during the period touched on the scandal, which drew more attention from Harry than any other topic during the years he coanchored the evening news. Howard Smith would be remembered for being the first prominent commentator to call for Nixon's resignation, but Harry was equally focused on how Watergate was hurting the nation.

As the scandal deepened in 1973, Harry looked on it with a mixture of scorn, bemusement, and sarcasm. Early in the year he observed that the affair would be the "funniest thing American politics ever produced" had the implications not been so serious, and then added: "We have a great new gallery of American portraits, crew-cut Rasputins, incompetent Machiavellis, fumbling crusaders. I hope it stays funny. It's the only saving grace of the whole sordid episode."[62] Later, he contended that greed separated the Teapot Dome oil leases scandal of the 1920s from Watergate. Nixon's men were motivated by "a deep desire to eliminate the untidiness of the American system—the slovenly tolerance of a loud opposition and a free press, the permission that the founding fathers carelessly gave people to hold wrong opinions." He concluded: "These clowns didn't think they were crooks. They thought they were crusaders."[63]

More than once Harry asked what the Watergate burglars had hoped to gain from the break-in. "It may, I suppose, come out," he told viewers, "but everything so far indicates that never in the history of politics was so much risked for so little."[64] Harry's distaste for Nixon, particularly the president's attacks on the press, surfaced more and more in commentaries as the months passed. With a rare touch of sarcasm, Harry said of Nixon: "He evoked a heartbreaking picture of a beleaguered leader, pilloried nightly on every newscast by the 'leers and sneers' of commentators....I think it is mostly the president who sneers. Which is, of course, his perfect right."[65]

Harry tended to look for something positive in any troublesome situation, an optimism he shared with viewers. The day after Howard Smith called on Nixon to resign, Harry told viewers he agreed with his coanchor's judgment. Yet he also noted that Nixon, while refusing to resign, was attempting to be conciliatory toward his critics. "The best thing to do would be for Mr. Nixon to resign or for Congress to remove him. But if that's not going to happen, and considering the chaos and disaster this man in some of his moods could bring us to, it is mildly encouraging that he seems to realize what a mess he has made and is trying to repair it."[66]

At times Harry offered a humorous bent to the bad news that seemed to flow so freely from Washington. After the White House tapes showed Nixon and others using vulgar language, he ended a commentary about the tapes by claiming that a fight between a Nixon partisan and a Lyndon Johnson partisan had broken out in a Third Avenue bar the previous night. "The bartender said the sentence that started it was, 'My president talks dirtier than your president,'" Harry told viewers, "but he doesn't know which one said it."[67]

When impeachment or resignation seemed inescapable, Harry spoke in favor of the balance of power and warned that the presidency itself should not be weakened because of Nixon's transgressions.[68] Three days before Nixon resigned, Harry suggested the president should be given some sort of amnesty from prosecution once he left office. "I say let him go, if he finds it in himself to go," Harry commented. "Give him amnesty and draw a curtain over this scene. Not for his sake. For ours."[69] When President Gerald Ford granted Nixon a pardon the following month, Harry was among those supporting the decision, although he asked that other Watergate offenders and draft dodgers and deserters be considered for pardons as well.[70]

Serious issues did not escape Harry's attention, nor did they dominate his thinking. What distinguished him from Howard Smith and CBS's Eric Sevareid was an interest in life beyond the nation's social and political ills. Harry often reflected on everyday matters, blessings, and annoyances. "Trivial is a

mean-sounding word," evening news producer Ernie Leiser said. "He preferred painting with a smaller brush."[71] Harry knew better than anyone that
he had established a following with light, thoughtful end pieces on *Calendar* and the Sunday night and evening news programs on CBS, and his ABC
commentaries carried similar themes of home and hearth.

Harry was drawn to eulogizing men who had had a positive impact on
American culture. Baseball player Jackie Robinson, jazz musician Duke El-
lington, aviator Charles Lindbergh, and former chief justice Earl Warren
were among those he honored. He even used the ABC airwaves to congrat-
ulate CBS president Frank Stanton upon his retirement and to mourn the
death of his CBS News colleague John Merriman.

Holidays were a favorite topic. The trend to create a three-day weekend by moving the day of commemoration to Monday annoyed Harry to no
end. Christmas was special to him, and he delivered variations of his favorite
Christmas essay twice on ABC.[72] As Thanksgiving approached, he reflected
on the relative lack of commercialism surrounding it. "It was created a holiday to mark gratitude for having gotten the harvest in," Harry noted, "but it
is also a somber gathering of the clan to note that a long winter lies ahead and
we still need all the help we can get from whatever gods are willing to smile
on this wide nation."[73]

As he had for years, Harry left his mind open to any bit of news, any event,
any offhand remark by a friend that could spark an idea for a commentary:

- The *New York Times* published its fifth article on the film *The Exor-
  cist*. Harry asked why "a cheap movie made from a cheap bad novel"
  had gained such intense publicity from a respected medium. "Based
  on this case and the evidence of much of the *Times*'s literary and dramatic criticism, I'm afraid the good old paper is possessed."[74]
- The predominantly white voters of Los Angeles elected its first black
  mayor, Tom Bradley. "For the first time a major American city has
  chosen a mayor on the basis of who seems to be the better man, without reference to color," Harry said. "The next major step, I suppose,
  would be to reject someone because he was obnoxious, even if black."[75]
- In May 1974 the news marked the twentieth anniversary of school
  desegregation. "As I grew to understand and love the South and
  Southerners of both races," Harry said, "I remember saying even
  then that when the argument over equality goes to the North it was
  going to be much nastier than it ever was in Birmingham. I'm sorry I
  was right."[76]
- The film *Last Tango in Paris* raised the hackles of censors. "Censorship
  is tempting because it is quite clear you can't rely on anybody's taste—
  not producers, who want to make money; not directors, who want to

push on to further sordid horizons; and certainly not actors, who will do anything if you promise somebody will watch them do it."[77]

A wry touch did not make for influential commentaries or enshrine Harry as one of broadcasting's eminent thinkers. Still, many viewers of a national newscast must have been delighted by reflections that at times avoided the onerous events of the day for their grist. How else to explain that, in the course of nearly eight years with ABC, no commentary by Harry drew as much response as his reflections on a new entry in fashion—men's panty-hose. "I know what the men's liberation people will say—that they are sick and tired of fooling around with girdles and garter belts and runs in their nylons, but I still say that a man who can't keep his socks up without hooking them on his pelvis is going to be in trouble out in the real competitive world," he said. "I appeal to my fellow men. Paint a racing stripe on your jockey shorts if you want to, but stay out of pantyhose."[78]

Within two days Harry received a pair from the manufacturer. He told viewers that night that the response to his comments had surprised him, especially since he had remarked on far more important topics without much reaction. He rejected the conclusion that people were shallow, preferring instead to believe that most people don't react to things about which they can do little or nothing. "They'll act to give money or to vote for something or even to go to war. But they have an understandable reluctance to brood about something they can't change," he said. "Pantyhose, on the other hand, they can change."[79]

Harry and Howard Smith shared the evening news and its bully pulpit for five years. For half of that period, however, Harry alone had the privilege of anchoring a second news broadcast nearly every week. In early 1973, as he entered his third year as coanchor of the evening news, ABC began to compete with its rival networks in another medium, the news magazine. Harry would be at the helm of this belated enterprise, coming as it did more than four years after CBS and NBC had begun their news magazines. ABC named it *The Reasoner Report* to make further use of its star broadcaster.

Harry would anchor the weekly program, introducing segments and offering a closing essay. It was *The Reasoner Report* that brought Ernie Leiser, frustrated and bored at CBS, to ABC News—a decision made easier by the offer of a great deal of money and the challenge to produce the network's premier news magazine. (Within a year news executives decided Leiser was needed more urgently at the evening news.) ABC hired a strong production staff that included writer and producer Andy Rooney, veteran ABC producer Arthur Holch, and also Joan Richman, who had left CBS News after twelve years to join Leiser in creating what had been presented to her as a kind of junior *60 Minutes*.[80] When *The Reasoner Report* aired its first segments on

February 24, 1973, Harry promised viewers a "substantial new journalistic entity."

The Reasoner Report was a laudable news program even if it did not break ground in the genre of the news magazine. The fare was the typical mixture of newsmaker and celebrity profiles, investigations, and human-interest features. In its first six months its correspondents profiled United States senator Sam Ervin as he led the Watergate investigation, astronaut-turned-missionary Jim Irwin, Jordan's King Hussein and his new queen, entertainer Josephine Baker, activist and singer Pete Seeger, and painter Thomas Hart Benton. The broadcast investigated rising meat prices, water pollution, food additives, school-bus safety, gasoline shortages, and contaminated meat. Retrospectives examined the My Lai massacre; the lunch counter sit-in at Greensboro, North Carolina, that helped spark the civil-rights movements; the murder of civil-rights worker Medgar Evers; and the twenty-fifth anniversary of the Berlin airlift. Its few soft features included the popularity of country music in Japan.

Yet ABC ultimately treated *The Reasoner Report* as a poor stepchild. The network allowed the broadcast only thirty minutes of airtime instead of a full hour. Its anchor retained the daily responsibility of the evening news, which severely diminished his ability to contribute to the program. Unlike *60 Minutes*, it had no stable of correspondents, instead relying on ABC News correspondents in the field. Finally, the network assigned the program an undesirable time slot, 6:30 Saturday evening, often following ABC's prized sports coverage. If a football game or other event ran long, *The Reasoner Report* gave up its time. Sports preempted the program twenty-four times in as many months; in some months it aired just twice. A related problem was the fact that not all affiliates chose to air the show, preferring to hold on to that half-hour for their own programming in order to keep all of the revenues from the sale of commercials.

These limitations hampered Leiser's efforts to mount a program that could be successful in terms of its quality and its ratings. "We tried to squeeze two pieces in a half an hour and it just doesn't work. You need to have seventeen minutes for the main pieces," he said. It was clear that sports programming, under the guidance of executive producer Roone Arledge, was the priority.[81]

With the evening news his main concern, Harry probably looked on *The Reasoner Report* as another broadcast he could entrust to a seasoned staff. For him, the airtime and the prestige of having a broadcast carry his name made the effort worthwhile. For the network, it was a reasonable distribution of a valuable resource: The staff put together the program while Harry provided what they could not—star power. Except for the closing essays, Harry did little more than tape his segments on Friday afternoons after lunch. "He was perfectly willing to have me and the others working on *The Reasoner Report* do all the legwork," Leiser said.[82] Not that the news magazine was without merit or produced without pride. "It was certainly the best work on ABC," Richman said. For ABC News correspondents, the broadcast provided their only opportunity to do longer pieces.[83]

While *The Reasoner Report* was still in its first year, Ernie Leiser left as executive producer to oversee the evening news. Harry and other ABC executives asked that Al Primo replace Leiser as the head of the news magazine. Primo, at the time vice president of news for the network's owned-and-operated stations, called affiliates not carrying the program to urge them to help make it successful by building its audience. Having worked for CBS as well as ABC, with experience in local and national news programs, Primo saw the value of trying to break news on *The Reasoner Report* in order to gain the broadcast both publicity and respect. He also believed that Harry, as the star of the program, needed a more prominent role and should report from the field whenever possible.[84]

Finding time in Harry's schedule was only one challenge facing Primo. The producer discovered that his anchorman could be difficult to engage. Having to coax Harry to abandon his post-lunch drink to be on the set for lighting and sound checks was a sign to Primo that *The Reasoner Report* was not terribly important to its anchor. "It became abundantly clear in a couple of weeks, basically, he was pretty much interested in his own indulgences and he wanted me there to make him look good, and that was fine," Primo said. Motivation became the key to getting Harry involved in the broadcast that carried his name. "He was so talented he didn't have to work as hard—and he knew it," Primo said. "I was always trying to find ways to get him up and excited about things. When he did he was absolutely brilliant."[85] To appeal to Harry's interest in country music, for example, Primo produced a segment on singer Tanya Tucker.

When the evening news sent Harry out of New York, *The Reasoner Report* tried to develop segments that he could do from that location. He did more field work for the news magazine in the second half of 1973, traveling to Niger to report on a deadly drought, to the Middle East for a segment on the Yom Kippur War, and to Belfast to examine the conflict between Protestants and Catholics.

The great coup of *The Reasoner Report* in its two years and four months on the air was an exclusive tour of Camp David, the president's retreat in the Catoctin Mountains of Maryland. Gerald Ford, who assumed the presidency after Nixon's resignation, had been in office only three months when *The Reasoner Report* visited him. No television news crew had been allowed on the heavily guarded grounds until Harry arrived to interview the new president for a segment broadcast on November 16, 1974. "He was actually nervous as a cat because it was a first and he was going to be one-on-one with the president of the United States," Primo recalled. "And all he kept saying was, 'Are you sure we covered everything? Have we got all the questions?' Of course, he must have had 400 questions, every question there was in the world." [86] First Lady Betty Ford joined Harry and the president as they strolled the grounds before sitting down for an interview.

Harry could make any question seem friendly. "I'd like to just tick off some of the chief criticisms of you, President Ford, including some from people who respond to you, normally. I suppose the basic one is that your administration so far seems rudderless, without direction; the feeling that you do not have the grip on it. Is there something in that?"

Ford responded as amiably by saying, "Harry, I of course disagree with that…" and then defending his administration.

Later in the interview, Harry used the same approach to broach the subject of Ford's nominee for vice president, Nelson Rockefeller, who had been criticized and investigated because of financial gifts to aides and state officials. "Very early on, I think in your first news conference, you said the ethical standards of this administration would be your ethical standard," Harry told Ford. "You don't see any problem in what has come out about Mr. Rockefeller? You don't see anything unethical in what he's done?"

Ford answered: "I do not, from what I know. And I think I know all of it." [87]

Although Harry had not pressed Ford on these and other sensitive subjects, he had challenged the president on his own turf. As were most Americans, he was willing to give Ford time to establish his own style in the White House. In an essay that closed the Camp David broadcast, he encouraged others to look on the accidental president with optimism. "We have had two immediate predecessors who took things much harder," Harry said. "Just possibly a man who likes his job, and likes his constituents, and puts his pants on one leg at a time, is what we need." [88]

Most of the commentaries Harry wrote for *The Reasoner Report* played off its segments, which saved him the time and effort required to develop ideas. While the war in Vietnam was winding down and the Watergate scandal slowly enveloped the Nixon administration, the program had aired numerous reports on both topics. On one 1973 broadcast Harry offered a mild rebuke of President Nixon for secretly bombing Cambodia. "By the president's own definition, the American people did not have a need to know what our bombers were doing in 1969," he said. "But there's another point. If it was necessary to keep a military secret, was it a need of policy to make a misstatement to the people that the president was elected to serve?" [89] On the occasion of the 1973 withdrawal of the last American soldiers, Harry told viewers that Vietnam had taught the United States that it cannot police the world or control world events. "We will not only not get involved in bad, unwinnable wars, we are not available to intervene in good, winnable wars, either, if there are such things," he said. "We are sadder and wiser; just possibly, and at insane cost, we have grown up a little." [90]

In the first eighteen months of *The Reasoner Report* the Watergate scandal evolved from the "third-rate burglary" it had once been called to the gravest threat to a presidential administration in half a century. Most of Harry's thoughts about Watergate aired on the evening news, but he used the news magazine as an additional forum. At first he appealed to caution, warning that important institutions could be damaged as the investigation continued. [91] He also believed there were positive developments to note: The scandal had reminded people that the system does good work and does respond, and that the functioning of the courts, the press, and honest politicians in both parties had impressed the young. An unfavorable development, he added, had been the partial paralysis of the presidency and the failure of Congress to provide a political counterweight. "That leaves the country leaderless," Harry said, "and that is no position for a strong country to be in." [92]

Rejecting criticism that the press was overemphasizing the investigation because it was biased against Nixon, Harry told viewers there was no conspiracy by journalists. "I am shocked and sickened by the revelations of Watergate," he said. "If a majority of people are not, if they believe this is the normal routine of politics, we are in trouble." [93] The festive air that surrounded the nomination of Gerald Ford to replace Spiro Agnew, who had resigned after being charged with receiving bribes, disturbed Harry and brought out a rare barb. "It might have been uncomfortable but proper if the president or somebody had once mentioned why this soiree was being held, and the name of the man who made it necessary," he commented. In the same broadcast, he offered a hopeful view for the future: "The next few months and years will tell if Gerald Ford has the capacity to be a healer. The thing I think we do know is that Ford—this amiable man—will do no further positive injury. In the tenth month of a year like this, that's progress." [94]

By May 1974 the Senate hearings into Watergate—Harry called them "a strange and long-running television soap opera"—had entered their second year. One theme marked Harry's remaining observations about the scandal that would bring about Nixon's resignation: the need for reform in campaign financing. Yet he sounded pessimistic about that possibility, concluding that "the Congress will not establish a pressure-proof campaign financing system. I believe the Congress has been honestly shocked at the year's revelations. They are not, for the most part, venal men. But they haven't been shocked enough to deal responsibly with the evils that made Watergate possible." [95] Harry rarely visited the same subject more than once, but he noted the need for campaign reform—and the likelihood it would not occur—two more times. [96]

Beyond Vietnam and Watergate, Harry reflected on a wide range of the subjects presented by *Reasoner Report* correspondents. His commentaries carried the familiar optimistic, populist tone and common-sense approach he used on the evening news:

- After a segment on contaminated water in rural America, Harry commented, "If we can't afford to make sure that everybody in this country has a glass of cool, clear, safe water, when he wants it, we can't afford anything." [97]
- Contending that the nation was giving up its history by celebrating national holidays on Mondays in order to create a three-day weekend, he said, "Almost all of our days and many of our institutions have now been degraded for reasons of either economics or public relations." [98]
- Following a segment on a clash at the American Indian reservation at Wounded Knee, Harry observed, "We cannot undo Custer, or the Trail of Sadness, or the broken treaties, but we ought to be able to give some generation of Indians some hope." [99]
- Lamenting that the homogenization of automobiles had taken the fun out of driving, he told viewers: "If the American love affair with our cars is over, it isn't our fault. We're ready to come back if the cars will go to the gym and slim down, get rid of the falsies and the mascaraed eyelashes, and look a little healthily tempting again." [100]

A mild tone marked Harry's work behind the camera on *The Reasoner Report*. He placed fewer demands on his producers than most anchors. Traveling with him, as Joan Richman did on trips to Japan, Poland, and the Soviet Union, could be delightful. "He had a wonderful way of looking at the world," she said. "He had a wonderful sense of humor. He was a great Irish storyteller. He was an easy person, wasn't prickly. He enjoyed food and drink. He enjoyed seeing places. He didn't want to work too hard, which made leisure time important, which is always kind of a nice relief." [101]

In spite of the freedom Harry gave his producers, Richman and others wished that Harry contributed more to assignments. "When you have to really think through how to make the piece work and how complicated it is and all those things," she said, "if there are two of you doing that, you are going to end up with a much better product." [102] Al Primo found Harry to be difficult at times. "He was a prima donna, but a quiet prima donna," Primo said. "Everything had to be quite right, he had to get the proper respect and all that sort of thing. He just wasn't very vociferous about it." [103] Arthur Holch remembered Harry as professional and good company but not having his heart in *The Reasoner Report*. "He relied a lot on producers," Holch said. "He had a reputation that wasn't quite what the truth was. Harry had a great voice and a great personality, but I think he was a very lazy guy." [104]

The Reasoner Report went off the air without fanfare after its broadcast of June 28, 1975, which featured highlights from its ninety-four programs. Its chief limitations—a half-hour, a distracted anchor, a weak time slot often overtaken by sports, and a lack of unanimity among the affiliates that the program was worth carrying—never abated during its twenty-eight months on the air. The CBS News expatriates on the program, like many of those who had left the network only to return, enjoyed the work but were soured by their experience at ABC. "It was a very cheap-jack organization," Ernie Leiser said in reflecting on the three unhappy years he spent at ABC News. "Although they paid me well, they didn't pay anybody else well. The lesser people were paid very badly. News was not respected very much." [105] Joan Richman, who had produced *The Reasoner Report*, was happy to return to CBS News at the first opportunity. "Look at how many of us went back home," she said. "Most of us did." [106]

Anchoring the evening news each weeknight, the news magazine nearly every week, and special events as they came along, and also serving as host for an occasional documentary, Harry was a regular presence on national television. ABC demanded even more from its star. To further extend the Reasoner brand, the network provided a third forum in which Harry expressed his views—or so the public likely believed. Each weekday ABC Radio carried a five-minute broadcast, also called *The Reasoner Report*. It was similar to the *Dimensions* commentaries at CBS News, except that Harry did not write for the broadcast. He acknowledged to those who asked that another writer produced the commentaries he read for radio because it was not practical for him to write them. [107]

How could Harry write a daily essay and perform his other duties? He could not. Recognizing this reality but still wanting his voice on the radio, ABC hired a writer to produce scripts for Harry to read for the broadcast. Otto Penzler, formerly a sports writer for the *New York Daily News*, was working as a publicist for ABC Sports in 1973 when he heard about an opening as Harry's radio writer. "The only test for the job was to write three reports," Penzler recalled. "If Harry liked them, you got the job, which I did." [108] Harry and his new radio persona met for the first time when Penzler's first essays were to be taped in the studio on Broadway.

The assignment was clear: Write an essay with a thirty-second opening, a three-minute middle, and a thirty-second closing. The challenge lay in choosing topics and crafting sentences that listeners would recognize as the Reasoner style. "Harry had a very, very easy style to pastiche. It was simplicity itself. If you read a report out loud, you could immediately pick up Harry's cadences and that sort of thing. That part came very easily to me,"

Penzler said. Typically, Harry took care of the broadcasts on Tuesday and Thursday afternoons, reading scripts live on those days and taping the essays for Monday, Wednesday, and Friday. At first Harry read Penzler's script closely, but once he was satisfied that the writer could deliver the essays that fit his persona he read them cold, whether live or on tape, and flawlessly.[109]

One of the attractions of the job for a writer, besides good money and making one's own hours, was the freedom to explore nearly anything. Finding something to write about day after day could be brutal. "It was the hardest job I've ever had in my life," Penzler said. "The writing was easy. I could write a report in twenty minutes and it sounded like Harry. But coming up with a new idea every day was really hard. It got to the point where I couldn't sleep anymore."[110] Penzler left *The Reasoner Report* after a year in order to begin a publishing company and retain his sanity.

His replacement, Peter Freundlich, stayed on for five years, until Harry returned to CBS News—and then followed him to CBS to write Harry's radio essays for another five years. "That was the job, to come up with a reasonably good idea every day and to put it in some memorable form. It leads to desperation. Some days there just aren't any ideas. The poor brain wears out and yet you need a script or a column anyway," Freundlich said. "And so with the taste of ashes in your mouth you proceed to work on something you know is not very good."[111]

Harry offered his radio writers few ideas, little encouragement, and no guidance. As a practical matter, *The Reasoner Report* was a distraction from his work for the evening news, which aired just a few hours after he taped his broadcasts for radio. In that way it fit his own aims to allow his radio writers to do the job without interference or oversight once they had gained his confidence, assuring them their work was fine if they were to ask. There was little concern about Harry's reading words and offering ideas that were not his own to millions of listeners. "I didn't see myself as part of any deception. I don't think Harry did," Freundlich said. "It's the industry practice."[112] Harry was not at all demanding and had no particular agenda to advance.

As writers for *The Reasoner Report*, Penzler and, to a much greater extent, Freundlich contributed to the public's image of Harry and his perspective. Penzler was right of center politically whereas Freundlich was left of center, and their work reflected their own views. For example, Penzler thought off-track betting was immoral and hypocritical and wrote at least three essays deriding it. Each believed he tilted Harry a bit toward his end of the political spectrum. Yet both writers understood that Harry was a man of mild opinion and that he preferred an unusual take on a small subject rather than a serious political point or a heavy philosophical discussion.

Freundlich viewed the essays as closer to the kind Russell Baker produced for his columns for the *New York Times* than the commentaries Eric Sevareid delivered on the evening news at CBS. "They made light of serious things," he said of the essays, "and made serious things light." [113] Given that different writers would be putting words into Harry's mouth, this approach was as necessary as it was in character for Harry.

When Harry did venture into observations that he did not want associated too closely with his own, he preferred to use a character, as he had in the *Dimensions* essays at CBS. Instead of "a man I know" he used a fictional neighbor named Gus, usually more blue-collar and old-fashioned than Harry wanted to appear. Gus also did not like change and tended to complain a lot. "Those were shows he liked to do," Penzler said. "Harry had a pretty clear identity about who he was, politically, philosophically, socially. If I thought Harry might be uncomfortable with a position that I was writing about, then I would frequently use Gus." [114]

There were few occasions when Harry would reject a script. Once, Penzler provided a virulently anti-union essay for a taped broadcast. Harry stopped about a third of the way through and told Penzler his audience would not accept it. He read a back-up essay in its place. Another time, Penzler had become incensed that people commenting on Watergate were calling two of President Nixon's embattled staffers, John Erlichman and H. R. Haldeman, "krauts" and "nazis." He provided Harry an essay asking, if those epithets were appropriate, then why was it not acceptable to use other slurs? The title was "Niggers, Spics, Jews, and Wops." Harry taped a back-up essay instead. Penzler recalled, "Even Gus couldn't get that one through." [115]

There was no going back when Harry read a Penzler essay that took prankish advantage of his inability to pronounce the words "million" and "airplane." He began telling listeners about millions and millions of tourists flying in airplanes, the words coming out as "myion" and "aeo-plane." Live, Harry could only keep going—and shake his fist at Penzler. [116]

The radio work came after Harry's usual lunch break, which included a few drinks. "You could smell it," Penzler said, "but it never, ever affected the way he sounded on air." [117] Penzler would not have given the drinking much thought—so many people enjoyed a taste of alcohol at lunch—but it seemed to him that everyone at ABC talked about Harry's drinking.

Colleagues at ABC were asking the same questions that had dogged Harry at CBS: Was their point man lazy? Was alcohol the reason? Was there even a problem? Viewers and those within the industry apparently did not see one. In 1974 Harry won the Emmy award for Outstanding Television News Broadcaster, beating out Walter Cronkite, Mike Wallace, and others.

The answers to questions posed about Harry within ABC, as at CBS, depended on who had been asked. "There was a very easygoing, rumpled way Harry had," producer Jeff Gralnick said. "He had no sharp creases. Harry always said about himself, 'If I buy a new suit it comes wrinkled.' Put all of that together and people concluded the man was lazy. Well, the man was not lazy." [118] His friend and producer Bernie Cohen contended: "Harry was never lazy. He was laid-back. People, especially at CBS, where obsessive compulsive disorder was part of your job description, the guys at CBS felt that if you weren't a saber-tooth tiger killer that you apparently were lazy. For many of their guys it wasn't enough to be successful, their competitors had to fail as well. That was the CBS attitude, and Harry was not part of the CBS attitude." [119]

News vice president Bill Sheehan knew what others said about Harry's work ethic but could not fault as lazy the man who anchored daily and weekly news broadcasts, wrote commentaries two to three times a week, broadcast a daily radio program, and represented the news division with affiliates and the public as needed. "He can't be totally lazy and carry that kind of a load. Even putting out, at the minimum, is a lot of work," Sheehan said. "I think that is certainly a story I have heard and you'll find a lot of people that'll say that. But I would not hang that on him absolutely. Some things I would, but not that." [120] Walter Pfister observed, "He was like a natural athlete who didn't train and could still do damn well, but he could have broken records if he had trained." [121]

No one who worked with Harry at ABC could be unaware of his drinking. He did not hide the martinis at lunch or the visits to the bar before and after the evening news. "Right before the broadcast he'd have a little shot just to relax or he'd pop into the des Artiste bar," his driver, Adam Schloss, remembered. [122] Bernie Cohen recalled: "Going on air was always kind of a tough experience. He'd always say, 'One for the show.' I never, ever saw it affect his work." [123] Howard Smith maintained that Harry actually drank during breaks of a broadcast. "A secretary or some aide would hand him a little paper cup with a little vodka in it and he would drink that in between the commercial periods when someone would slip him this paper cup and he would sip it and then it would disappear when we came back to the camera," Smith said. [124]

Harry's colleagues debated the impact on the broadcast of any drinking. Sam Donaldson recalled that Harry did slur at times on the air and contended that a member of the staff would be assigned to keep him as far from the des Artiste as possible before airtime. "Some nights, the story would go, he essentially failed his duty," Donaldson said. [125] Others disputed whether Harry drank during breaks or needed a watchdog, and even Smith and Donaldson agreed the drinking had little or no effect on his performance. "He behaved beautifully," Smith said. "As soon as the camera came on, he was that gray, warm, likable personality, a wise one you could count on. He was an outstanding personality—restricting the word to personality." [126] Evening news producer Av Westin recalled one or two times that drinking led to a problem for the broadcast, but not major trouble. "I never really felt comfortable lecturing somebody, particularly a man of his stature, to straighten up and fly right because it never really got down to a point where we were blowing anything that was extraordinary," Westin said. "It was an 'Oh, there's Harry again' kind of thing rather than 'God, this guy is fucking up.'" [127]

Perceptions may have made the drinking seem a greater problem than it actually was. "Harry's drinking never affected any program that I did," producer Walter Pfister said, "and I did a lot of programs with Harry."[128] Still, people were concerned about the impact Harry's drinking could have on their work. It certainly was taken as an explanation for his relative lethargy. "When one of the things you have to do is to make sure he doesn't get near the bar, that becomes difficult," producer Jeff Gralnick said. "You get tagged with a reputation, for good or for ill, true or not true, it's yours. Harry was known to take a drink and Harry was known, at times, to be hurt by the drinking."[129] ABC executives turned the other way rather than deal with a problem that did not show itself on the air. "He was very effective as a broadcaster," Ernie Leiser observed. "They put up with his idiosyncrasies or his misbehaviors, if you will, because he was so much better than the other people they had around."[130]

So much better, in fact, that ABC agreed in 1975 to renegotiate his second three-year contract before it had ended. Harry had not wanted to offend Howard Smith by declining to be coanchor when he arrived in late 1970. "Harry didn't like sharing," said his agent, Ralph Mann.[131] The new agreement, however, asked for the one thing Harry coveted: the anchor desk without a partner. He believed he had earned the chance to be the sole anchor of the evening news. More important, at least from the ABC side of negotiations, was the plateau the ratings had reached by that time. ABC decided the partnership had attracted all the viewers it could.[132]

ABC gave Harry what he wanted—plus $400,000 a year, the going rate for anchormen, it seemed, as media reports claimed CBS's Walter Cronkite and NBC's John Chancellor were making about the same salary. When Sheehan, now the news division president, told Smith that ABC was ending its dual-anchor format, the veteran newsman thought he would remain at the anchor desk, not Harry. "Howard did not take it well," Sheehan remembered. "He felt the broadcast was on the move and that things were going well and why do we change it."[133] Smith stayed on as a commentator.

Harry now had it all. Just a year shy of his twentieth anniversary in television news he was the undisputed leader of a national network news program, the professional equal of Walter Cronkite at last. His strongest critics may have been left incredulous, but for Harry the ABC decision confirmed the high regard he had for his own abilities. It certainly indicated that he should change nothing about the way he worked. He had reached the top doing things his way. With the position he had long sought—anchorman—came the perquisites of wealth, influence, and celebrity. How Harry responded to their accompanying pressures and pleasures would color not only the remainder of his ABC years but all those that followed.

CHAPTER EIGHT

Trouble, Turmoil, and Barbara Walters

If you had looked forward to a time of quietness when passions would disappear and you could live in ease with the world around you, it's a little disappointing to find you get roughed up just as much in your fifties as you do in your twenties.   **H. R.**

V iewers may not have realized the power they wielded at ABC News. A shift of just a few ratings points could elevate an anchorman to greater prominence or throw his career into chaos. Ratings were the most important sign of success for Harry, to be sure, but there were issues of pride and prestige to consider as well. Aside from bringing stability and viewers to the evening news, Harry had enhanced the credibility of the entire news organization. Over the years his perspectives gained in prominence among his peers and the public. He was sought more as a public speaker, received more honors and accolades, and tended to be quoted more in the press on matters of the profession.

When in 1974 a public television station in New York, WNET-TV, aired a roundtable program called "The Anchormen" as a segment of its journalism series *Behind the Lines,* Harry joined CBS's Walter Cronkite and NBC's John Chancellor. They discussed the state of broadcast news with host Harrison Salisbury, a Pulitzer Prize–winning reporter and editor for the *New York Times.* Asked to look back on former vice president Spiro Agnew's attacks on the press, Harry agreed with Cronkite's view that Agnew had a few valid points. "In a way, it's too bad that he turned out to be a crook," Harry said, "because it blurred the issues. We went through a period of introspection and defending ourselves and wondering whether we were doing our job properly. And all of a sudden, Mr. Agnew resigns in disgrace and we may have come out of it looking better than we deserved to look. Some honest men should criticize us sometime."

Even in discussing his profession Harry could be playful. Salisbury, noting that the three networks often covered the same events each evening, asked the anchormen, "You don't call up your colleagues every afternoon to say, 'What shall we play tonight?'" Harry glanced at Cronkite and Chancellor and remarked, "We agreed to deny that, didn't we?" [1]

Journalism benefited from an articulate, respected ambassador in Harry— and during a period when the profession was under fire for its reporting on the Nixon administration. In his evening news and *Reasoner Report* commentaries, he encouraged viewers to consider a point of view that championed journalism but also demanded fairness and responsibility from such a powerful institution. "There are frequently a lot of reasons for not liking a free press," he commented on the evening news one night. "A free commercial press can be venal, corrupt, inaccurate, and irritating. The only thing worse than a free commercial press is its absence."[2] He lacked the arrogance of many of his peers and was willing not only to acknowledge that the press made mistakes, but even to chastise his profession for misusing its mandate to provide independent oversight of government.

Harry rejected the notion that the press had been tougher on the Nixon administration than it would have been on the administration of a Democratic president. "Reporters are interested in news," he assured viewers, "even when it hurts, even when it hurts people individual reporters may be in sympathy with. Unconvinced? Ask George McGovern. Or Thomas Eagleton."[3] Admitting that he, too, was tired of news leaks and unnamed sources in reports about Watergate, he pointed out that little could be done except demand that such reports meet reasonable tests of accuracy. "It is not for journalism to conceal things it knows," he said. "Self-censorship is the worst kind of censorship, and I think the press should avoid it."[4]

Taking a dim view of advocacy journalism, Harry supported his generation's principles that called on reporters to report rather than participate in events. His sharpest criticism of the profession came in March 1974 when he accused *Time* and *Newsweek* of being unprofessional in their Watergate reporting. "Week after week their lead stories on the subject have been more in the style of pejorative pamphleteering than objective journalism," he said on the evening news, "and since they are highly visible and normally highly respected organs of our craft, they embarrass and discredit us all." He accused the newsweeklies of patronizing their readers by spoon-feeding them conclusions about Watergate. "We are going through a substantial national tragedy and journalists have been among the few heroes of the epoch," he concluded. "Let's not tarnish our pride in that."[5]

The evening news was the most prominent forum for his views on the press, but Harry also touched upon his profession when he traveled the country giving speeches to various groups. He told an audience of advertising executives in Kansas City that there may have been bias in reporting on Agnew and, if so, that was bad. "We don't always live up to our goals," he said. "As you know, publishers and owners of television stations tend to be conservative and Republican while reporters tend to be liberal and Democratic. I just hope they can keep their politics out of the news business."[6] Earning $3,000 for such appearances, Harry added to his income and promoted ABC News and its affiliates, much to their delight. In his public presentations he usually reviewed the state of American society, taking an unsurprisingly optimistic view when answering the question posed by the title of the speech, "Can We Survive the Seventies?"

Harry himself was a survivor of sorts. By fall 1975 he had remained at the anchor desk for nearly four years, a modern record at ABC second only to the six years Howard K. Smith had lasted. Now he appeared alone, just as he had when Smith had been on vacation. To the press he dismissed the rumor that ABC was considering pairing him with a woman as coanchor. "I'm anxious to try the ABC news on my own, without a coanchor of any sex," he told a reporter.[7] Other than a new set and a screen behind him that flashed graphics and allowed for chatter with correspondents, little of substance was different. That made Harry the only variable to be linked to success or failure.

One change in the evening news format was significant for Harry. Now with Smith providing only commentary, Harry turned more and more to the sort of end pieces he had enjoyed writing for the Sunday night news. They often relied on irony for their humor and usually required nothing more from Harry than a deadpan delivery and what viewers took for a wisp of a smile and a twinkle in the eyes:

- When Japanese Emperor Hirohito visited the United States, an aide said the emperor wanted to meet John Wayne, one of his favorite actors. "He didn't say on the basis of what movies Wayne is a Hirohito favorite," Harry observed. "Presumably not *Operation Pacific*, *They Were Expendable*, or *The Sands of Iwo Jima*."[8]
- On the birthday of Millard Fillmore, the thirteenth president, Harry commented: "I'm not quite sure why Millard Fillmore has always seemed such a funny name. He was not renominated by his party after he became president following the death of Zachary Taylor, but he didn't start any wars and he had something to do with the Compromise of 1850, which delayed if it didn't prevent the Civil War. Also, he put the first bathtub in the White House and we've had a cleaner presidency ever since. There have been presidents who've done less."[9]
- On the Friday before daylight savings time would begin Harry told viewers: "Don't be careless. Remember, at two a.m. Sunday, get up and set your clocks an hour different."[10]

In retrospect, Harry should not have eased away from commentary on the evening news. It had separated him from Cronkite and Chancellor, who left commenting on the news to others. With the *Reasoner Report* gone and the radio program a venue only for his voice, the evening news commentary had offered Harry the only regular outlet for his writing—and the main intellectual discipline in a job in which he could get by doing little but reading in front of the camera. With Vietnam over and Watergate concluded, the times were relatively quiet.

More worrisome, however, was that Harry was growing weary of anchoring the evening news each night. "It is a grinding job and it takes a daily, meticulous devotion," he later wrote in his memoir. "Maybe I didn't give it that." [11] In hindsight, he thought it might have been a mistake for ABC to split up the Reasoner-Smith team. It was a surprising admission of error, given the fact that he had demanded the change and had long sought the opportunity to be on his own. Harry felt the broadcast was losing its momentum for other reasons but admitted he no longer put it nearly first in his life. Just as he needed all of his energies to succeed on his own, he found himself going through a period of soul-searching both at work and at home. Later, Harry wondered if he had been experiencing a midlife crisis. [12]

Others wondered as well, including his wife, Kay. Their marriage had appeared solid to most of their friends and outside observers. Within the family the relationship had seemed strained at times since the 1960s. Why was not clear. "They were both very strong personalities," their daughter Elizabeth recalled, "strong and competitive." [13] While Harry had built a career in the public eye, Kay had put aside her career aspirations to raise their children and maintain a home for her husband. It had been a good life for both Harry and Kay. Their children remember their home as a happy place in which to grow up.

All that had been threatened when, in the mid-1960s, Kay had been diagnosed with a tumor at the base of her spine. Although it was slow-growing and benign at the time, to remove the tumor and the surrounding organs would have reduced the quality of life Kay desired. She opted instead for what became a series of surgical procedures over her lifetime. Stoic as well as private and proud, Kay seldom discussed her health. Her daughter Jane said, "The phrase I remember her using was that she did not want to engage in a 'litany of complaints.'" [14] Kay refused to let the illness and subsequent surgeries—one every few years—prevent her from enjoying her family, her volunteer work, or her life in the church. Looking back, Ann and Elizabeth thought their mother's illness may have pushed aside problems troubling the marriage. "Here they were sort of struggling with their issues," Elizabeth observed, "and then she was going to die. They really thought she wasn't going to make it through, and several times after that. I think that changed the whole thing. I think they were not able to help each other." [15]

As with money matters, Harry and Kay did not discuss marital issues with their children, even the older ones who had left the home. Harry remained the supportive father he had always been. "We had great freedom to choose sort of who we were and what we did," Elizabeth said. "There were standards he held—he wanted us to have self-respect and integrity and a sense of humor. But that really could pretty much take any form or go in any direction we wanted."[16] Harry was not judgmental and tried to be patient and sensitive to his children's concerns. "When you were having a bad time he would just have the perfect thing to say," Ellen remembered. "I wasn't afraid to go to him, I wasn't afraid to talk to him. Even if you were embarrassed or you felt bad, he would make you feel better."[17]

No one questioned whether Harry loved Kay—"It was a very intense and passionate relationship," Elizabeth maintained—and it is doubtful he could have seriously considered leaving her while she suffered with her illness. That did not mean Harry was a faithful husband. In his memoir *Before the Colors Fade* he made veiled references to liaisons with other women. At times he discussed conquests with friends, and an affair with a woman at CBS before Kay had become ill was widely known by their colleagues.[18] As he observed in his book, Harry was no "hot dog" when it came to women, but in 1974 he began an affair that eventually led to the end of his marriage and the prospect of another.

It started with a fan letter. Tamara Newell had worked in television news herself, for WPLG in Miami, and in print journalism in her hometown of Kokomo, Indiana, and had recently begun a new career in public relations in Coral Gables, Florida. She wrote to Harry to praise a report on the Dominican Republic. Months later, she visited producer Bernie Cohen at ABC News in New York. Cohen introduced her to Harry. "I have a letter from you I've been meaning to answer," Harry told her. A stunned silence followed—Newell could hardly believe he remembered her letter—and Cohen remarked, "He gets 10,000 letters a week."[19]

Newell later met Harry for a drink. "Knowing Harry after the first night was as natural as knowing someone in my own family," she recalled. "We just hit it off. I think we had similar backgrounds—small town, Midwest."[20] The difference in their ages (Tamara was twenty-five years younger than Harry) did not matter. They began meeting around the country as Harry traveled for his job, and at times they went abroad together. Where the relationship was heading neither knew.

Personally and professionally, Harry felt adrift even as he told the press he was enjoying his new responsibilities as point man for ABC News. "It is kind of interesting to do the show by myself," he told a television writer in St. Louis. "The only part I don't like is it ties me down. There is less chance to go out in the world and play reporter."[21] He talked at times of writing another novel—"I'd rather be a good journalist than a self-conscious novelist"—or of putting into a book the wisdom he wished he had imparted to his children.[22] There was even the idea for a book in which Harry and Tamara Newell would tell their stories of their love affair, each describing events from their own point of view. (That project got at least as far as a few pages typed on the back of ABC News stationery.) If not completely content, and even bored at times, Harry was not particularly motivated to do anything that might bring turmoil into his life.

Turmoil came, as it usually does, at the least expected time and from a surprising source. Having gained a new contract and a substantial salary from ABC, Harry probably thought he had two or three years to see whether the ratings would rise, fall, or remain stable—or stagnant, as corporate executives were likely to see a lack of motion in the numbers. "If you're maintaining the status quo, you're losing," producer Bob Siegenthaler said. "You try to do something that will get off the plateau and start a perceptible rise." [23] Nothing but improvement in the ratings would prevent network executives from pondering changes in format and personnel for the evening news.

As it turned out the ratings did not change significantly with Harry alone at the desk. In the first three months of 1976, ABC's evening news reached just 19 percent of viewers while the CBS share stood at 27 percent and NBC's at 25 percent. [24] The numbers did not raise alarm or create fear that ABC would return to the bad old days before Harry had arrived. No one could have been surprised that Harry sans Howard was not the sort of change that would attract more viewers. The ABC News president who had brought Harry to the network, Elmer Lower, later observed, "Harry alone…he just wasn't a strong enough personality." [25]

Still, just six months had passed when ABC News president Bill Sheehan told Harry the plan its executives had devised to improve the evening news. It involved two firsts in broadcasting, for once allowing ABC to be ahead of CBS and NBC.

The ABC evening news would expand to sixty minutes, with the affiliates giving up local airtime for the first hour-long national news program. Harry would share the additional chores of anchoring with a unique partner: Barbara Walters, the host of NBC's *Today* show and the most prominent woman in television journalism. In joining Harry she would become the first woman to anchor a national evening news program.

It would have been a bold proposal coming from any network. All three national news operations had dreamed of airing a one-hour newscast each night. With thirty more minutes ABC correspondents would report in greater depth, Harry would have time for longer essays, and Barbara would provide the kind of interviews with which she had built a strong following among viewers. Sheehan assured Harry that ABC was not unhappy with his work as anchor but saw the opportunity to add value to the broadcast. [26] ABC News, for so many years the joke of broadcast journalism, would be an innovator at last.

Harry—stunned, angry, and defensive—did not buy any part of it. "He was a very proud guy," ABC producer Al Primo said. "He read that whole thing as, 'Oh, you don't think I can do it.'" [27] Harry felt he had not had time to develop his own program and to build a following. Looking back just a few years later, he thought he may not have been providing the energy the broadcast needed and questioned his request to drop Howard Smith as a partner. But at the time ABC began wooing Barbara Walters, Harry still had his pride and sense of self-worth. He did not want to share the desk with anyone; he did not want to share it with a woman; and he did not want to share it with *that* woman.

Accepting a partner meant, in Harry's eyes, that he had failed. "He didn't want to be paired with anybody, whether it was a man, a woman, or a talking duck," said producer Bob Siegenthaler.[28] At one point ABC had approached CBS News correspondent Roger Mudd about joining the network and perhaps coanchoring with his old friend. When they met for lunch Harry let Mudd know he was not welcome. "He said, 'You know, I hate to say this but as much as I like you I don't want you to come coanchor with me because I've been waiting all these years to have my own broadcast,'" Mudd recalled. "I understood completely."[29] Tired he may have been, but the idea that others thought he could no longer handle the job jolted Harry.

A woman was on the verge of coming to ABC News, and her partner was no feminist. Nearly a year before ABC began laying its plans to bring Barbara Walters to the evening news, the three network news anchors had been asked by Harrison Salisbury of the *New York Times* whether the day would come when an anchorwoman would be on the air. "Oh, sure," said NBC's John Chancellor. When Salisbury asked why there was no anchorwoman at that time, Chancellor responded, "Because we're all holding on to our jobs." Salisbury continued: "Well, is this the next step forward?" Harry chimed in, "If it would be a step forward...."[30]

For a man who loved women, supported civil rights, and raised five daughters, welcoming the first woman to the anchor desk should have been a privilege. Yet this was the workplace—his workplace—and there was a hesitation. Harry had worked with women throughout his broadcasting career but never as an equal. The important figures in his career had all been men. One of the few women with whom he worked in news, producer Joan Richman, thought Harry was old-fashioned in this respect. "He was from a generation that was not used to working with women, and it took him a long time to decide that a woman was trustworthy and that a woman could be a sort of a buddy in the way that men producers were buddies," Richman said.[31] Harry once told ABC producer Av Westin he had hired too many women in the newsroom.[32]

In the early 1970s, Harry had not minded being considered a chauvinist. In fact, he referred to himself that way on the air and admitted to being out of step with the women's movement. Years before Walters came to ABC he had annoyed and angered feminists with his tendency to see women and their issues in terms of gender and sex instead of equality. When he closed Andy Rooney's script for *An Essay on Women* on CBS in 1967, Harry said: "We have no quarrel with women. Our feeling is, although we're willing to admit we may be wrong, our feeling is that they are better people than men and we don't understand their dissatisfaction with their own virtues. We wish they would stop following us around, imitating our worst characteristics and demeaning their own attributes. We wish they would stop believing, or acting as if they believe, that man's goals are the ones worth achieving."[33]

Harry enjoyed poking fun at any person or institution that he thought took itself too seriously, including the women's movement. Beneath the humor, he opposed the Equal Rights Amendment and questioned nearly anything that he thought made women less feminine and alluring. "I have spoken with something less than complete respect for the militant members of women's liberation groups," he remarked one night on the ABC evening news. "I accept a large percentage of their contentions but reject the part that seems to be destructive of what, overall, are attractive distinguishing features between the sexes." He went on to criticize advertising that made women appear helpless and feminine and concerned only with household chores and the like, adding that he did not care for male stereotypes either.[34]

When the first issue of the new magazine *Ms.* appeared, Harry called it "pretty sad" and predicted it would fail after a few issues. He claimed the magazine lacked good writing, among other things, and condescendingly referred to "the girls who are putting out *Ms.*" as being prettier than H. L. Mencken if not as good when it came to editing.[35] (Six years later Harry, always a good sport, appeared in an ad for *Ms.* in the *New York Times* admitting he had been wrong when he predicted the magazine would not last more than a few months.)[36] In another commentary, he dismissed the suggestion that women could do a better job of leading the world, calling gender no more of a virtue than color. He contended that the leaders of Israel, India, and Ceylon, all women, did not seem to do much better than similarly qualified men, particularly in the case of India. "The Third World turns out to be much like the other two, as the second sex politically turns out much like the first," he said on the evening news. "The frailties of mankind turn out to be the frailties of personkind."[37]

If viewers criticized Harry's views on women, he apologized for offending them, but not wholeheartedly. He told a *Reasoner Report* audience that he disdained efforts by stewardesses to shed their "geisha girl" image. "I don't want a sex object in the narrow aisle," he said. "But I don't want a surly union member either. I want someone youthful and illusory who looks like she thought flying was fun, even if she knows more about emergency evacuation of airplanes than I'd like to think about." He went on to quote "another male chauvinist I know" who declared that being a stewardess should not be a career, certainly not for a married woman or a mother. "They should remain patches of color in the business of flying. They should be there for a few years and then, like the clouds outside the windows, be replaced with soft and fluffy new ones."[38] Two weeks later Harry told viewers the mail ran nine to one against his views. "Do I have any defense? Only that I didn't mean to be sexist about it," he said. "I have worked with and for women a good deal of my life and I have found them no worse than men."[39]

Mainly, though, women's issues earned little serious attention from Harry. "I suppose it is a woman's own business if she wants to wear pants," he remarked once on the *Reasoner Report*. "And a decision that men should accept gracefully. One woman explained, they are much more comfortable, no stockings, and no concern about how you sit. You can sit any way you want to, she said, and no one will notice. I don't want to carp, but that didn't use to be the idea."[40] When Harry later claimed his unhappiness with a woman coanchor had nothing to do with her gender, his words did not ring true given his other public pronouncements.

Then there was Barbara Walters. If a woman were to take the anchor's chair, becoming the equal of Walter Cronkite and John Chancellor as well as Harry, one could imagine the selection of a woman with a long career in broadcast journalism or, at least, a career marked by excellence in news reporting. No one could claim that Barbara Walters brought to the desk the experience of her male counterparts. "He didn't like Barbara," Elmer Lower said. "He didn't think she knew anything about the news, and he was very blunt in saying so. I don't think it was because she was a woman. She may say that, but I don't know."[41] More disturbing to many in the profession, Walters came from the entertainment side of television.[42]

Entertainment had been a part of Walters's life from the beginning. Born in 1929, she was raised in New York by a father who owned popular nightclubs. Broadway openings and celebrity friends were normal for the Walters household. One of her first jobs after graduating from Sarah Lawrence College in 1951 was promoting clients for a public-relations firm in New York. The *Today* show hired her in 1961 to write for the broadcast and to conduct pre-interviews with guests and develop ideas for segments. Within a year she was gaining on-camera assignments, including joining the press corps for First Lady Jacqueline Kennedy's tour of India and Pakistan in 1962. The president's assassination brought Walters greater exposure and attention. In 1964, at age thirty-five, she was named a *Today* reporter. She even substituted for talk-show host Johnny Carson on the *Tonight Show*.

Intimate interviews with celebrities became the Walters trademark. Then, at the dawn of the Nixon administration, she began to persuade government officials to sit in the chair across from hers. Nixon himself gave Walters an exclusive interview in 1971, and she used her good relations with the president to score interviews with Britain's Prince Philip and Nixon adviser Henry Kissinger, with whom she later attended social occasions and became linked in gossip columns. Walters was one of only three women among the nearly ninety journalists who traveled to China with Nixon in 1972.

True, Walters lacked the old-school credentials of Walter Cronkite, David Brinkley, John Chancellor, Harry Reasoner, and other men who formed the bedrock of broadcast journalism at the time. Cronkite and Chancellor had worked in morning shows, too, as had Harry, but they had established their careers in news before those assignments. Yet Walters had worked as a reporter in television for fifteen years, could deliver news-making interviews, and knew how to use the tools of her trade effectively. She was also relentless when it came to her job, always preparing, always working. However, her brand of personal journalism—the journalist was an integral part of the story—did not sit well with traditionalists. It may have been acceptable and even desirable for a morning show and a magazine broadcast, but not for the evening news, the television version of the news of record.

There was another rub against her. Barbara Walters was what the evening-news anchors feared becoming: a celebrity. That perception overshadowed her credentials and accomplishments. It also raised concern in the profession—not just in the mind of Harry Reasoner—that the evening news at ABC was moving toward entertainment.

Walters's contract with NBC was set to end in September 1976. In March, ABC Television president Fred Pierce learned from her agent that she was interested in new challenges and might entertain an offer from ABC. In just two seasons Pierce had helped ABC advance in entertainment and sports, and adding Barbara Walters to its news division might energize its fortunes as well. The asking price of one million dollars did not seem too high if the result were to weaken *Today*, the leader among morning shows, and to earn the publicity certain to come with her to ABC.[43] Sheehan agreed to try to bring Walters to the news division, especially when Pierce said the entertainment division would pay half of her million-dollar salary.

For the deal to be made and the partnership to succeed, both Harry and Barbara had to come to terms with ABC—and with each other. She had had a wearing relationship with *Today* host Frank McGee—another hidebound newsman—and Barbara did not want another adversary as a colleague. In early spring Barbara and Harry met several times, out of the public eye, to see whether they could make it work.[44] The negotiations with the network were laborious. In the end, according to news president Bill Sheehan, Harry and Barbara believed the hour-long format would create enough room for both of them.[45]

And, of course, there was the money. Barbara would earn $500,000 as coanchor of the evening news and another $500,000 to produce specials and to appear on other ABC broadcasts. In that regard the partnership brought about another first: No one, man or woman, had ever been signed for a million dollars. Barbara would become television's highest-paid journalist. Harry benefited from her groundbreaking deal; his salary would rise from $400,000 to $500,000 in order to equal hers. When the press began calling Barbara a "million-dollar baby" many people mistakenly thought Barbara was paid more than Harry, but they were equals in terms of salary for their evening news duties. By doing nothing more than sitting beside Barbara, Harry would be taking home twenty-five percent more money. Press reports later speculated that Cronkite and Chancellor likely would seek a raise in their own pay.

Barbara had a special pay scale, but Harry had a special agreement with Sheehan. If he were not satisfied with the pairing, he would be free to leave ABC before his contract ended in 1980. Harry later called it his "Barbara Walters escape clause." With that assurance, he approved the partnership. "He didn't like it," recalled his agent, Ralph Mann, "but he agreed to be a good fellow and go along with it." [46] Harry was a realist. He probably recognized that if he did not agree to coanchor with Walters, another plan to boost the ratings would take its place, one potentially more damaging to his standing and to his ego—and unlikely to be as lucrative for him.

Word of the negotiations eventually found its way into the press, but it was not until April 22, 1976, that ABC made it official. That night on the evening news, Harry told viewers the Reasoner-Walters team would make its debut in October. "Many of the stories said that I had some reservations when the idea came up," Harry told viewers. "If I did, they have been taken care of, and I welcome Barbara with no reservations." He praised her by claiming that there was no better candidate to be the first woman anchor, and he promised to "get the place shined up, Barbara, and we look forward to your arrival." In true Reasoner form, he ended on a wry note: "There are, inevitably, certain problems…for instance, the matter of billing. Confirming my longtime non-sexist grace and courtesy, I suggest we do it alphabetically …by last names." [47]

Soothed by an extra $100,000, the prospects of an hour-long broadcast, and the promise that he could bail out if things went wrong, Harry indeed may have been sincere when he said he welcomed Barbara without reservation. "I think it will be interesting," he told the *New York Daily News* that day. "I'll stay on the show and help her in any way I can." [48] More telling of the trouble ahead for Walters was the *Daily News* headline on its front page that day: "Doll Barbie to learn her ABCs." [49]

Criticism of Walters's hiring focused on her salary, but at times the context of a woman in broadcast journalism's top job seemed close at hand. "It's ridiculous," said the chairman of the Senate Communications Subcommittee, Senator John Pastore of Rhode Island. "The networks come before my committee and shed crocodile tears and complain about their profits. Then they pay this little girl a million dollars. That's five times better than the President of the United States makes." Most of the time, though, Walters's peers questioned whether television journalism would change for the worse with million-dollar paychecks. The ombudsman for the *Washington Post*, Charles Seib, sounded resigned to the fact that entertainment-style salaries had invaded journalism. "We might as well face it," Seib said. "The line between the news business and show business has been erased forever. It was a mighty thin line at best, so not much has been lost." Eric Sevareid worried that the struggle to keep the packaging from dominating the contents of the package had been lost.[50]

Whether Barbara Walters would be taken seriously as a network news anchor was not Harry's concern. His contribution to the new format would be shaking people, especially reporters, of the notion that he neither liked Barbara nor respected her. Both tried to play down questions about their compatibility.[51] Yet the damage had been done. Once the word got out that Harry had reacted negatively to the partnership, people would be watching for any signs of friction between the two no matter what they said in public.

At the end of May, when ABC affiliates gathered in Los Angeles, Harry and Barbara appeared together for the first time in public to promote the new format, its debut scheduled for October. She defended her salary and criticized those who thought one million dollars was too much for a journalist. "We know that news makes money," she said, adding that large salaries in entertainment are common and accepted. "There is a theory that if you're a news person you should be too pure to think about things like that." Harry contended that the success of the broadcast depended upon the anchors, of course, but also required a commitment to news by the network and its affiliates. "We won't be cute, and we won't be catty," he said, "and if we don't like each other, nobody out there will know it."[52] Nevertheless, questions regarding how Harry really felt about Barbara arose almost immediately.[53]

Less attention was paid to the negative reaction from affiliates unhappy with the prospect of losing from fifteen minutes to a half-hour of their time—and the accompanying advertising revenue—to a longer newscast. "If they're proud to have Barbara Walters aboard, I'm happy for them," one affiliate representative told *Broadcasting*, the industry's trade magazine. "But I resent their trying to take *my* time to help *them* pay *her*, especially since they didn't consult us affiliates in the first place."[54] NBC and CBS began discussing a similar move to avoid being left behind. Throughout the summer the industry debated whether affiliates could afford a national newscast longer than thirty minutes.[55] By the fall, NBC determined it would not expand its national news. Soon, ABC reversed itself and announced it too would leave its newscast at thirty minutes, a damaging blow to the Reasoner-Walters partnership.[56]

ABC had gambled and lost. All top network executives had been behind the change, and a popular entertainment schedule, plus an invigorating format featuring two strong personalities, made for powerful incentives for the affiliates to go along. "Our people felt that with that strength they could go to the stations and force it on them," Bill Sheehan recalled. "It turned out they couldn't."[57] ABC News had already hired an executive producer for the hour-long broadcast and had developed its format. Sheehan said, "We had to go back to Harry and Barbara after Barbara had signed up and after Harry had agreed that this would be something he would be willing to do and tell them the affiliates wouldn't clear it."[58] In spite of the news Barbara remained positive, and Harry betrayed no feelings either way.[59] Now they would be competing for airtime. It was not just a matter of egos: One anchor could not be off camera for too long without throwing the broadcast out of balance.

The coanchors spent the last two weeks of September in rehearsals. Among those watching from the sidelines, if from Washington, was Howard K. Smith. He would remain on the broadcast to provide commentary, but his anchoring days, even as a substitute, were all but over. Smith could understand better than anyone Harry's reluctance to have a coanchor, and he believed Walters was in for trouble from the partner he had found to be impersonal. He invited her to his home and offered a warning.

"You're going to have a rough time," he told her, "do you know that?"

Barbara responded, "I'm beginning to think so."

Smith added, "Be strong and stand up to it, but he's not going to treat you well."[60]

That prescient advice aside, Smith may have been closer to Harry in his view of women in the workplace than he realized. On the evening news broadcast that preceded the debut of the new team, Smith closed with a farewell that was patronizing at best. After calling Walters "network television's first female anchorman, a lady whose beauty sometimes disguises a talent rarely equaled in this craft," he noted that his agent was a woman, the producer of the documentary series he was undertaking was a woman, and even the person behind the camera at that moment was a woman. "Now on this report I will answer to a lady anchorman, Barbara," Smith told viewers. "Any bruise to male ego is assuaged by the thought that if you've got to go, then being a male island in a sea of pretty women, well, what a way to go."[61]

Everyone expected the ABC evening news to draw huge ratings on October 4, 1976. The fact that an anchorwoman would attract national attention and curiosity showed the tenor of the times when it came to women in a man's world. Other than a new set—how many sets had ABC gone through over the years?—nothing had changed except the gender of one of the people reading the news.

That night Harry opened the broadcast with a report on the resignation of Agriculture Secretary Earl Butz, who had been under fire for telling a racial joke in private. "Closer to home, I have a new colleague to welcome," he told viewers. "Barbara?"

"Thank you, Harry," Walters said. "Well, tonight has finally come to me and I'm very pleased to be with you, Harry, and with ABC News."

After a report on the resignation, Walters noted that when she had interviewed Butz that day the former official had said he thought Jimmy Carter, the Democrat running against President Ford, should withdraw for his indiscreet comments to *Playboy* magazine. Harry turned to Barbara and remarked, "I suppose, uh, I suppose the Carter people would object to having one verbal indiscretion linked to a racial joke."

"Uhmm," Walters responded. "Let me tell you a little bit more about what Earl Butz said..." They continued to discuss the resignation, underscoring a new approach for ABC's evening news. Its anchors were freer to talk to each other—Howard had been in Washington, not at Harry's side—and to comment immediately on a news report. Yet their discussion sounded slightly forced or, at the least, awkward. Neither seemed comfortable at the moment. But it was a beginning.

Later the broadcast aired the first segment of Walters's exclusive interview with Egypt's president, Anwar Sadat. Of equal if not greater interest to the millions tuning in were her words, and Harry's, about their partnership. Barbara went first, promising that she and Harry would bring viewers essential information and she a closer look at people through her interviews. She also noted that she would try to deal with issues of particular interest to women. She closed by saying, "We hope that if you've watched tonight out of curiosity, you'll return to watch us tomorrow out of conviction. Mr. Reasoner?"

Harry appeared as inscrutable as ever as he addressed the camera. He admitted he was not sure how to welcome her, not wanting to sound sexist, patronizing, or sycophantic. "The decision was to welcome you as I would any respected and competent colleague of any sex," he said, "by noting that I've kept time on your stories and mine tonight. You owe me four minutes ..."

Barbara laughed with surprise at the reference to their efforts to keep airtime equal, and Harry betrayed a smile as he signed off. A long shot showed the two talking to each other, and he appeared to be chuckling.[62]

The second part of Barbara's taped interview with Sadat aired the next night. At the end of the segment, after she had thanked Sadat for appearing, he surprised her by saying: "Thank you, Barbara. Uh, how do you like a million-dollars job?" Walters laughed as Sadat added: "I must tell you quite frankly, you know the salary of my job. It is twelve thousand only—and I'm working day and night, Barbara!" [63]

Harry's end pieces did not guarantee him the last word. On their third night together, he reported on the shopping spree of an oil sheik who bought sixteen cars, eight refrigerators, twelve hundred pieces of luggage, twenty thousand pounds of auto tools, and two grapefruit trees. Barbara added enthusiastically, "I want to meet him!" [64]

In its first three nights the new ABC evening news had given fans and critics alike exactly what they wanted. Those who enjoyed a relaxed broadcast found the coanchors employing the easy chatter growing in popularity on local newscasts. Critics could deplore the introduction of "happy news" to a national news program. Harry had offered his typical droll commentary, and Barbara had questioned a world leader in keeping with her reputation for getting the big interview. On a negative note, people looking for any trace of animosity could point to Harry's crack about keeping time. Those who thought Walters was unprofessional and insipid could find their evidence in her comment following Harry's end piece.

The opening nights of the broadcast also highlighted the way in which having a partner diminished Harry's unique personal style. His ability to look into the camera lens as if he were looking into the viewer's eyes accounted for a large part of his appeal. When he ended a broadcast with a bit of whimsy or a light joke or a touching observation, he connected directly with viewers. A partner at the desk, offering light banter or commenting on what Harry had read, became an intruder who interrupted the connection he had developed with the audience. Barbara Walters was not the problem. Harry was at his best when he alone broadcast the evening news.

Whatever the analysis, ABC had to hope that, over time, viewers would judge Harry and Barbara by the quality of their newscast and not by the perceptions of critics looking for any tear in the seam that joined them. As it turned out, the most corrosive criticism came from within ABC News.

Partisans quickly took their places around Harry and Barbara, each feeding the concerns that proper respect was not being paid by one to the other. Bob Siegenthaler saw it the first night after Harry had joked about the time Barbara owed him. "He had some puckish little witticism which in a perfect world would have been seen as that. But it was magnified immediately as, 'Oh, that was a zinger and he was trying to score on her.' That became a problem throughout," Siegenthaler remembered. Both would have been better off not to listen. "In a less hyper-heated atmosphere it might not have been seized by people," Siegenthaler said. "But of course Barbara's people said, 'See, he's putting you down.' And Harry's people said, 'Good, good, you scored on her.' The two cliques were impossible." [65]

Over time a particular exchange stood out because it could be used as ammunition by either camp. One night, after a story about Henry Kissinger, Barbara turned to her coanchor and said, "You know, Harry, Kissinger didn't do too badly as a sex symbol in Washington." Harry responded, "Well, you'd know more about that than I would."[66] (Barbara, after all, had been on Kissinger's arm at social functions in the past.) Reasoner partisans could point out that Walter Cronkite would never have made such a comment about a man or woman, that Walters was taking the broadcast to a lower level, that she just did not understand the difference between anchoring the news and serving as host of a morning talk show. On the other side, Walters's defenders could be aghast that Harry had been rude to her on the air and had injected a personal sexual aside into the program.

The exchange also pointed to what was becoming obvious: A newscast designed to be more personal would emphasize any lack of warmth between its coanchors.

Election night 1976 came just a month after Harry and Barbara had begun working together. Special-events producer Walter Pfister had already heard the chatter that the duo was in trouble. "That buzz started about two weeks afterwards," Pfister remembered. "It was a mismatch of personalities. We knew that at the time, but we thought professionalism would prevail. We knew that they weren't going to hug each other and put their arms around each other at the end of the program but that they would be sensible and do their thing." During election coverage each anchor had a script and tended to it. The atmosphere between them was professional but cool. "He didn't talk to her unless it was absolutely necessary," Pfister said. "There was no chit-chat between them, any banter, unless it was initiated by Barbara."[67]

Cool and professional. Those words may best describe the relationship between Harry and Barbara for the twenty-one months they worked together. "I did not see any personal unpleasantness," news president Bill Sheehan said. "There was professional distance between them, but not personal unpleasantness."[68] Producers who worked with them each day dismissed the notion of ugly confrontations or harsh words. "There was perceivable coolness, which waxed and waned from day to day," Bob Siegenthaler recalled. "Some days it was not as cool, some days it was cool. It was a very interesting situation."[69] Walter Porgess, who wrote the news for both anchors, thought a neutral relationship developed over time. "There was never a voice raised as far as I determined. Maybe they raised it in the sanctity of an office, but I never heard it," Porgess said. "Maybe they were cold to each other. They certainly weren't very warm to each other as I remember."[70]

There were light moments. One day as they watched a piece of tape from an affiliate, a buxom, pretty woman appeared on camera to deliver the weather report.

"Oh, Harry," Barbara said, "there's your next partner."

Moments later a newsman with a toupee filled the screen, prompting Harry to remark, "There's yours."

Not to be outdone, Barbara said, "I can always wear a sweater."

Harry replied, "I can always get a toupee."

Relating the exchange to a reporter, Barbara observed: "This is the sort of thing nobody ever expected of us. Maybe we should put it on the air."[71] It was a telling comment: Barbara did not appreciate the point of view that the sort of "happy talk" that suited a morning show like *Today* was out of place, in the eyes of many, for the evening news.

Most days Harry and Barbara avoided each other and came to the set no sooner than necessary. They could talk about baseball but little else. "He sort of basically ignored her and sort of sulked in his office and would spend a minimal amount of time with her," recalled producer Dick Richter. "Harry tended to like to be convivial, so that this was very noticeable."[72] Bernie Cohen, a producer and a close friend of Harry's, dismissed the gossip of a bad relationship between the coanchors and contended Harry had been professional and courtly to Barbara. "I never heard a bad word between them, never heard an argument. He never even said to me or his friends something like, 'Gee, she's a pushy bitch.' I never heard him say that even in the bar when we hung out together. Never said a bad word," Cohen said years later. "Harry wouldn't hesitate to say to his close friends, 'What a pain in the ass.' He never, ever did. Harry only treated her with courtesy and decency."[73]

When Harry and his friends went out for a drink and left Barbara behind, some saw it as yet another slight. Barbara declined Harry's invitations to join the group, Cohen remembered, but not out of spite or pique. "Barbara is a driven person. She went home and worked on a script, made phone calls, tried to get stories lined up," Cohen said. "That's what Barbara does every minute she gets, she works. Barbara was very driven and Harry was very laid-back."[74]

Harry resisted attempts by others to improve his relationship with Barbara. At one point Bob Siegenthaler suggested that the coanchors try to have a Spencer Tracy–Katharine Hepburn relationship, bringing to mind the barbed but respectful banter of the movie couple. "I don't think so, Bob," Harry said.[75] Cohen joked about Barbara's serious demeanor and would come up with ways Harry could lighten her mood. "Goose her under the desk," he suggested. Harry responded, "I can't reach that far."[76]

Instead of being a spectacular success or a dismal failure with viewers, the new anchor team drew an ambivalent response. For the last quarter of 1976, which represented the first three months Harry and Barbara worked together, the ABC evening news gained a single percentage point, rising to 19, for its share of the evening news audience. CBS rose from 27 to 29 while NBC fell from 26 to 25 percent. More people were watching the news, boosting the ABC numbers, but more new viewers were choosing CBS.[77]

The news executives began tinkering with the program. "They tried to put lighter things on, they tried to put heavier things on, they tried to do more investigative pieces," producer Bernie Cohen said. "If it didn't work, it didn't work. There wasn't really anything you could do about it."[78] In time Bill Sheehan and others realized the ratings would not rise with Harry and Barbara at the desk. Too many viewers simply did not tune in. "Harry and Barbara were two different people," Sheehan said, "and I think they came off on the broadcast as two different people, not as a team."[79]

The partnership that seemed so promising, the bold stroke that would put ABC News on top, had turned into a very public embarrassment. Relief in the form of higher ratings appeared unlikely, discouraging all involved and making it easier for those inside and outside of the newsroom to criticize the decision to bring in Walters.

A few newspapers, most notably the *New York Times*, examined whether ABC News had erred in creating a less formal newscast, one that gave viewers more soft news with a personal touch instead of the traditional news-of-record approach. Writing for the *Times*, media reporter Jeff Greenfield noted that the evening news was using a conversational writing style and airing more interviews and features. "Clearly Barbara Walters can deliver that kind of approach to the news," Greenfield concluded, "but whether, without the news credibility of a Reasoner or similar figure, the audience wants that kind of news show is a question very much in doubt."[80]

The philosophy of news did not gain the same attention from the press and public as the chilly relationship that had developed between the evening news coanchors. Lips may have been loosened by the belief that the broadcast was slowly sinking. Unidentified insiders told the *Times* that Harry remained skeptical about Barbara's credentials to anchor the newscast as well as the personal approach she used. As early as February 1977, insiders claimed Harry was exploring how to leave the broadcast if he were to remain tied to Walters.[81] On the record, Harry was only mildly supportive of the status quo. "We get along fine," he told Greenfield. "We're not great drinking buddies, but then there's no reason why we should be." Walters was equally restrained in her comments, noting that her partner had been unhappy from the beginning. "I think he's feeling more comfortable with me," she told Greenfield. "And if he leaves, where will he go?"[82]

Adding Barbara Walters to the evening news had brought controversy and negative publicity to the broadcast rather than a significant number of viewers. In the ABC newsroom, Harry bore the brunt of the failure, at least in the eyes of many of his colleagues, because he seemed to devote little effort to making the broadcast succeed. Barbara was as hard-driving as usual, always trying to get the elusive interview and to improve her performance on air. Harry was disengaged more than ever, spending much of his time in his office with friends. His visits to the des Artiste bar did not abate.

In the press, Barbara, as the million-dollar woman in a man's job, drew the heavier criticism. Harry was not under scrutiny; he had been in the anchor's chair for years. Barbara was the highly paid novice who stumbled over her words at times. Worse, the cool reception extended into the newsroom and beyond Harry. "No one talked to me," she said in an interview with CNN in 1999. "The technicians didn't talk to me. I would pick up the paper every day and read what a flop I was." [83] No one could blame Walters for feeling unwanted or unappreciated. "Barbara was very sensitive about it," Sheehan recalled. "There seemed to be stories that were not pleasant coming up every other day in one form or the other, in some publication or the other, that we just as soon would not have seen. There was a period that was very intense that made your stomach churn regularly." [84]

ABC seemed ready to abandon Walters in February 1977 when the *Chicago Daily News* reported that the network was considering sending her to Washington to coanchor the broadcast. "The $1-million on-air marriage of Harry Reasoner and Barbara Walters is on the rocks," television columnist Frank Swertlow reported. "Harry and Babs may be heading for the divorce court after only four months together." [85] Sheehan had told Swertlow such a move was being considered, an admission he soon regretted. The report angered Walters, and she told the press that she would not move to Washington. ABC said no more about it. Further damaging to Walters was Swertlow's assertion that sources believed she could be dropped from the broadcast altogether by the summer.

As winter turned to spring the notion of a sour relationship between Harry and Barbara turned from rumor to accepted fact—and fodder for humor. Columnist Russell Baker suggested they receive counseling in order to "save their relationship and assure them of a long, happy, and meaningful life of reading the news together." He then offered examples of how David Brinkley and John Chancellor had worked out their differences (they had argued, he claimed, over whether Brinkley should read the news barefoot) and how Walter Cronkite had found happiness running the only bachelor news show on the air. "As for Barbara and Harry," Baker wrote, "their refusal to come forth and ask for counseling makes it difficult to explain their unhappiness. We know, of course, that Barbara has the money, and it may be that Harry, a model of virility if there ever was one, resents having to ask her for $10 every time he wants to go bowling with the camera crew." [86]

Satirist Art Buchwald imagined what the ABC evening news would be like if only Harry and Barbara could overcome their "domestic strife." First, the set would change. Instead of the anchor desk, they would be in a loveseat holding hands. She would call him "Hal" and he would call her "Babs." In Buchwald's world, they would tell each other the news as if they were an intensely happy couple. Even more cutting, Buchwald worked in references to the actual issues behind the unhappiness: Barbara's lack of news experience, Harry's chauvinism, and the turn toward a softer, personalized news style.

"What a wonderful story, Hal. Only somebody like you could dig it up."

"Babs, that's what I get paid for. I don't earn as much as you, but then again you have all those specials you have to produce."

"I think the most marvelous thing about you, Hal, is that you're truly liberated. Most anchormen would be furious if they thought they were making less than their anchorwoman."

"All I want is for us to have a good news program. The fact that we're happy doing the show together means more to me than the $675,987.50 extra you get every year."[87]

Neither Harry nor Barbara could survive lackluster ratings and public humiliation for the full extent of their contracts. She had signed on for five years, and his contract would not end until 1980. It would be intolerable for all. Yet the coanchors were not the first casualties of what Harry later called "the wreckage of Fred Pierce's judgment."[88] In May 1977, as part of a general shake-up of the news division, Roone Arledge replaced Bill Sheehan and carried dual responsibilities as president of both ABC News and ABC Sports.

Arledge was the top television producer in sports, having created *Wide World of Sports* and *Monday Night Football* for ABC. Yet he had always been in awe as well as envious of news, which he viewed as the higher calling for a television network. It was news, after all, that covered the events that made history and brought a network its prestige. Arledge had been the executive producer of ABC's coverage of the terrorist attack during the Munich Olympics in 1972, and the excitement he felt was unlike any sporting event he had covered. In the wake of the failure of the Reasoner-Walters partnership and with his contract in negotiations at ABC, Arledge decided to pursue an off-hand remark by ABC President Fred Pierce that he should run the news division. Only Arledge wanted to be president of both news and sports.[89]

The announcement of Arledge as ABC News president brought a reaction similar to the hiring of Barbara Walters. Critics called him more a showman than a journalist and warned that television news was taking another step toward entertainment if Arledge created a sort of *Wide World of News* broadcast. Inside ABC News, correspondents Peter Jennings and Ted Koppel were among those who asked Pierce to reconsider the appointment. (Both later owed Arledge a boost in their careers. Jennings became evening news anchor in 1983 and Koppel anchor of the Arledge-created *Nightline* broadcast in

1980.) For his part, Arledge promised to get the news division more money but also expected people to work harder than ever to turn around the division's reputation with viewers and within the broadcasting industry itself.[90]

Barbara reacted to the hiring of Arledge with an act she had avoided for six months: She gave an interview to a reporter. She called her new boss a man of "intelligence, integrity, and style" and saw a parallel in the criticism that greeted his arrival to ABC News. "Roone is being described in exactly the same way I was, as show biz," she told Judy Flander of the *Washington Star*. "I'm afraid he'll bend over backward too far the other way, just as I did. People are expecting miracles from him, just as they did from me."[91] Barbara, it seemed, hoped she had found a soul mate. They had been casual friends while she was working at NBC and had kept in touch since she joined Harry at ABC. Roone had heard directly from Barbara of her unhappiness with the situation.[92]

Arledge admired Harry, even envied him his status as a newsman America trusted. He also thought Harry was an excellent anchor and had not been treated fairly when he was forced to take Barbara Walters as a partner. But after they lunched together he knew he would have to remove Harry from the evening news. "One of them had to go," Arledge wrote in his memoir years later. "Deciding which was coldly simple. Barbara was the future of ABC News, Harry wasn't. Because while there were other Harry Reasoners in television, there was only one Barbara Walters."[93] Still, Arledge believed Barbara was a weak news anchor and simply did not appear comfortable delivering the news. Harry remained, in Arledge's eyes, a valuable property for ABC. He was confident he could find the right vehicle for her—and he thought he could find something to keep Harry at ABC.

Harry, for his part, remembered his first meeting with Arledge differently. He later said he wasted no time in exercising his "Barbara Walters escape clause": the first time they met after Arledge took over the news division, Harry told Arledge he wanted to leave ABC.[94] But Arledge was not about to lose the coanchor of the nightly news without a replacement. He refused Harry's request to honor Bill Sheehan's oral agreement but, at the same time, began laying plans for a complete revamping of the evening news. First, he needed to bandage the wound that had so injured the broadcast.

Arledge brought in Av Westin to serve once more as the executive producer of the evening news and issued a single order: "Your job is to get them off the air while we develop their replacement." Upon his return to the broadcast, Westin found the newsroom divided into two camps. "The whole thing was such a mess," he remembered. "The two of them had been pissing at each other. We knew that we were going to replace them." One of Harry's associates told Westin that Barbara owed him four and a half minutes of airtime, a sign to Westin of how silly things had become.[95]

What appeared on camera was Westin's chief concern. "They both wanted out of it, too," he said. "Barbara was unhappy, Harry was unhappy. Harry's male chauvinism was rampant. He was just contemptuous, particularly on air. That's why we split them apart." Previously, both Harry and Barbara had been shown at the anchor desk at the beginning of the broadcast. They had handed off stories, often signaling the change by speaking the other person's name, and Harry had ended the broadcast by saying, "That's the news. For Barbara and me, good night." Now, however, the anchors no longer appeared in the same shot. It was as if they were in different locations. Nor did they acknowledge each other's presence, even at the end of the program.[96]

Later in the fall Frank Reynolds became part of the anchor lineup introduced each night, and Howard K. Smith soon made it a foursome to further diminish the impact of the failed duo. Harry and Barbara alternated days off during the week, and assignments away from the newsroom put more distance between them. These machinations were nothing more than a short-term approach to a problem that could not be solved until Harry and Barbara left the evening news for good. Until that time, ABC limped along in third place and its evening news existed in an electronic purgatory.

Distractions large and small helped keep Harry's mind off the quiet battle-ground that had become his workplace. For instance, he accompanied President Carter on his trip to Europe in May 1977 and in August joined Sam Donaldson for an interview with the president at his home in Plains, Georgia. That fall he attended the retirement party of Eric Sevareid. He wrote an introduction for a book on photojournalism, picking up a quick $750.[97] He earned another $50 from *Reader's Digest* for a joke he had submitted to the magazine: An English professor was addressing his senior seminar. "There are two words," he said, "which I will not permit in this class. One is 'swell' and the other is 'lousy.'" "Fine," said a voice from the back of the room. "What are the words?"[98]

Arledge was busy devising the next incarnation of the evening news. He envisioned a team of correspondents rather than a single or dual anchor. Frank Reynolds, the anchor fired in 1970, would be the primary anchor and report from Washington, where nearly half of the evening news reports originated. Peter Jennings, the anchor alumnus from the 1960s, would anchor the foreign news from London. Max Robinson would move from WTOP in Washington to ABC's Chicago bureau to anchor domestic news. Howard K. Smith would continue to provide commentary, and Barbara Walters would serve the broadcast as its primary interviewer and reporter.[99] There was no room in this new evening news format for Harry. Yet Arledge believed that Harry was too valuable to let go and considered him for the host of the new magazine program he was planning, *20/20*.[100]

In public Harry had continued to express his desire to leave, although he did not cite the failed partnership with Barbara Walters as the reason. He told the Associated Press in January 1978 that he was considering abandoning the anchor desk because being a correspondent was more glamorous. "I'm not suddenly complaining," he told the AP. "I don't particularly object to doing less work, but you get bored."[101] Within days of the story ABC executives told their counterparts at CBS that, in spite of what Harry had said, his contract kept him at ABC until April 1980.[102]

Arledge unveiled his plans for the evening news on April 19, 1978. While acknowledging that Harry would not be part of the broadcast, he declined to comment on what role, if any, Harry would have at ABC News. Meanwhile, Harry was offered the position of host of *CBS Reports* by his old network. ABC still would not release him from his contract. During a news conference a month later, a reporter asked Arledge, "Why are you tormenting Harry Reasoner if he doesn't figure in your plans and if he has a job waiting for him at CBS News?" Arledge responded, "How can you say we are tormenting someone who receives $500,000 a year?"[103] The reason may have been pique on Arledge's part—CBS executives had derided his takeover of ABC News, and NBC had made ABC wait months for its contract with Walters to end before she could begin her work at ABC. It also may have been gamesmanship, denying a competitor something it wanted.[104] Harry had been reduced to a mere pawn in a game for which he had little interest.

Finally, more than a year after Harry had asked to be freed from his contract, ABC announced in May 1978 he would be allowed to go.[105] With planning for the replacement broadcast completed, Arledge gave Harry what he wanted. "I no longer needed his high-profile dissidence, on or off the air," Arledge later wrote.[106] The network had gained one important concession: Harry Reasoner would not anchor the evening news anywhere else in the first months after his departure.[107] Harry did not care. More than anything, he wanted to get out of ABC. The day after the announcement CBS signed Harry to be the anchor of *CBS Reports* beginning in the fall season. He was going home at last.[108]

Why had the ABC evening news with Harry Reasoner and Barbara Walters failed? The simple answer is that viewers did not turn from CBS and NBC to ABC in sufficient numbers. Nor did enough new viewers choose to tune in to the broadcast. Which factors were stronger—among them, the mismatched personalities of the coanchors or the perceived hostility they had for each other or just the intractable viewing habits of the television audience—is impossible to gauge. Not to be overlooked is the flawed execution of the original concept. Harry and Barbara were to share an hour-long newscast; the half-hour format did not accommodate their different styles. Creating the broadcast without having secured the additional time was a mistake from which the evening news never recovered.

One quality of the criticism that befell both Harry and Barbara spoke poorly of American culture at the time. So much was made of a man and woman anchoring the news together. Gender played far more of a role than may have been expected in the mid-1970s. When Harry and Barbara showed signs of a strained relationship, professional reasons were not nearly as often the subject of reflection as a perceived battle between the sexes. They were "on the rocks" and "headed to divorce court" and needed counseling. She made more money. A woman reading the news on a national network was a barrier that had yet to be crossed, and doing so brought forth a jumble of reactions. Harry as well as Barbara suffered as their audiences gained a new maturity in their outlook concerning how men and women worked together in broadcast journalism.

Postmortems by ABC producers and others, from the perspective of a quarter-century, focused on the lack of chemistry in the partnership as well as the lack of effort on the part of Harry. In the best light, Harry was depicted as the victim of an unfortunate pairing in a broadcast that no one could foretell would not work until it actually aired. At worst, he was remembered as a lazy sexist who did very little to try to make the team a success.[109]

Barbara Walters declined to be interviewed for this book. Her feelings—or how she stated them publicly—about what she came to call "the worst period in my life" changed over time. At first she placed blame for the failure on the chauvinism she and others believed turned Harry against the pairing. "I will never know if it would have been the same with Harry Reasoner had my name been Tom Brokaw instead of Barbara Walters, and I don't want to know," she said while accepting a Women in Communications award in 1979. "Our careers are no longer intertwined, and we enjoy each other now as friends, and I think so much of what happened last year is leftover remnants of misunderstanding about women and of fear about women and fear about their world and communication."[110]

Later, Walters looked back on her partnership with Harry in the deeper context that only time—and great success—could allow. "I don't think he disliked me. I think he didn't want a partner," she told CNN's Larry King in 1999. "And here was this girl who had come off the *Today* show, who didn't have the Associated Press or United Press credentials, because I was of the generation that was educated in television, as so many are now. He didn't want a partner, and he wasn't able to fake it."[111]

Nothing more than speculation can answer a lingering question: Why did Harry risk his salary, reputation, and career by not doing all he could to make the broadcast successful? Walters may be right—he simply could not pretend to be happy with it. Perhaps, though, Harry also thought that if the partnership were to fail, then he would remain as the sole anchor. After all, Harry's abilities were never faulted. If Barbara were the problem, as many thought she was, then it only made sense that she would leave and he would stay on. (Indeed, when the partnership of Dan Rather and Connie Chung foundered in 1995, it was Chung, not Rather, who left the CBS evening news.) Arledge, however, realized that, in the long run, Walters had more to offer ABC. Time proved correct his decision to retain Barbara and let Harry go.

For his part, Harry never wavered from his belief that the pairing had been a mistake, an attempt to gain ratings for the wrong reasons. In the wake of the disaster, he told reporters his differences with Walters had been exaggerated.[112] When his memoir *Before the Colors Fade* appeared in 1981, Barbara interviewed him for a segment of *20/20*. "If I could have known five years ago that we would be sitting here like this, it sure would have made it easier for both of us," she said. Harry responded: "Well, I don't know. Maybe I didn't behave very well. I never did resent you. You know that. I'm not a chauvinist. And I'm certainly not anti-Barbara. But I did have the feeling that whatever the case was that people out there were going to think we were engaged in a stunt at the network, and they did. And I don't think anything you or I could have done would have changed that."[113]

Harry's final broadcast for the evening news took place on July 7, 1978. He took fewer than thirty seconds to wrap it all up. He had been through the mill in the last two years, and ABC had made it difficult for him to take his leave when he had wished. He could have concluded his ABC career with the sort of barbed, bitter observations Frank Reynolds had employed in 1970. But that was not his way. He simply thanked everyone at ABC and bid viewers farewell.[114] It was no surprise that many viewers wished Harry well, writing to tell him that they had enjoyed his newscasts and his commentaries.[115]

Whatever his faults, Harry had improved the fortunes of ABC News. Eventually its network news operation surpassed CBS and NBC in ratings and prestige. Yet it had been Harry's star power that had allowed ABC to gain the foothold it needed to survive and prosper. "There were a whole lot of guys, regardless of what anybody tells you, who made a contribution, and he's one of them," retired news president Elmer Lower said. "There's no doubt that Harry Reasoner made a contribution to ABC's improvements in its standings. The station clearance went up and the size of the audience went up, and the revenue the sales department was able to earn went up too."[116]

There was no overlooking the fact that Harry was taking a step down in the broadcast news hierarchy by serving as host of *CBS Reports*, the respected, honored, venerable documentary series that so few people watched. His salary for this initial assignment was just $250,000, half of what he had been earning as news anchor at ABC.[117] He had lost money and prestige but not his sense of humor. With his new contract signed, Harry sent to Ralph Mann a Steuben glass apple along with a note that read, "To the agent who broke his balls getting less for me."[118]

CHAPTER NINE

A Rocky Return to CBS

I came back a lot calmer, a lot easier in relations with my colleagues. Maybe, sometime in your fifties or sixties, even people like me begin to grow up.   **H. R.**

Nearly eight years had passed since Harry had left CBS for ABC. At first the change had been a boon to his career in terms of money and exposure. But on the August morning in 1978 when he walked into the Broadcast Center as a new employee, he was returning to CBS for less than half the salary he had been earning and tainted by the kind of exposure best avoided by a newsman. Bad luck had followed Harry ever since his chance to be solo anchor at ABC had turned sour with mediocre ratings and had grown worse with the Barbara Walters pairing.

His fortunes seemed no better when an old nemesis, Bill Leonard, succeeded Richard Salant as president of CBS News just a few months before Harry returned to the network. Salant had respected Harry and had been distressed by his move to ABC. In the 1960s it was Leonard who had taken the lead in criticizing Harry to the point that Harry began looking for greener pastures. Their friendship never recovered from the blow of a professional disagreement that, for Harry, was quite personal.[1]

With Bill Moyers leaving, those who worked on *CBS Reports* were anxious to see how the new correspondent would operate. To put them at ease, Harry assembled his colleagues and told them he was proud to be working with them and would be pleased to take all of the credit for all of the work they would be doing. "It was said in a way that was designed to reflect his understanding in the role he was assigned," one of the producers, George Crile, remembered. "It was a nice gesture to the people who were going to be doing the primary reporting and writing."[2]

In addition to working on *CBS Reports*, Harry spent his initial weeks on the job anchoring special reports for the network, including stories on the death of Pope Paul VI and the election of his successor. Near the end of the month he anchored a prime-time retrospective on the tenth anniversary of the year 1968. On radio, Harry would be back to recording *The Reasoner Report*, written by someone else as it had been at ABC and, at times, at CBS years earlier. It was as though he had stepped back in time to the 1960s when he had moved from assignment to assignment.

Another executive might have been content to leave Harry on these light duties and *CBS Reports*, seeing him merely as a failed evening-news anchor not known for working hard serving as host of a broadcast prestigious in the industry but not popular with audiences. Leonard, however, understood where Harry's talents and interests lay and how they could be tapped. He also knew that Harry remained an audience favorite second only to Walter Cronkite. Sentencing a popular broadcaster to a low-rated program would be foolish. Leonard decided to move Harry from *CBS Reports* to *60 Minutes*, the program Don Hewitt had created for a broadcaster of Harry's talents.

There was another benefit to the switch: annoying Roone Arledge. The ABC News chief believed the negotiations to allow Harry to do more than anchor *CBS Reports* but not to appear on the evening news had been a ruse to open the way for Harry's return to the magazine broadcast.[3] CBS denied such subterfuge, but it is likely people at the Broadcast Center enjoyed the idea that Arledge thought he had been had. (Over time Harry would become annoyed himself by the accolades paid to Arledge for rescuing ABC News while he, Howard K. Smith, and Elmer Lower were all but ignored for having begun the turnaround.)

At last Harry's luck had changed. The return to *60 Minutes* gained him the first positive press he had in years. "They needed a fourth man, and I can get along with Don Hewitt," he told the *Chicago Sun-Times* when CBS announced the new assignment near the end of August. "And I'm someone who can tolerate Mike Wallace."[4] With Harry back to tweaking Wallace, it seemed like old times.

The fortunes of *60 Minutes* had improved during Harry's absence. In the decade since Harry and Mike Wallace had introduced its first segment, the broadcast had survived personnel changes, low ratings, a deadly Tuesday-night time slot, and a biweekly schedule. Its foundation had remained stable: Wallace was still chief correspondent and Hewitt executive producer. Replacing Harry and replicating the chemistry produced by the Reasoner-Wallace team had not been easy in 1970. Charles Kuralt was the first candidate, but he did not want to leave his "On the Road" assignment for the evening news to join a broadcast that drew fewer than one out of five viewers and was headed toward its worst ratings yet. Hewitt approached Morley Safer, the network's London correspondent whose urbane countenance would balance Wallace's street-smart personality. Safer agreed to join the broadcast if he could return to London once CBS canceled the show.[5] Cancellation seemed likely at the end of the 1970–1971 season when *60 Minutes* finished 101st out of 103 programs and scored a lowly 9.7 rating.[6]

Few people tuned in, but in its first three years *60 Minutes* earned acclaim from critics and more and more awards for its investigations. The network

could no longer abide such a poor showing among viewers but was unwill-
ing to end a program that brought it respect and prestige. In fall 1971 the
network took *60 Minutes* off the prime-time schedule and sent it to Sunday
nights, a television desert. Instead of competing against *Marcus Welby, M.D.*,
every other Tuesday, *60 Minutes* would face family-oriented programming
at six o'clock every Sunday night. Another slight came with the move: pro
football coverage would eat into *60 Minutes*'s airtime whenever a game lasted
longer than expected. The sixty minutes for which Hewitt had once pleaded
could become forty minutes if a game went into overtime.

Sunday night proved to be the place for *60 Minutes* to connect with viewers. Its rating rose by a third, from 9.7 to 12.7, and its share increased by
nearly half, to 25.[7] The broadcast itself had hardly changed. Wallace and
Safer continued to present a gallery of heroes and villains, offering pieces
that amused or interested viewers and others designed to make them angry
about waste and unfairness. The new weekly schedule forced Hewitt to recruit more contributing correspondents, Charles Collingwood, Eric Sevareid, and Robert Trout among them. The pace was brutal for the regulars,
and even the energetic Wallace found himself so strained that at times he
considered quitting the broadcast.

For the next few years CBS experimented with the *60 Minutes* time slot.
When it moved from Sunday nights to Friday nights for two summer months
in 1973 the number of viewers fell. Fewer viewers tuned in the following summer when the program moved to later in the evening on Sunday. The pattern repeated itself in the summer of 1975. Finally, in fall 1975 CBS placed
60 Minutes in the seven o'clock slot on Sunday night, a piece of prime time
where it was left alone to build an audience interested in more than the *Wonderful World of Disney* on NBC and *Swiss Family Robinson* on ABC.

That same year Hewitt added a third regular correspondent, Dan Rather,
in order to ease the burden on Wallace and Safer. On the spectrum of personalities Rather, the longtime CBS News White House correspondent, was
closer to Wallace's hard-driving, brash brand of reporting. All three correspondents were excellent reporters who could handle a wide range of stories,
yet all were distinct personalities who gave their work a unique flavor. The
broadcast itself gained notoriety for its investigations, and the image of a
miscreant exposed by Wallace or Rather or Safer became its signature.

By fall 1978 the broadcast had become a ratings standout, that rare nonfic-
tion broadcast popular with viewers. It had risen from the eighteenth-most-
watched program to the fourth.[8] The program had become popular enough
for CBS to allow it to be aired in its entirety rather than to be truncated by
sporting events. Pro football, once the program's albatross, became an effective way to retain the adult audience it tended to garner. In addition, if

60 Minutes threw off the entire night's schedule by a few minutes, viewers were more likely to stay tuned to CBS than change channels to a show already under way on either ABC or NBC.

Hewitt decided to bring in a fourth correspondent. He considered Ed Bradley, who had distinguished himself in Vietnam and was working with *CBS Reports*. As a black man Bradley would have provided another point of view to a program featuring only white males. When Harry rejoined CBS, however, Hewitt could not pass up the opportunity to bring him back to the broadcast. "We were delighted to have Harry back. Harry was part of our youth," Hewitt said.[9] The same year saw another addition: the closing essays with writer Andy Rooney. *60 Minutes* was more like a print magazine than ever.

For Harry, the move was a homecoming. "He was so happy to be back here," Mike Wallace remembered. "There was a certain amount of turmoil in his life and, to some degree, in his professional life."[10] The professional battering Harry had suffered at ABC had been very public, but few of his colleagues knew his marriage had been equally bruised. Harry and Kay had stayed together even as Harry had spent more and more time with Tamara Newell. "I'm not crazy about being cast as 'the other woman,' but I was," Newell said in reflection. Harry had told her he would not leave Kay while she was ill.[11] With Kay's health on an upswing, he was moving closer to a decision to end their marriage.

First, though, Harry had to find his footing at *60 Minutes*. Not lost on him was the critical role of the producer in the *60 Minutes* system. The producer still served as the reporter for the story, usually coming up with the idea, doing nearly all of the legwork and initial interviewing, developing questions for the correspondent, and providing a first draft of a script. "He could write well, but he didn't really enjoy doing it," producer Jim Jackson said of Harry. "He much preferred the producer writing the entire script and then he would go over it and change a few things—mostly for style and for greater simplicity."[12] If a producer turned in a weak script, Harry rewrote it even though the extra work annoyed him. He had retained his uncanny ability to read a script once, commit the lines to memory, and deliver it flawlessly on camera.

Harry began his second tour of duty surrounded by able producers, mainly men with whom he had enjoyed working, old hands like Jackson, Bill McClure, Paul Loewenwarter, and a friend brought over from ABC, Drew Phillips. Eight years had passed since Harry and Loewenwarter had worked together, but Harry acted as if they had never been apart. "Harry had this kind of relationship with people," Loewenwarter said, "but there was a cutoff point and it never went on very deeply beyond that point."[13] Still, Harry was as friendly and amenable a companion as he had been in the early years. "He was good company on the road—rarely complaining," Jackson said, "but he did want to break for a proper lunch—none of this eating a sandwich in the parking lot on a ten-minute break. He had been doing this sort of thing for a number of years and he insisted that the whole experience on the road be as civilized as possible and with reasonable hours." [14]

The stories Harry reported in his first years back provided *60 Minutes* with many of its lighter features, the human-interest pieces that balanced the heavier investigative reports. There was the story of a teen-ager in Florida who was sentenced to seven years in prison for stealing five dollars, and a report on the use of snake venom to treat multiple sclerosis. Harry and his producers were drawn to profiles of unusual institutions, such as the French Foreign Legion, the precision flying team the Thunderbirds, and Soviet television. Just as Mike Wallace occasionally did personality profiles, Harry occasionally reported on scams and investigations, including the abuse of wills and estates and the polluted Love Canal area.[15]

Unlike Mike Wallace, Harry's television persona was warm and friendly and did not cause fear and trepidation for his interview subjects. Criticism, never Harry's forte, usually came in the off-camera narration rather than in the one-on-one interviews. Confrontation seldom occurred. When it did, Harry was so easygoing that people responded honestly, even sheepishly, while explaining their motivations no matter how wrong their actions may have been.

For a 1979 segment on illegal copying of movies onto videotape, Loewenwarter and cameraman Bob Peterson brought a hidden camera into a lower Fifth Avenue video store to record their efforts to buy current films on tape. For forty dollars apiece, they were offered a tape of *Superman* and tapes of other films recorded illegally. Later, Harry and a *60 Minutes* camera crew paid a visit to the store to confront its owner. Sam Adwar cheerfully, if nervously, told Harry he had begun copying the pornographic movie *Deep Throat* as a favor for his customers and eventually branched into feature films.

"You think—you were thinking of yourself as a legitimate businessman?" Harry asked.

"Definitely," Adwar replied.

"Running a—a nice business, making a little profit?"

"Right."

"But you're technically," Harry continued, "you're technically flirting with a felony, aren't you?"

Adwar replied, "I guess so, right."[16]

The confrontation, such as it was, ended there. One can imagine Mike Wallace grilling Adwar with questions, yet Harry's approach probably kept the exchange going longer than it would have under more pointed interrogation. "Harry was never in pursuit in the way that Mike Wallace is, or Dan

Rather, for that matter," Loewenwarter said. "Harry would record what a person said and be helpful in making that person tell his story but not be confrontational." [17] If the person's claims were not born out by the record, the narration would note the discrepancy. Unlike Wallace or Rather, Harry would seldom challenge a person.

In part, *60 Minutes* thrived on such different styles. Phil Scheffler noted, "What Don has always been looking for at *60 Minutes* is people who can tell a story well and who therefore can attract people to look at the stories, that is, to say, 'I'm interested in the story that Harry Reasoner is telling me to-night or that Mike Wallace is telling tonight.' " [18] Perhaps it was the presence of Harry and his wry smile that allowed an interview subject to let down his guard and speak more frankly than he would have had the other chair been occupied by the likes of Wallace. "Sometimes it requires a little softness to get inside the door. If you don't get inside, you aren't going to meet the sub-jects," producer Bill McClure said. "That's why sometimes Harry would get the opportunity to do a story that Mike might not because people would not want to be assaulted by Mike." [19] The interviews worked best when the sub-ject took a question from Harry and just talked. If the subject were cantan-kerous and otherwise uncooperative, or merely uninspired by the experience, the interview would go nowhere.

Senator Barry Goldwater, the outspoken Arizona Republican, needed no prodding to say something controversial. Harry had interviewed the former presidential candidate in 1967 for a program about his beloved state. In the 1980s he appeared three times on *60 Minutes*, always stating his mind. In a 1980 interview with Harry, Goldwater said of Richard Nixon: "Mr. Nixon hurt the Republican Party and he hurt America and, frankly, I don't think he should ever be forgiven. He came as close to destroying this country as any one man in that office ever has come." [20] (In another interview, Goldwater called Nixon "probably the most dishonest man I ever knew in politics. I'm glad he quit.")[21]

Two years later, Goldwater broke with many conservatives by criticizing the military buildup favored by President Ronald Reagan and by support-ing abortion rights. Harry asked Goldwater what kind of president he would have been had he been elected in 1964.

"I can tell you one thing, or several things," Goldwater said. "We would have quit spending money that we didn't have and the war in Vietnam would have ended about a week after I became president."

"By a victory," Harry asked, "or a withdrawal?"

"By a victory," Goldwater said. "And there wouldn't have been enough left of North Vietnam to plant rice on." [22]

One example of a mediocre interview was Harry's 1979 profile of Ted Turner. A year or two away from creating CNN, Turner was known as a colorful and bombastic yachtsman, sports franchise owner, and cable television station mogul. Rather than challenge him about his image as "Captain Outrageous," Harry tossed easy question after easy question, accepting the answers and saving the controversial analysis for the connecting narration recorded out of earshot of Turner. More to the point, perhaps, would have been to ask about Turner's widely reported arrogance and fetish for control.

That was not Harry's style. Instead, he concluded the segment by telling viewers: "I left that baseball field liking Ted Turner. I'd hate to have to keep up with him, and I'd hate to have to be that driven myself, but I liked him. He's a talented man with a very large ego, not unheard of in American business and show business. And when you look at his accomplishments, maybe you can't blame him. He's just convinced he can do almost anything he sets out to do, and so far he's been right."[23] It was the sort of lightweight personality piece that viewers enjoyed in large part because Harry brought it to them.

The Turner profile came during Harry's first year back at *60 Minutes*. If the broadcast had improved with age since he left it in 1970, the same could not have been said of Harry. "When he came back from ABC it was like he'd had a lobotomy or something," Sanford Socolow, a longtime CBS News producer, said. "He was a different guy."[24] Harry had slowed down, as one might have expected of a man of fifty-five who had never been energetic. "I don't think he was prepared when he came back to work nearly as hard as he had before he left," producer Phil Scheffler recalled.[25] Harry had given up the job of anchor at ABC News, where he was coddled and carried to a great degree, to rejoin one of the more demanding broadcasts in television news. "If you talked to producers who worked with him, Harry was less than active on a story," producer Norman Gorin said. "He had to be sort of dragged around and would do only what was required. The other end of the spectrum is Mike Wallace. He wants to be involved in everything. Mike was driven. Harry was not."[26]

To the chagrin of his colleagues, Harry's bad old habits—drinking, smoking, and relying too much on other people to do the work—had grown worse with time. They thought part of the problem was an unhappy home life. Don Hewitt observed, "It's very difficult to be at your best professionally when there are personal problems tugging at your heartstrings and poking you with a pitchfork."[27] Laying the problems on his home life, however, ignored the years, the decades, Harry had worked in a similar fashion.

Harry and Kay's marriage had reached its final crossroad. When a *60 Minutes* assignment sent Harry to Scotland in June 1979, Kay accompanied her husband. Producer Bill McClure sensed a strain had developed between the couple as he and Harry reported for a segment about Texas oil workers living among the Scots near an offshore drilling project.[28] The chill was so pronounced that McClure came to believe he had witnessed the final act of the Reasoners' marriage. In fact, he had. By September their attorneys were discussing the terms of a separation agreement.[29] "In a way it was a shock," their daughter Jane said. "In other ways, of course, I could see some of the things that weren't working. I don't think it was probably an easy decision for them to make. They had stayed together through some pretty rough times."[30] Kay continued to live in the Long Lots house.

That same summer Harry and Tamara traveled together to San Antonio for a *60 Minutes* piece about William Martin, a Rice University professor and preacher who reviewed churches for *Texas Monthly* magazine.[31] His effort to explain other religions, from Buddhism to Islam, had intrigued producer Paul Loewenwarter. Martin spent several days with the producer as they filmed services at two Protestant churches in Dallas. When they filmed a mariachi Mass in San Antonio, Martin met Harry for the first time. "I was struck by how much he appeared in private to be as he appeared to be on the screen," Martin remembered. "There were no surprises. He was easygoing, genial, wry, insightful, very, very comfortable to be with." As they strolled and chatted along the river walk in downtown San Antonio, people recognized Harry's voice and turned to greet him. "He was very gracious and friendly to people and seemed grateful that they were so friendly to him," Martin said. "There was nothing of the stereotypical star syndrome. Kind of rumpled and easygoing, the way he was dressed and the way he just shambled along."[32]

What did surprise Martin was Harry's frankness about his relationship with Tamara. In the lounge of the La Mansión del Rio, Harry told Martin and his wife, Patricia, that his relationship with Tamara was no dalliance and that he had given her a ring. Martin thought Harry, knowing he was in the presence of a preacher and a professor of religion, felt compelled to tell him their relationship was neither casual nor promiscuous. "I took it as something of a compliment," Martin said, "but also as a mark of integrity, that though it was obviously a bit irregular, that he wanted me not to think of him as a person who simply brought along a sexual playmate."[33] Others may have thought Harry had been doing just that since he had begun the affair, but their relationship had grown into a commitment. They lived together in a Central Park South apartment, a private couple but not a secret one.

At one point in their relationship Harry and Tamara had been trailed by *National Enquirer* photographers eager to catch them together. He had never tried to conceal their relationship by avoiding the Biarritz and other favorite places. "Harry was interesting that way," Newell remembered. "It was never hiding in back booths. He was always up front, forward. I would go to Madam's, everyplace. And nobody commented on it. Then it went to the *Enquirer*, the *Globe* and all that kind of stuff." The attention paid to the difference in their ages did bother Harry. Once, a woman asked Harry, "Oh, are you here with your daughter?" Newell said, "It would devastate him."[34]

The news that Harry had left Kay, and for a woman the age of his children, stunned and saddened many of their old friends. "He lost a lot of points when he did that," Phil Scheffler said. "It was sort of like he left his wife at a time when she needed him."[35] When talking to friends Kay blamed the end of her marriage on the cancer, Harry's difficulties at work, and a classic midlife crisis she believed he had been suffering.[36] She became embittered about the end of the marriage and never reconciled with Harry, whom she seldom saw over the ensuing years.

Harry wrote briefly about the break-up in his memoir. "Whenever you see a man in his fifties decide to leave a long-time wife, you can hardly be wrong in your judgment of him and your pity or contempt for him," he asserted. He also believed that he and Kay might be better off apart than they had been together. "I have not been intimate with a lot of women," he added. "But I have known an incredibly classy group. And in a lot of the ways that make men and women important to each other, Kay stood alone."[37] For a wife of nearly thirty-five years who bore seven children, oversaw their upbringing at the expense of her own career aspirations, and held together a household over years of illness, the compliment seemed inadequate at best. Yet Kay had her faults, too, and Harry had been too private and too much a gentleman to embarrass her further by airing his grievances in public. Leaving his wife likely was not how Harry envisioned himself as a husband and as a father. "He sort of failed in his ideals," Elizabeth Reasoner said of her father. "He had a fault that he was not happy living with—and very publicly."[38] When he learned the reference to the end of their marriage in *Before the Colors Fade* had disturbed her, Harry wrote an apology to Kay admitting that to have included those observations had been a mistake.[39]

Breaking up with Kay and moving in with Tamara did not end his problems at *60 Minutes*. Time clouded recollections of the timing of events, but his colleagues looked back at the period immediately following his return to *60 Minutes* with disappointment. Harry was lethargic and required too much prodding to work. "He didn't really want to get on the bus or get on the next plane or hustle off to do something with the same energy that Wallace had," Loewenwarter said. "That's really the measure of it."[40] With marital strife no longer a factor, his colleagues turned to the usual suspicion—a lackadaisical attitude fueled by too much alcohol—when trying to fathom why Harry was not as involved in his work as the other *60 Minutes* correspondents. Less a mystery was why Don Hewitt would have tolerated it. "With a talent that big you put up with a lot of crap," said Esther Kartiganer, who produced segments for *60 Minutes* and became its senior editor and senior producer. "He did well even in spite of it. Allowances were made."[41]

Wallace contended that working with Harry had become so problematic that Hewitt considered suspending him from *60 Minutes* the first year or so after he had returned.[42] Asked by a reporter about that period, Harry later said: "When I came back, I suppose there was a period…when there was a question of whether or not I still had my legs, as a baseball manager would say."[43] Years later, Hewitt acknowledged that Harry's drinking had become a problem for the broadcast but described any talk of removing Harry as a tactic to encourage him to seek help.[44]

Harry did improve—for a time. The quality of his work was adequate at the least, and the positive aspects of working with him remained consistent: He was pleasant, self-effacing, and easygoing. "It was impossible to fire Harry," Kartiganer said. "Everybody loved him. Nobody was going to fire him."[45] An ebb and flow marked his work. Some stories interested Harry more than others, and some days he was more energetic than others.

Success protected Harry more than the goodwill of his colleagues. *60 Minutes* finished the 1979–1980 season as the Number One program in television. It was in second place for the next two years before returning to the top spot in 1982–1983. In the remaining years Harry was on the broadcast, *60 Minutes* never fell out of the top ten programs.[46] No producer or news executive would meddle with a formula that had produced such results.

How much of the success of *60 Minutes* was due to Harry's presence? There was no question he drew viewers to the program each Sunday night. In 1979, as CBS pondered how it would replace Walter Cronkite as anchor of the evening news, a polling organization asked one thousand people whom they preferred to succeed Cronkite. Harry was the choice of more people than any other CBS News correspondent, drawing 19 percent to Roger Mudd's 11 percent and Dan Rather's 10 percent. "Reasoner appears to share many of Cronkite's on-camera qualities," the polling organization commented, "projecting maturity, quiet competence, and a relaxed warmth that television viewers value in deciding on their favorite news anchor personalities."[47]

It is doubtful, however, that CBS executives seriously considered Harry for the job he once coveted. One reason could have been practical: Harry was just seven years younger than Cronkite, meaning he would have to be replaced himself far too soon. Longevity had been part of the anchor position—only Douglas Edwards and Cronkite had been the evening news anchors since its inception in 1948. Both in their forties, either Mudd or Rather would have been worth the long-term investment. Another reason could have been the uncertain future of Harry's health. No one could have ignored the incessant smoking and drinking. Considering the other complaints, news president Bill Leonard and others in the executive offices of CBS could not have paid much attention to viewer preferences for Harry when deciding to replace Cronkite with Rather.

Doubtful, too, is whether Harry would have wanted to be anchor by that time: *60 Minutes* allowed him flexibility he could never have enjoyed on the evening news. Free from the demands of a high-profile daily broadcast, Harry did not want to go back. He now claimed he had the best job in journalism.[48]

Once he corrected his behavior enough to stave off threats of being pulled from the broadcast, Harry established a consistent work pattern for the next few years. He gave his producers free reign in deciding which stories to pursue and left them alone. "He was the easiest guy to work with," recalled Sanford Socolow, who joined *60 Minutes* as a producer in the mid-1980s. "It was much easier to work with him. Whether that made for a better product or not is another question, but it was much, much easier."[49] Harry wrote and revised scripts when it suited him, and he traveled as necessary.

Producers learned not to expect too much from Harry, even if their reputations—and his—were at stake. Paul Loewenwarter's investigation of cost overruns in Illinois Power and Light's construction of a nuclear power plant near Clinton, Illinois, needed a strong public advocate when the report came under the most effective counterattack ever mounted against *60 Minutes*. Harry was not up to the task.

Broadcast in November 1979, "Who Pays? You Do" examined charges of mismanagement that the segment claimed led to multimillion-dollar losses every month. Illinois Power had followed the *60 Minutes* cameras with a camera crew of its own, recording Harry's interviews with its officials. Its hour-long video, *60 Minutes—Our Reply*, took issue point by point with assertions Harry had made in the report. It showed the entire segment but stopped at various points to raise a question of fact, play a part of an interview that had been omitted from the *60 Minutes* piece, and otherwise contend that the broadcast had been erroneous and misleading. Later, CBS News acknowledged errors in the report but maintained that it had been accurate overall, especially in the forecast of huge cost overruns for the project.[50] "We had made a couple of mistakes along the way," Loewenwarter said. "On the very large points we were right."[51] The real question, he contended, was whether the errors in the segment were important errors.

Illinois Power argued that all the errors, taken together, cast grave doubts on the credibility of the piece. The company then distributed hundreds of copies of *60 Minutes—Our Reply* across the country, mostly to other utility companies, with the encouragement to show it to key people in their communities. "They spread it all over everywhere, and nobody had ever dared challenge *60 Minutes* this way before," Loewenwarter said. "They were very, very effective."[52] Although it conceded some points to Illinois Power, CBS News dismissed most of the power company's rebuttal in a statement.

Loewenwarter accepted the criticism for the errors because he had been the producer of the segment. Harry let him stand alone. CBS News President Bill Leonard nearly fired Loewenwarter over the controversy that threatened to tarnish the news division's gem.⁵³ Had Mike Wallace been a part of a segment under fire, he likely would have been on the front lines defending the piece. In that regard, Harry was missing in action.⁵⁴ Loewenwarter was the expert on the subject, not Harry. Given the nature of the *60 Minutes* assembly line, Harry had been the on-camera talent for the segment, not its principal reporter and writer. Yet he was the face of the segment and took the public criticism that followed.

The grass-roots campaign conducted by Illinois Power worked. Many people who saw *60 Minutes—Our Response* believed the CBS report had been a fraud. Dozens expressed their ire to Harry, some accusing him of misrepresenting the facts and questioning what else the broadcast had aired that was slanted.⁵⁵ Those who wrote received a brief typed letter from Harry, actually a form reply, that merely noted their concern. His office attached a copy of a five-page letter from news Vice President Bob Chandler to the chairman of Illinois Power that argued the credibility of the segment.⁵⁶

For the next several years the Illinois Power response made its way around the country, and as late as 1985 Harry received letters from outraged viewers. Meanwhile, Loewenwarter kept track of the cost overruns, which continued in spite of the company's effort to damage the credibility of the report. When Phil Scheffler spoke to groups he was prepared for questions about the Illinois Power story and the company's reply. "They did a wonderful if inaccurate response to it," Scheffler said. "I would say the only mistake we made was in understating the degree of the overrun and the number of years it would take for the thing to be finished."⁵⁷ The Illinois Power controversy confirmed for many in the *60 Minutes* shop that Harry was not the best correspondent for a piece that would entail detailed reporting and could engender controversy.

Lighter fare and subjects that appealed to him, such as the film director Billy Wilder and the country music star Johnny Cash, brought out Harry's own appealing personality and raised his level of interest.⁵⁸ "He was not the best interviewer on the show—he simply could not be aggressive," producer Jim Jackson said. "He was at his best when the subject had a sense of humor and we were trying to bring that out on camera—not easy to do—but Harry's own sense of humor would feed right into the subject's humor and the results were always amusing."⁵⁹ Harry often tossed out an impish question. When he interviewed the French actor Yves Montand, he asked: "What makes you attractive to women? Is there anything I can learn?" Montand laughed and suggested Harry ask them.⁶⁰

As much as he enjoyed *60 Minutes* assignments that took him abroad,

Harry could be terribly provincial. "He was shy, actually, with foreigners," said a French producer for *60 Minutes*, Anne de Boismilon. "Harry was so deeply American. He felt so much at home in America, more than the other correspondents, more than Mike or Lesley [Stahl] or all the other people who were more international. Harry was not international at all. He was more deeply American." De Boismilon found Harry to be less interested in other countries and cultures than she had expected of a journalist. "He didn't want to be confronted with a culture he didn't understand and he didn't feel comfortable with," she said. "Talking to foreigners, finding out about their problems, finding out about themselves…Harry didn't show any interest." [61] At the end of the workday he preferred to have a drink or dinner with the crew. Always anxious to return home, he insisted on only one story per trip rather than working on multiple segments.

Harry enjoyed visiting France and Switzerland. *New York Times* food critic Craig Claiborne joined Harry for a 1980 segment that recalled their piece twelve years earlier on dining in New York. "The Best Restaurant in the World" took them to the restaurant Girardet in Switzerland. The two rode in a Rolls-Royce, Claiborne assuring Harry he would see the most beautiful food in his lifetime. "Am I going to feel uncomfortable and wonder which fork?" Harry asked.

Throughout several courses, Harry took the opportunity to joke about the elegant surroundings and act like a small-town Iowan who had won a prize. After Claiborne raved about the creative and innovative dishes, Harry asked, "But in the meantime, sometimes don't you want a cheeseburger?" Surprisingly, Claiborne admitted he often craved a hamburger upon returning from Europe.

Later, Harry asked, "Why would you think this place was better than the greatest restaurant in Toledo?" Claiborne explained that Europeans tended to be more sophisticated and more demanding and had food of higher quality. "For the first time," he added, "I know that we're living in the greatest age of gastronomy in the world." At the close of the piece Harry noted that the $220 check was eleven times what CBS authorizes for lunch in Europe. [62]

In a profile of an international celebrity, Placido Domingo, Harry observed the opera star had his own groupies. Domingo admitted to Harry that it was not easy for his wife, Marta, to see women coming to his performances to swoon over her husband. Harry asked, "She has justified confidence in your fidelity?"

"Yes," Domingo said. "The fidelity, the love that I feel for my wife is there. And I am faithful to her, absolutely."

"Never tempted?" Harry asked.

"Oh, tempted? Yes, many times. And I am saying," Domingo continued with a laugh, "I'm faithful inside, I am faithful in my soul, and I'm not going to answer any more." [63]

Harry exuded an everyman quality even when he seemed at a loss for words. A segment titled "Inside the Vatican" explored the structure and operation of the headquarters of the Roman Catholic Church. Harry and his *60 Minutes* crew had front-row seats in a large hall across the street from St. Peter's Cathedral for a message from Pope John Paul II. As the pope greeted people in the front row, Harry identified himself and conducted an impromptu interview. "Any message for America?" he asked.

"God bless America," a smiling John Paul II responded. "It is—it is the shortest."

"And Poland," Harry continued, "do you have any advice for me there? Will I find signs of hope?"

"Oh, yes, you—you will—you will say you have seen him."

Harry seemed unsure of what to say next. "You know, I will say—I will bring that message."

"You have met him here in the Vatican..."

"How is—how is the state of the church after three years of a Polish pope? It has survived?" Harry could not help but laugh as he finished his question.

"It's the Holy Ghost who knows that," the pope replied. [64]

The charm and rapport Harry brought to his interviews did not always bridge the cultural gap with his subjects. In 1984 Anne de Boismilon gained permission for a rare interview with the spiritual leader of militant Sikhs in India, Jarnail Singh Bhindranwale. His meeting with Harry took place in a spectacular setting, the Golden Temple of the Sikhs in the city of Amritsar in the state of Punjab, as armed followers surrounded them.

Harry had been given a list of questions formulated by de Boismilon but had not put them in any kind of order as she had requested. To her embarrassment—and fear—Harry asked first, "Well, where is the money coming from?" Even the interpreter knew the question was out of bounds and refused to translate it. The interview stumbled along accordingly, Harry asking questions and the interpreter deciding which to translate. Events transformed the mediocre exchange into an exclusive report: Within three weeks of the *60 Minutes* interview Indian government troops took over the temple and killed more than 500 people, including Bhindranwale and many others Harry had interviewed. De Boismilon quickly prepared the segment for broadcast the following week. [65]

Not only could it make Harry feel out of place, travel abroad could limit his indulgences. To his annoyance he had not been allowed to smoke in the presence of the Sikh leader. Before he traveled to Libya to interview Moammar Gadhafi in 1980, Harry learned he would be entering a Muslim nation that forbade alcohol. Ordering a gin and tonic would be difficult if not impossible in Tripoli. While packing for the trip, Harry poured out the contents of a bottle of hair tonic and replaced it with gin. "I don't know where he got the tonic," producer Bill McClure remembered, "but he said he had the gin." [66]

Harry was more at home when he interviewed the jazz singer Anita O'Day. She had been working at Michael's Pub in New York in 1980 when Harry, a fan, approached her about a television interview. She had never watched *60 Minutes* and had never seen the white-haired man before her. "He fell off the chair backwards, straight down," O'Day recalled nearly twenty years later. "Couldn't believe somebody had never heard of him." [67] Her agent persuaded her that a *60 Minutes* gig would help her comeback.

Harry interviewed O'Day at her Los Angeles home for a segment that came to be titled "Canary." [68] He drank some of her vodka, and they chatted while her music played. None of his questions about her fall from popularity and drug and alcohol abuse bothered her. "The way he worded them," she said, "he had a little class." Two days later, O'Day received a case of vodka as a gift of thanks. "How many people repay you for a few drinks? Nobody," she said. "He had to be the nicest man around." [69]

When a producer offered Harry a story that interested him, he could apply his talents for writing, interviewing, and broadcasting in ways that were nothing short of brilliant. The segment he would be best remembered for among his colleagues came in 1981 when he presented "The Best Movie Ever Made?", a piece about his and millions of others' favorite film, *Casablanca*. He interviewed its producer, Hal Wallis, and its two living stars, Ingrid Bergman and Paul Henreid, who shared stories of an unhappy Humphrey Bogart, an unfinished script, and uncertainty about the quality of the film that would later win an Oscar as Best Picture.

If ever there was a personal story for Harry on *60 Minutes*, it was "The Best Movie Ever Made?" He recalled for viewers how he had first seen the picture in Minneapolis at the age of nineteen, but he did not mention his date with high-school crush Maura Anderson. "In 1943," he told viewers, "the kids didn't know they were beginning a nearly forty-year tradition: seeing *Casablanca*, falling in love with love or with the person next to you, memorizing a hundred lines of dialogue—dialogue which, with the spareness of good Hemingway, said a lot more than it seemed to."

As a young man Harry had daydreamed about *Casablanca*. Now, sitting among the props from the Rick's Café set in the Burbank Studios in Hollywood, he wore the kind of white dinner jacket that Bogart wore in the film. Harry toasted the movie and his love of four decades earlier. "I don't suppose then or now young men wind up for good with the young women with whom they first saw *Casablanca*. I didn't. The story seems to lead to bittersweet endings in real life too. But you never forget who you first saw it with. I wonder if she remembers. If she does, here's looking at you, kid." [70]

Harry had been in a reflective mood for some time when he wrote his tribute to *Casablanca*. A month before *60 Minutes* aired the segment the publisher Alfred A. Knopf released his memoir *Before the Colors Fade*. He had been writing the book, off and on, for two years. It had been a struggle. He had been part of a team for so long that he had forgotten how lonely sitting at the typewriter could make him feel.[71] "I like having written," he told the *Los Angeles Times* when the book appeared, "but the writing process itself is a chore."[72] Harry promoted *Before the Colors Fade* with appearances in New York, Minneapolis, Los Angeles, and a few other cities. Television interviews with Phil Donahue, Charlie Rose, and a few others followed, and even Barbara Walters talked about the book with Harry on a segment of her ABC series *20/20*, an invitation that had surprised him.

In just 205 pages, Harry presented his life in the news in the sort of once-over-lightly style that had marked his end pieces and essays for radio. Hardly mentioned were his parents—their premature deaths not at all—or other aspects of his youth and his personal life. Tamara Newell later observed, "He was not of the new generation of people who bared their souls to everyone."[73] The book focused squarely on his career in print and broadcast journalism. In brief chapters he presented vignettes about his work and the people he covered. He dedicated the book to Don Hewitt, an act of gratitude that surprised the long-time producer.[74] Tamara photographed Harry for the book jacket and, though unnamed in the text, was credited with persuading Harry to go back to CBS and for rebuilding his professional ego.

Harry never shared with readers or viewers the fact that their relationship failed to weather tough times. Harry and Tamara did not marry as once planned. She had a drinking problem of her own and left Harry and New York to get help. She later married and had a child but, after a separation of a few years, began seeing Harry again. "He was a lot of fun. He was so bright," Tamara said. "I learned so much from him. He was probably, in a complicated way, the great love of my life."[75] They would never marry, in spite of his willingness, but would remain close friends for the rest of Harry's life.

Critics who read *Before the Colors Fade* were divided over whether the thin volume was the product of a lack of pretension or a lack of effort. "The book is ultimately too muffled and soft hitting," the *Washington Post* commented. "It would have been a better book if Reasoner had opened his mouth a little wider." The *Toledo Blade* countered: "Maybe that's why *Before the Colors Fade* is such an enjoyable book. It's as light as a bubble and every bit as uplifting. It has none of the pontification that usually bogs down the ponderous books by most veteran correspondents." *Newsday* pronounced it "amiable if superficial," and *Kirkus Reviews* summed up by saying, "Lots of zest, shrewd pacing, spotty reporting."[76]

Before the Colors Fade went into multiple printings and was the second book written by Harry to become a Book of the Month Club selection. He told those who asked about his next book that he was working on a novel to prove to himself that he could write another. If he could, he did not. He might have been more successful trying to write another memoir, perhaps about his childhood in Iowa and Minneapolis and his experiences in college and the army. Had he lived to see more of the 1990s, Harry might have joined Walter Cronkite, Dan Rather, David Brinkley, and other broadcasters who wrote best sellers about their lives. It is likely, though, that Harry did not want to revisit the sad times that came with the memories of happier ones. In *Before the Colors Fade* he seemed most at ease reflecting on the events and people he had observed as a correspondent rather than thinking so much about himself.

If Harry thought he could avoid the burdens of celebrity by not discussing his private life in detail in his book, the *National Enquirer* and gossip writers ended any hope of that. His divorce had been reported by the mainstream press in 1981 when it became a matter of public record. Being the subject of published gossip was altogether different.

Once Harry became an item for the columns, his private life was treated as fair game. Marilyn Beck of the *New York Daily News* reported in May 1981 that Harry had been "keeping company" with actress Angie Dickinson. A month later the *Enquirer* published a story, "Love-Struck Angie Dickinson Flips for *60 Minutes* Host Harry Reasoner," claiming they were seen in New York and Los Angeles holding hands.[77] There could be no question the actress was just the type of woman Harry enjoyed, blond and beautiful and good company. They met in New York and Los Angeles off and on during the early to mid-1980s. She sent to Harry a Guindon cartoon published in the *Los Angeles Times* in 1982. It showed a middle-aged woman sitting on the lap of a balding man in a restaurant. "This is my husband, Jesse," the woman says. "In my fantasy he's Harry Reasoner."[78]

In spite of the reports, people close to Harry disagreed with the gossip about the depth of the relationship with Dickinson. Tamara Newell described the actress as a friend of Harry's who enjoyed the publicity she gained from being seen with the newsman.[79] One of his daughters remembers Dickinson as a good friend of her father's, not a serious romance. Dickinson, however, later called Harry "the love of my life."[80]

Mike Wallace could not pass up an opportunity to needle Harry about his supposed fling with the actress. One day in the *60 Minutes* suite of offices, Harry walked into the hallway after a nap, looking disheveled with his shirttail hanging out. Wallace was walking by and shook his head but then stopped a deliveryman in the hallway. "Sir," Wallace asked, "do you know who this man is?" The deliveryman admitted he did not. "Uh-huh," Wallace continued, "do you know who Angie Dickinson is?" Of course, the man nodded. "Would it surprise you to learn," Wallace said, "that this is the sort of man Angie Dickinson can't keep her hands off?"[81]

At the time he turned sixty in 1983, Harry was still a valuable asset to CBS News. He was one of the stars of the most popular program the news division had ever aired. Another poll had reminded his colleagues that, whatever his faults, he had strong marquee value. When *TV Guide* asked its readers the previous fall whom they trusted most in television news now that Walter Cronkite had retired, Harry had been their choice. He earned a confidence rating of 56 percent, just ahead of David Brinkley, by then of ABC, with 54 percent, John Chancellor of NBC with 50 percent, and Mike Wallace with 49 percent—and well ahead of the 38 percent scored by Barbara Walters of ABC. Viewers appeared to trust most broadcast journalists who were older, the magazine reported, and those who had held more than one news-related job and on more than one network.[82]

If that was not enough of an endorsement, CBS founder William S. Paley had told Harry in a letter that he believed Harry was part of the strongest quartet of correspondents in television history.[83] Well-wishing fans seemed to be everywhere. Harry had met Cary Grant at a Friar's Club gathering honoring the actor, and he later wrote to Harry that he and his wife tried never to miss seeing him on Sunday nights.[84]

Within the *60 Minutes* shop, however, the problem with Harry was nearing another state of critical mass by the middle of the decade. Worse, the press was paying attention to his troubles. Gary Deeb, a syndicated television writer in Chicago, reported in June 1984 that Harry would be replaced on the broadcast by Diane Sawyer, calling it a virtual certainty and reporting that CBS had wanted to move Harry off the program for nearly two years. "That's too bad," Deeb wrote. "Reasoner's only 61, but his superiors think he's too laid-back and soft-spoken and they'd like him to retire."[85]

Deeb was half right. Diane Sawyer joined *60 Minutes* in fall 1984, but Harry remained on the program. Those who told Deeb they wanted Harry off the broadcast may have hoped he would leave of his own accord. From Harry's perspective, why should he have retired? The complaints he was hearing carried the empty echoes of decades. He had shrugged off the naysayers before and his career had continued to rise. With *60 Minutes*, he was at the top once more. "Those stories about Reasoner's leaving the broadcast are simply not true," Mike Wallace told *Playboy*. "Harry just came through the best year he's had since he came to *60 Minutes*. How that story got into circulation I have no idea."[86]

Harry may not have realized—or he may have simply denied to himself—the extent of the frustration felt by the people who worked with him.

"Harry was always there, ready for work," producer Paul Loewenwarter said. "But present is quite different from being there at full speed."[87] Producers were beginning to shy away from working with him.[88] Others found that Harry was of little help after he had enjoyed his noontime martinis. He was at his best just half the day. "After lunch things became a little slower, speech became a little slurred," recalled Joel Dulberg, who recorded sound for *60 Minutes* and other broadcasts. "For the most part I'd say he was pretty good. But there were times we had to do an occasional entire read over again just to get a cleaner, more distinct read from him so it was not apparent that his speech had become somewhat slurred. That became more prevalent as the years rolled on."[89]

In the eyes of most observers, drinking was the culprit. Tamara Newell, looking back, was among those who believed that Harry probably was suffering from depression. "If he were alive today somebody would have him on Prozac or a similar thing," she said. "I think he was definitely depressed. Depressed people learn how to treat their depression with alcohol and depress themselves further."[90] Tamara and Drew Phillips, who had much in common with Harry in terms of their outlook on life and their fondness for a drink, decided to organize an intervention to persuade Harry to seek help. Too few people would participate, so they confronted Harry themselves. Although Alcoholics Anonymous had helped her, she could not persuade Harry to join the twelve-step program. "He doubted the fact that he would remain anonymous. That was important to him," she said. "He felt the trust level would go down. There would be value judgments placed on him."[91]

It was the sort of logic that an alcoholic in denial would formulate: Getting help could ruin his career even though his career was in jeopardy and his health, without question, was being ruined. Years of drinking were affecting his liver and inflaming the nerve endings of his hands and feet. Debilitating gout may have been another side effect of his drinking. At the same time, the arthritis in his hands was becoming difficult to ignore.

Why Harry stopped drinking is unclear even if the reasons to do so would be many. He may have finally accepted that he could not continue to drink without hurting himself and those around him. He may have been frightened by a doctor's prognosis that his liver could not take much more abuse. "This is not a moral problem," he told his daughter Jane. "This is a liver problem."[92] Tamara's insistence or encouragement from his children may have had an impact. But at some point in the early to mid-1980s—neither his friends nor family remember exactly when—Harry actually turned away from alcohol. "He was like a little kid," Ellen Reasoner remembered. "I mean, he was happy, he was joking, he had a lot more energy. I don't think it was a pleasant thing for him to do, but I think he was really happy he had done it."[93]

His other damaging vice was another matter entirely. Years earlier Harry had wagered a friend $1,000 he could stop smoking. Within days he lost their bet.[94] Over the years he had learned to order his life to accommodate his desire to have a cigarette. He arranged plane flights to guarantee he could smoke on board. He avoided restaurants that did not allow smoking. When asked at a restaurant if he preferred a table in the smoking or nonsmoking section, his favorite response—"Smoking. I hear that's where the action is"—always got a laugh.[95] Harry told friends he could quit drinking but could not quit smoking. And he never did.

CHAPTER TEN

Behind the Camera, a Difficult Farewell

The idea of trying to outguess life to avoid everything that might conceivably ever injure your life is a peculiarly dangerous one, I think. Pretty soon you are existing in a morass of fear.... It may not be wise or manly to act only to stay alive: the odds are that you will die anyway.   **H. R.**

For three decades Harry had been a constant presence on national television—and a welcome one. People on the sidewalk, in airports and restaurants, and passing through other public places often recognize the faces of the men and women who bring them the news. No one at CBS News was greeted with more warmth and affection than Harry. "It wasn't just that they recognized him and admired him," producer Jim Jackson said. "They genuinely liked him and they had to come over to tell him how much they liked him."[1] A shy and private man, Harry still appreciated the goodwill he had earned with the public. "Doesn't that aggravate you," his son Stuart asked after a well-wisher had approached him, "having these people come up?" Harry replied, "Well, it pays very well."[2] He signed autographs, joked with people, and made them happy he had passed their way.

To his colleagues, even those who had worked with him nearly all his career, Harry remained an enigma of sorts. He was extremely talented but did not always put his talent to its best use. He was likable and friendly but did not let most people grow too close, not even longtime friends like Mike Wallace. "We weren't that kind of close," Wallace said. "We were office close, and we would visit each other's homes. But we weren't inside each other's souls."[3] Don Hewitt had known Harry practically from the day Harry began working at CBS News in 1956. "Harry Reasoner always struck me as being the last person I would have thought would have been haunted by devils," Hewitt said. "There must have been some haunting him."[4]

If dark spirits did indeed follow Harry, he kept them to himself rather than share them with everyone around him. "You could see that his habits— smoking, drinking—were killing him. And he couldn't stop," said Lowell Bergman, a *60 Minutes* producer. "And he came out of a world, like Hewitt and like Wallace, where it was difficult to admit weakness. You didn't admit those things. It's a generational thing."[5]

Just coping with life was a challenge. In 1986, Kay Reasoner's long struggle with illness ended. The divorce five years earlier had hardly diminished the impact Kay had had on his life. "The loss of my mother was not insignificant," Elizabeth said. "He came to her funeral with us."⁶ As he often did when facing grief, Harry found a light moment amid the sadness. Jane had tickets to a Mets game to be played just two days after Kay's death, and she asked Harry to join her at Shea Stadium. The morning after the game she received a things-to-do note from Harry concerning arrangements to take place after the funeral. In the list she found the notation, "Trade top three hitters, move Santana to No. 4." It was Harry's way of reassuring his daughter there was no need to feel odd for wanting to go to the game.⁷

For a time, Harry won the battle with alcohol. He seemed addicted to Coca-Cola as he got through the day without a martini. "He went on the wagon at one point and was an insufferable bore about your body being a palace," producer Sanford Socolow recalled. "He'd make fun of the rest of us who were drinking while he was on soda water or something. But that didn't last long."⁸ Harry probably remained sober longer than many people had expected. "If he hadn't thought he had a problem," Tamara Newell observed, "I don't think he would have spent that time sober."⁹

Lowell Bergman remembers Harry proposing to do a *60 Minutes* segment on alcoholism, focusing on his own struggle. Hewitt, Harry told Bergman, vetoed the idea. "I think that really hurt him," the producer said.¹⁰ Harry did do several segments on smoking and its dangers even as he continued to imperil his health with cigarette after cigarette. His own addiction to nicotine was never mentioned. "The role of the correspondent is to be the invincible storyteller," Bergman noted.¹¹ Indeed, the correspondents on *60 Minutes* never showed any weaknesses. (When Mike Wallace revealed he had suffered from depression, he discussed the illness on other programs, not his own.)

Memories differed on how much time passed before Harry began drinking again. Some remembered him abstaining from alcohol for several months while others marked the period at several years. Tamara Newell contended only six months had passed before Harry began drinking again, not years as some recalled. If people thought he was sober, that was fine with him. "He wanted people to think that," Newell said.¹² One of Harry's daughters, Elizabeth, set the time at nearly five years. The difference in his personality when he was sober surprised her. "I don't know that I would have thought that my father was a man either affected by drinking or with a drinking problem or any of that until I saw what he was like when he did not drink," Elizabeth said. "I had always loved and admired him and enjoyed him, but it was just better. It was much more comfortable. I felt more respect from him."¹³

Watching him turn back to alcohol distressed his friends. Norman Gorin and Jim Jackson had joined Harry at a bar in California when he ordered a drink for himself. "Jim and I were stunned," Gorin said. "Jim, who knew him and worked with him, had not seen him drink in years. It was certainly the first time I had seen Harry drink in years."¹⁴ Slowly, Harry reverted to a pattern all too familiar to his colleagues. "I think it dulled him," Esther Kartiganer said of Harry's drinking. "That's what it did. It dulled his energy, it dulled his wit, it made him a slug. He didn't have those kinds of personality changes that made you not want to be around him." [15]

Still, there was work to be done. Harry was not incapacitated. He did not lose his ability to read a script and edit it or to conduct an interview or to deliver his lines on camera. But the process was taking longer, and his level of participation was falling. More important, the producers assigned to him were growing tired of the extra burdens they assumed with Harry as correspondent. "A lot of times the producers felt that Harry was mailing it in, that he really wasn't doing his homework, that he wasn't studying the story, that he was just getting by," Phil Scheffler said. "And it was true. He wasn't performing up to his full capacity. And yet his presence on the air was still as pleasant as it always had been." When Scheffler talked to him about the problem, Harry responded with a shrug and admitted he was doing as much as he cared to do. [16]

Harry was more ill than anyone, including himself, realized. The years of smoking that had begun in his teens had damaged his lungs, of course, but the extent of the damage became clear in June 1987, when he underwent surgery for lung cancer. Until then he had never spent a night in a hospital. [17] Recovering from the operation took more time than expected. At first Harry had little energy and appetite. Doctors discovered he was short of blood, and his health improved after he received a transfusion. When Joe Wershba visited Harry at Norwalk Hospital he found his old friend smoking a cigarette. "Jesus, no!" Wershba cried. "What are you doing?" Harry explained that the doctors told him nothing worse could happen now that they had removed the diseased part of his lung and that he had decided to quit drinking instead of quit smoking. [18] Out of the hospital he did neither.

A second surgery in less than two years was another blow. "Maybe he realized he wasn't going to make it," Jim Jackson said, "and he thought, 'What the hell, I might as well enjoy myself.'" [19] The cancer took its toll on his health and his outlook. "I don't think he ever felt really great after the first surgery," his daughter Jane recalled. "Once he had the diagnosis of lung cancer, I don't think he was very optimistic." [20] Given the family history with the disease—cancer had killed his mother, sister, and former wife—optimism would have been difficult. Alcohol later became such a problem that his children arranged an intervention to try to persuade Harry to stop. [21] At CBS he was threatened with firing if he did not curtail his drinking. [22] Harry managed to cut back enough to satisfy everyone for a time.

Working with Harry became an even greater challenge after he had cancer. His appearance had changed over the years. He had already required makeup to hide his red nose and the areas of his face turned ruddy by rosacea. Now the camera avoided filming his hands, which had been knotted by arthritis and at times quivered and shook. Breathing with just one good lung, he moved even more slowly.

The most effective *60 Minutes* producers who worked with Harry in his last few years on the broadcast were those able to use his liabilities to their advantage. Those who wanted a free hand and no interference from the correspondent knew Harry was the correspondent who would give them the least grief. Lowell Bergman observed, "I got to do some things with him easily, that he went along with, that I might have to fight with Mike Wallace to do or I might have to try to manipulate Diane Sawyer into doing."[23] Bergman preferred investigative segments and, in effect, turned Harry into an investigative reporter when they worked together.

"Patient Zero" reported on a study that explored the nature of AIDS and how the virus spread. In "Local 560" Harry presented the unusual case of the first Teamsters local to be taken over by the federal government under an antiracketeering law. Harry and Bergman went to Costa Rica for a segment about its president, Oscar Arias Sánchez, who had won the Nobel Peace Prize, and later to Cuba for the thirtieth anniversary of the revolution that had put Fidel Castro into power.[24] Bergman wrote the scripts and Harry revised them so he sounded like himself. "He was very much the writer's rewriter," Bergman said. "Harry really worked it to try to make it better." As grueling as the job could be—going from place to place—Bergman never heard Harry complain.[25]

In another investigative segment, Bergman spotlighted the case of Elmer "Geronimo" Pratt, a Black Panther leader convicted in 1972 of robbing and killing a young white woman four years earlier. From his cell in San Quentin, Pratt admitted to killing only Viet Cong soldiers when he served with distinction as a sergeant in the 82nd Airborne. "You get back here," he told Harry, "and it's used against you. You're a cold, calculated killer, so send him to prison."[26] Bergman's reporting exposed to the largest audience yet the details of the case, including how Pratt had become a suspect on the word of an FBI informant inside the Black Panthers and other questionable tactics the FBI had used to subvert the radical group. Other evidence that might have helped Pratt had been kept from his lawyers.

Still, his efforts to win a new trial or to be released on parole after seventeen years of good behavior continued to fail. Pratt refused to admit to the crime even though an admission probably would help him win his freedom. He told Harry, "You don't put no murder on me that I didn't do."[27] Ten more years passed before a judge ordered Pratt's release in June 1997.

Like Bergman, George Crile had less of a problem working with Harry than other producers. "If you were looking for someone to write the stuff and all the rest...Harry was obviously so very capable," he said. "I wasn't really looking for that." Crile preferred to do the writing and all aspects of a story himself and used Harry as the on-camera talent. "It was rough to get a full narration out of him. We used to have to piece together different parts of the whole business in the end to make it work."[28]

At times there was a trouper quality to Harry even as his health worsened. In 1988 he traveled with Crile to Afghanistan for a segment on a Texas congressman, Charlie Wilson, who helped gain federal funding for the Afghan resistance of Soviet troops.[29] The Americans accompanied Afghan fighters who entered a Soviet fort just a day after the invaders had abandoned it. "The vodka was still in the glasses, they had moved so fast," Crile recalled. "All these Mujahadeen are all around. And Harry had to shuffle—he really couldn't walk—shuffle around to view all these old captured enemy weapons and weapons the CIA had put in there and all. He was wearing one of those funny hats. He said he looked like one of the Seven Dwarfs."[30]

At one point the Mujahadeen handed Wilson a rocket launcher as part of a ceremony to thank him for supporting their cause. "The camera moved perfectly, as it should do, from the congressman to the freedom fighter and then swept down to Harry, which is the dream of the correspondent, to be portrayed in such a loving light, participating to the hilt," Crile said. "And he was asleep. Harry was asleep because it had been pretty rough for him. But he always had that same look on his face. No matter where he was he put the exact same look on his face and kept in there, in whatever circumstance. He was just wonderful."[31] Within days of his return home Harry checked into the hospital. He was treated for dehydration and dysentery brought on, he assumed, by a meal he had shared with the rebels in their camp.[32]

With his health precarious and his career in a slow decline, few high points remained for Harry. One came in 1988 when he married Lois Weber. He had met Lois in a New York restaurant one night while dining with Bernie Cohen. She was just Harry's type, young and blond. (At times friends confused her with Tamara Newell.) Lois had been trained as a nurse and was working for an insurance company. After they had agreed to marry, Harry and Lois arranged a prenuptial agreement that called for her to receive $300,000 in the event they divorced. If Harry died while they were married, Lois would receive either $300,000 or one-eighth of his estate, whichever she chose.[33]

While deciding where to conduct the ceremony, Harry had had a brainstorm: his adopted hometown of Humboldt, Iowa. His last public appearance there had been July 4, 1983, when he had served as marshal of the Fourth of July parade. He wanted Lois to see Iowa as he remembered it, including Napier and the two-story frame house next to the consolidated school where his parents had worked. Most of all, he wanted her to visit Humboldt, the town he remembered so fondly from his childhood and still called "the best place in the world." Lois was no stranger to Iowa, having spent a year working at

Iowa Methodist Hospital in Des Moines. Harry asked his Humboldt cousin Peg Reasoner Hansen to make the arrangements for the following June.

Harry's happiness was not shared by his children, some of whom had deep misgivings about the union. Ann had asked him, "What do you see in this lady?"[34] Ellen, for one, had a bad feeling about the woman her father was preparing to marry. When Harry told her he was marrying Lois, his young-est daughter burst into tears. "I'm sorry," he said. "I don't mean to make you cry, but I deserve to be happy, too." Lois had had a hard life, he explained, and he wanted to make life better for her. "Nobody could understand the attraction, why this happened," Ellen remembered. "People would meet her and say, 'What is he doing?'"[35] Shortly before the wedding, Harry told Tamara Newell that he just could not stand to be alone.[36]

Regardless of any reservations, all of the children joined Harry, Lois, and nearly two dozen other members of the Reasoner clan for the wedding at the Congregational United Church of Christ on May 28, 1988. Peg's husband, Ron, served as best man. "I like to get to Humboldt once in a while," Harry told a reporter from the local paper. "My kids haven't seen as much of it as I wished they had. Altogether, it seemed liked a good idea."[37]

The following year Harry made another nostalgic pilgrimage to the Mid-west. He received a degree from the University of Minnesota—not an hon-orary degree, but a bachelor of arts degree. The university had honored him with a distinguished alumnus award in 1970, but Harry had remained un-lettered because he had never finished the degree requirements. He practi-cally flunked out of the university before entering the Army in 1943. Once he returned to Minneapolis and started a family he tried taking a few classes, but he could not stay with school and build the career he wanted. In 1986 a Minnesota dean suggested the journalism school grant Harry a degree and invite him to speak at commencement. Journalism professor Irving Fang led the cause, arguing to the faculty that Harry's professional experience made up for the fact that he was short credits in basic reporting, journalism history, and four additional courses. Others, however, thought granting a degree to someone who had not completed the degree requirements would set a bad precedent, and the faculty tabled the proposal.[38]

Several months later, Fang was passing through the airport at Nairobi, Kenya, when he came across Harry, on his way to Uganda. Fang mentioned to Harry that an effort to grant a degree to him had failed, but Harry brushed off the matter as of no consequence. He had a different attitude, however, when he returned to the university for a ninetieth birthday celebration hon-oring his beloved professor, Mitchell Charnley. In remarks at dinner Harry wryly noted that he thought he had earned his degree and wanted to have it. "When Reasoner speaks he has such a jocular way about him you think he's joking even when he's serious," Fang said, "and I sensed that he was really serious."[39]

The university had a program that allowed for credit based on equivalent knowledge gained through experience. Fang went to work. For the basic reporting course, Harry submitted scripts for *60 Minutes*. For the history course he submitted a copy of *Before the Colors Fade*. Commentaries he had written for broadcast applied to credit for opinion writing. "One way or another," Fang said, "other material came together and we provided the material for the six courses."[40] Faculty graded Harry's work and awarded him five A's and a B. At last Harry had earned his degree, which he called "the oldest B.A. in the history of the University of Minnesota."[41]

Five thousand people attended commencement on June 11, 1989. Harry thanked university officials and then addressed his remarks "to my fellow students..."; the audience cheered.[42] Later, as students received their degrees, some began leaving the reception line to shake hands with Harry. More and more came to his chair and, in spite of his arthritic hands, Harry smiled and congratulated each one.[43]

At *60 Minutes* it was only a question of when and how Harry would leave the broadcast. His weakened state could still be hidden from viewers. "If you have two cameras and a relatively unlimited budget, you can make anybody look like they're coherent," Lowell Bergman said. "You'd be surprised what you can do with a little film editing."[44] Producers avoided photographing him in direct sunlight, and silk screens helped improve his appearance on film. His work behind the cameras took more time. "Looking at him through the glass wall here to the announce booth," Joel Dulberg remembered, "to watch the shaking of the hand, the quiver in the voice, to hear the slurred speech and just look at the gauntness of his face, if you will, was upsetting to me. Looking back through the years, I had a great deal of respect for Harry Reasoner and I think a lot of people did."[45]

In the field Harry was genial but lethargic. His profile of jazz musician Miles Davis—a fascinating encounter between an easygoing correspondent and a mercurial musician—was a nightmare behind the camera for its producer, Anne de Boismilon. Once a producer for French television, she had worked as an assistant to Bill McClure since 1981 and knew Harry could be an excellent writer and could look very good on camera. She had been assigned to Harry after correspondent Diane Sawyer had left the broadcast for ABC News. With Harry she reshot a segment on the Swiss Army she had prepared with Sawyer and then undertook the Davis profile.

Miles Davis was ill himself and not particularly interested in the interview, but he also would not cancel it. An on-camera session in New York had gone well, but then Harry and de Boismilon waited for days for Davis to sit down for another interview, this time at his home in Los Angeles. Harry was of no help in persuading Davis. "Harry would not use his authority—be Harry Reasoner—and say, 'Miles, come on, we have to do the interview,'" de Boismilon remembered. On the fifth day, she lost her temper. To the amusement of both men, she threatened to leave town if the interview did not take place at two o'clock that afternoon. Davis finally agreed.[46]

The segment was unusually tense for a Reasoner piece. When Harry asked if black musicians were genetically better than white musicians, Davis responded: "Not better, but they play different. White musicians seem to lag behind the beat, you know. I don't know why."

"'Cause black musicians hurt more?" Harry asked.

"What do you mean, 'hurt more'?" Davis asked. When Harry tried to explain, Davis interrupted him. "It's not that cliché."

Harry continued. "It's not that easy to say that because you came out of slavery, you lay on the beat."

"No, no, no," Davis said. "Don't have nothing to do with it."

"All right," Harry said.

Perhaps it was Harry's agreeable tone and his willingness to allow Davis to speak his mind, but the musician seemed to open up. "I told a schoolteacher of mine like that in Juilliard," he continued. "She started talking about, 'Well, you know, black people were despondent at night and they say that's where the blues came from.' So I raised my hand and I said, 'Listen, my father's rich, my mama's good-looking, all right? And I can play the blues. I've never suffered and don't intend to suffer.'"

Davis challenged Harry throughout their interview. Harry, at one point, observed that Davis did "bad things" when he was addicted to heroin. "Like what?" Davis asked.

"Well," Harry said, "you said you were pimping for a while—"

"Is that bad?" Davis asked. "Is that bad?"

"Well, now," Harry replied, "you're right. I made a judgment on a word and I shouldn't have. You did a lot of things, different things ..." Davis then acknowledged having had some sort of relationship with prostitutes.

Other exchanges between Harry and Davis were uncomfortable at times, touching as they did on race (he admitted to seldom liking white people), drugs (he quit heroin by spending five days alone in a cabin), and women (American women, he asserted, watched too much television and acted as they saw women act in soap operas).[47] Harry ended up with one of the better interviews to air in his final years with *60 Minutes*.

One portion of the segment showed Davis and Harry walking along the beach, the only shot of the two in motion. "They walked like ninety-year-olds," de Boismilon remembered. "I asked them five times to walk. I told them, 'Listen, you walk like dead bodies, I'm sorry. You look so old. Could you give me just a little bit of energy?' Finally, they were laughing because I was so much out of my mind."[48]

People who encountered Harry were understanding and forgiving of his weakened state. For a segment on a community clinic that served rural poor in Tutwiller, Mississippi, Harry spent a day or two interviewing its doctor, herself a Catholic nun, and her colleagues.[49] The producer, Josh Howard, had warned people that Harry was recovering from illness. He tired easily but did not look ill, recalled Sister Maureen Delaney, a clinic worker and among those Harry interviewed on camera. "He asked good things and made you want to talk. People liked him," she said. "I think he was very warm. His eyes spoke to you. He seemed like he was very interested in you and what you had to say. That kind of came across. It didn't seem like an act. He seemed like he was really interested."[50]

The power of *60 Minutes* showed itself when orders for quilts—handmade by local women who shared the profits with the clinic and a community center—soared to more than six hundred in each of the next two years. "We were getting seven trays of mail a day for weeks," Sister Maureen said. "We were overwhelmed with things—things that people sent us and quilt orders and donations. We thought we would never get out from under all this goodness."[51] Harry's office received nearly thirty letters, some with checks of $25 to $100 for the Tutwiller clinic.

Within the *60 Minutes* shop, producers avoided working with Harry if they could and no longer made a secret of it. When one of his favorites, Patti Hassler, left his team for Morley Safer's, Harry was crushed. "I think it said to him that if she was leaving him, then things were coming to a close," Lowell Bergman said. Anne de Boismilon recalled: "This break was a terrible offense to him and he never accepted that. I think he felt betrayed."[52] Others eventually begged off of working with Harry, including Bill McClure. Harry's lack of preparation and his inability to conduct adequate interviews had become embarrassing. "Frankly, I couldn't go on because it was affecting my productivity, and I had to work with other people," McClure said. "I asked to work with other people. I didn't ask for it until everyone knew he was ill and not able to contribute. I always felt I was deserting him and I did try my best not to desert him."[53] Losing longtime colleagues hurt Harry but did not persuade him to retire.

Someone had to work with Harry, even if under duress. "There are a lot of crosses that producers at *60 Minutes* have to bear," Phil Scheffler said, "and Harry was one of them."[54] In 1990 de Boismilon produced four more segments with him. He showed no interest in the piece about the inferior status of women in the Soviet Union.[55] "Harry was unable to write the script," she said. "Harry felt so weak, so sick. It was so painful. You cannot imagine how he looked." Saying nothing to Harry, de Boismilon took her script to Don Hewitt and worked with him on the revision. As much as she liked Harry and wanted him to do well, she too had had enough. "You want to get the most out of your own time, too, and you don't want to be held back. It's like being held back by an invalid," she said. "He was ill, he was truthfully ill."[56]

Harry's attitude while working on a report on alcoholism in the Soviet Union surprised de Boismilon.[57] He seemed comfortable with the subject, almost totally detached from it. "Harry behaved like these people have really a problem and like he didn't have any," she said. "He never mentioned his problem. He was looking at them like they were very sick people, and they were, but Harry was too."[58] The segments in the Soviet Union were their last together, except for a French television report *60 Minutes* aired with Harry's narration.[59] One story, a lighthearted look at the secret of the Italian seduction, never aired, she believed, because Hewitt did not like it and Harry did not fight for it. "My *60 Minutes* years, especially my years with Harry, were the best in my life. I have no bitterness," de Boismilon said. "But for his producers, believe me, these years were very, very hard."[60]

Her experience was not unique. David Turecamo had been an editor with *60 Minutes* for eleven years before he produced three segments in 1990 with Harry, all among his last work for broadcast. Turecamo knew the Harry of the past—a fine writer, a wonderful companion, and a joy as a human being in so many ways. "Had this guy been a prick, everybody would have just stood by and greased the skids for him. It would have been just a delight to see him crash," Turecamo said. "But I think that was Harry's tragedy. Everybody did have such respect for him and liked him so much that when you saw this guy start to go again, it just was crushing. And everybody at the end, a lot of people around him …it was devastating. We all kind of tried to keep it manageable. But it just wasn't."[61]

By this point Turecamo knew the quality of Harry's work was unpredictable even if Harry himself was good company. His interviews with laid-off workers at a nuclear weapons plant—all knew they probably were fatally ill with radiation poisoning—could not have been more empathetic and revealing. But when Harry failed to press film industry representative Jack Valenti about the validity of the movie ratings system for another report, Turecamo felt frustration mixed with sadness.[62] "You have a job to do, and at that point I was struggling to survive up there," he said. "I realized this was going to cost me a livelihood, too. It was tough."[63]

Why had Don Hewitt allowed Harry to continue? "Do you realize Harry was a hero of all of ours?" Hewitt asked in response to the question. "To turn your back on Harry would be like turning your back on your brother."[64] Yet Hewitt had talked many times with Phil Scheffler and others about Harry's leaving the broadcast.[65] Still, Harry kept working. "I think it was a kind of inertia," Scheffler said. "One of the things that keep us working, besides the fact that we like what we do, is that our lives are so inexorably bound up in journalism that we're not exactly sure whether we can survive without it."[66]

Some *60 Minutes* producers, their careers dependent upon the quality of their work, were sympathetic to Harry's plight but critical of the way they felt Hewitt ignored the problems Harry presented them. "We didn't get any support from Don Hewitt," de Boismilon said. "Don didn't want to acknowledge that Harry had become a problem for all his *60 Minutes* producers. He knew that, but he didn't want to acknowledge it. It's part of Don's personality—he's always attracted by what looks great, what is healthy and young and glamorous. Don at the end was not talking to Harry, was not trying to help Harry, was not acknowledging the problems we had working with Harry, and actually was not supportive of Harry." [67]

Producers and correspondents were always in conflict at *60 Minutes*, in large ways and small. Lowell Bergman believed Harry's star power and Hewitt's concept of the correspondent as the star of the program had kept Harry on the broadcast. "The show's consistency is to keep the same faces as long as possible. You start changing the faces, at least in his theory of the show, and it causes problems with the audience. And Harry had a big following," Bergman said. "The bottom line is, he was a recognizable personality. He had a talent for writing and he could keep people watching because of who he was, and so that was worth it to Hewitt." [68]

The end of Harry's career came in late October 1990. Turecamo was producing a segment on direct marketing and was waiting in San Francisco, where Harry would interview people at a trade convention. Then Harry's assistant called on the phone to say he was not up to traveling from New York. As Turecamo tried to figure out how to make the segment work without its correspondent, Don Hewitt called. "David, come home," Hewitt told him. "It's over." [69] Harry was leaving the broadcast.

How hard Hewitt and others at CBS had to push for Harry's retirement is a matter of speculation. Harry himself had decided in the fall of 1990 that he would not seek a renewal of his contract, which would end the following spring. Money would not be a reason to attempt to continue the grueling pace. His attorney, Stuart McKeever, had developed a retirement plan that would net Harry an estimated $250,000 a year. With speeches, narrations, and other uses of his talents he could continue to live comfortably for the rest of his life and still leave a generous estate. [70]

What annoyed and hurt Harry, however, was the way in which he was being rushed to leave. His son Stuart recalled: "I had a sense that he was retired before he wanted to be and was not at all happy about that. He sure didn't seem very happy the last few years of his life." [71] Reacting to what he considered a lack of respect, Harry sought an immediate termination of his contract. [72] "He said he wanted out," said his agent, Ralph Mann. "I told him I thought he was totally wrong and that we ought to work something out—and it was already done. He was a guy, when he decided something, that's the way it was going to be. He just decided he wanted out." Mann wanted to negotiate a settlement that included a long-term agreement that would allow

Harry to have some participation in programs and still be paid. Harry did not care about the terms. "He just wanted to get the hell out of there. Those were not happy days," Mann said. "He went home and he stayed home. I think he expected to die."[73]

When asked if he pushed Harry into retirement, Hewitt responded: "He pushed himself. He kept wandering off to God knows where. I was always bringing him back. Nobody pushed Harry over the edge. He sort of wandered off the reservation and got lost out there in Big Sky country. It was a sad moment for all of us."[74] Harry spoke little about the situation to friends or even to family.

Whatever the impetus, in an agreement dated December 4, 1990, CBS promised to pay Harry $471,153.76 within a week of accepting the terms.[75] As of January 1 he would become an "independent contractor" for the next two years, serving as a post-retirement adviser and consultant to CBS. Harry would be required, among other things, to make not more than ten public appearances per year for the network and would appear up to five times per year for interviews on documentaries and special broadcasts.

In exchange Harry would receive $50,000 for each of the two years. Compared to the multimillion-dollar deal Walter Cronkite had reportedly negotiated with CBS upon his retirement, Harry left the network with a pittance. At *60 Minutes*, sentiment brought about the designation "editor emeritus" for Harry.[76] Hewitt hoped that his friend and colleague, not faced with a full load, could be revitalized in some way. "Harry was treated, I thought, pretty bad," Mann said. "He was never asked to be part of anything. They only gave him a minimum send-off."[77] Except for the segments that had yet to air, Harry never again appeared on the broadcast he had helped to launch.

After the network announced on November 8 that Harry was entering semiretirement as editor emeritus of *60 Minutes*, colleagues at both CBS and ABC and viewers around the country praised him and wished him well.[78] Avoiding sentiment himself, Harry was as wry as ever when he told reporters, "I've been waiting for Mike to retire first, and I realized it wasn't going to happen."[79]

The difficulties that had become inherent in working with Harry were put aside when *60 Minutes* broadcast a tribute to him on May 19, 1991, the program airing again the *Casablanca* piece. Granted, it would have been bad public relations to unceremoniously drop him without comment from television's most successful program. But the goodwill people held for Harry was genuine and strongly felt. After Mike Wallace, Morley Safer, Andy Rooney, and others toasted him, Harry sat before the camera once more to bid viewers farewell after thirty-five continuous years on the air:

> I can't imagine anything I could have done that would have been so rewarding, particularly the people, all the people in this shop and a lot of

you out there in the country—in a lot of countries, actually—is to me like having literally millions of close friends.

I could go on and on but I might cry, and Mike hates to see me cry.

I'm Harry Reasoner. Most of us will be back next Sunday with another edition—Volume 23, Number 36, to be exact—of *60 Minutes*. Good night.[80]

In the months that followed Harry considered what would come next. When daughter Elizabeth asked him what he would be doing in ten years, a question he had posed to her, Harry responded, "Living, I hope."[81] At first he looked forward to pending projects, including delivering speeches to groups and appearing at corporate seminars, which would net a sturdy income. (His speaking fee was approaching $25,000 per appearance.) As he explored other opportunities to make money, such as reading books on tape, he also began planning the management of his retirement income. For years he had contemplated writing a book called *Letters I Never Wrote*, planned as a series of observations he had wanted to share with his children. He bought his first word processor to begin writing again, but he never put it to much use.[82]

More and more Harry spent his time at home reading or just watching baseball on television. "On the one hand I do think he thought he was going to die," Jane Reasoner said of her father. "On the other hand, I remember him being pleased about the speeches and stuff and having some plans to put his papers, his things at home, in order, all the awards he had. I think a part of him didn't see it as imminent, anyway."[83] As far as his children knew, Harry did not have a recurrence of cancer. But Jane believed something was affecting his health. For example, there were spring days he could not stay warm.

Life at home could be difficult. Relations between Lois and Harry's children had not warmed in the years they had been married. In their eyes, Lois had become increasingly demanding and confrontational. Ellen recalled that Lois set limits on where her siblings were allowed on the Long Lots property, even where they were allowed to park their cars, and often said hurtful things to them. More important, Ellen believed Lois was not taking care of her father and was damaging his relationship with his family. She would visit Harry for breakfast before Lois had come downstairs and then would leave as soon as Lois appeared. Others felt uncomfortable around Lois and began staying away from Harry in order to stay away from her. "The only way I can sum up Lois is 'poison,'" Ellen said. "She poisoned his life, and that's how I look at it."[84] Having avoided confrontation all his life, Harry would have been an unlikely peacemaker.

The *60 Minutes* shop celebrated the end of the 1990–1991 season with lunch at the Russian Tea Room on June 4, 1991, and turned it into a retirement salute to Harry. The bittersweet nature of the gathering turned more somber when people saw him. "Everybody understood that Harry was very sick, and he understood it," Phil Scheffler remembered. "He made a very sweet talk. I can't remember the words, but it was very sweet and very moving."[85] Many people felt the mixed emotions of wishing Harry well and believing they were seeing him for the last time.

Others may have thought Harry had given up, but not Andy Rooney. He had recently talked with Harry about death—Harry's and his own—and did not believe Harry had any intention of dying. His actions did not show a man idly waiting for the end. He had agreed to appear June 13 on CNBC's Dick Cavett show. Plus, he had season tickets to see the Mets.

The week after the retirement party Jane visited her father at the Long Lots house in Westport. Watching television without even a Coke to drink or a cigarette burning in the ashtray, Harry did not seem to be himself that morning. Nor did he appear to be drinking. "He was very—kind of unresponsive. One of the things I have wondered since is—if he had some kind of event in his brain going on, some funny mix of medications," Jane said. "Something was not right."[86] When Ellen visited the house for a swim later that afternoon, she also noticed her father was not drinking.[87]

The next morning, Stuart McKeever called the Long Lots house to discuss a financial matter with Harry. Lois answered the phone. "You know he's not here," she told McKeever.[88] At the same time, a call came into the office from Jane. Norwalk Hospital had contacted her to request permission to perform emergency neurosurgery on her father. It was the first any of the children had learned that Harry had been critically injured at his home the night before.[89]

Harry had fallen down the narrow stairway in back of the kitchen, according to Lois, cracking his head on a tile floor. She later said she called Harry's doctor for help—and he told her to call an ambulance immediately. Emergency personnel who arrived at Long Lots found him unconscious and lying in a pool of blood. Lois did not ride to the hospital with her husband, arriving there by herself some hours later, and afterward explained that she could not reach any of the children by phone to alert them to their father's state, according to McKeever.[90]

The injury required surgery in order to remove a blood clot that had formed in his brain. Harry remained in intensive care for weeks. He came out of a coma, the first sign that he might be able to recover from the damage. On occasion he recognized people and attempted to speak to them. "It was just a few times that he spoke clearly. There was one day when he was just talking nonstop, but he was very hard to understand," Jane said.[91] On another day, with the television tuned in to a baseball game, Harry became visibly excited when the Mets got a hit. Still, he could not communicate clearly. "I didn't really see him at any time where I would describe him as really clear and coherent," Jane said.[92] The family sensed Harry would never be completely himself but might be able to come home one day and improve with therapy.

For a time it appeared Harry would escape the fate that had taken his father from him along the Lake Superior shoreline all those years ago. He was in the rehabilitation unit of the hospital when doctors detected a pulmonary embolism, a blood clot in his lung. He was sent back to intensive care, and his body began to fail. He contracted pneumonia, aspirated liquid, became septic—everything seemed to be going wrong. Then something occurred—Jane remembered it being described to her as "a major event" in his brain—and it soon became apparent Harry would not survive.[93] He died in Norwalk Hospital on August 6.

Under state law in Connecticut, the assistant medical examiner assigned to the hospital was required to investigate the circumstances surrounding the death. An autopsy usually would not be required for an accidental death at home unless questions had been raised. Six weeks had passed since Harry had fallen, however, clouding the fact that the injury leading to death had occurred outside the hospital. "As occasionally happens when there is a long interval between injury and death, the private physician signed him out on a private death certificate and didn't report it to us. Technically, this is illegal," said H. Wayne Carver II, the state's chief medical examiner. "It's a screw-up. It happens to little old poor people, too. I really do not assign any evil motives to the physician who did this other than he just screwed up. It's common enough."[94] With the death certificate completed, officials released the body for burial.

The mistake of not calling the medical examiner's office came to light several months later, after the Reasoner children continued to question how their father had been injured. They never fully accepted Lois's account of the accident and what took place before the ambulance arrived. Westport police did not come to the house the night of the accident and never interviewed Lois. Stuart McKeever, as executor, conducted an investigation on behalf of the estate. Experts reconstructed the fall and, among other things, analyzed the original blood patterns on the floor to determine how long Harry had lain there before emergency workers were called to treat him. McKeever presented the results of the investigation to police and the state attorney's office.[95]

Nearly a year had passed since Harry had died when, on July 21, 1992, the state attorney's office asked Carver, as medical examiner, to look into the fatal fall. In early October the *Westport News*, in a story carried by the Associated Press, reported that authorities in Iowa and Connecticut were considering an exhumation in order to conduct an autopsy.[96] Westport police told the newspaper the Reasoner family had requested an inquiry even though there was no indication of foul play in the death.

The *National Enquirer* lent its voice to the investigation with a headline on its October 6 cover: "Family Fears Harry Reasoner Was Murdered." (In keeping with the lurid style of the publication, the first two words appeared in type just half the size of the rest.) The *Enquirer* focused on the sensational elements of the probe, including quotes from Lois denying she had killed her husband. It was becoming just the sort of public spectacle Harry detested as a private citizen but understood as a journalist.

In the course of his investigation, Carver reviewed more than 1,000 pages of medical records and nearly 200 X-rays as well as reports about the fall. "It was my conclusion that he died as the complication of head injuries, that they were accidental in nature and resulted from a fall," he said. "It wasn't sexy enough for the tabloids to publish."[97] Carver amended the certificate of death accordingly.

Did Harry's drinking play a role in the fall? Carver determined that alcohol could not be cited as a contributing factor.[98] Nor did he believe an autopsy would provide additional evidence. In the six weeks Harry lay hospitalized, tissue would have healed sufficiently to make difficult any reliable determination about the nature of the injuries he had suffered.[99] No exhumation occurred, and authorities in Connecticut and Iowa ended their probe. The Reasoner children no longer pursued answers to the questions they believed were left unresolved. "The family made a conscious decision not to let their father be dragged into the morass of tabloid journalism," McKeever said. "There will always be a mystery surrounding his fall."[100]

In time the Reasoner children severed all ties with Lois. Her contact with the family ended with the disposition of Harry's estate, which was valued at around $4 million. Under the terms of the prenuptial agreement, Lois had the choice of a $300,000 payment or one-eighth of the estate. She accepted the former, which would be paid much faster than any claims on the estate; years passed before it was settled.[101]

After CBS had announced Harry's death on August 6, 1991, friends and colleagues at the networks where he had worked paid tribute to him. Dan Rather called him "an American original. He was an influential and important voice in American journalism that will be sorely missed." Eric Sevareid observed, "He was a gentle and thoughtful man in a rough-and-tumble business, but I never knew him to do a poor job at anything." Morley Safer contended that Harry's most important contribution to American journalism had been "showing that it is possible to excel while not being an egotistical fool." Barbara Walters also issued a statement: "Harry and I had our differences many, many years ago but they were never personal and they never lingered. His death saddens us all. He was a superb journalist and a gentle and humorous man."[102] Both networks aired obituaries on the evening news programs he had once anchored.

On Saturday, August 10, friends and family gathered at St. Luke's Catholic Church in Westport for a service. That Sunday night's edition of *60 Minutes* (it would be the most-watched television broadcast that week)[103] featured a tribute to Harry written by his friend and collaborator Andy Rooney. "Harry was an infinitely complex person," Rooney told viewers. "He wasn't like any-one I ever knew. If you think you know what he was like because you saw him so often here on *60 Minutes*, you're wrong. No matter what you thought he was like, I can promise you he wasn't like that." The segment recalled their work together at CBS and ABC—*Calendar*, the essay broadcasts, and others. Rooney bristled, though, when he thought of the years he would not share with Harry. He ended the piece with these words: "Harry was the smartest correspondent there has ever been on television, but he did more dumb things than most of them, too. How does the smartest man I have ever known lose a lung to cancer and continue smoking two packs of cigarettes a day? I'm sad, but I'm angry, too, because Harry was so careless with our affection for him." [104]

The next day, on August 12, mourners gathered for private services at the Congregational United Church of Christ in Humboldt. Three hundred people had attended a public visitation. The church service was simple. A flutist played "Amazing Grace," and soloists performed "Going Home," "His Eye Is On the Sparrow," and "The Lord's Prayer." (Three weeks later, on September 5, a memorial service at Lincoln Center would draw 350 people, many of them his colleagues from broadcasting.)

Harry had once said a person should be buried in the ground where his roots are. Later that day at Union Cemetery, his body was laid in a grave near those of his sister, Esther, and the brother who had died the day he was born. Beside him were the graves of his parents, Eunice and Harry Ray. An honor guard from Veterans of Foreign Wars Post 5240 saluted Harry, the army sergeant, with military rites. One of the men presiding lost his place in the ceremony and muttered, "Aw, shit," just loud enough for some of the mourners to hear him. "It was one of the funniest things, so typical for Harry," said his friend and agent, Ralph Mann. "I thought, 'Jesus, Harry would have laughed, and he must be up there laughing now.'" [105]

Moments of sorrow had challenged Harry when he was writing for radio and television. The end of a life often moved him even though he was in a profession accustomed to the passing parade. He could not be called on to place his death and life in perspective. Looking back, an essay Harry wrote in 1965 for *Calendar*—one that rationalized smoking, of all things—carried a suitable epitaph to his own life in the news:

A man makes a sort of deal with life. He gives up things because they are undignified or piggish or immoral; if life asks him to cringe in front of all reasonable indulgence, he may at the end say life is not worth it. Because for the cringing he may get one extra day or none; he never gets eternity. If eternity exists, it is available not on the basis of how hard you hold to life but how generous you are with it. [106]

CONCLUSION

CBS News celebrated its first fifty years in television in 1998 with a two-hour, prime-time retrospective and, each night for a week, a look back on the evening news. Edward R. Murrow, understandably, dominated the early history of the news operation. Most prominent in the evening news segments were the three men who anchored the broadcast during those five decades: Douglas Edwards, Walter Cronkite, and Dan Rather. Most of the attention was paid to Cronkite and Rather, both of whom were on hand to commemorate the past. Harry Reasoner, dead for seven years, received scant mention in either venue in spite of his contributions to both.

There are people who transcend their roles as news givers. Murrow lives on because he was the voice and then the face of CBS News during early broadcasting's coverage of American crises—and the conscience of the entire profession. Longevity guarantees Cronkite and Rather a presence whenever events whose news coverage they anchored are revisited. Howard K. Smith is remembered whenever the first presidential debates are recounted. The footage of Cronkite breaking the news that President Kennedy has died appears destined for broadcast immortality.

Harry has only a few small measures of immortality. As long as *60 Minutes* remains on the air, he will be remembered as one of its initial correspondents. The clip of Harry and Mike Wallace sitting in front of the program's iconic stopwatch is a part of every *60 Minutes* retrospective. He appears a few times in the Oscar-winning documentary *The Fog of War* (2003), interviewing Defense Secretary Robert McNamara and reading the news from the anchor's desk. More snippets of Harry on the air are likely as documentaries exploring the 1960s and 1970s use anchor reports to illustrate the period.

Harry's presence in television news began fading soon after his death. He was remembered fondly when *60 Minutes* turned twenty-five in 1993, two years after Harry had left the popular broadcast. He was a lesser presence on the broadcast's thirtieth anniversary program, which gave most of its attention to the correspondents still contributing to it. Unlike three of his colleagues—Cronkite, Rather, and Wallace—he was never the subject of a prime-time program about his career. Time also allowed each of them to write more about themselves. Cronkite's autobiography was a best seller in 1996, a forerunner to a spate of books from television broadcasters. Had Harry used his insight and writing skill to revisit his youth—the period in his life he ignored in his memoir—he likely would have produced a best seller in retirement. Far too soon he was gone.

So was the kind of television news he and others in that first generation had known. The change was under way in 1980 when CNN began broadcasting news every minute of every day. As more all-news networks followed, the voracious appetite of the twenty-four-hour channels redefined news itself as well as how people received it. Today, only a third of those watching television are tuned in to one of the three traditional evening news shows. The audience that Harry garnered in 1975 as ABC's sole anchor was deemed too small at the time, but now even the most popular of the newscasts are challenged to reach as many people. The Internet, putting an untold number of news sources at a person's fingertips, further fragmented the audience for which the evening news had once been a shared experience.

It can be argued, of course, that Harry simply did not leave a large enough mark on television news to be remembered along with the likes of Murrow and Cronkite. At CBS, Sig Mickelson and Don Hewitt designed the presentation of news for television, Murrow set its ethical dimensions, and others, including Harry, applied their skills within that model. "He was, in terms of pure intellect, the brightest correspondent I have ever known in television," his friend Andy Rooney contended, "and I've known all of them."[1] However, Harry was no innovator when it came to shaping television news itself.

Would Harry have had a more lasting impact at CBS and ABC had he worked harder, as so many of his colleagues wished he had? Not with his focus on writing and broadcasting. Lasting impact lay more with the broadcast executives, such as Richard Salant at CBS and Roone Arledge at ABC, those who hired staff, set policy, and determined the look of the evening news and the news division's other programs. Harry had no interest in the executive suite.

Impact aside, he was hardly inconsequential to either network. Nor could his career be dismissed as a case of what could have been. "It seems to me given his talents, given his flaws, he was at the top of his game," CBS News correspondent Roger Mudd observed. "If I had lived Harry's life and at the end I looked back, I don't think I would have sold myself short. I think he did everything."[2] Reporter, morning show host, White House correspondent, specials host, evening news anchor, news magazine correspondent—Harry was the jack-of-all trades, the man who could do any task well.

How well he did those tasks was the rub, and the criticism leveled at Harry was not unfounded. Yet, when the forces behind television news had a message to send, they often chose him to carry it. They turned to Harry because millions of viewers placed their confidence in him. He gave the news its most important quality: credibility. His audience sensed that he could be trusted to report the news accurately and fairly and even offer worthwhile commentary about it. "He was a glorious writer," Mike Wallace said. "What people didn't realize, in his reading he did an equivalent amount of thinking."[3] His voice and words carried the credibility of an honest man who tried to make sense of things. Through a life and career marked by study and reflection, Harry gained the confidence of his audience—and never betrayed it.

Television news has a woefully short memory when it comes to its own history—and to honoring the men and women who spend their careers telling millions of viewers about their world. There is an ephemeral quality to the medium that, in a way, gives a reassuring message: The news itself is more important than the people who report it. For his part, Harry Reasoner took good care of television news and the public trust that came with his role as reporter and anchorman. Others follow him, and the news goes on.

NOTES

Introduction

1. Walter Cronkite interview, September 29, 1998.
2. "Viewers Place Most Trust in Harry Reasoner," *Kansas City Star*, September 21, 1982.
3. Dan Rather interview, April 22, 1998.
4. Andrew A. Rooney, *Sweet and Sour* (G. P. Putnam's Sons, 1992; Berkely Books, 1994), 303–305.
5. Don Hewitt interview, March 23, 1998.

Chapter One. The Most Wonderful Place in the World

Epigraph quotation is from Joyce Wagner, "Harry Reasoner: Beneath the Placid Exterior, Ambition and Competitiveness," *Kansas City Star*, March 12, 1972.

1. A family history of the Reasoners is among the Ellen Reasoner Papers (ERP). Although undated and uncredited, its author appears to be a female cousin of Harry Reasoner; she refers to Frederick William Reasoner as her grandfather.
2. Hazel A. Schelper to the author, July 15, 1999. The registrar of Buena Vista University in Storm Lake, Iowa, she confirmed data from Harry Ray Reasoner's college records.
3. The Reasoner family is listed in the 1920 Census for Humboldt County, Iowa. It is available on microfilm T625, Ed. No. 157, Vol. 38, through the National Archives in Kansas City, Missouri.
4. The book *Bellevue College, 1880–1919: A Brief History* (Hastings, Nebraska, 1962) lists Eunice Nicholl and her brother William as graduates of the class of 1904. For other details of her education and teaching background, see "Funeral Rites for Mrs. R. Reasoner Tuesday Afternoon," *Humboldt Independent*, February 4, 1936.
5. See Peg Reasoner Hansen interview, November 11 and 13, 1997; and HR to Tom Wolf, March 12, 1971. In Memos (Carbons) ABC, 1971–1972 file, Box 4Ja15, HRP.
6. See the 1920 Census for Humboldt County, Iowa, National Archives.
7. See "Funeral Rites for Mrs. R. Reasoner Tuesday Afternoon," *Humboldt Independent*, February 4, 1936, for details of her education and teaching background.
8. See Humboldt County Birth Records, Book Three, 111, and "Humboldt Personals," *Humboldt Republican*, October 22, 1920.
9. "Humboldt Personals," *Humboldt Republican*, April 22, 1923.
10. Peg Reasoner Hansen interview with the author.
11. For information on salaries of teachers and administrators and other Varina school data, see *Report of the Department of Public Instruction, For the Biennial Period ending June 30, 1924* (Des Moines: State of Iowa, 1924), 5. For details of the Rea-

soner family's life in Varina during this period, see the unpublished autobiography by Chester Newby, *My Recollections, 1911–1984*, 28–29. Newby, a native of Varina, later became a business partner of Harry Ray Reasoner and the husband of Esther Reasoner, Harry's sister. A copy of *My Recollections* was provided to the author by Newby's widow, Arlene.

12. Newby, *My Recollections*, 28.

13. Ibid., 32.

14. Ibid., 32–33, 44–45.

15. Ibid., 46–67.

16. Peg Reasoner Hansen interview.

17. James Egan, "The Boyhood Joys of Christmas," *Good Housekeeping*, December 1971, 44.

18. Egan, "Boyhood Joys of Christmas," 45.

19. Donna O'Hare Hopkins interview, May 27, 1998.

20. Schelper to the author, July 15, 1999.

21. See Ed Marsh to HR, January 21, 1966; Mrs. Kenneth Porath to HR, circa 1966; and Merle Garton Phillips to HR, August 19, 1966, in manila envelope, ERP.

22. For information on salaries of teachers and administrators and other Napier school data, see *Report of the Department of Public Instruction, For the Biennial Period ending December 31, 1928* (Des Moines: State of Iowa, 1928), 127.

23. HR to Jonathan Helm, March 24, 1969. In first 1968–1969 file, Box 4Ja15, HRP. Helm, a fourth-grader from Newark, Delaware, had written the broadcaster to ask for his memories of school when he was a child.

24. Untitled manuscript, dated April 7, 1952. In manila envelope marked "dormant HTR," Box 4Ja38, HRP.

25. Newby, *My Recollections*, 71.

26. Harry Reasoner, "Family Secrets I'm Happy to Share," *Guideposts*, February 1972, 3–6.

27. Newby, *My Recollections*, 82.

28. A copy of the flier is in Box 4Ja39, HRP.

29. Newby, *My Recollections*, 81.

30. Ibid., 87–111.

31. Ibid., 115–120.

32. Ibid., 144–145. A commemorative yearbook for the Napier Consolidated School, 1919–1955, lists Eunice Reasoner among the teachers for the Class of 1934. However, state school records do not list Eunice among Napier faculty after 1932. Still, Chester Newby recalled that Harry and his mother moved to Minneapolis in 1935, and Harry's eighth-grade transcript lists his first term as beginning in 1935.

33. See *Minneapolis City Directory* (Minneapolis: Minneapolis Directory Company), 1931, p. 1102, and 1932, p. 1184.

34. Newby, *My Recollections*, 169.

35. See Newby, *My Recollections*, 169–172, and a photocopied newspaper clipping advertising Harry Ray Reasoner for speaking engagements in 1933, source unknown. In the green scrapbook, Box 4Ja39, HRP.

36. Paul Reasoner interview, February 26, 1998.

37. Peg Reasoner Hansen interview.

38. Donna O'Hare Hopkins interview.

39. Peg Reasoner Hansen interview.

40. Paul Reasoner interview.

41. Newby, *My Recollections*, 168.

42. Ibid., 192.

43. The school transcript from his Emerson and Jefferson school years was provided to Elizabeth Reasoner by the Minneapolis School District and then forwarded to the author. For his reaction to leaving the rural school, see HR to Jonathan Helm, March 24, 1969, in first 1968–1969 file, Box 4Ja15, HRP; and Edith Efron, "The Reasoner Touch," *TV Guide*, July 25, 1964, 15–17.

44. Newby, *My Recollections*, 228.

45. Harry Reasoner, "The Merry Company," an unpublished manuscript dated February 26, 1940. In Box 4Ja38, HRP.

46. Peg Reasoner Hansen interview.

47. Reasoner, "The Merry Company."

48. Newby, *My Recollections*, 198–202.

49. Harry Reasoner, *Tell Me About Women* (New York: Beechhurst Press, 1946), 55.

50. Peg Reasoner Hansen interview.

51. Ibid.

52. Paul Reasoner interview.

53. Newby, *My Recollections*, 213–215.

54. Ibid., 217.

55. Transcript from Emerson and Jefferson schools, Minneapolis School District.

56. The school transcript from West High School was provided to Elizabeth Reasoner by the Minneapolis School District and then forwarded to the author.

57. Harry Reasoner, "Migration," *West High Times*, April 6, 1938. The school paper is on microfilm at the Minnesota Historical Society Library, St. Paul.

58. See "Chance to Express Opinions is Gained in Writing Essays," *West High Times*, November 17, 1937; and "Force Pushing Man forward is Belief Nothing is Certain," *West High Times*, February 9, 1938.

59. The description of the Script Club comes from the yearbook *Hesperian* (Minneapolis: West High School, 1938), 89. In the Minnesota Historical Society Library.

60. Betty Alexander James interview, September 3, 1998.

61. Ibid.

62. James Cooke Brown interview, August 22, 1998.

63. Paul Reasoner interview.

64. Alden Chamberlin interview, February 24, 1998.

65. Jerry Rapp interview, December 8, 1997.

66. Alden Chamberlin interview.

67. Jerry Rapp interview.

68. Paul Norby interview, September 15, 1998.

69. Paul Reasoner interview.

70. Bill Landis interview, November 11–12, 1998.

71. West High School transcript, Minneapolis School District.

72. Newby, *My Recollections*, 212–216.

73. Ibid., 220–222.

74. Ibid., 220.

75. Ibid., 221–225.

76. A copy of the program for *The Music Master* was provided to the author by Bill Landis.

77. Bill Landis interview.

78. Harry Reasoner, "Milestone in Alkali," published in *Atlantic Contests for High School Students, Minnesota Winners, 1939–1943* (Boston: Atlantic Monthly Company, 1939–1943), 3–4. In the Minnesota Historical Society Library.

79. See James Cooke Brown and Paul Norby interviews.

80. Paul Norby interview.

81. James Cooke Brown interview and Newby, *My Recollections*, 224.

82. James Cooke Brown interview.

83. Harry's diploma, dated January 1940, is among the Reasoner Papers. The fact that his high-school graduation date was 1940 and he attended Stanford from 1939–1940 has confused biographers.

84. A copy of the commencement program, which does not list Harry's name, was provided to the author by Bill Landis. Betty Alexander James, in an interview with the author, recalled the jokes about Harry's graduation status.

85. Paul Reasoner interview.

86. Newby, *My Recollections*, 233.

87. Ibid., 233–234.

88. See Newby, *My Recollections*, 233–234; and "Vacationist Dies in Fall off Cliff on North Shore," *Duluth News-Tribune*, August 15, 1939.

89. Joyce Wagner, "Harry Reasoner: Beneath the Placid Exterior, Ambition and Competitiveness," *Kansas City Star*, March 12, 1972.

90. Reasoner, *Tell Me About Women*, 55.

91. Andrew A. Rooney, *Sweet and Sour* (G. P. Putnam's Sons, 1992; Berkely Books, 1994), 303–305.

92. See interviews with Dermot Doran, June 20, 1998; Elizabeth Reasoner, August 21, 1998; and Stuart Reasoner, January 19, 1999.

93. Edith Efron, "The Reasoner Touch," *TV Guide*, July 25, 1964, 15–17.

Chapter Two. A Comfortable Life Upended

Epigraph quotation is from a letter Harry Reasoner wrote to his sister Esther Newby, September 27, 1943 (Ellen Reasoner Papers).

1. Unpublished autobiography by Chester Newby, *My Recollections, 1911–1984*, 234–235.

2. Ibid., 235–236.

3. Ibid., 236–244.

4. Ibid., 243.

5. A transcript of Harry's year at Stanford University was provided by the university to his daughter Elizabeth Reasoner, who provided a copy to the author.

6. Joyce Wagner, "Harry Reasoner: Beneath the Placid Exterior, Ambition and Competitiveness," *Kansas City Star*, March 12, 1972.

7. Newby, *My Recollections*, 243.

8. Ibid., 244.

9. Ibid., 245.

10. See interviews with Victor Cohn, September 22, 1998; Glenn Hanson, September 22, 1998; and George Gates, September 22, 1998.

11. George Gates interview.

12. See Newby, *My Recollections*, 252, and the University of Minnesota transcript of Harry's coursework. A copy was provided by the university to Elizabeth Reasoner, who provided a copy to the author.

13. Job application, United States Information Agency. The undated application, which Harry completed in 1951, lists his employment history from 1943 to 1951. A copy of the application was provided to the author under a Freedom of Information Act request to the National Personnel Records Center in St. Louis.

14. Newby, *My Recollections*, 250.

15. George Gates interview.

16. Victor Cohn interview, September 22, 1998.

17. Harry Reasoner, "Horror Play Is Season's Best," *Minnesota Daily*, November 13, 1941.

18. Harry Reasoner, "Don't Miss the Faculty Follies," *Minnesota Daily*, March 6, 1942.

19. Harry Reasoner, "First French—Now Swedish," *Minnesota Daily*, May 14, 1942.

20. Harry Reasoner, "Some Notes on Formal Dress," *Minnesota Daily*, May 20, 1942.

21. Harry Reasoner, "Homecoming," as published in *Max Shulman's Guided Tour of Campus Humor*, Max Shulman, ed. (Garden City, New York: Hanover House, 1955), 56–58.

22. Carole A. Potter, "Harry, You're On Your Own," *TV Preview, Battle Creek Enquirer and News*, July 20, 1975, 3.

23. HR to EN (Esther Newby), September 15, 1943, ERP.

24. See Newby, *My Recollections*, 252, and transcript from the University of Minnesota.

25. Newby, *My Recollections*, 250.

26. HR to EN, April 14 and May 20, 1943.

27. This unsigned, undated letter to Chet Newby is among the army-era letters, ERP.

28. Harry Reasoner, *Tell Me About Women* (New York: Beechhurst Press, 1946), 56.

29. Job application, USIA.

30. Ibid.

31. *Reasoner Report* script, May 8, 1967. Reasoner essays file, Box 4Ja39, HRP.

32. Harry Reasoner, "Under Your Hat," *Minneapolis Times*, November 30, 1942.

33. Ibid., December 7, 1942.

34. Jack Weinberg, "Under Your Hat," *Minneapolis Times*, March 4, 1943.

35. Harry Reasoner, "Under Your Hat," *Minneapolis Times*, December 17, 1942.

36. Ibid., January 11, 1943.

37. Ibid., January 19, 1943.

38. Ibid., March 1, 1943.

39. Ibid., December 30, 1942.

40. Maura Anderson interview, November 3, 1998.

41. Ibid.

42. HR to EN, April 6, 1943, ERP.

43. Harry Reasoner, "Under Your Hat," *Minneapolis Times*, March 10, 1943.

44. Harry's army service record was provided to the author under a Freedom of Information Act request to the National Personnel Records Center in St. Louis.

45. Unpublished novel, unlabeled file, Box 4Ja38, HRP.

46. HR to EN, March 23, 1943, ERP.

47. Army service record.

48. HR to EN, March 29, 1943, ERP.

49. See HR to EN, March 30 and April 1, 1943, ERP.

50. See HR to EN, April 4, 5, 6, 8, 11, 13, and 14, 1943, ERP.

51. HR to EN, May 25, 1943, ERP.

52. HR to EN, April 19, 1943, ERP.

53. HR to EN, April 30, 1943, ERP.

54. HR to EN, May 4, 6, 11, 13, 17, 1943, ERP.

55. HR to EN, May 20, 1943, ERP.

56. HR to EN, June 4, 1943, ERP.

57. HR to EN, June 8, 1943, ERP.

58. HR to EN, June 21 and 26, 1943, ERP.

59. HR to EN, July 8, 1943, ERP.

60. HR to EN, July 12, 1943, ERP.

61. HR to EN, July 16 and 20, 1943, ERP.

62. HR to EN, August 19, 1943, ERP.

63. HR to EN, November 9, 1943, ERP.

64. HR to EN, December 4, 1943, ERP.

65. HR to EN, August 6 and 18, 1943, ERP.

66. HR to EN, August 9, 1943, and June 13, 1944, ERP.

67. HR to EN, August 8, 1943, ERP.

68. HR to EN, August 25, 1943, ERP.

69. HR to EN, September 23, 1943, ERP.

70. HR to EN, September 23, 1943, ERP.

71. HR to EN, September 2, October 18, November 15, 1943; and May 19, 1944, ERP.

72. HR to EN, October 5 and 8, 1943, ERP.

73. HR to EN, September 29, 1943, ERP.

74. HR to EN, November 19, 1943, ERP.

75. HR to EN, December 19, 1943, ERP.

76. HR to EN, February 25 and March 4, 1944, ERP.

77. See "Wins Trip to GOP Convention," *Los Angeles Examiner*, June 24, 1944; and "Former Times Reporter, in Army, Wins GOP First Voter Essay Prize," *Minneapolis Times*, June 9, 1944.

78. HR to EN, May 5, 1944, ERP.

79. A recording of the NBC Radio broadcast is in the holdings of the Center for American History at the University of Texas, Austin.

80. HR to EN, August 14, 1944, ERP.

81. Walt Kingsley interviews, July 28 and September 1–2, 1998.

82. Ibid.

83. Ibid.

84. Ibid.

85. HR to EN, March 10, 1945, ERP.

86. HR to EN, January 8, 1945, ERP.

87. Army service record and HR to EN, April 6, 1945, ERP.

88. Kingsley interview.

89. Ibid.

90. Army service record.

Chapter Three. Secure at Home, Adrift at Work

Epigraph quotation is from the transcript of an interview with Francesco Scavullo dated April 18, 1977. Scavullo file, Box Ja40, HRP.

1. *Reasoner Report* script, May 8, 1967. Box 4Ja39, HRP.

2. Barbara Flanagan interview, November 13, 1998.

3. Ibid.

4. Ibid.

5. Untitled manuscript, dated October 21, 1951, in dormant manuscript file, Box 4Ja38, HRP.

6. Script dated May 9, 1967. In Reasoner essays file, Box 4Ja39, HRP.

7. Script dated December 14, 1966. In Reasoner essays file, Box 4Ja39, HRP. In the essay Harry refers to "a man I know" who worked as a reporter. Often in his radio essays he used the device to talk about himself or his opinions.

8. Joyce Hartment to HR, September 7, 1945. Unmarked file, Box 4Ja38, HRP.

9. Eleanor King to HR, November 13, 1945. EK file, Box 4Ja38, HRP.

10. BOMC News, May 1946, 16. In a scrapbook in Box 4Ja39, HRP.

11. EK to HR, February 4 and March 6, 1946. EK file, Box 4Ja38, HRP.

12. Olive Carruthers, "Maturing in Confusion," *Chicago Sun Book Week*, April 28, 1946.

13. John K. Sherman, "Reasoner's Novel Vivid Chronicle of Young Love," *New York Herald Tribune*. An undated clip in the green scrapbook, Box 4Ja39, HRP.

14. Clip Boutell, "Authors Are Like People," *New York Post*. The clipping is dated sometime in April 1946; it is in the green scrapbook in Box 4Ja39, HRP.

15. Maura Anderson interview, November 3, 1998.

16. Harry Reasoner, *Tell Me About Women* (New York: Beechhurst Press, 1946), 56.

17. EK to HR, December 19, 1945. EK file, Box 4Ja38, HRP.

18. EK to HR, April 30, 1946. EK file, Box 4Ja38, HRP.

19. EK to HR, July 26, 1946. EK file, Box 4Ja38, HRP.

20. The untitled manuscript is in the Harry Reasoner Papers.

21. Lynn Carroll interview, April 23, 1998.

22. The unpublished memoir of Chet Newby, *My Recollections, 1911–1984*, 284.

23. Dennis Newby interview, June 4, 1998.

24. Chet Newby, *My Recollections*, 285.

25. Lynn Carroll interview.

26. Ibid.

27. *Reasoner Report* script, September 26, 1966. In Reasoner Reports July–August–September 1966 file, Box 4Ja27, HRP.

28. Harry Reasoner, "Color Shots and Folk Song Hits Make 'Smoky' Pleasing," *Minneapolis Times*, July 12, 1946.

29. Harry Reasoner, "Cole Porter's Music Alone Puts 'Night and Day' Over," *Minneapolis Times*, August 2, 1946.

30. Ibid.

31. Harry Reasoner, "'Canyon Passage' Beautiful, Enjoyable Adventure Film," *Minneapolis Times*, August 9, 1946.

32. Harry Reasoner, "'Anna and King of Siam' to Rate With Year's Best," *Minneapolis Times*, August 16, 1946.

33. Harry Reasoner, "'O.S.S.' Plausible Picture of Undercover Agents," *Minneapolis Times*, August 23, 1946.

34. Harry Reasoner, "Claude Rains Steals Show in 'Angel on My Shoulder,'" *Minneapolis Times*, October 18, 1946.

35. Harry Reasoner, "'Sister Kenny' Fine Movie Made By Excellent Cast," *Minneapolis Times*, November 1, 1946.

36. Ibid.

37. See Harry Reasoner, "Bogart and Bacall Keen Team in New Loop Thriller," *Minneapolis Times*, September 13, 1946; "Jimmy Stewart Heads for Loop in Grand New Movie," *Minneapolis Times*, December 20, 1946; "'Miracle on 34th Street' Does Difficult Job Neatly," *Minneapolis Times*, July 11, 1947.

38. "Times Merges Monday With Star and Tribune," *Minneapolis Times*, May 15, 1948.

39. Job application, USIA file.

40. *Reasoner Report* script, May 8, 1967, Box 4Ja39, HRP.

41. Ibid.

42. Newby, *My Recollections*, 285.

43. Job application, USIA files.

44. Stephen E. Mills, *More Than Meets the Sky: A Pictorial History of the Founding and Growth of Northwest Airlines* (Seattle: Superior Publishing Company, 1972), 88.

45. Ibid., 103.

46. Harold Peyer interview, July 1, 1999.

47. Ibid.

48. Ibid.

49. Eileen Peyer interview, July 1, 1999.

50. Harold Peyer interview.

51. Ibid.

52. Hugh Harrison, "6 of 8 Want Change in Liquor Licensing," *Minneapolis Tribune*, May 5, 1949.

53. "Complete City Vote Results," *Minneapolis Tribune*, May 11, 1949.

54. Harold Peyer interview.

55. Job application, USIA files.

56. University of Minnesota transcript.

57. Charles F. Sarjeant, ed., *The First Forty: The Story of WCCO Radio* (Minneapolis: T. S. Denison, 1964), 66.

58. Ibid., 9.

59. Ibid.

60. Allen Gray interview, July 5, 1998.

61. Benedict E. Hardman, *Everybody Called Him Cedric* (Minneapolis: Twin Cities Federal Savings and Loan, 1976), 73–74.

62. Hardman, *Everybody Called Him Cedric*, 327.

63. "Cedric Adams Tells of Early Start in Journalism Career," *West High Times*, November 17, 1937.

64. *Cedric Adams Album: Celebrating 25 Years with Radio and Newspaper*, 48. No publisher is listed in this 1951 booklet. In the Minnesota Historical Society Library.

65. Ibid.

66. Job application, USIA file, National Personnel Records Center.

67. Gray interview.

68. *Cedric Adams Album*, 48.

69. Joyce Lamont interview, June 26, 1998.

70. Ibid.

71. Sarjeant, *First Forty*, 13.

72. Lamont interview.

73. Sig Mickelson interview, November 17, 1997.

74. Transcript, Minneapolis High School.

75. Job application, USIA file.

76. Memo, February 23, 1951, USIA file.

77. Judson H. Lightsey to HR, August 15, 1951, USIA file.

78. HR to EN, November 14, 1951, ERP.

79. HR to EN, November 19 and December 13, 1951, ERP.

80. *Reasoner Report* script, September 18, 1967. Reasoner essays file, Box 4Ja39, HRP.

81. Ken Landgren interview, March 4, 1998.

82. Bob Thompson interview, December 4, 1997.

83. HR to EN, November 19, 1951, ERP.

84. Landgren interview.

85. HR to EN, January 2 and January 11, 1952, ERP.

86. Lynn Landgren and Ken Landgren interviews, March 4, 1998.

87. Carroll interview.

88. HR to EN, October 9, 1951, ERP.

89. HR to EN, October 17, 1951, ERP.

90. HR to EN, December 9, 1951, ERP; Dermot Doran interview, June 20, 1998.

91. Kay Reasoner to EN, March 31, 1952, ERP.

92. KR to EN, March 24, 1952, ERP.

93. KR to EN, March 27, 1952, ERP.

94. The photocopied clipping in the HRP is undated and uncaptioned.

95. HR to EN, January 21, 1952, ERP.

96. *Reasoner Report*, December 29, 1966. Reasoner essays file, Box 4Ja39, HRP.

97. HR to EN, July 22, 1952, ERP.

98. HR to EN, July 16, July 7, and August 14, 1952, ERP.

99. See inspectors' efficiency reports dated November 13 and December 22, 1952, and April 16 and May 13, 1953, USIA file.

100. Thompson interview.

101. See inspectors' efficiency reports dated November 13 and December 22, 1952, and April 16 and May 13, 1953, USIA file.

102. These manuscripts are in an envelope marked "dormant manuscript" in Box 4Ja38, HRP.

103. Edith Efron, "The Reasoner Touch," *TV Guide*, July 25, 1964, 15–17.

104. HR to EN, October 24, 1952, ERP.

105. KR to EN. This undated letter was probably written in late 1952 or early 1953. ERP.

106. HR to EN, June 1, June 16, October 9, and October 12, 1953, ERP.

107. HR to EN, July 16, July 7, and August 14, 1953, ERP.

108. HR to EN, March 25, 1953, ERP.

109. HR to EN, March 31, 1953, ERP.

110. Undated manuscript in Box 4Ja38, HRP.

111. Bob Thompson interview, December 4, 1997.

112. HR to EN, April 13, 1954, ERP.

113. Mickelson interview.

114. HR to Hampton E. Brown, August 31, 1954, USIA file.

115. Memo, September 18, 1954, USIA file.

116. Bob Fransen interview, September 17, 1998.

117. Stuart Armstrong interview, August 28, 1998.

118. Glenn Smith interview, June 26, 1998.

119. Ibid.

120. John Cashman, "TV's Top Newscasters: Harry Reasoner," *New York Post*, January 28, 1965.

121. Armstrong interview.

122. Cashman, "TV's Top Newscasters," *New York Post*, January 28, 1965.

123. Bill Crawford interview. June 15, 1998.

124. Jack Horner interview, July 21, 1998.

125. Fransen interview.

126. Horner interview.

127. Armstrong interview.

128. Will Jones, "Radio Wins Back a TV Beachhead," *Minneapolis Tribune*, November 3, 1955.

129. Will Jones, "News Peddlers, Not Newsmen, Dominate TV in the Twin Cities," *Minneapolis Tribune*, November 6, 1955.

130. Tom Carlyon interview, June 18, 1998.

131. See interviews with Jane Purcell, June 24, 1998, and Tom Carlyon.

132. See undated newspaper clipping, Box 4Ja39, HRP, and Harry Reasoner, *Before the Colors Fade* (New York: Alfred A. Knopf, 1981), 12–13.

133. Review, "The Invisible Fence," *Variety*, June 6, 1956.

134. The award citation is in a green scrapbook, Box 4Ja39, HRP.

135. "5 Radio and TV Stations Win News Awards," *Minneapolis Tribune*, Feb. 11, 1956.

136. Carlyon interview.

137. Undated interview with Peter Costa of United Press International, Box 4Ja26, HRP.

138. Carroll interview.

139. Memo, March 15, 1956, USIA file.

140. Mickelson interview.

141. Ibid.

142. Purcell and Horner interviews.

143. Horner interview.

144. Armstrong interview.

145. Reasoner, *Before the Colors Fade*, 15.

146. Unheadlined article, *Minneapolis Star*, July 13, 1956.

Chapter Four. Taking a Chance at CBS News

Epigraph quotation is from Joyce Wagner, "Harry Reasoner: Behind the Placid Exterior, Ambition and Competitiveness," *Kansas City Star*, March 12, 1972.

1. HR to EN, Aug. 13, 1956, ERP.

2. Robert L. Hilliard and Michael C. Keith, *The Broadcast Century and Beyond: A Biography of American Broadcasting*, 3rd ed. (Boston: Focal Press, 2001), 63.

3. Edward Bliss Jr., *Now the News: The Story of Broadcast Journalism* (New York: Columbia University Press, 1991), 219.

4. Christopher H. Sterling and John M. Kittross, *Stay Tuned: A Concise History of American Broadcasting*, 2nd ed. (Belmont, CA: Wadsworth Publishing, 1990), 209.

5. Bliss, *Now the News*, 219.

6. Ibid., 220.

7. Sterling and Kittross, *Stay Tuned*, 208–209.

8. Ibid., 369.

9. See Bliss, *Now the News*, 222.

10. Philip Scheffler interview, November 17, 1998.

11. Wendell Hoffman interview, January 18, 1998.

12. Bill Crawford interview, June 15, 1998.

13. Ralph Paskman interview, September 22, 1998.

14. Ibid.

15. Scheffler interview.

16. David Buksbaum interview, September 3, 1998.

17. Paskman interview.

18. Walter Cronkite interview, September 29, 1998.

19. HR to EN, Oct. 28, 1956. ERP.

20. Elizabeth Reasoner interview, August 21, 1998.

21. Ann Reasoner interview, September 9, 1998.

22. Cronkite interview.

23. Memo by John Day, dated Nov. 26, 1957. Old Comment file, Box 4Ja38, HRP.

24. Harry Reasoner, *Before the Colors Fade* (New York: Alfred A. Knopf, 1981), 24.

25. See interviews with Stuart Reasoner, January 19, 1999; Jane Reasoner, October 13, 1998; Ellen Reasoner, September 12, 1998; and Elizabeth and Ann Reasoner.

26. Press release dated February 28, 1958. Old Comment file, Box 4Ja38, HRP.

27. The honorary membership card is in the Old Comment file, Box 4Ja38, HRP.

28. "Earl Wilson Says," *Des Moines Register*, November 3, 1958.

29. A copy of the tax form is in an unlabeled file in Box 4Ja38, HRP.

30. Crawford interview.

31. Scheffler interview.

32. Robert Wussler interview, March 20, 1998.

33. Ernest Leiser interview, December 9, 1997.

34. Sanford Socolow interview, May 29, 1998.

35. Reasoner, *Before the Colors Fade*, 47–48.

36. Claude Sitton interview, October 12, 1999.

37. Scheffler interview.

38. Reasoner, *Before the Colors Fade*, 27.

39. Wussler interview.

40. Reasoner, *Before the Colors Fade*, 98–99.

41. Hoffman interview.

42. Paskman interview.

43. Socolow interview.

44. Dan Rather interview, April 22, 1998.

45. John Shanley, "Reasoner: Anti-Cliché Newsman," *New York Times*, April 2, 1961.

46. Reasoner, *Before the Colors Fade*, 71–72.

47. Jack Gould, "'Eyewitness to History' and Harry Reasoner Get Behind the Scenes," *New York Times*, March 12, 1961.

48. Irv Drasnin interview, May 28, 1998.

49. Reasoner, *Before the Colors Fade*, 76–77.

50. Drasnin interview.

51. Ibid.

52. Harry Reasoner, *The Reasoner Report* (New York: Doubleday, 1966), 17–18.

53. Drasnin interview.

54. Reasoner, *Before the Colors Fade*, 75.

55. John Kiermaier interview, January 31, 1998.

56. Madeline Amgott interview, December 18, 1997.

57. Kiermaier interview.

58. Ibid.

59. Amgott interview.

60. Mel Ferber interview, June 1, 1998.

61. Kiermaier interview.

62. Ibid.

63. Mary Fickett interview, December 16, 1997.

64. Ibid.

65. John Mosedale interview, March 31, 1998.

66. See entry for Andy Rooney, *Current Biography 1982*, Charles Moritz, ed. (New York: H. W. Wilson, 1983), 364–367.

67. John Sack interview, February 10, 1998.

68. Mosedale interview.

69. Ferber interview.

70. Drasnin interview.

71. Ferber interview.

72. Jack Gould, "TV: Daily 'Calendar,'" *New York Times*, October 3, 1961.

73. Ron Bonn interview, June 29, 1998.

74. Bonn interview.

75. Mosedale interview.

76. Drasnin interview.

77. Amgott interview.

78. Mosedale interview.

79. Bob Siller interview, June 25, 1998.

80. Andrew A. Rooney interview, March 23, 1998.

81. Script dated February 12, 1962. Unmarked file. In Box 4Ja38, HRP.

82. Script dated March 27, 1962. Unmarked file. In Box 4Ja38, HRP.

83. Script dated April 25, 1962. Unmarked file. In Box 4Ja38, HRP.

84. Script dated April 17, 1963. Unmarked file. In Box 4Ja38, HRP.

85. Rooney interview.

86. Drasnin interview.

87. Bonn interview.

88. Fickett interview.

89. Rooney interview.

90. Broadcast of July 10, 1962. A tape of the broadcast is in the collection of the Museum of Television and Radio in New York and Los Angeles.

91. Bonn interview.

92. Fickett interview.

93. Amgott interview.

94. Ferber interview.

95. A notebook listing shows and guests is in Box 4Ja22, HRP.

96. Amgott interview.

97. HR to EN, Aug. 2, 1962. A postcard in envelope labeled miscellaneous correspondence. ERP.

98. Bonn interview.

99. Drasnin interview.

100. Mosedale interview.

101. Siller interview.

102. Bonn interview.

103. Ibid.

104. Jane Reasoner interview.

105. A copy of the tax form is in the 1963–1965 personal file, Box 4Ja51, HRP.

Chapter Five. On the Air and Everywhere

Epigraph quotation is from Joyce Wagner, "Harry Reasoner: Behind the Placid Exterior, Ambition and Competitiveness," *Kansas City Star*, March 12, 1972.

1. Harry Reasoner to Richard Salant, January 4, 1963. Box 4Ja51, HRP.

2. Salant to Margaret Miller, April 30, 1963. File marked 1963–1965 personal. Box 4Ja51, HRP.

3. HR to Salant, January 4, 1963. Box 4Ja51, HRP.

4. Salant to Bob Dale, Oct. 11, 1963. In 1963–1965 personal file. Box 4Ja51, HRP.

5. Raymond A. Schroth, *The American Journey of Eric Sevareid* (South Royalton, Vermont: Steerforth Press, 1995), 291–292.

6. Bob Siller interview, June 25, 1998.

7. Ibid.

8. Hal Haley interview, June 16, 1998.

9. Ibid.

10. Norman Gorin interview, September 23, 1998.

11. Harry Reasoner, *Before the Colors Fade* (New York: Alfred A. Knopf, 1981), 79.

12. Script dated November 7, 1965. In Sunday News outstanding broadcasts 1965. Box 4Ja51, HRP.

13. Script dated December 5, 1965. In Sunday News outstanding broadcasts 1965. Box 4Ja51, HRP.

14. Script dated October 17, 1965. Box 4Ja28, HRP.

15. Script dated August 15, 1965. In Sunday News outstanding broadcasts 1965. Box 4Ja51, HRP.

16. Gorin interview.

17. See Gary Paul Gates, *Air Time: The Inside Story of CBS News* (New York: Harper and Row, 1978), 228; and John Mosedale, *The First Year: A Retirement Journal* (New York: Crown, 1993), 129; and Gary Paul Gates interview, January 24, 1998.

18. Gates, *Air Time*, 79–81.

19. Ibid., 82–91.

20. Edward J. Bliss Jr., "And That's the Way it Was," *The Quill*, June 1973, 41–43.

21. Ibid.

22. Ed Bliss interview, June 18, 1998.

23. Bill Crawford interview, June 15, 1998.

24. Gates, *Air Time*, 7.

25. Leslie Midgley interview, May 11, 1998; and Midgley, *How Many Words Do You Want?: An Insider's Story of Print and Television Journalism* (New York: Birch Lane Press, 1989), 177–179.

26. Script dated November 23, 1963. In Box 4Ja38, HRP.

27. Siller interview.

28. Dan Rather interview, April 22, 1998.

29. Robert Wussler interview, March 20, 1998.

30. Don Hewitt, *Tell Me A Story: Fifty Years and 60 Minutes in Television* (New York: Public Affairs, 2001), 76.

31. Bliss interview.

32. Sanford Socolow interview, May 29, 1998.

33. Bliss interview.

34. John Mosedale interview, March 31, 1998.

35. Socolow interview.

36. Bliss interview.

37. Gates, *Air Time*, 106–109.

38. Reasoner, *Before the Colors Fade*, 132.

39. Dan Rather and Mickey Herskowitz, *The Camera Never Blinks: Adventures of a TV Journalist* (New York: William Morrow, 1977), 160–161.

40. Reasoner, *Before the Colors Fade*, 123.

41. Ron Bonn interview, June 29, 1998.

42. Stuart Reasoner interview.

43. Elizabeth Reasoner interview.

44. Jane Reasoner interview.

45. Wussler interview.

46. Robert Pierpoint interview, May 11, 1998.

47. Ibid.

48. George Herman interview, June 1, 1998.

49. Rather and Herskowitz, *The Camera Never Blinks*, 158.

50. Script dated February 18, 1965, in the March 1965 file. Box 4Ja27, HRP.

51. Script dated June 23, 1965, in the June–July 1965 file. Box 4Ja27, HRP.

52. Script dated October 28, 1965. August–September–October 1965 file. Box 4Ja27, HRP.

53. Reasoner, *Before the Colors Fade*, 127.

54. Pierpoint interview.

55. Gary Paul Gates and an announcer in the Washington bureau of CBS News, Kim Gregory, recalled Harry telling this story to them on separate occasions. Whom Johnson called was not clear. One version had it that Johnson called Katharine Graham, the *Washington Post* publisher whose company also owned WTOP. "I don't remember it happening and I don't think it could have happened," Graham told the author during an interview on May 14, 1998. She said that she did not have that kind of influence with the station and that its executives would not have taken orders to put a program on the air. However, she contended that it was not beyond Johnson to attempt such a move or to tell Harry he had done so. "Johnson could say anything," Graham said. "Certainly it wasn't beyond conception that he would have called."

56. Pierpoint interview.

57. Reasoner, *Before the Colors Fade*, 128–129.

58. Script dated October 11, 1965. August–September–October 1965 file. Box 4Ja27, HRP.

59. Script dated October 19, 1965. August–September–October 1965 file. Box 4Ja27, HRP.

60. Bill Small interview, June 16, 1998.

61. Pierpoint interview.

62. Crawford interview.

63. Herman interview.

64. Kim Gregory interview, May 7, 1998.

65. Small interview.

66. Gordon Manning interview, March 27, 1998.

67. Bill Moyers to the author, April 22, 1998.

68. Reasoner, *Before the Colors Fade*, 125.

69. Gates, *Air Time*, 122–127.

70. HR to Naomi Burton, August 5, 1966. In Correspondence—Doubleday and Co. Box 4Ja15, HRP.

71. Harry Reasoner, *Tell Me About Women* (New York: A. S. Barnes and Co., 1964), 5.

72. Undated memo from A. S. Barnes and Co. to HR. In Artists Agency Corp. II, 64–66 file, Box 4 Ja51, HRP.

73. Lucia Staniels to HR, January 6, 1967. File marked Doubleday and Co., 1966 and 1967. Box 4 Ja51, HRP.

74. A copy of the tax form is in the 1963–1965 personal file, Box 4 Ja51, HRP.

75. Scripts carrying their names are in Box 4 Ja27, HRP.

76. Script dated October 1, 1964. Unfiled in Box 4 Ja27, HRP.

77. Script dated October 22, 1964. Unfiled in Box 4 Ja27, HRP.

78. Harry Reasoner, *The Reasoner Report* (New York: Doubleday, 1966), 22.

79. See script dated September 3, 1965, in the August–September–October 1965 file, Box 4 Ja27; and the script dated November 7, 1967, in the October–November–December 1967 file, Box 4 Ja28, HRP.

80. See script dated January 26, 1968, in January 1968 file, Box 4 Ja28; and script dated September 21, 1966, in July–August–September 1966 file, Box 4 Ja27, HRP.

81. Elizabeth Reasoner interview.

82. Script dated January 18, 1965, in Box 4 Ja27, HRP.

83. Undated script provided to the author by Andy Rooney. Labeled an end piece, the comment may have come on the Sunday night news broadcast that followed King's murder.

84. Script dated April 5, 1968, in April 1968 file, Box 4 Ja28, HRP.

85. John Sack interview, February 10, 1998.

86. Herman interview.

87. Ibid.

88. Script dated March 8, 1964, Andy Rooney Papers.

89. The citation can be found at the Web site for the George Foster Peabody Awards, www.peabody.uga.edu.

90. Rooney interview.

91. Poem signed "Charles Ku-ralt" was typed on a news release. It is in the Kuralt file, Box 4 Ja46, HRP.

92. Rooney interview.

93. The programs and their air dates are *McNamara and the Pentagon*, September 25, 1963; *The Harlem Temper*, December 11, 1963; *The Crisis of Presidential Succession*, January 8, 1964; *The Catholics and the Schools*, February 5, 1964; *Cigarettes: A Collision of Interests*, April 14, 1964; *After Ten Years: The Court and the Schools*, May 13, 1964; and *The Press and the Law*, January 18, 1965.

94. *Young Mr. Eisenhower* aired on September 13, 1966.

95. The programs and their air dates are *JFK: The Childhood Years*, October 13, 1967; *What About Ronald Reagan?* December 12, 1967; and *Eisenhower and Bradley on Vietnam*, November 28, 1967.

96. Reasoner, *Before the Colors Fade*, 145.

97. Ed Fouhy interview, May 27, 1998.

98. Ibid.

99. Barry Zorthian interview, June 11, 1998.

100. Fouhy interview.

101. Reasoner, *Before the Colors Fade*, 148–154.

102. Irv Drasnin interview, May 28, 1998.

103. Transcript dated Oct. 20, 1966. In scripts miscellaneous file, Box 2K122, CBS Evening News Archives, CFAH.

104. Rather interview.

105. Siller interview.

106. Walter Cronkite interview, September 29, 1998.

107. Bill Leonard, *In the Storm of the Eye: A Lifetime at CBS* (New York: G. P. Putnam's Sons, 1987), 148–149.

108. Gordon Manning interview.

109. Ibid.

110. Rooney interview.

111. HR to Bill Leonard, November 4, 1968. In Box 4Ja22, HRP.

112. Rather interview.

113. Reasoner, *Before the Colors Fade*, 174–175.

114. Manning interview.

115. Reasoner, *Before the Colors Fade*, 173.

116. Hewitt, *Tell Me A Story*, 106.

Chapter Six. 60 Minutes *and a Bruised Ego*

Epigraph quotation is an on-air comment from Harry quoted in one of the obituaries broadcast upon his death. See "Newscasts of Harry Reasoner's Death," Box 4Ja47, HRP.

1. Susan and Bill Buzenberg, eds., *Salant, CBS, and the Battle for the Soul of Broadcast Journalism: The Memoirs of Richard S. Salant* (Boulder, CO: Westview Press, 1999), 59–60.

2. See Don Hewitt, *Tell Me a Story: Fifty Years and 60 Minutes in Television* (New York: Public Affairs, 2001), 106, and Bill Leonard, *In the Storm of the Eye: A Lifetime at CBS* (New York: G. P. Putnam's Sons, 1987), 144.

3. Leonard, *In the Storm*, 144.

4. Ibid., 142–143.

5. Hewitt, *Tell Me a Story*, 104–106.

6. See program schedule in Tim Brooks and Earle Marsh, *The Complete Directory to Prime Time Network and Cable TV Shows, 1946–Present*, 7th ed. (New York: Ballantine Books, 1999), 1172.

7. Leonard, *In the Storm*, 146–147.

8. Ibid., 144–145.

9. Ibid., 147.

10. Harry Reasoner, *Before the Colors Fade* (New York: Alfred A. Knopf, 1981), 158.

11. Gordon Manning interview, March 27, 1998.

12. Reasoner, *Before the Colors Fade*, 159.

13. Leonard, *In the Storm*, 147.

14. Don Hewitt, *Minute By Minute* (New York: Random House, 1985), 29.

15. For Wallace's background, see the biographical entry in Vol. 3, *Museum of Broadcast Communications Encyclopedia of Television*, ed. Horace Newcomb (Chicago: Fitzroy Dearborn, 1997), 1782–1785.

16. Leonard, *In the Storm*, 148.

17. Mike Wallace and Gary Paul Gates, *Close Encounters* (New York: William Morrow, 1984), 109–111.

18. Mike Wallace interview, March 24, 1998.

19. Wallace and Gates, *Close Encounters*, 87.

20. Wallace interview.

21. Hewitt, *Tell Me a Story*, 108–109.

22. Wallace interview.

23. Broadcast of September 24, 1968.

24. Ibid.

25. Review, *Variety*, October 2, 1968.

26. Transcript dated November 26, 1968.

27. Reasoner, *Before the Colors Fade*, 162.

28. Transcript dated January 21, 1969.

29. Transcript dated February 24, 1969.

30. Transcript dated September 30, 1969.

31. Transcript, December 16, 1969. Box 4Ja20, HRP. The *60 Minutes* version of the essay differs from the *Calendar* and ABC evening news versions in terms of organization and in some wording but not in its key ideas. The *Calendar* version can be found in *The Reasoner Report* and *Before the Colors Fade*; the ABC evening news broadcast took place on December 23, 1971.

32. Frank Coffey, *60 Minutes: 25 Years of Television's Finest Hour* (Los Angeles: General Publishing Group, 1993), 235.

33. See the top-thirty programs list in Brooks and Marsh, *Complete Directory to Prime Time Network and Cable TV Shows*, 1249.

34. Walter Cronkite interview, September 29, 1998.

35. Gary Paul Gates interview, January 24, 1998.

36. Ed Bliss interview, June 18, 1998.

37. Broadcast of September 2, 1968.

38. Broadcast of December 31, 1968.

39. Broadcast of September 9, 1968.

40. Broadcast of April 21, 1969.

41. Broadcast of July 3, 1969.

42. Broadcast of April 9, 1969.

43. Broadcast of July 25, 1969.

44. Bliss interview.

45. Marie Louise Vaillant interview, March 24, 1998.

46. Ibid.

47. See Harry Reasoner, "What Makes Our Decade Different," a reprinting of a speech he gave to the American Society for Medical Technology in Minneapolis on June 11, 1971, in Box 4Ja51, HRP. A similar telling of the anecdote appeared in printed comments delivered at the annual meeting of the Connecticut Public Expenditure Council on May 11, 1972, in Box 4Ja46, HRP.

48. Broadcast of April 16, 1969.

49. Gates interview.

50. Merv Block interview, June 16, 1998.

51. Ibid.

52. Andy Rooney interview, March 23, 1998.

53. Ralph Mann interview, March 18, 1998.

54. Gates, *Air Time*, 234.

55. Mann interview.

56. See HR to Bill Leonard, October 27, 1969, and HR to Marvin Josephson, both in the Marvin Josephson–IFA file, Box 4Ja46, HRP. Harry had traveled to a speaking engagement on his day off, making him unavailable for some unscheduled *60 Minutes* work. Leonard admonished him in a memo and asked that he clear future speaking appearances with him. Harry, angry because he heard about the memo before he received his copy, canceled three appearances and asked his agency not to book any others.

57. See the contract with IFA Lectures dated March 31, 1970. In file marked "dead speeches," Box 4Ja51; and William C. Riddervold to HR, August 9, 1971, Riddervold file, Box 4Ja40, HRP.

58. Stuart Reasoner interview.

59. Elizabeth Reasoner interview.

60. Jane Reasoner interview.

61. See top-thirty programs list in Brooks and Marsh, *Complete Directory to Prime Time Network and Cable TV Shows*, 1250.

62. For ABC News history, see Marc Gunther, *The House That Roone Built: The Inside Story of ABC News* (Boston: Little, Brown, 1994), 34–37.

63. Bob Siller interview, June 25, 1998.

64. Gunther, *The House That Roone Built*, 35.

65. Howard K. Smith, *Events Leading Up to My Death: The Life of a Twentieth-Century Reporter* (New York: St. Martin's, 1996), 283–284.

66. Elmer Lower interview, June 29, 1998.

67. Robert Siegenthaler interview, June 29, 1998.

68. Sam Donaldson interview, June 5, 1998.

69. Block interview.

70. Lower interview.

71. Bill Sheehan interview, June 18, 1998.

72. Gates, *Air Time*, 236.

73. Lower interview.

74. Mann interview.

75. Howard K. Smith interview, June 15, 1998.

76. Siegenthaler interview.

77. Sheehan interview.

78. Sanford Socolow interview, May 29, 1998.

79. Roger Mudd interview, February 16, 1999.

80. Manning interview.

81. David Buksbaum interview, September 3, 1998.

82. Broadcast on December 4, 1970.

83. Broadcast on November 5, 1970.

84. Gates, *Air Time*, 237.
85. Broadcast on November 6, 1970.
86. See Lyndon Johnson to HR, November 7, 1970; Hubert Humphrey to HR, November 14, 1970; and Richard Nixon to HR, November 23, 1970. In file marked Correspondence—Letters of Congratulations, Box 4Ja56, HRP.
87. Gates interview.

Chapter Seven. At ABC, New Duties and Old Habits

Epigraph quotation is from Glenda Gilmore, "Informality Has Its Place, Reasoner Feels," *Tampa Tribune*, July 26, 1972.
1. "The Age of Reasoner," *Time*, November 16, 1970, 54.
2. Broadcast on December 7, 1970.
3. Elmer Lower interview, June 29, 1998.
4. Joan Richman interview, November 10, 1998.
5. Gary Paul Gates, *Air Time: The Inside Story of CBS News* (New York: Harper and Row, 1978), 240.
6. Paul Jones, "Reasoner Style Starts at 6," *Atlanta Constitution*, December 20, 1971.
7. Ernest Leiser interview, December 9, 1997.
8. "Gentle Persuasion for ABC Affiliates," *Broadcasting*, May 10, 1971, 31.
9. Lawrence Laurent, "The Salary Changes But Reasoner Doesn't," *Washington Post TV Channels*, August 20, 1972, 5.
10. Phil Strassberg, "Reasoner's Happy He Switched to ABC," *Arizona Republic*, August 13, 1972.
11. Wade H. Mosby, "As I See It," *Milwaukee Journal*, July 9, 1972.
12. Adam Schloss interview, September 5, 1998.
13. Susan Colleen Engelhart, *Harry Reasoner, ABC News Correspondent: The Philosophy of a Television News Broadcaster*, master's thesis, University of Akron (June 1977), 126.
14. Walter Porgess interview, May 11, 1998.
15. Engelhart, *Harry Reasoner, ABC News Correspondent*, 127.
16. Av Westin interview, June 22, 1998.
17. Dick Richter interview, June 27, 1998.
18. Bill Sheehan interview, June 18, 1998.
19. Av Westin, *Newswatch: How TV Decides The News* (New York: Simon and Shuster, 1982), 132.
20. Engelhart, *Harry Reasoner, ABC News Correspondent*, 125–126.
21. Bernie Cohen interview, July 23, 1999.
22. Howard K. Smith interview, June 15, 1998.
23. For Smith's background, see the biographical entry in Vol. 3, *Museum of Broadcast Communications Encyclopedia of Television*, Horace Newcomb, ed. (Chicago: Fitzroy Dearborn, 1997), 1508–1510.
24. Smith interview.
25. Richter interview.
26. Lower interview.

27. Smith interview.

28. Walter Pfister interview, August 28, 1998.

29. Porgess interview.

30. Robert Siegenthaler interview, June 29, 1998.

31. Leiser interview.

32. Broadcast March 13, 1972.

33. Broadcast April 24, 1972.

34. Broadcast March 27, 1972.

35. Smith interview.

36. Ibid.

37. Porgess interview.

38. Pfister interview.

39. John J. Archibald, "Television, News and Harry Reasoner," *St. Louis Post-Dispatch*, June 30, 1972.

40. Pfister interview.

41. Siegenthaler interview.

42. Ron Powers, "TV picture a triumph, but commentary flawed," *Chicago Sun-Times*, February 21, 1972.

43. Commentary, February 22, 1972.

44. Commentary, February 24, 1972.

45. Commentary, June 24, 1974.

46. "Reasoner Became Delivery Boy When Russians Pulled Plug," *Baltimore Sun*, July 8, 1974.

47. Richter interview.

48. Bishop-Jones memo, May 12, 1971, in Reasoner's F.B.I. file, which the author received through a Freedom of Information Act request, is otherwise unremarkable. Most of the file is made up of a bureau investigation prompted by Harry's application to the United States Information Agency in 1951. Agents found no evidence that Harry was anything but a good and loyal American.

49. Mosedale interview.

50. Howard K. Smith, *Events Leading Up to My Death: The Life of a Twentieth-Century Reporter* (New York: St. Martin's, 1996), 326–328.

51. Cohen interview.

52. Commentary, December 10, 1970.

53. Commentary, April 23, 1971.

54. Schloss interview.

55. Commentary, March 1, 1971.

56. Commentary, April 28, 1971.

57. Commentary, May 13, 1971.

58. Commentary, January 31, 1972.

59. Commentary, April 17, 1972.

60. Commentary, June 17, 1971.

61. Commentary, February 15, 1972.

62. Commentary, April 20, 1973.

63. Commentary, May 2, 1973.

64. Commentary, June 14, 1973.

65. Commentary, September 6, 1973.

66. Commentary, November 1, 1973.

67. Commentary, May 3, 1974.

68. See commentaries, July 8 and July 30, 1974.

69. Commentary, August 6, 1974.

70. Commentary, September 10, 1974.

71. Leiser interview.

72. See commentaries, December 23, 1971, and December 24, 1974.

73. Commentary, November 25, 1971.

74. Commentary, January 28, 1974.

75. Commentary, May 31, 1973.

76. Commentary, May 17, 1974.

77. Commentary, January 16, 1973.

78. Commentary, November 30, 1971.

79. Commentary, December 2, 1971.

80. Richman interview.

81. Leiser interview.

82. Ibid.

83. Richman interview.

84. Al Primo interview, May 7, 1998.

85. Ibid.

86. Ibid.

87. Transcript, *Reasoner Report*, November 16, 1974.

88. Ibid.

89. Transcript, *Reasoner Report*, August 25, 1973.

90. Transcript, *Reasoner Report*, March 13, 1973.

91. Transcript, *Reasoner Report*, March 3, 1973.

92. Transcript, *Reasoner Report*, June 16, 1973.

93. Transcript, *Reasoner Report*, May 19, 1973.

94. Transcript, *Reasoner Report*, October 13, 1973.

95. Transcript, *Reasoner Report*, May 18, 1974.

96. See transcripts, *Reasoner Report*, June 8 and 22, 1974.

97. Transcript, *Reasoner Report*, April 7, 1973.

98. Transcript, *Reasoner Report*, May 26, 1973.

99. Transcript, *Reasoner Report*, November 17, 1973.

100. Transcript, *Reasoner Report*, April 6, 1974.

101. Richman interview.

102. Ibid.

103. Primo interview.

104. Arthur Holch interview, November 4, 1998.

105. Leiser interview.

106. Richman interview.

107. Engelhart, *Harry Reasoner, ABC News Correspondent*, 147.

108. Otto Penzler interview, May 26, 1998.

109. Ibid.

110. Ibid.

111. Peter Freundlich interview, March 25, 1998.

112. Ibid.

113. Freundlich interview.

114. Penzler interview.

115. Ibid.

116. Ibid.

117. Ibid.

118. Jeff Gralnick interview, May 29, 1998.

119. Cohen interview.

120. Sheehan interview.

121. Pfister interview.

122. Adam Schloss interview, September 5, 1998.

123. Cohen interview.

124. Smith interview.

125. Sam Donaldson interview, June 5, 1998.

126. Smith interview.

127. Westin interview.

128. Pfister interview.

129. Gralnick interview.

130. Leiser interview.

131. Ralph Mann interview, March 18, 1998.

132. Sheehan interview.

133. Ibid.

Chapter Eight. Trouble, Turmoil, and Barbara Walters

Epigraph is from the transcript of an interview with Francesco Scavullo dated April 18, 1977. Scavullo file, Box Ja40, HRP.

1. Transcript, *Behind the Lines*, December 12, 1974.

2. Commentary, December 26, 1974.

3. Commentary, May 10, 1973.

4. Commentary, October 2, 1973.

5. Commentary, March 12, 1974.

6. Howard Pankratz, "For New Goals, Old Values," *Kansas City Star*, December 15, 1971.

7. Elaine Markoutsas, "ABC-TV Gets Into 'Good News,'" *Chicago Tribune*, August 25, 1975.

8. Commentary, October 10, 1975.

9. Commentary, January 7, 1976.

10. Commentary, April 23, 1976.

11. Harry Reasoner, *Before the Colors Fade* (New York: Alfred A. Knopf, 1981), 185.

12. Ibid., 185–186.

13. Elizabeth Reasoner interview, August 21, 1998.

14. Jane Reasoner interview, October 13, 1998.

15. Elizabeth Reasoner interview.

16. Ibid.

17. Ellen Reasoner interview.

18. Friends and colleagues shared this information in interviews with the author.

19. Tamara Newell interview, December 1, 1998.

20. Ibid.

21. Pete Rahn, "Harry Reasoner Enjoying Hectic Job As Solo Anchor," *St. Louis Globe-Democrat*, October 31, 1975.

22. Leo Seligsohn, "A Reasoner Report: He'll Solo," *Newsday*, July 13, 1975.

23. Robert Siegenthaler interview, June 29, 1998.

24. Harry F. Waters, "The $5 Million Woman," *Newsweek*, May 3, 1976, 78.

25. Elmer Lower interview, June 29, 1998.

26. Bill Sheehan interview, June 18, 1998.

27. Al Primo interview, May 7, 1998.

28. Siegenthaler interview.

29. Roger Mudd interview, February 16, 1999.

30. Transcript, *Behind the Lines*, December 12, 1974.

31. Joan Richman interview, November 10, 1998.

32. Av Westin interview, June 22, 1998.

33. Broadcast of January 24, 1967.

34. Commentary, January 13, 1972.

35. Commentary, December 21, 1971.

36. *New York Times*, June 20, 1977.

37. Commentary, November 4, 1971.

38. *Reasoner Report*, March 10, 1973.

39. *Reasoner Report*, March 24, 1973.

40. *Reasoner Report*, April 21, 1973.

41. Lower interview.

42. For detailed information and perspective on Walters's career, see Jerry Oppenheimer, *Barbara Walters: An Unauthorized Biography* (New York: St. Martin's Paperbacks, 1990), and Barbara Lewis and Dan Lewis, *Barbara Walters: TV's Superlady* (New York: Pinnacle, 1976).

43. Oppenheimer, *Barbara Walters: An Unauthorized Biography*, 335–337.

44. Ibid., 341–342.

45. Bill Sheehan interview.

46. Ralph Mann interview, March 18, 1998.

47. Broadcast, April 22, 1976.

48. Kay Gardella, "Barbara Walters, ABC Reach Pact," *New York Daily News*, April 23, 1976.

49. Gardella, *New York Daily News*, April 23, 1976.

50. These and other views of the Walters salary are in "The Supersalaried Superstar: Eyebrows Are Up Everywhere Over Walters's High Price Tag," *Broadcasting*, May 3, 1976, 30–31.

51. Michael Pousner, "Barbara and Harry: A Dynamite Duo?" *New York Daily News*, May 5, 1976.

52. "Together For the First Time on Any Stage," *Broadcasting*, May 31, 1976, 58.

53. Walter Saunders, "Channel 9's 'Expressions' Displays Art of TV," *Rocky Mountain News*, May 31, 1976.

54. "Walters Deal the Opener for Longer Network News?" *Broadcasting*, April 26, 1976, 19–20.

55. "Longer News a Bitter Pill Stations Brace to Swallow," *Broadcasting*, June 28, 1976, 19–21.

56. "Odds Growing Longer on Longer News," *Broadcasting*, November 1, 1976, 19–20.

57. Sheehan interview.

58. Ibid.

59. Siegenthaler interview.

60. Howard K. Smith interview, June 15, 1998.

61. Broadcast, October 1, 1976.

62. Broadcast October 4, 1976.

63. Broadcast October 5, 1976.

64. Broadcast October 6, 1976.

65. Siegenthaler interview.

66. The exchange is cited in Barbara Matusow, *The Evening Stars: The Making of the Network News Anchor* (Boston: Houghton Mifflin, 1983), 184.

67. Walter Pfister interview, August 28, 1998.

68. Sheehan interview.

69. Siegenthaler interview.

70. Walter Porgess interview, May 11, 1998.

71. Judy Flander, "Barbara Walters: No Vapors, Frills or Hostility," *Kansas City Star*, May 15, 1977.

72. Dick Richter interview, June 27, 1998.

73. Bernie Cohen interview, July 23, 1999.

74. Ibid.

75. Siegenthaler interview.

76. Cohen interview.

77. Jeff Greenfield, "Conflict More Philosophy Than Personality," *Kansas City Star*, February 27, 1977.

78. Cohen interview.

79. Sheehan interview.

80. Greenfield, "Conflict More Philosophy Than Personality," *Kansas City Star*.

81. Ibid.

82. Ibid.

83. Transcript, *Larry King Live*, CNN, November 29, 1999.

84. Sheehan interview.

85. Frank Swertlow, "ABC May Split Reasoner, Miss Walters," *Kansas City Star*, February 4, 1977.

86. Russell Baker, "A news team can find happiness," *Kansas City Star*, March 27, 1977.

87. Art Buchwald, "The Babs and Hal Show," *Kansas City Star*, March 1, 1977.

88. Reasoner, *Before the Colors Fade* (New York: Alfred A. Knopf, 1981), 188.

89. Roone Arledge, *Roone: A Memoir* (New York: HarperCollins, 2003), 153–157.

90. Ibid., 163–167.

91. Flander, "Barbara Walters: No Vapors, Frills or Hostility," *Kansas City Star*.

92. Arledge, *Roone: A Memoir*, 176–177.

93. Ibid., 176.

94. Reasoner, *Before the Colors Fade*, 188.

95. Westin interview.

96. Ibid.

97. Al Garfin to HR, August 5, 1977. Garfin represented Newsweek Books, the publisher of *The Best of Photojournalism II*. Newsweek Books–Al Garfin file, Box 4Ja46, HRP.

98. Catherine Conklin to HR, November 8, 1977. *Reader's Digest* file, Box 4Ja40, HRP.

99. "ABC stays with Miss Walters," *Kansas City Star*, March 3, 1978.

100. Arledge, *Roone: A Memoir*, 189.

101. "Anchorman Unhappy With Role," *Kansas City Star*, January 5, 1978.

102. David W. Burke of ABC to Donald Hamilton of CBS, January 24, 1978. In ABC contract file, Box 4Ja39, HRP.

103. Les Brown, "Reasoner is a hostage of the TV competition game," *Kansas City Star*, May 14, 1978.

104. Ibid.

105. "Reasoner Gets Release," *Kansas City Star*, May 12, 1978.

106. Arledge, *Roone: A Memoir*, 191.

107. The Reasoner Papers include a memo dated April 22, 1976, the period in which Walters was being brought to ABC as coanchor. Notes on Harry's meeting with Bill Sheehan, taken by Ralph Mann, record that as of June 1, 1978, Harry could leave ABC as long as he did not anchor elsewhere for three months, did not leave without good reason, and did not use the option to seek more money. The notes also said Leonard Goldenson had given oral approval of the arrangement. The memo is in the Ralph Mann file, Box 4Ja46, HRP.

108. See the agreement dated May 12, 1978. In folder marked Departure letters from ABC summer of 1978, Box 4Ja24, HRP.

109. See interviews with Sheehan, Lower, Siegenthaler, Pfister, Richter, Porgess, and Cohen; and Jeff Gralnick interview, May 29, 1998.

110. Suzanne Levine and Harriet Lyons, eds., *The Decade of Women: A Ms. History of the Seventies in Words and Pictures* (New York: Paragon Books, 1980), 38.

111. Transcript, *Larry King Live*, CNN, November 29, 1999.

112. Tom Jory, "Reasoner finding change bittersweet," *Kansas City Star*, August 25, 1978.

113. *20/20*, broadcast November 19, 1981.

114. Broadcast July 7, 1978.

115. See Helen Carroll to HR, undated; and Helen Carr to HR, July 9, 1978, Departure letters from ABC summer 1978, Box 4Ja24, HRP.

116. Lower interview.

117. See the agreement dated May 12, 1978. In folder marked Departure letters from ABC summer of 1978, Box 4Ja24, HRP.

118. Mann interview.

Chapter Nine. A Rocky Return to CBS

The epigraph quotation is from Harry Reasoner, *Before the Colors Fade* (New York: Alfred A. Knopf, 1981), 198.

1. Bill Leonard, *In the Storm of the Eye: A Lifetime at CBS* (New York: G. P. Putnam's Sons, 1987), 149.

2. George Crile interview, October 6, 1998.

3. Sally Bedell, "What Made Harry Reasoner Switch Back to CBS?" *TV Guide*, January 27, 1979, 28 (24–28).

4. Frank Swertlow, "You Can Go Home Again," *Kansas City Star*, August 30, 1978.

5. Frank Coffey, *60 Minutes: 25 Years of Television's Finest Hour* (Los Angeles: General Publishing Group, 1993), 39–46.

6. Ibid., 235.

7. Ibid.

8. Ibid.

9. Don Hewitt interview, March 23, 1998.

10. Mike Wallace interview, March 24, 1998.

11. Tamara Newell interview, December 1, 1998.

12. Jim Jackson to author, June 10, 1998.

13. Paul Loewenwarter interview, July 1, 1998.

14. Jackson to author.

15. The segments and the dates they aired are "The $5 Bill," October 7, 1979; "Snake Venom," December 16, 1979; "The Foreign Legion," November 18, 1979; "The Thunderbirds," January 20, 1980; "CCCP-TV in Moscow," January 6, 1980; "Where There's a Will," February 24, 1980; and "Warning: Living Here May Be Hazardous to Your Health," May 25, 1980.

16. Transcript, "Who Stole Superman?" July 1, 1979.

17. Loewenwarter interview.

18. Philip Scheffler interview, November 17, 1998.

19. Bill McClure interview, July 2, 1998.

20. Transcript, "Barry Goldwater," March 9, 1980.

21. Transcript, "Barry Goldwater," May 11, 1986.

22. Transcript, "Barry Goldwater," April 18, 1982.

23. Transcript, "Ted Turner," April 22, 1979.

24. Sanford Socolow interview, May 29, 1998.

25. Scheffler interview.

26. Norman Gorin interview, September 23, 1998.

27. Hewitt interview.

28. The segment, "Deep in the Heart of Scotland," aired October 21, 1979.

29. Stuart McKeever to George Constantikes, September 20, 1979. In the Stuart McKeever file, Box 4Ja46, HRP.

30. Jane Reasoner interview.

31. The segment, "Judgment Day," aired September 23, 1979.

32. William Martin interview, July 16, 1998.

33. Ibid.

34. Newell interview.

35. Scheffler interview.

36. Kay Reasoner made these observations in a letter to Jane Purcell. Jane Purcell interview, June 24, 1998.

37. Harry Reasoner, *Before the Colors Fade* (New York: Alfred A. Knopf, 1981), 195–196.

38. Elizabeth Reasoner interview.

39. Jane Reasoner interview.

40. Loewenwarter interview.

41. Esther Kartiganer interview, October 12, 1998.

42. Mike Wallace and Gary Paul Gates, *Close Encounters* (New York: William Morrow, 1984), 355–356.

43. Morgan Strong, "Playboy Interview: 60 Minutes," *Playboy*, March 1985, 58.

44. Hewitt interview.

45. Kartiganer interview.

46. Coffey, *60 Minutes: 25 Years of Television's Finest Hour*, 235.

47. Press release from Consensus, Inc., dated May 1, 1979. In Box 4Ja33, HRP.

48. Bob Lundegaard, "Harry Reasoner: He's Riding High with Rest of '60 Minutes' Crew," *Minneapolis Star Tribune*, Decemer 23, 1979.

49. Socolow interview.

50. J. Bednarski, "Utility Firm Turns Cameras on '60 Minutes,'" *Kansas City Star*, February 24, 1980.

51. Loewenwarter interview.

52. Ibid.

53. Ibid.

54. Ibid.

55. See Jane Martigoni to HR, February 21, 1980; Bruce Speidel to HR, March 6, 1980; and Janice Skinner to HR, undated. In 1980 correspondence file, Box 4Ja52, HRP.

56. HR to L. P. Bragg, March 14, 1980. In 1980 correspondence file, Box 4Ja52, HRP.

57. Scheffler interview.

58. The segments and their air dates are "Billy Wilder," February 28, 1982, and "Johnny Cash," May 8, 1982.

59. Jackson to author.

60. Transcript, "Yves Montand," May 20, 1982.

61. Anne de Boismilon interview, October 6, 1998.

62. Transcript, "The Best Restaurant in the World," October 12, 1980.

63. Transcript, "Placido Domingo," July 22, 1984.

64. Transcript, "Inside the Vatican," February 21, 1982.

65. The segment, "The Sikhs," aired November 4, 1984.

66. McClure interview.

67. Anita O'Day interview, September 2, 1998.

68. The segment, "Canary," aired June 22, 1980.

69. O'Day interview.

70. Transcript, "The Best Movie Ever Made?" November 15, 1981.

71. HR to Chuck Elliott of publisher Alfred A. Knopf, October 17, 1978. In Chuck Elliott file, Box 4Ja46, HRP.

72. Cecil Smith, "Reasoner's Minutes—Unfaded and Unfazed," *Los Angeles Times*, October 1, 1981.

73. Newell interview.

74. Hewitt interview.

75. Newell interview.

76. The reviews appeared in Don Shirley, "Regarding Reasoner," *Washington Post*, September 28, 1981; Ron Miller, "Reasonable Contented Man," *Toledo Blade*, November 8, 1981; Nina King, "Flirtatious Memoirs of a TV Journalist," *Newsday*, September 17, 1981; and *Kirkus Reviews*, August 15, 1981.

77. See Marilyn Beck, "Mariette Kills Improper Ad For 'Improper Channels,'" *New York Daily News*, May 20, 1981; and Cherie Hart and Alan Braham Smith, "Love-Struck Angie Dickinson Flips for *60 Minutes* Host Harry Reasoner," *National Enquirer*, June 23, 1981.

78. See the *Los Angeles Times*, March 20, 1982.

79. Newell interview.

80. "He Was the Love of Her Life," *Des Moines Register*, September 9, 1991.

81. Wallace interview.

82. "Viewers Place Most Trust in Harry Reasoner," *Kansas City Star*, September 21, 1982.

83. William S. Paley to HR, January 26, 1981. In William S. Paley file, Box 4Ja46, HRP.

84. Cary Grant to HR, June 13, 1982. In Cary Grant file, Box 4Ja46, HRP.

85. Gary Deeb, "'60 Minutes' May Ease Out Harry Reasoner," *Grand Rapids Press*, June 20, 1984.

86. Strong, "Playboy Interview: 60 Minutes," *Playboy*, 58.

87. Loewenwarter interview.

88. Socolow interview.

89. Joel Dulberg interview, June 1, 1998.

90. Newell interview.

91. Ibid.

92. Jane Reasoner interview.

93. Ellen Reasoner interview.

94. Jane Reasoner interview.

95. Lowell Bergman interview, November 10, 1998.

Chapter Ten. Behind the Camera, a Difficult Farewell

The epigraph quotation is from Harry Reasoner, *The Reasoner Report* (New York: Doubleday, 1966), 165–166.

1. Jim Jackson to author, June 10, 1998.

2. Stuart Reasoner interview, January 19, 1999.

3. Mike Wallace interview, March 24, 1998.

4. Don Hewitt interview, March 23, 1998.

5. Lowell Bergman interview, November 10, 1998.

6. Elizabeth Reasoner interview, August 21, 1998.

7. Jane Reasoner interview, October 13, 1998.

8. Sanford Socolow interview, May 29, 1998.

9. Tamara Newell interview, December 1, 1998.

10. Bergman interview.

11. Ibid.

12. Newell interview.

13. Elizabeth Reasoner interview.

14. Norman Gorin interview, September 23, 1998.

15. Esther Kartiganer interview, October 12, 1998.

16. Philip Scheffler interview, November 17, 1998.

17. Elizabeth Reasoner interview.

18. Joe Wershba interview, February 2 and 10, 1998.

19. Jackson to author.

20. Jane Reasoner interview.

21. Ellen Reasoner interview, September 12, 1998.

22. Stuart McKeever interview, June 23, 2003.

23. Bergman interview.

24. The segments were "Patient Zero," November 15, 1987; "Local 560," February 14, 1988; and "Costa Rica Is Different," November 6, 1988.

25. Bergman interview.

26. Transcript, "Geronimo Pratt," November 29, 1987.

27. Ibid.

28. Crile interview.

29. The segment, "Charlie Did It," aired October 30, 1988.

30. Crile interview.

31. Ibid.

32. Jane Reasoner interview.

33. McKeever interview.

34. Ann Reasoner interview, September 9, 1998.

35. Ellen Reasoner interview.

36. Newell interview.

37. "Harry Reasoner Comes Home," *Humboldt Independent*, June 7, 1988.

38. Irving Fang interview, February 13, 1998, and Mike Peltier, "Journalism Faculty Split Over B.A. for Reasoner," *Minnesota Daily*, October 29, 1986.

39. Fang interview.

40. Ibid.

41. Unheadlined article, *Kansas City Star*, June 2, 1989.

42. Bob Ehlert, "Harry Reasoner: 'He Was Always A Man of Dignity,'" *Minneapolis Star Tribune*, August 7, 1991.

43. Fang interview.

44. Bergman interview.

45. Joel Dulberg interview, June 1, 1998.

46. De Boismilon interview, October 6, 1998.

47. Transcript, "Miles," November 12, 1989.

48. De Boismilon interview.

49. The segment, "Dr. Brooks," aired September 23, 1990.

50. Maureen Delaney interview, July 16, 1998.

51. Ibid.

52. See Bergman and de Boismilon interviews.

53. Bill McClure interview, July 2, 1998.

54. Scheffler interview.

55. The segment, "Moscow Mystique," aired March 10, 1991.

56. De Boismilon interview.

57. The segment, "Na Zdorove," aired November 18, 1990.

58. De Boismilon interview.

59. The segment, "Playing War," aired May 12, 1991.

60. De Boismilon interview.

61. David Turecamo interview, September 4, 1998.

62. The segments were "Body Snatchers?" January 13, 1991, and "I Know It When I See It," October 28, 1990.

63. Turecamo interview.

64. Hewitt interview.

65. Scheffler interview.

66. Ibid.

67. De Boismilon interview.

68. Bergman interview.

69. Turecamo interview.

70. McKeever interview.

71. Stuart Reasoner interview.

72. McKeever interview.

73. Ralph Mann interview, March 18, 1998.

74. Hewitt interview.

75. The ten-page agreement is in Box 4Ja42, HRP.

76. Hewitt interview.

77. Mann interview.

78. See Eric Sevareid to HR, May 24, 1991, and Dan Rather to HR, undated. In Box 4Ja42, HRP.

79. Jill Brooke, "Reasoner to Step Down," *New York Post*, November 9, 1990.

80. Broadcast May 19, 1991.

81. Elizabeth Reasoner interview.

82. See interviews with daughters Jane and Ellen Reasoner.

83. Jane Reasoner interview.

84. Ellen Reasoner interview.

85. Scheffler interview.

86. Jane Reasoner interview.

87. Ellen Reasoner interview.

88. McKeever interview.

89. Ibid.

90. Ibid.

91. Jane Reasoner interview.

92. Ibid.

93. Ibid.

94. H. Wayne Carver II interview, August–September 1998, date unrecorded.

95. McKeever interview.

96. "Report Says Reasoner's Body May Be Exhumed," *Fort Dodge Messenger*, October 3, 1992.

97. Carver interview.

98. Ibid.

99. Ibid.

100. McKeever interview.

101. Ibid.

102. The tributes appeared in Seth Amgott, "CBS' Harry Reasoner Dies At 68," *Stamford Advocate*, August 7, 1991.

103. " '60 Minutes' Boosts CBS," *Washington Post*, August 14, 1991.

104. Transcript, "Harry Reasoner," August 11, 1991.

105. Mann interview.

106. Harry Reasoner, *The Reasoner Report* (New York: Doubleday, 1966), 165–166.

Conclusion

1. Andy Rooney interview, March 23, 1998.

2. Roger Mudd interview, February 16, 1999.

3. Mike Wallace interview, March 24, 1998.

BIBLIOGRAPHY

Archives

Harry Reasoner Papers (HRP). Center for American History. University of Texas, Austin.
The archive holds more than forty boxes of materials taken from Reasoner's office at the time of his death. Materials include transcripts of *60 Minutes* and other television broadcasts, original scripts from his *Dimensions* radio broadcasts for CBS News, and original commentaries for ABC News.

Unpublished Material

Newby, Chester. *My Recollections, 1911–1984*. Privately published memoir. A copy was provided to the author by Mr. Newby's widow.
Ellen Reasoner Papers (ERP). Privately held by HR's daughter Ellen. Material includes an unpublished, undated family history and correspondence from Harry Reasoner to his sister, Esther Newby (EN).

Dissertations

Engelhart, Susan Colleen. *Harry Reasoner, ABC News Correspondent: The Philosophy of a Television News Broadcaster*. Master's thesis. June 1977. University of Akron.

Correspondence

Jackson, Jim. Letter to the author. June 10, 1998.
Moyers, Bill. Letter to the author. April 22, 1998.
Reasoner, Harry. Letters to his sister, Esther Newby (EN), circa 1943–1946 and 1951–1953. Ellen Reasoner Papers (ERP).
Schelper, Hazel A. Letter to the author. July 15, 1999.

Books

Arledge, Roone. *Roone: A Memoir*. New York: HarperCollins, 2003.
Bellevue College, 1880–1919: A Brief History. Hastings, Nebraska: 1962.

Bliss, Edward, Jr. *Now the News: The Story of Broadcast Journalism*. New York: Columbia University Press, 1991.

Brooks, Tim, and Earle Marsh. *The Complete Directory to Prime Time Network and Cable TV Shows, 1946–Present*, 7th ed. New York: Ballantine Books, 1999.

Buzenberg, Susan and Bill, eds. *Salant, CBS, and the Battle for the Soul of Broadcast Journalism: The Memoirs of Richard S. Salant*. Boulder, CO: Westview Press, 1999.

Cedric Adams Album: Celebrating 25 Years with Radio and Newspaper. No publisher is listed in this 1951 booklet located in the Minnesota Historical Society Library.

Coffey, Frank. *60 Minutes: 25 Years of Television's Finest Hour*. Los Angeles: General Publishing Group, 1993.

Gates, Gary Paul. *Air Time: The Inside Story of CBS News*. New York: Harper and Row, 1978.

Gunther, Marc. *The House That Roone Built: The Inside Story of ABC News*. Boston: Little, Brown, 1994.

Hardman, Benedict E. *Everybody Called Him Cedric*. Minneapolis: Twin Cities Federal Savings and Loan, 1976.

Hesperian, 1938. Yearbook. Minneapolis: West High School, 1938.

Hewitt, Don. *Minute By Minute*. New York: Random House, 1985.

———. *Tell Me A Story: Fifty Years and 60 Minutes in Television*. New York: Public Affairs, 2001.

Hilliard, Robert L., and Michael C. Keith. *The Broadcast Century and Beyond: A Biography of American Broadcasting*. 3rd ed. Boston: Focal Press, 2001.

Leonard, Bill. *In the Storm of the Eye: A Lifetime at CBS*. New York: G. P. Putnam's Sons, 1987.

Levine, Suzanne, and Harriet Lyons, eds. *The Decade of Women: A Ms. History of the Seventies in Words and Pictures*. New York: Paragon Books, 1980.

Lewis, Barbara, and Dan Lewis. *Barbara Walters: TV's Superlady*. New York: Pinnacle, 1976.

Matusow, Barbara. *The Evening Stars: The Making of the Network News Anchor*. Boston: Houghton Mifflin, 1983.

Midgley, Leslie. *How Many Words Do You Want? An Insider's Story of Print and Television Journalism*. New York: Birch Lane Press, 1989.

Mills, Stephen E. *More Than Meets the Sky: A Pictorial History of the Founding and Growth of Northwest Airlines*. Seattle: Superior Publishing Company, 1972.

Minneapolis City Directory, 1931. Minneapolis: Minneapolis Directory Company, 1931.

Minneapolis City Directory, 1932. Minneapolis: Minneapolis Directory Company, 1932.

Moritz, Charles, ed. *Current Biography 1982*. New York: H. W. Wilson, 1983.

Mosedale, John. *The First Year: A Retirement Journal*. New York: Crown, 1993.

Newcomb, Horace, ed. *Museum of Broadcast Communications Encyclopedia of Television*, vol. 3. Chicago: Fitzroy Dearborn, 1997.

Oppenheimer, Jerry. *Barbara Walters: An Unauthorized Biography*. New York: St. Martin's Paperbacks, 1990.

Rather, Dan, and Mickey Herskowitz. *The Camera Never Blinks: Adventures of a TV Journalist*. New York: William Morrow, 1977.

Reasoner, Harry. *Before the Colors Fade*. New York: Alfred A. Knopf, 1981.

———. "Homecoming." In *Max Shulman's Guided Tour of Campus Humor*, ed. Max
Shulman. Garden City, NY: Hanover House, 1955.

———. "Milestone in Alkali." In *Atlantic Contests for High School Students, Minnesota
Winners, 1939–1943*. Boston: Atlantic Monthly Company, 1939–1943.

———. *Tell Me About Women*. New York: Beechhurst Press, 1946. Reprint, New
York, A. S. Barnes and Co., 1964.

———. *The Reasoner Report*. New York: Doubleday, 1966.

*Report of the Department of Public Instruction, For the Biennial Period ending June 30,
1924*. Des Moines: State of Iowa, 1924.

*Report of the Department of Public Instruction, For the Biennial Period ending December 31,
1928*. Des Moines: State of Iowa, 1928.

Rooney, Andrew A. *Sweet and Sour*. New York: G. P. Putnam's Sons, 1992; Berkely
Books, 1994.

Sarjeant, Charles F., ed. *The First Forty: The Story of WCCO Radio*. Minneapolis:
T. S. Denison and Company, 1964.

Schroth, Raymond A. *The American Journey of Eric Sevareid*. South Royalton, VT:
Steerforth Press, 1995.

Smith, Howard K. *Events Leading Up to My Death: The Life of a Twentieth-Century
Reporter*. New York: St. Martin's, 1996.

Sterling, Christopher H., and John M. Kittross. *Stay Tuned: A Concise History of
American Broadcasting*. 2nd ed. Belmont, CA: Wadsworth Publishing, 1990.

Wallace, Mike, and Gary Paul Gates. *Close Encounters*. New York: William Morrow,
1984.

Westin, Av. *Newswatch: How TV Decides the News*. New York: Simon and Schuster,
1982.

Journals and Periodicals

"5 Radio and TV Stations Win News Awards," *Minneapolis Tribune*, February 11,
1956.

" '60 Minutes' Boosts CBS," *Washington Post*, August 14, 1991.

"ABC stays with Miss Walters," *Kansas City Star*, March 3, 1978.

"The Age of Reasoner," *Time*, November 16, 1970, 54.

Amgott, Seth. "CBS' Harry Reasoner Dies At 68," *Stamford Advocate*, August 7, 1991.

"Anchorman Unhappy With Role," *Kansas City Star*, January 5, 1978.

Archibald, John J. "Television, News and Harry Reasoner," *St. Louis Post-Dispatch*,
June 30, 1972.

Baker, Russell. "A news team can find happiness," *Kansas City Star*, March 27, 1977.

Beck, Marilyn. "Mariette Kills Improper Ad For 'Improper Channels,'" *New York
Daily News*, May 20, 1981.

Bedell, Sally. "What Made Harry Reasoner Switch Back to CBS?" *TV Guide*, January 27, 1979, 28 (24–28).

Bednarski, J. "Utility Firm Turns Cameras on '60 Minutes,'" *Kansas City Star*, February 24, 1980.

Bliss, Edward J., Jr., "And That's the Way it Was," *The Quill*, June 1973, 41–43.

Brooke, Jill. "Reasoner to Step Down," *New York Post*, November 9, 1990.

Brown, Les. "Reasoner is a hostage of the TV competition game," *Kansas City Star*, May 14, 1978.

Buchwald, Art. "The Babs and Hal Show," *Kansas City Star*, March 1, 1977.

Carruthers, Olive. "Maturing in Confusion," *Chicago Sun Book Week*, April 28, 1946.

Cashman, John. "TV's Top Newscasters: Harry Reasoner," *New York Post*, January 28, 1965.

"Cedric Adams Tells of Early Start in Journalism Career," *West High Times*, November 17, 1937.

"Complete City Vote Results," *Minneapolis Tribune*, May 11, 1949.

Deeb, Gary. " '60 Minutes' May Ease Out Harry Reasoner," *Grand Rapids Press*, June 20, 1984.

"Earl Wilson Says," *Des Moines Register*, November 3, 1958.

Efron, Edith. "The Reasoner Touch," *TV Guide*, July 25, 1964, 15–17.

Egan, James. "The Boyhood Joys of Christmas," *Good Housekeeping*, December 1971.

Ehlert, Bob. "Harry Reasoner: 'He Was Always A Man of Dignity,' " *Minneapolis Star Tribune*, August 7, 1991.

Flander, Judy. "Barbara Walters: No Vapors, Frills or Hostility," *Kansas City Star*, May 15, 1977.

"Former Times Reporter, in Army, Wins GOP First Voter Essay Prize," *Minneapolis Times*, June 9, 1944.

"Funeral Rites for Mrs. R. Reasoner Tuesday Afternoon," *Humboldt Independent*, February 4, 1936.

Gardella, Kay. "Barbara Walters, ABC Reach Pact," *New York Daily News*, April 23, 1976.

"Gentle Persuasion for ABC Affiliates," *Broadcasting*, May 10, 1971, 31.

Gilmore, Glenda. "Informality Has Its Place, Reasoner Feels," *Tampa Tribune*, July 26, 1972.

Gould, Jack. " 'Eyewitness to History' and Harry Reasoner Get Behind the Scenes," *New York Times*, March 12, 1961.

———. "TV: Daily 'Calendar,' " *New York Times*, October 3, 1961.

Greenfield, Jeff. "Conflict More Philosophy Than Personality," *Kansas City Star*, February 27, 1977.

Harrison, Hugh. "6 of 8 Want Change in Liquor Licensing," *Minneapolis Tribune*, May 5, 1949.

"Harry Reasoner Comes Home," *Humboldt Independent*, June 7, 1988.

Hart, Cherie and Smith, Alan Braham. "Love-Struck Angie Dickinson Flips for *60 Minutes* Host Harry Reasoner," *National Enquirer*, June 23, 1981.

"He Was the Love of Her Life," *Des Moines Register*, September 9, 1991.

Heinrich, Ken. "Beautiful People Minispecial Showed Difference Between GOP, Democrats," *Miami News*, August 23, 1972.

Holston, Noel. "Reasoner Hunts New Audience," *Orlando Sentinel Star*, September 13, 1976.

"Humboldt Personals," *Humboldt Republican*, October 22, 1920.

———. April 22, 1923.

"The Invisible Fence," *Variety*, June 6, 1956.

Jones, Paul. "Reasoner Style Starts at 6," *Atlanta Constitution*, December 20, 1971.

Jones, Will. "News Peddlers, Not Newsmen, Dominate TV in the Twin Cities," *Minneapolis Tribune*, November 6, 1955.

———. "Radio Wins Back a TV Beachhead," *Minneapolis Tribune*, November 3, 1955.

Jory, Tom. "Reasoner finding change bittersweet," *Kansas City Star*, August 25, 1978.

King, Nina. "Flirtatious Memoirs of a TV Journalist," *Newsday*, September 17, 1981.

Laurent, Lawrence. "The Salary Changes But Reasoner Doesn't," *Washington Post TV Channels*, August 20, 1972, 5.

"Longer News a Bitter Pill Stations Brace to Swallow," *Broadcasting*, June 28, 1976, 19–21.

Lundegaard, Bob. "Harry Reasoner: He's Riding High With Rest of '60 Minutes' Crew," *Minneapolis Star Tribune*, December 23, 1979.

Markoutsas, Elaine. "ABC-TV Gets Into 'Good News,'" *Chicago Tribune*, August 25, 1975.

Miller, Ron. "Reasonable Contented Man," *Toledo Blade*, November 8, 1981.

Mosby, Wade H. "As I See It," *Milwaukee Journal*, July 9, 1972.

News item. *Kansas City Star*, June 2, 1989.

———. *Kirkus Reviews*, August 15, 1981.

———. *Los Angeles Times*, March 20, 1982.

———. *Minneapolis Star*, July 13, 1956.

———. *New York Times*, June 20, 1977.

"Odds Growing Longer on Longer News," Broadcasting, November 1, 1976, 19–20.

Pankratz, Howard. "For New Goals, Old Values," *Kansas City Star*, December 15, 1971.

Peltier, Mike. "Journalism Faculty Split Over B.A. for Reasoner," *Minnesota Daily*, October 29, 1986.

Potter, Carole A. "Harry, You're On Your Own," *TV Preview, Battle Creek Enquirer and News*, July 20, 1975, 3.

Pousner, Michael. "Barbara and Harry: A Dynamite Duo?" *New York Daily News*, May 5, 1976.

Powers, Ron. "TV picture a triumph, but commentary flawed," *Chicago Sun-Times*, February 21, 1972.

"Quadrennial Overkill," *Newsweek*, July 24, 1972, 85–86.

Rahn, Pete. "Harry Reasoner Enjoying Hectic Job As Solo Anchor," *St. Louis Globe-Democrat*, October 31, 1975.

Reasoner, Harry. "'Anna and King of Siam' to Rate With Year's Best," *Minneapolis Times*, August 16, 1946.

———. "Bogart and Bacall Keen Team in New Loop Thriller," *Minneapolis Times*, September 13, 1946.

———. "Canyon Passage Beautiful, Enjoyable Adventure Film," *Minneapolis Times*, August 9, 1946.

———. "Carson at His Funniest in 'Two Guys From Milwaukee,'" *Minneapolis Times*, September 6, 1946.

———. "Chance to Express Opinions is Gained in Writing Essays," *West High Times*, November 17, 1937.

———. "Claude Rains Steals Show in 'Angel on My Shoulder,'" *Minneapolis Times*, October 18, 1946.

———. "Cole Porter's Music Alone Puts 'Night and Day' Over," *Minneapolis Times*, August 2, 1946.

———. "Color Shots and Folk Song Hits Make 'Smoky' Pleasing," *Minneapolis Times*, July 12, 1946.

———. "Don't Miss the Faculty Follies," *Minnesota Daily*, March 6, 1942.

———. "Family Secrets I'm Happy to Share," *Guideposts*, February 1972, 3–6.

———. "First French—Now Swedish," *Minnesota Daily*, May 14, 1942.

———. "Force Pushing Man Forward is Belief Nothing is Certain," *West High Times*, February 9, 1938.

———. "Horror Play Is Season's Best," *Minnesota Daily*, November 13, 1941.

———. "Jimmy Stewart Heads for Loop in Grand New Movie," *Minneapolis Times*, December 20, 1946.

———. "Migration," *West High Times*, April 6, 1938.

———. "'Miracle on 34th Street' Does Difficult Job Neatly," *Minneapolis Times*, July 11, 1947.

———. "'O.S.S.' Plausible Picture of Undercover Agents," *Minneapolis Times*, August 23, 1946.

———. "'Sister Kenny' Fine Movie Made By Excellent Cast," *Minneapolis Times*, November 1, 1946.

———. "Some Notes on Formal Dress," *Minnesota Daily*, May 20, 1942.

———. "Sultry Hedy Goes Over Big in 'Strange Woman,'" *Minneapolis Times*, November 22, 1946.

———. "Tracy and Hepburn Score in Grim, Gripping Movie," *Minneapolis Times*, April 25, 1947.

———. "Under Your Hat," *Minneapolis Times*, November 30, 1942; December 7, 1942; December 17, 1942; December 30, 1942; January 11, 1943; January 19, 1943; March 1, 1943; March 4, 1943; March 10, 1943.

"Reasoner Became Delivery Boy When Russians Pulled Plug," *Baltimore Sun*, July 8, 1974.

"Reasoner Gets Release," *Kansas City Star*, May 12, 1978.

"Report Says Reasoner's Body May Be Exhumed," *Fort Dodge Messenger*, October 3, 1992.

Saunders, Walter. "Channel 9's 'Expressions' Displays Art of TV," *Rocky Mountain News*, May 31, 1976.

Seligsohn, Leo. "A Reasoner Report: He'll Solo," *Newsday*, July 13, 1975.

Shanley, John. "Reasoner: Anti-Cliché Newsman," *New York Times*, April 2, 1961.

Shirley, Don. "Regarding Reasoner," *Washington Post*, September 28, 1981.

Smith, Cecil. "Reasoner's Minutes—Unfaded and Unfazed," *Los Angeles Times*, October 1, 1981.

Strassberg, Phil. "Reasoner's Happy He Switched to ABC," *Arizona Republic*, August 13, 1972.

Strong, Morgan. "Playboy Interview: *60 Minutes*," *Playboy*, March 1985, 58.

"The Supersalaried Superstar: Eyebrows Are Up Everywhere Over Walters's High
  Price Tag," *Broadcasting*, May 3, 1976, 30–31.
Swertlow, Frank. "ABC May Split Reasoner, Miss Walters," *Kansas City Star*, Febru-
  ary 4, 1977.
———. "You Can Go Home Again," *Kansas City Star*, August 30, 1978.
"Times Merges Monday With Star and Tribune," *Minneapolis Times*, May 15, 1948.
"Together For the First Time on Any Stage," *Broadcasting*, May 31, 1976, 58.
"Vacationist Dies in Fall off Cliff on North Shore," *Duluth News-Tribune*, August
  15, 1939.
Variety, October 2, 1968.
———. February 28, 1973.
"Viewers Place Most Trust in Harry Reasoner," *Kansas City Star*, September 21,
  1982.
Wagner, Joyce. "Harry Reasoner: Beneath the Placid Exterior, Ambition and Com-
  petitiveness," *Kansas City Star*, March 12, 1972.
"Walters Deal the Opener for Longer Network News?" *Broadcasting*, April 26,
  1976, 19–20.
Waters, Harry F. "The $5 Million Woman," *Newsweek*, May 3, 1976, 78.
Weinberg, Jack. "Under Your Hat," *Minneapolis Times*, March 4, 1943.
"Wins Trip to GOP Convention," *Los Angeles Examiner*, June 24, 1944.
Woodruff, Al. "Under Your Hat," *Minneapolis Times*, May 9, 1944.

Interviews

Amgott, Madeline. December 18, 1997.
Anderson, Maura. November 3, 1998.
Armstrong, Stuart. August 28, 1998.
Bergman, Lowell. November 10, 1998.
Bliss, Ed. June 18, 1998.
Block, Merv. June 16, 1998.
Bonn, Ron. June 29, 1998.
Brown, James Cooke. August 22, 1998.
Buksbaum, David. September 3, 1998.
Carlyon, Tom. June 18, 1998.
Carroll, Lynn. April 23, 1998.
Carver, H. Wayne II. August–September 1998, date unrecorded.
Chamberlin, Alden. February 24, 1998.
Cohen, Bernie. July 23, 1999.
Cohn, Victor. September 22, 1998.
Crawford, Bill. June 15, 1998.
Crile, George. October 6, 1998.
Cronkite, Walter. September 29, 1998.
De Boismilon, Anne. October 6, 1998.
Delaney, Maureen. July 16, 1998.
Donaldson, Sam. June 5, 1998.
Doran, Dermot. June 20, 1998.

Drasnin, Irv. May 28, 1998.
Dulberg, Joel. June 1, 1998.
Fang, Irving. February 13, 1998.
Ferber, Mel. June 1, 1998.
Fickett, Mary. December 16, 1997.
Flanagan, Barbara. November 13, 1998.
Fouhy, Ed. May 27, 1998.
Fransen, Bob. September 17, 1998.
Freundlich, Peter. March 25, 1998.
Gates, Gary Paul. January 24, 1998.
Gates, George. September 22, 1998.
Gorin, Norman. September 23, 1998.
Gralnick, Jeff. May 29, 1998.
Gray, Allen. July 5, 1998.
Gregory, Kim. May 7, 1998.
Haley, Hal. June 16, 1998.
Hansen, Peg Reasoner. November 11 and 13, 1997.
Hanson, Glenn. September 22, 1998.
Herman, George. June 1, 1998.
Hewitt, Don. March 23, 1998.
Hoffman, Wendell. January 18, 1998.
Holch, Arthur. November 4, 1998.
Hopkins, Donna O'Hare. May 27, 1998.
Horner, Jack. July 21, 1998.
James, Betty Alexander. September 3, 1998.
Kartiganer, Esther. October 12, 1998.
Kiermaier, John. January 31, 1998.
Kingsley, Walt. July 28 and September 1–2, 1998.
Lamont, Joyce. June 26, 1998.
Landgren, Ken. March 4, 1998.
Landgren, Lynn. March 4, 1998.
Landis, Bill. November 11–12, 1998.
Leiser, Ernest. December 9, 1997.
Loewenwarter, Paul. July 1, 1998.
Lower, Elmer. June 29, 1998.
Mann, Ralph. March 18, 1998.
Manning, Gordon. March 27, 1998.
Martin, William. July 16, 1998.
McClure, Bill. July 2, 1998.
McKeever, Stuart. June 23, 2003.
Mickelson, Sig. November 17, 1997.
Midgley, Leslie. May 11, 1998.
Mosedale, John. March 31, 1998.
Mudd, Roger. February 16, 1999.
Newby, Dennis. June 4, 1998.
Newell, Tamara. December 1, 1998.

Norby, Paul. September 15, 1998.
O'Day, Anita. September 2, 1998.
Paskman, Ralph. September 22, 1998.
Penzler, Otto. May 26, 1998.
Peyer, Eileen. July 1, 1999.
Peyer, Harold. July 1, 1999.
Pfister, Walter. August 28, 1998.
Pierpoint, Robert. May 11, 1998.
Porgess, Walter. May 11, 1998.
Primo, Al. May 7, 1998.
Purcell, Jane. June 24, 1998.
Rapp, Jerry. December 8, 1997.
Rather, Dan. April 22, 1998.
Reasoner, Ann. September 9, 1998.
Reasoner, Elizabeth. August 21, 1998.
Reasoner, Ellen. September 12, 1998.
Reasoner, Jane. October 13, 1998.
Reasoner, Paul. February 26, 1998.
Reasoner, Stuart. January 19, 1999.
Richman, Joan. November 10, 1998.
Richter, Dick. June 27, 1998.
Rooney, Andrew A. March 23, 1998.
Sack, John. February 10, 1998.
Scheffler, Philip. November 17, 1998.
Schloss, Adam. September 5, 1998.
Sheehan, Bill. June 18, 1998.
Siegenthaler, Robert. June 29, 1998.
Siller, Bob. June 25, 1998.
Sitton, Claude. October 12, 1999.
Small, Bill. June 16, 1998.
Smith, Glenn. June 26, 1998.
Smith, Howard K. June 15, 1998.
Socolow, Sanford. May 29, 1998.
Thompson, Bob. December 4, 1997.
Turecamo, David. September 4, 1998.
Vaillant, Marie Louise. March 24, 1998.
Wallace, Mike. March 24, 1998.
Wershba, Joe. February 2 and 10, 1998.
Westin, Av. June 22, 1998.
Wussler, Robert. March 20, 1998.
Zorthian, Barry. June 11, 1998.

INDEX